MW00719667

Emerging from the Mist

Surrey School District
APPROVED

Pacific Rim Archaeology

This series is an initiative of UBC Laboratory of Archaeology and UBC Press. It provides a source of scholarly reporting on significant new archaeological research along the entire Pacific Rim, spanning the region from Southeast Asia to western North America and Pacific Latin America. The series will publish reports on archaeological fieldwork in longer monograph form as well as edited volumes of shorter works dealing with contemporary themes.

The general editors of the series are Michael Blake and David Pokotylo, both faculty members in the Department of Anthropology and Sociology at the University of British Columbia.

Emerging from the Mist: Studies in Northwest Coast Culture History is the third volume in the series. The first was *Hidden Dimensions: The Cultural Significance of Wetland Archaeology,* edited by Kathryn Bernick, and the second was *Since the Time of the Transformers: The Ancient Heritage of the Nuu-chah-nulth, Ditidaht, and Makah,* by Alan D. McMillan.

SURREY SD# 36

4794227

*Edited by R.G. Matson, Gary Coupland,
and Quentin Mackie*

Emerging from the Mist:
Studies in Northwest Coast Culture
History

UBCPress · Vancouver · Toronto

Aboriginal Education Department
12772 - 88 Avenue, Surrey BC V3W 3J9
RESOURCE CENTRE

© UBC Press 2003

All rights reserved. No part of this publication may be reproduced, stored in a retrieval system, or transmitted, in any form or by any means, without prior written permission of the publisher, or, in Canada, in the case of photocopying or other reprographic copying, a licence from Access Copyright (Canadian Copyright Licensing Agency), www.accesscopyright.ca.

09 08 07 06 05 04 03   5 4 3 2 1

Printed in Canada on acid-free paper that is 100% post-consumer recycled, processed chlorine-free, and printed with vegetable-based, low-VOC inks.

Pacific Rim Archaeology (ISSN 1483-2283)

National Library of Canada Cataloguing in Publication Data

Main entry under title:
  Emerging from the mist : studies in Northwest Coast culture history /
  edited by R.G. Matson, Gary Coupland, and Quentin Mackie.

  (Pacific Rim archaeology, ISSN 1483-2283)
  Includes bibliographical references and index.
  ISBN 0-7748-0981-7 (bound). – ISBN 0-7748-0982-5 (pbk.)

  1. Indians of North America – Northwest Coast of North America – Antiquities.
2. Indians of North America – Material culture – Northwest Coast of North
America. 3. Northwest Coast of North America – Antiquities. I. Matson, R. G.
(Richard Ghia), 1944- II. Mackie, Quentin, 1962- III. Coupland, Gary, 1953-
IV. Series.

E78.N78E43 2003   979.5'01   C2003-911044-3

Canadä

UBC Press gratefully acknowledges the financial support for our publishing program of the Government of Canada through the Book Publishing Industry Development Program (BPIDP), and of the Canada Council for the Arts, and the British Columbia Arts Council.

This book has been published with the help of a grant from the Humanities and Social Sciences Federation of Canada, through the Aid to Scholarly Publications Programme, using funds provided by the Social Sciences and Humanities Research Council of Canada, and with the help of the K.D. Srivastava Fund.

UBC Press
The University of British Columbia
2029 West Mall
Vancouver, BC V6T 1Z2
604-822-5959 / Fax: 604-822-6083
E-mail: info@ubcpress.ca
www.ubcpress.ca

To Donald Hector Mitchell,
  archaeologist, ethnohistorian, anthropologist

Contents

Illustrations

Acknowledgments

The editors wish to express their appreciation to everyone who helped make this book a reality. It began with a suggestion by Leland Donald in February 1994, and he continued to help with it up to the very end. There were many people who participated in the symposium on "Ethnohistory and Archaeology on the Northwest Coast: Papers in Honour of Donald H. Mitchell" at the Canadian Archaeology Associations in May 1998 at Victoria, who are not contributors to this volume but still encouraged it into being. First among these is Bjorn Simonsen, the organizer of the meetings, who found the time and space for the largest and best attended symposium yet on Northwest Coast archaeology. Kenneth Ames, Michael Blake, Morley Eldridge, Rick Garvin, Eric McLay, Dorothy Kennedy, and Rob Whitlam, all presented papers not included in this volume. The editors of Pacific Rim Archaeology, Michael Blake and David Pokotylo, read an early draft, made significant comments, and kindly forwarded it to UBC Press as a candidate for their series. Two anonymous reviewers provided commentary, much of which was prompt, thorough, and informed, and we thank them for their efforts. At UBC Press, Jean Wilson saw the volume through from an idea to getting it accepted by the editorial board, and through the subventions committee of the Humanities and Social Sciences Federation of Canada, even though we did not number the pages as instructed. Darcy Cullen managed the production, Joanne Richardson was appreciated as having the right touch in her copy editing, and Deborah Kerr's meticulous proofreading was much appreciated. Susan Matson produced many of the figures in this book, often from ill-conceived drafts, fixed up many photographs, and only occasionally was properly paid for her efforts. Finally, it was up to the contributors to produce their papers, respond to sometimes-contradictory reviews, and to do so in a timely fashion, and we appreciate their efforts, which made this book possible.

Emerging from the Mist

1
Introduction:
The Northwest Coast in Perspective
R.G. Matson

> As Dr. Boas informs us, there are in all the tribes three distinct
> ranks – the chiefs, the middle class, and the common people – or
> as they might perhaps be more aptly styled, nobles, burgesses, and
> rabble. The nobles form a caste. Their rank is hereditary; and no
> one who was not born in it can in any way attain it. The nobles
> have distinction and respect, but little power ... The lowest class,
> or rabble, is therefore a veritable residuum ... [including] – in
> those tribes which practise slave-holding – slaves and their
> descendants.
>
> – Hale 1890:4-5

When ethnographic examples of complex hunter-gatherers are given, they
are almost invariably from the Northwest Coast of North America (e.g.,
Burch and Ellana 1994; Kelly 1995; Netting 1977, 1986; Johnson and Earle
1987; Fried 1967; Lee and Devore 1968). The Northwest Coast is commonly
conceded to be second only to the Southwest in ethnographic importance
among North American culture areas. The Northwest Coast has a corre-
spondingly prominent place in theories about the development of social
complexity (Fried 1967; Johnson and Earle 1987; Service 1971, 1975). This
positioning of Northwest Coast cultures is partly the result of the rich ethnographic accounts, their many exotic aspects, and the lack of descriptions of
equivalently complex hunters and gatherers.

In contrast to the prominent placement of Northwest Coast ethnography, Northwest Coast archaeology is rarely cited. The first book-length published account of Northwest Coast prehistory as a whole became available
only recently (Matson and Coupland 1995), while A.V. Kidder's ground-
breaking *Introduction to the Study of Southwestern Archaeology* was first published in 1924. The relatively low visibility of archaeology in the literature
is not in accord with its theoretical importance (for if the ethnographic

pattern is important, then it follows that the record of its development will be a test of ideas about the development of cultural complexity). The same holds true of the visibility of the quantity and quality of archaeology carried out in the last thirty years along the Northwest Coast, and of the relatively important changes in our understanding of the nature of the ethnographic pattern that have occurred in the same period. This volume is an attempt to rectify this situation, reporting not only on the archaeology of the Northwest Coast and its implication for cultural evolution but also on aspects of our current understanding and the extent of the Northwest Coast ethnographic pattern.

Many recent archaeological investigations have assumed that the general pattern presented by Wayne Suttles (1951, 1987a, 1990b) is valid for the Northwest Coast as a whole, in contrast to the alternative views put forward by investigators such as Drucker and Heizer (1967) and Rosman and Rubel (1971). To many, the decisive research supporting Suttles's view is the ethnohistoric research presented by Donald Mitchell (1981, 1983, 1984, 1985) and Leland Donald (1983a, 1985, 1990, 1997) (see also Mitchell and Donald 1985, 1988; and Donald and Mitchell 1975, 1994). Almost all the chapters in this volume share this orientation, and almost all also make good use of early historic accounts.

It will also be noted that these archaeological chapters share an interest in anthropological concerns, like that maintained by Donald Mitchell throughout his career (Mitchell 1968, 1971a, 1979, 1988, 1990). The reason for these commonalities is that these chapters originated in a session (although they constituted only a small portion of those delivered) of the Canadian Archaeological Association Annual Meetings in May 1998 in Victoria, British Columbia, in honour of Donald Mitchell. This was the largest such session on Northwest Coast archaeology to date. At the same meeting, Professor Mitchell was also honoured with the Canadian Archaeological Association Smith-Wittemberg Award.

In order to provide a context for the following chapters, I give an overview of the culture area and the current important issues. I begin by briefly reviewing the area and the ethnographic pattern, and then turn to more specific concerns. By using a single set of terms defined in this book we hope to reduce confusion and unnecessary redundancy in the chapters that follow.

Setting

The Northwest Coast has been defined in a variety of ways over the years, but the first detailed description, given by Wissler in 1917, holds up well today. Both the judgmental evaluation made by Kroeber (1939) – and, following him, Drucker (1955b, 1965) – and the statistical evaluation made by Jorgensen (1980) support the same basic classification that was followed by Suttles (1990a) in *Handbook of North American Indians,* Volume 7, *Northwest*

Coast. In all these cases the Northwest Coast is seen as extending from the Tlingit at Yakutat Bay to at least the Tolowa in northern California. The place of the Eyak north of the Tlingit, and the Karok and Yurok south of the Tolowa, remains problematic. The region south of the Columbia River has long been recognized as having less complex cultures than the region further north. Some (e.g., Mitchell and Donald 1988) have in fact defined it as being outside of the Northwest Coast. Matson and Coupland (1995) called this section the "South Coast," and that is the term we will use here (Figure 1.1).

In the last chapter in this volume Leland Donald investigates whether the "South Coast" area can be fully considered an integral portion of this culture area. Whatever the evaluation, Donald points out that the South Coast is clearly distinctive in a number of important ways. Matson and Coupland (1995:259) suggest that the Northwest Coast pattern was still spreading south at contact and that contact may well have terminated the southern spread.

Somewhat more arbitrarily, Matson and Coupland (1995) defined the "Central Coast" (Figure 1.1) as extending from the Columbia River to the north end of Vancouver Island, and the "North Coast" as the area from the north end of Vancouver Island to Yakutat Bay. The commonalities in settings from one end of the Northwest Coast to the other, though, include a coastal environment with a generally mild but wet climate and year-round access to coastal resources. Fish, particularly Pacific salmon, are clearly the most important resource. It is no accident that the inland penetration of the Northwest Coast cultures is along such major salmon streams as the Columbia, Fraser, Skeena, and Nass rivers. Other fish, particularly cod, herring, rockfish, halibut, and other flat fish are also important. Shellfish, both burrowing clams and rocky-foreshore-dwelling mussels are also often major dietary items. Marine mammals are also locally significant, including, at some places on the outer Central Coast, whales, as is detailed in the contribution by Monks. Large trees of splitable wood are also a common presence, with redwood in the south, red cedar on the Central Coast, and red and yellow cedar on the North Coast. Douglas fir is abundant in the south, and is joined by hemlock along the Central Coast and replaced by Sitka spruce on the North Coast. Donald gives a much more detailed look at the distribution of some of these important trees and their geographical correlation with cultural traits.

The importance of these resources varies from place to place, but the large-scale processing of salmon in late summer and fall for preservation and use in the winter is a near constant. Low values for land mammals and birds are typical, although this is variable. Except for berries, vegetable foods do not contribute significant calories beyond the South Coast, where acorns are abundant.

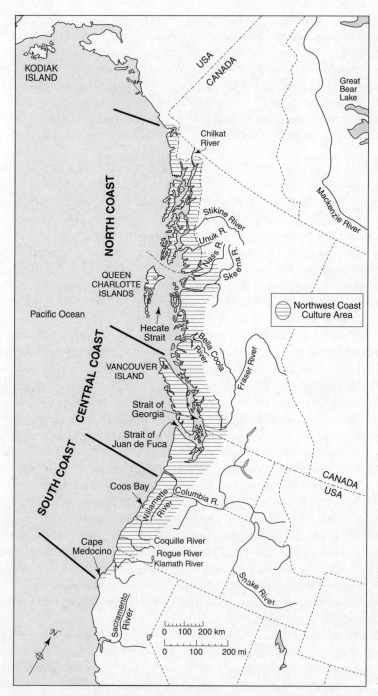

Figure 1.1   Northwest Coast culture area according to Kroeber (1939), with Matson and Coupland (1995) subdivisions.

Cultures

Spread out along this coast are very unusual hunters and gatherers; the numerous large households lived in spacious planked permanent houses in large villages, displaying intricate ceremonies and elaborate decorative arts, all reflecting a complex society with inherited social statuses. All these attributes contrast with the usual pattern seen for people making their living without agriculture.

In our training, many of us received as conventional wisdom the fact that these cultures were "rank societies," in Fried's (1967) term, that there were statuses present that were limited by heredity and not open to all but that real inequities in access to the material means of life did not exist. Further, these status differences existed mainly within kingroups/households and not between them. That was not the view of such earlier workers as Wissler (1917) or Hale (1890), as the quotation at the top of this introduction indicates, nor is it the understanding that has developed in the last twenty years, following Ruyle (1973); Suttles (1973, 1987a); Suttles and Jonaitis (1990), and Donald (1985, 1990, 1997). Work by Mitchell (1985) and Donald (1983, 1997; Mitchell and Donald 1985) has shown that numerous slaves existed in early historic times in some of these groups, and it is very difficult to see slaves, whose very lives were at the whim of their owners (as discussed in Donald's contribution to this volume), having "equal access to the material needs of life." Close inspection indicates that even groups without numerous slaves had inherited inequities with regard to access to the material needs of life, indicating that, in general, the ethnographic Northwest Coast cultures should be more properly thought of as low-level "stratified," "class," or "class divided" societies in Donald's (1985, 1997) terms, rather than as "rank" societies (Ames 2001).

Although this image of the Northwest Coast appears solid for the ethnographic present (i.e., the situation inferred to exist immediately before contact) – at least until the next time the pendulum swings – the situation for the last 2,000 or 3,000 years is not nearly so clear. Matson and Coupland (1995) report on several lines of evidence that indicate that the ethnographic pattern is either a recent development or unstable. This is a common theme in this volume, a recognition that we cannot assume that something approximating the ethnographic pattern was present on the Central and North coasts for the last 2,000 years – a view that would have had significantly more support twenty years ago. Matson and Coupland further suggest that the South Coast might best be viewed as a "rank society" in contrast to the socially stratified Central and North coasts, a position consistent with Donald's contribution.

In contrast to the undoubted high degree of social stratification, Northwest Coast political complexity is generally low. The Northwest Coast "chief" is better thought of as "head of household" or "head of kinship group."

There is very little evidence for a formal position for chief of the community and almost none for a political position incorporating several communities. Mitchell (1983a) and Miller and Boxberger (1994) have looked at some of the best known claims for these and soundly rejected them. There are, though, several exceptions that appear to be tied to postcontact developments, and Chapter 2, Martindale's contribution, is a careful and full examination of perhaps the best known counter-example in early historic times along the Skeena River (Figure 1.1).

A Northwest Coast "chief," then, had the allegiance of his household, but beyond that, political power rested in his own abilities and alliances with other household leaders. This lack of political complexity contrasts with the much less socially complex California "tribelets" but is clearly a distinctive feature of the Northwest Coast. Coupland (1988a) points out that communities did frequently act as cooperative groups in defence of their members and of community-controlled resources; but beyond this, community-wide corporate activities are typically not seen.

The high degree of social stratification and the low degree of political complexity is a reason that the Sahlins-Service-Earle (Service 1971, 1975; Sahlins and Service 1960; Johnson and Earle 1987) political evolutionary scheme involving "chiefdoms" is little used in this area, although, as pointed out above, the common alternative (Fried's [1967]), also needs major modification in order to fit our current understanding of the ethnographic present. One wonders about the dominant scheme if it does not allow for the Northwest Coast case, yet this scheme is frequently used as if it is the only process by which cultural complexity can develop. Arnold (1993:77), for instance, defines "complex" as including a hierarchical political organization on a multicommunity scale and seems to believe that, without this, other aspects of complexity cannot exist among hunters and gatherers. Can one turn around and say that the Northwest Coast case invalidates this popular scheme? At the UCLA symposium on Complex Hunter-Gatherers of the World (1994) my impression was that there was a general disbelief among those unfamiliar with the Northwest Coast that social complexity could exist without political complexity, and an apparent willingness to force archaeological data into the Sahlins-Service scheme, which, at the very least, is not validated for the hunting-gathering case.

Another contrast between the Northwest Coast and most of its surrounding areas involves the number of languages present. This was recognized early (Hale 1889, 1890) and appears to be a result of very high population density and stability of subsistence, which allows groups of sufficient size to be biologically stable and to exist in relatively small geographical areas (Martin 1973). The pattern of many distinct linguistic groups also occurs to the south, in California, probably for the same reasons along with the additional factor of ecological diversity.

The Northwest Coast cultures are clearly "logistic collectors," moving resources collected at specialized processing sites to the winter village site for use during the winter. It is not generally recognized that these same societies can also have a high degree of residential mobility (Mitchell 1994). The "permanent" winter village structures are often only frames from which the planks are removed for use in spring, summer, and fall camps. Curiously, the structures are larger and less permanent on the Central and North coasts than they are on the South Coast. The exploitation and processing of salmon are the most important of the resource activities, and this has continued at least for the last 3,000 to 3,500 years (Matson 1992) on the Central Coast, which is consistent with the evidence collected by Moss, Erlandson, and Stuckenrath (1990) for fish weirs on the North Coast.

In Chapter 3 Dale Croes focuses on what the perishable remains from the Hoko River site on the Washington shores of the Strait of Juan de Fuca (Figure 1.1) indicate about the development of subsistence technology. Most archaeology investigations of subsistence patterns – which are crucial to understanding the Northwest Coast – are based on faunal and floral remains, and that is true for the coast as a whole. Equally important, but not usually as visible, is the technology involved. The presence of numerous wet sites on the Northwest Coast allows a unique way to explore this topic, and Croes's chapter points to how these remains can be used to evaluate subsistence issues.

Households and Household Archaeology

The main economic organization for these activities is the household. The household has been traditionally seen as consisting of twenty to twenty-five individuals (Mitchell and Donald 1988) for the Central and North coasts. Families and individuals of different social statuses were said to be located in different areas of the house. This structure was also used for the large-scale storage of food, which was necessary to surviving the long, wet winters. On the South Coast, a smaller household of perhaps eight to twelve individuals lived in a smaller planked house. On the Central Coast, a number of households may be present in a single shed-roofed house, which might be several hundred feet long (Suttles 1991).

The size and nature of the household are not clear for the contact period, let alone for the past. How the household came to be is another question that is not understood. These questions can be answered only through household archaeology; thus many of the chapters in this volume deal with aspects of the prehistoric household.

In Chapter 4 I examine the remains of a relatively recent Coast Salish shed-roof house on Valdes Island in the Strait of Georgia (Figure 1.1) and look not only at its architectural structure and possible social organization but also at likely household sizes. In the Coast Salish shed-roof house, a number of households may share the same structure. In Chapter 5 Al Mackie and Laurie Williamson present new information about the physical makeup of similar early historic houses on the southern west coast of Vancouver Island (Figure 1.1). This is the first detailed description, including measurements, of these houses and will undoubtedly be much used by future researchers. Of particular interest is the very large size of these structures and the variety of their architectural features.

In contrast to the very large shed-roof houses, on the North Coast the usual rule was a single household to a smaller gable-roof house, although sometimes a single "household" might include two "houses." My investigation indicates that the common "household/compartment" size within the shed-roof house is about the same size as are many North Coast houses.

In Chapter 6 Coupland, Colten, and Case look at the differences in remains found in front of and behind houses at McNichol Creek, near the mouth of the Skeena River (Figure 1.1), as well as some suggestive differences between houses of varying sizes and even limited information on differences within a single house. Although these findings need to be confirmed elsewhere, they indicate significant differences in activities and access to resources – all in accord with the general "Suttles" model.

The full package – ascribed status differences; large, permanent winter households and villages; logistically organized economy, usually centred around stored salmon – found in the ethnographic accounts is what Matson and Coupland (1995) have referred to as the "Developed Northwest Coast Pattern." One of the outstanding issues in the development of the Northwest Coast pattern is the establishment and nature of the large household. Matson and Coupland (1995) found surprisingly little evidence for the antiquity of large houses on the North Coast, given the conventional archaeological wisdom that the ethnographic present was established there 2,000 years ago. Coupland points out that the evidence on the North Coast is more in accord with a smaller multifamily household, with perhaps ten to twelve individuals. Matson and Coupland (1995) found that, even on the South Coast, the archaeological houses were smaller than one would expect from the ethnographic record. This evidence casts doubt on the common archaeological assumption that the Developed Northwest Coast Pattern has been present for the last 2,000 years. In the chapter by Coupland, Colten, and Case it is interesting to note that most of the houses are much smaller than one would expect from ethnographic accounts and what is present on some early historic sites. What features of the ethnographic present are the results of early contact (Acheson 1995)? One of the houses at McNichol Creek is much larger than the others, possibly indicating a different social organization than present ethnographically on the Northwest Coast.

In Chapter 7 Grier looks at the possible advantage of having a large household 1,500 or 2,000 years ago. In the Gulf of Georgia area large households are found at that time, and Grier has been investigating one at the Dionisio Point site (very near the Valdes Island site upon which I report). It is, though, in an area without significant salmon resources today, and Grier explores the possibility that the ethnographic pattern of moving seasonally to the Fraser River for access to salmon occurred at this time as well as why that might have been allowed by the Fraser River inhabitants. He argues that "labour for salmon" exchange may have been occurring with benefits for both groups. This would be a different pattern than that seen ethnographically, again indicating a willingness to move outside of ethnographically recorded patterns to explain the archaeological record.

Unique Northwest Coast Activities

Two of the most unusual characteristics of Northwest Coast peoples were whaling and the use of metal. In Chapter 8 Monks looks at the archaeological remains of sea mammals found in excavations carried out by McMillan, St. Claire, and himself on the west coast of Vancouver Island as well as at those recovered from Ozette (Samuels 1994) to see how whales were used. At the very least, this chapter contains useful data for further investigation; however, its conclusions that the archaeological use varies from the ethnographic description and that this has been the case for a substantial length of time are very interesting. In particular, the ethnographic descriptions of the ownership of different parts of the whale and sources of oil need to be re-evaluated.

Metal using appears to go back at least 2,000 years on the Northwest Coast, and the early explorers were impressed with the amount and range of metals in use at first contact. In Chapter 9 Acheson analyzes these accounts for information about the nature and extent of precontact metal use and arrives at the conclusion that this technology has deeper and broader roots than is conventionally recognized.

It is only very recently that ethnic groups have been traceable with any reliability in archaeology. Two chapters look at this subject from very different perspectives: Kathryn Bernick (Chapter 10) focuses on the identification of a particular basketry technique that will aid ethnic identification of recent Coast Salish material; Alan McMillan (Chapter 11), explores the old question of the spread of Wakashan (ancestral Nootka and Kwakiutl speakers) people along the west coast of Vancouver Island and finds that some rethinking is in order to account for the latest archaeological information. Dale Croes's chapter also uses basketry to look at some of these issues, although he employs a rather different style of analysis than does Bernick. Together these chapters show that tracing ethnic groups is becoming much more feasible than it was in the past, and they point to the future development of culture history.

All the above chapters use relatively conventional assumptions and techniques, fitting within the "Suttles" and "processual archaeology" paradigms as followed by Donald Mitchell throughout his career (although he would probably disagree with the latter placement [Mitchell 1998]). In Chapter 12 Quentin Mackie points to a future, albeit a complementary one, with new assumptions, new paradigms, and new techniques. He looks at the settlement patterns on the west coast of Vancouver Island but in terms of "central place" or "travelling salesman" perspectives and links this to the post-structural idea of practice theory (Bourdieu 1977, 1990). He is able to show that, if one looks for the five to nine most "central place sites," they turn out to be much larger than expected. This is explained as the result of long-term "practice" rather than as a result of cultural or ecological reasons. I believe this approach is even more complementary to the rest of this volume than the author indicates. For instance, he contrasts practice theory with "culture" but with a "culture" of "norms" and "intentionality" that is not very prominent elsewhere in this volume. Further, while the investigator cites settlement pattern investigations from Alaska that do not find correlations between resources and sites and, particularly, site size, Eric McLay (1999), who also presented a paper at the 1998 symposium in Victoria, found both relationships on Valdes Island, off the east coast of Vancouver Island. Finally, although Mackie argues that his large central places cannot be explained by traditional central place notions, it was commented at the Victoria symposium, that good "base camp" locations would be expected to have these characteristics. Are these five to nine "central" places particularly good base camps – or number of local groups? What advantages do these new techniques and theories have over the "old" ways, and how do they link to these more "grounded" ideas about settlement patterns and more traditional ideas of culture? I see some interesting research ahead as these questions are investigated from both directions.

Chapter 13, by Leland Donald, reviews the Northwest Coast as a culture area, reexamining Kroeber's (1923, 1939) definition and description in light of current knowledge. It is interesting to see that Kroeber early recognized the high degree of social stratification and low degree of political complexity emphasized in this introduction. Perhaps more important, Kroeber (and Donald) stress the uniqueness of the Northwest Coast among North American culture areas, a point often overlooked by those of us immersed in its wonderful complexities. Although Kroeber's ideas of historical development – as Donald points out – are no longer relevant, both because of the emergence of Northwest Coast archaeology and developments in the understanding of cultural processes, many of his other ideas are still relevant, as this chapter demonstrates. Donald's discussion of the distribution of several important cultural and ecological "traits" gives support to both the idea of the Northwest Coast as a group of cultures sharing important characteristics and to the validity of the "culture area" concept. As he points out, though, neither the shared characteristics nor the area involved are constant, with the culture area likely expanding to the north (de Laguna 1972) and to the south (Matson and Coupland 1995:259) at the time of European contact. However, Donald suggests that the spread to the north was probably reaching the limit possible with the technology present in the seventeenth century.

This book ends with Donald's "Epilogue," which gives his perspective on the other contributions. Although most of the chapters do share many assumptions about the nature of Northwest Coast society and, therefore, about what are the important questions, there are many topics that are not touched. Still, our understanding is now dramatically different from what it was twenty years ago, which leads to the prominence of new questions and, therefore, different sorts of research. It is clear that our knowledge of Northwest Coast society is much better grounded now, and this, as represented by the chapters in this book, has allowed for the rapid, interconnected progress we have made in our understanding of the past.

2

A Hunter-Gatherer Paramount Chiefdom: Tsimshian Developments through the Contact Period

Andrew R.C. Martindale

The Tsimshian of the eighteenth and nineteenth centuries have been described as a complex hunting and gathering society, in part because they possessed cultural characteristics normally associated with agricultural economies. These included intensive subsistence production that operated at sufficient per capita rates to achieve the year's food supply in only six or seven months, a system of land tenure, a relatively high population density for hunter-gatherers, permanent architecture, economic and social inequality, specialized technologies and occupational specialization, regional economic redistribution, and slavery (Boas 1916; Coupland et al. 2001; Drucker 1965; Garfield 1951; Halpin and Seguin 1990; Martindale 1999a; Miller 1997; Roseman and Rubel 1977; Seguin 1984a). It was first suggested by Garfield (1951:33) that the Tsimshian were a rare example of a hunting and gathering society organized into a paramount chiefdom, a political system in which the paramount chief had regional control over a suite of subservient leaders. Recently, Tsimshian cultural complexity has been noted (Halpin and Seguin 1990; Miller 1997) but that this complexity went beyond the system of ranked society has not been discussed. In this paper, I argue that the Tsimshian did develop a paramount chiefdom but only after contact with Europeans which began in AD 1787.

Nature of a Paramount Chiefdom

The argument that the Tsimshian developed a paramount chiefdom in the late eighteenth and early nineteenth centuries assumes that their culture underwent a qualitative shift from one type of society to another. Cultural typologies have been criticized for their association with neo-evolutionary theory. However, as Wason (1994:13) argues, we can use cultural typologies without assuming evolutionary causes. A typological structure such as proposed by Sahlins (1958), Service (1962), Fried (1967), Johnson and Earle (1987), or Wason (1994) provides useful descriptions of cultural patterns that themselves do not necessarily presuppose any particular causality. In this chapter, I follow Firth's (1951:53) and Sahlins's (1958) terminology and describe Tsimshian society of the early eighteenth century as a ramage-type system that developed into a paramount chiefdom.

Although it reflects an older terminology, a ramage-type system is a good description of traditional Tsimshian society. In its earliest uses, a ramage was synonymous with a lineage, a descent group, a clan, or a tribe (Firth 1951). Sahlins (1958:140) refined the definition to "a non-exogamous, internally stratified, unilineal descent group." Ramages form nested, hierarchical structures such that the segments of a ramage are themselves ramages. In the Tsimshian case, the village group is a ramage: it has a hierarchical structure of lineages in which the leader of the highest ranked lineage is the village group leader, or chief, and the leaders of the other lineages form his/her core of noble counsellors. In addition, the lineages that comprise the village group are themselves ramages. Each lineage is composed of matrilineally related families within which rank is usually associated with distance from the core line of primogeniture descent. Although both are ramages, their structuring rules are different: the lineage-ramage is structured around rules of descent, while the village group ramage is based on rank determined by inherited and achieved levels of status (Rosman and Rubel 1971:13-14). While the village group ramage is not based on kinship, it is analogous to a lineage and the counsellors are thought of as junior siblings to the village group leader.

A paramount chief is the leader of a chiefdom, a common typological concept in anthropology most familiar from the work of Service (1971) but updated recently by Johnson and Earle (2000:265-302). Chiefdoms are characterized by a large regionally organized population, hierarchical authority organized along kinship lines, centralized economic control of surplus production, and a hierarchical settlement pattern around a regional centre. Chiefdoms are rare but not unknown in hunter-gatherer societies; the fifteenth-century Calusa of southern Florida are one example (Widmer 1988).

A paramount chiefdom is formed by the creation of a third ramage operating at a larger, regional scale. The ramage structure of hierarchy within an autonomous descent group is reproduced between village groups. The village groups become stratified under a regional leader or paramount chief. The relationship between the paramount chief and the village group leaders is again analogous to the relationships between siblings in a descent group. The structuring principles of the Tsimshian paramount chiefdom are, like the village group organization, based on ranked levels of status. However, as described below, new mechanisms of generating wealth through the introduction of the European market economy were the means by which paramount chiefs consolidated their regional authority.

Wason (1994) has argued that the difference between a ramage system and a paramount chiefdom (in his terminology, a ranked system and a chiefdom) is the level of entrenchment of inequality. Entrenchment of inequality produces relationships of dominance (Berreman 1981:8), which are recognized as different positions of status. Differences of status exist even in so-called egalitarian societies, and these are usually based on an individual's abilities. These can be institutionalized along lines of age and gender, for example. In Fried's (1967:33) terms, inequality based on the character and characteristics of individuals creates as many high-status positions as there are people capable of filling them. A higher level of entrenchment produces what Wason (1994:37) calls "kin/role" distinctions. In this situation, an individual's status is dependent on his or her position in the kinship group or on his/her role in an organization (such as a military or religious group). Kin/role based inequalities tend to produce ranked societies in which status is ascribed. In rank societies such as the ramage-type system, fewer status positions exist than people to fill them (Fried 1967:109). Selection is based on strict rules of heredity, although there are ways to circumvent these rules (Wason 1994:46). The highest level of unstratified, ranked society is the chiefdom. Here, the status positions themselves are organized into a rigid hierarchy in which there is a single highest ranked, or paramount, position. Chiefdoms are usually regionally linked segments of ranked societies, so the increase in status is concurrent with an increase in the regional size of the chief's authority.

The criterion by which different levels of social complexity can be resolved is the increasingly arbitrary entrenchment of inequality. In weakly ranked societies, inequality is based on inherent characteristics such as gender and age. In ranked societies it becomes related to kinship or position, which are usually functions of an individual's genealogy. In stratified societies, it is related to a number of arbitrary distinctions such as class, race, and caste. Significantly, with increased entrenchment of inequality comes increased control over economic resources. In the first threshold (to ranked societies), higher status individuals have economic control of non-subsistence resources only. At the second threshold (to stratified societies), this control includes subsistence goods.

The principle of increasing social inequality and its economic correlates is the basis of social complexity. Why this is so is beyond the scope of this chapter. We can imagine how a society in which complex characteristics, such as a regional distribution of economic resources with a stable exchange between subsistence and manufactured goods, exists in the absence of social inequality. However, to my knowledge, this has never been observed. This definition of social complexity, then, is somewhat dystopian. As societies become more complex, fewer individuals have power (the control of resources or people's labour), authority (the control over a territory), and prestige (the accumulation of material wealth) (Berreman 1981:12).

Were the Tsimshian a Paramount Chiefdom?

The term "Tsimshian" refers primarily to a Penutian linguistic phylum comprised of two major language groups: Coast/Southern Tsimshian and Nisga'a/ Gitk'san (Dunn 1976:3-6; Thompson and Kinkade 1990:31, 45). These four language variants had discrete territories around the Skeena and Nass Rivers of northern British Columbia (Figure 2.1). It is tempting to think of these linguistic areas as synonymous with cultural and/or political boundaries, but the issue is not so straightforward. Tsimshian people participated in cultural relationships on different levels and at different scales, many of which crossed linguistic boundaries and created relationships that did not correspond directly with archaeological notions of culture area. An individual belonged by birth to at least five levels of nested social organization – phratries, clans, village groups, lineages, and families – each of which was composed of multiple divisions. The largest of these (the phratry) extended to other language groups, while the smallest (the family) was co-resident throughout the annual seasonal round from coast (winter) to interior (summer). The maximum unit of political organization is generally believed to have been the village (or local) group, which was composed of separate extended family lineages which, for the lower Skeena Tsimshian (Coast Tsimshian speakers), shared a coastal winter village and a separate interior territory. The local group coastal villages and interior territories of the Coast and Southern Tsimshian-speaking people are shown in Figure 2.1. As Seguin (1984b:x) writes: "The major subdivisions of the Tsimshian rarely functioned as political or economic units, though there were some long-term alliances, particularly among the Coast Tsimshian near the mouth of the Skeena. In general, each village was an independent territorial, economic, and political unit."

What is uncertain is whether there was any political office above that of leader (also referred to as chief) of the village group. Were the Tsimshian organized as hierarchically ranked but autonomous village groups that shared cultural and linguistic traditions? Or was there a paramount regional chieftainship?

The uncertainty of the issue begins with the major Tsimshian ethnographers, Boas and Garfield. The maximum level of political authority that Boas (1889:823; 1916:429-434, 496) identifies is that of the village group leader, the highest ranked member of the highest ranked lineage in a village group. All village group leaders were ranked, and the highest ranked of these enjoyed preferential treatment as a consequence of high status, although the role had no additional political or territorial authority. Garfield (1939:

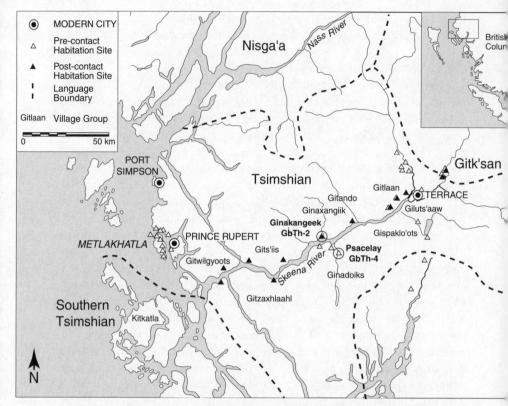

Figure 2.1   Archaeological sites and village group territories in the Tsimshian area.

182-191) also refers to village group leaders and identifies Ligeex (a.k.a. Legaix, Legaic) of the Gispaklo'ots as the highest ranked of the lower Skeena village group leaders. However, in a later work, she argues that regional, multi-village chiefs (a paramount chieftainship) developed among the Tsimshian during the late eighteenth century, about the time of European contact:

> However, the Tsimshian of the lower Skeena and Nass Rivers are unique. They developed lineage political leadership into village chieftainship, probably early in the eighteenth century. *Before the beginning of the nineteenth century this had developed further into tribal chieftainship.* As far as we know they had the only overall tribal organization headed by a chief that was found in northwestern North America. (Garfield 1951:33, emphasis added)

Most modern analyses follow Boas (see, for example, Halpin and Seguin 1990) and rely on his ethnographic data. Donald Mitchell (1983a) has made a convincing argument using documentary evidence from European sources that the Tsimshian were not organized into a paramount chiefdom. Dean (1994) has argued in a similar vein that Ligeex's influence has been overstated. Nevertheless, the perception that Ligeex was a paramount chief of the Tsimshian persists in overviews of Tsimshian history (Fisher 1977:47; Wolf 1982:189).

In this chapter, I refer to archaeological data, documentary sources, and evidence from Tsimshian oral traditions in an attempt to resolve this issue. I argue, that prior to European contact in AD 1787, the Tsimshian were not organized into a paramount chiefdom but a short-lived paramount chiefdom did develop under Ligeex during the early contact period, a development that disappeared after AD 1840.

Archaeological Evidence of Change

I have discussed the archaeological developments of the Tsimshian contact era in more detail elsewhere (Martindale 1999a, 1999b, 2000), but they can be summarized as follows. In the absence of a single, deeply stratified, multicomponent site in the lower Skeena Valley, I have devised a three-period, five-phase archaeological chronology for the interior zone of Tsimshian territory based primarily on habitation sites and settlement patterns, as shown in Table 2.1.

For this discussion, our interest is the transition from the precontact period (late phase [about 500 BP to AD 1787]) to the contact period (protocontact phase [1787-1850]). Prior to contact, Tsimshian local groups followed a seasonal cycle of residential mobility between interior territories in the watershed of the lower Skeena River and coastal villages located at a place called Metlakhatla, near the modern city of Prince Rupert. The interior zone was occupied in the summer and fall months and was the source of most of the annual food supply, primarily anadromous fish, land mammals, and plant foods. Food stores collected from the interior supplied the majority of food consumed during the winter months on the coast. Archaeological examples of winter villages are common (MacDonald and Inglis 1981), but only recently has the precontact interior settlement pattern come to light (Martindale 1999a). Interior habitation sites contained only one or two houses and were located throughout the tributary valleys of the Skeena River watershed. Excavations at the site of Psacelay (GbTh-4) revealed many characteristics of the ethnographic Tsimshian, including extended family households composed of family subunits (that had differential access to economic surpluses and wealth items), surplus production of interior resources, and occupation of the interior zone during the summer and fall months. This settlement pattern allowed each household to distribute itself within the village group resource territory during the summer months when staple food resources were most abundant. Thus, it was well suited to an economy based on the surplus production of subsistence resources.

Table 2.1

Tsimshian interior zone archaeological sequence

Period	Phase	Description
Contact	Modern (AD 1850-present)	• Appearance of industrial sites such as canneries, sawmills, mining camps, roads, rail lines, docks, and rock-fill quarries.
		• Continued occupation of interior villages, though with much reduced population.
		• Houses adopt increased European design elements such as glass windows and metal nails.
		• Increased use of interior zone by coastal residents for short periods of hunting and fishing; construction of special-use cabins.
	Protocontact (AD 1787-1850)	• Large village sites of up to 17 houses located on flat riverside terraces; satellite camps at fishing and hunting locations.
		• House sizes approximately 6 × 8 m; incorporation of European design elements.
		• Villages located at confluences of tributary rivers and the Skeena River; cabins located at fishing locations or access points into high hunting grounds.
Late pre-contact	Traditional (1000-163 BP)	• Corresponds to traditional Tsimshian society.
		• Seasonal mobility between coast (winter) and interior valleys (summer-fall).
		• Small habitation sites of 1 to 2 houses located on flat riverside terraces.
		• Houses approximately 10 × 16 m.
		• Sites located throughout tributary valleys.
Early pre-contact	Regional (1700-1000 BP)	• First evidence of coast-to-interior similarities.
		• Year-round occupation of interior valleys.
		• Small habitation sites of 1 to 2 small houses cut into valley slopes.
		• Houses approximately 4 × 6 m.
	Interior (2500-1700 BP)	• Sites located throughout tributary valleys of the Skeena River.
		• Ground stone technology.
		• Year-round residence in interior valleys.
		• Rock shelter is only known habitation site type.
		• Lithic flake technology, using quartz and basalts.

Source: Martindale 1999a.

After contact, the settlement pattern of the interior changed to include larger habitation sites containing multiple houses. These new interior villages, containing as many as fourteen houses, were located within each local group territory along the Skeena River. Psacelay continued to be occupied into the contact period, but one of its two houses was abandoned. The development of interior villages analogous to the coastal villages of the precontact period appears to be part of a shift towards regionalization and increased settlement hierarchy. Prior to contact, the settlement pattern contained two levels of sites: agglutinated coastal villages and small interior habitation sites. This changed to three levels of site types after contact: interior habitation sites, agglutinated interior villages, and a new regional indigenous centre at Laxhlgu'alaams, near the Hudson's Bay Company trading post at Fort Simpson (now known as *Port* Simpson). The identification of Laxhlgu'alaams/Fort Simpson as an indigenous regional centre is based on evidence form European documentary sources and Tsimshian oral traditions and is discussed in more detail below.

These changes in the archaeological record of the contact period have three implications. First, they indicate a shift away from the subsistence resources territories in favour of occupation along the main interior-to-coast trade route, the Skeena River. Second, they imply a decrease in the significance of subsistence resources in favour of economic activity within the trade economy. In its place, as we shall see below, was increased participation in the European trade economy. Third, they indicate a change in house size. When the large houses (about 150-200 m²) of Psacelay disappeared, new, smaller houses (about 75-100 m²) were constructed at Ginakangeek (GbTh-2). The spatial organization of the traditional plank house at Psacelay is evidence of a relatively large extended family of about forty people. The houses at Ginakangeek were smaller, forming a considerably smaller social and economic unit. The reasons for the reduction in household size are unknown. Population decrease may have been a factor. Such a decrease in population may have been a result of smallpox epidemics, the first of which killed an estimated one-third of the Tsimshian population in 1836 (Dean 1994:58-59). Alternatively, the extended family household may have maintained its social ties but split into its constituent nuclear families, each living in a smaller house at a different location in order to maintain representation in each of the economically significant areas: the interior resource territory for subsistence production and the interior Skeena River area for interior-to-coast trade.

These three developments (increased settlement hierarchy, increased participation in the trade economy at the expense of the subsistence economy, and reduction in house size) are indicative of fundamental changes in Tsimshian social and economic organization. Such changes were a consequence of contact with Europeans; however, as I have argued elsewhere (Martindale 1999a), during the early decades of contact Tsimshian society was insulated from the more destructive aspects of European colonization because of the lack of permanent European settlements in the area. This meant that furs, though valuable, could not be exchanged for food, and, as a consequence, the traditional Tsimshian subsistence economy remained the only source of food until the 1840s. Thus, the changes of the protocontact phase appear to consist of adaptations to the market economy rather than an erosion of indigenous society due to the deleterious effects of colonialism. This interpretation is based on evidence from documentary sources.

Data from Historic Documents

We do not know who the first Europeans to meet the Tsimshian were. When Captain Charles Duncan and James Colnett of the British Royal Navy sailed into Kitkatla in 1787, the Tsimshian there "already had trade goods and were eager for more" (Halpin and Seguin 1990:281). The first recorded European expedition to arrive off the coast of British Columbia was that of Juan Perez in 1774 (Fisher 1977:1; Wagner 1968:172-173). Commissioned by the Spanish government to explore the continent north of the outpost of San Blas, on the California coast, Perez, in his frigate *Santiago*, sailed to the Queen Charlotte Islands before turning south due to poor weather. On his return trip, he stopped at a cove on the west coast of Vancouver Island, which may have been Nootka Sound, and returned to San Blas (Beals 1989:88-89; Wagner 1968:173). Although he encountered Haida people off the Queen Charlottes and Nuu-chah-nulth people on Vancouver Island, Perez made little contact. Later voyages by Maurelle (in 1775), Cook (in 1778), and Martinez (in 1788) were conducted before an armed Spanish fort was constructed on Nootka Sound on the west coast of Vancouver Island in Nuu-chah-nulth territory.

An explanation for the foreknowledge of European trading among the Kitkatla Tsimshian, and probably among the Haida, may have a Russian source. Vitus Bering, a Russian explorer, reached the Aleutian Islands in 1728 and the Alaskan coast in 1741. In the 1741 expedition, Bering, captaining the *St. Peter*, made landfall on the Alaska coast in the area of Mount St. Elias. Bering was taken ill with scurvy, but his officers mapped the coastline of Alaska north and west. Bering died when the *St. Peter* beached on an island halfway between the Aleutian Islands and the Kamchatka Peninsula, and the crew was forced to over-winter on this barren island (Beals 1989:16). The survivors rebuilt the remains of the *St. Peter* into a makeshift vessel and sailed home. Alexei Chirikov, captain of the *St. Paul*, had left Russia with Bering but set his own course for the Northwest Coast after the two ships had been separated in a storm. Chirikov made landfall off the Alaska coast at Baranof Island, about 400 kilometres south of Bering, where he encountered indigenous people, probably Tlingit. Chirikov sent a party of ten men ashore but none ever returned; after six days he set sail back to the Russian coast (Bancroft 1884:30; Gough 1992:25). Thereafter, however, the rich sea otter populations of the Northwest Coast drew Russian hunters. Nevochikov returned in 1745 and Glotov in 1763-65, although it is unclear how many Russian hunting expeditions were mounted or how far south they reached.

Early Contact: Maritime Fur Trade

In 1792 Jacinto Caamano led an expedition to explore the waters north of the fort on Nootka Sound. His journals (Wagner and Newcombe 1938) indicate that he sailed around the Queen Charlottes, east to the Tsimsean Peninsula, and south to Pitt Island before encountering any indigenous people. On Pitt Island he was met by its inhabitants, whose village, Ksidiya'ats, remains identifiable today as an ancient habitation site (Halpin and Seguin 1990:281). That Caamano did not encounter any Tsimshian out of Metlakhatla may be because his trip through their territory occurred in late July, a time of year when most of the Metlakhatla Tsimshian would be at their interior territories in the lower Skeena watershed. Caamano exchanged beads and small metal ornaments with the Tsimshian, a pattern that Kendrick (1985:97) argues was characteristic of the early trading between European explorers and indigenous peoples.

Despite the fact that European governments at the time were only beginning to map the area, Caamano encountered an American brigantine, the *Hancock*, anchored off the Queen Charlottes. It was a Boston-based trader that had returned from China, the main importer of sea otter pelts (Wagner and Newcombe 1938: 265). Although documentary evidence of this shadow contact between the Tsimshian and private trading vessels is slim, it appears to have been an early and significant relationship. The potential of trading sea otter furs from the Northwest Coast to China had been revealed in 1784 when Cook, in published accounts of his 1778 trip, had noted that sea otter pelts were worth $120 in China (Fisher 1977:2). He had seen such pelts for sale in Canton but did not reveal their source (Kendrick 1985:97). The first recorded American fur trading expedition to the Northwest Coast occurred in 1785 when John Hanna captained the merchant vessel the *Sea Otter*. Hanna's first trading venture garnered him 560 pelts worth over $20,000. Soon others followed (Fisher 1977:3). In 1787 George Dixon arrived as captain of the *Queen Charlotte*. Through his exchanges with the Haida, he acquired 1,821 furs (1997:3). In 1788 Kendrick and Grey left Boston in the *Columbia Rediviva* and the *Lady Washington*, respectively, to ply the Northwest Coast-to-China trade route. By 1790 other vessels, including the *Hancock* and the *Hope*, had joined them. In 1791 the *Grace* and the French vessel *Solide* were active in the sea otter trade. By 1792 twenty-one merchant vessels were working the Northwest Coast-to-China route (Wolf

1982:182). Between 1785 and 1825 records indicate that at least 330 merchant vessels visited the Northwest Coast (1982:185).

The effect of these merchant vessels, and their demand for sea otter pelts, was to create a new industry among Northwest Coast peoples, including the Tsimshian. Within a decade of 1785, the sea otter trade had become the primary forum for European contact with indigenous peoples. The enormous profits of the 1780s were quickly reduced when indigenous peoples inflated the price of pelts. By 1792 the price of a sea otter pelt had quadrupled; it would eventually reach ten times its original value (Fisher 1977:5). The increase in price was due to three factors, all of which reveal the increasing scale of the trade. First, the early success of the 1780s had attracted greater numbers of merchant ships, each prepared to deal almost exclusively in sea otter pelts. Although indigenous production increased to meet this demand, it remained a seller's market. When multiple ships were anchored at a trading harbour, indigenous sellers would move from buyer to buyer looking for the highest price. Fisher (1977:9) states that "even captains of solitary vessels who felt that Indian prices were exorbitant were informed that other traders would soon follow who would be willing to pay what was asked."

Second, the reciprocal trade in metal had, conversely, saturated the market (1977:6). Demand for metal remained but was soon accompanied by an interest in blankets, rum, tobacco, molasses, and firearms. Occasionally, ornaments of different types were in high demand, but their value was largely a result of their rarity, and, as supply increased, the demands of fashion shifted and their value dropped. Indigenous traders maintained a consistent demand for quality and rejected goods they deemed to be of inferior value (1977:7).

The third factor that created the inflationary market was the economic savvy of the indigenous traders. We know, for example, that they recognized and even worked to create a seller's market. It is also likely that they used the merchants' desire to be under sail to Asian markets to their own advantage by drawing out bargaining negotiations over pelts for days while, as Fisher (1977:10) puts it, "affecting the utmost indifference as to whether they sold them or not." What is only suggested in the European accounts is that, in many areas, indigenous traders were themselves wholesalers who were being supplied by many different producers. Access to Europeans was frequently in dispute, conflicts that were eventually resolved so that the majority of trade to the Europeans was conducted through a few indigenous leaders operating out of a small number of entrepots (Fisher 1977:13; Harris 1997:34-35). In the Tsimshian area, there were three initial trading harbours: Big Bay, Tugwell Island, and near the communities of Metlakhatla in Venn Passage (Marsden and Galois 1995:171). Later, the primary anchorage of merchant vessels became the Nass River estuary.

Fisher (1977:17) argues that, because of the fundamental indigenous control over the market in terms of the location of trade, the pace of negotiations, the quantity of furs available and, to a large extent, the price, the sea otter trade did not produce a lopsided power structure. As a consequence, he argues, indigenous society was not significantly disrupted by the sea otter trade. According to him, wealth from the sea otter trade was not distributed evenly either within the indigenous trading group or between different groups. This led to discrepancies in wealth on a greater scale than was possible prior to contact. Drucker (1943:27) noted this phenomenon and argued that this "fluorescence of native culture" was especially evidenced by the development of indigenous communities at trading depots. Barbeau (1917:508) even argued that this increased wealth triggered a fluorescence in elite art forms such as ceremonial pole carving. Although the detrimental effects of disease, violence, land encroachment, and wage labour eventually appeared, the initial effect of the early contact period appeared to have been economic prosperity, at least for some sectors of indigenous society.

Established Contact: Interior Fur Trade

By 1805 the sea otter trade had begun to collapse (Marsden and Galois 1995:172). The cause was declining sea otter populations which, by 1810, would be severely depleted and by 1830 would be hunted to near extinction. From the European point of view, the loss of this commodity was compensated for by an increase in the appearance of inland terrestrial mammal pelts, especially beaver. That these interior commodities began to appear in coastal markets as the frequency of sea otter pelts declined is rarely an issue of note in European documents (see, for example, Wolf 1982:189). The rise of the interior fur trade coincided with two new European initiatives. Both were a consequence of the arrival of the North American trading cartels, the North West Company and the Hudson's Bay Company, which merged in 1821 into the Hudson's Bay Company (HBC). The first initiative was the scheduled appearance of company vessels and, later, the establishment of permanent trading posts in areas of high-volume trading on the coast. The second was the appearance of trading posts in the interior, connected to overland trade routes.

The trading cartels were a different type of consumer for the indigenous markets. With their influence in government and the resources of their companies behind them, they were able to embark upon and secure long-term trading relationships with indigenous groups. Unlike the earlier merchant ships, they offered a variety of goods for exchange, including subsistence foodstuffs. They sent experienced, armed operatives whose responsibilities included governance as well as trade. And, finally, they facilitated regular contact between indigenous peoples and a variety of Europeans, including missionaries.

The HBC's move into the Northwest Coast was a response to two perceived threats to its business interests. American traders, by shipping directly to China, were bypassing the European markets. The HBC wished to extend its influence over this aspect of the fur trade and to redirect Northwest Coast furs through its own eastern distribution system. Second, trading relationships between northern Northwest Coast indigenous peoples and Russian traders were also sapping furs out of the eastern market (Dean 1994:45). The HBC was also aware of the efforts of indigenous traders, who were manipulating the availability of pelts in order to maintain a high price. In response, the company sent the HBC vessel *William and Anne* into Tsimshian territory in 1825. In their first trading mission with Tsimshian and Nisga'a peoples, the master trader (Henry Halwell) and his clerk (Alexander Mackenzie) encountered an indigenous population familiar with European products and trade. Most of the Nisga'a had guns, and many wore European items of clothing. They also possessed more tobacco than the Europeans, a deficit the Nisga'a recognized and tried to exploit by offering their own at an exorbitant price (1994:46). Halwell and Mackenzie noted that four American brigs had visited the coast that season and that their annual trade amounted to about a thousand beaver pelts per year (1994:47).

American traders had developed a pattern of arriving off the Nass River estuary in early spring to begin trading for pelts. Although they may not have known it, they had essentially been incorporated into the traditional Tsimshian springtime gathering for trading eulachon grease. In 1828 HBC employee Aemilius Simpson noted as much in a letter to his London head office. Simpson described items commonly traded at the Nass, including slaves, guns, rum, beads, bracelets, and dentalia shells (1994:48-49). In 1831 the HBC began construction of a northern trading post on the coast. It chose a location on the Nass River estuary, as this was the most active trading entrepot in the area (Fisher 1977:26). After Fort Nass's completion in September 1832, the company maintained it for two years before abruptly moving it thirty kilometres west to Laxhlgu'alaams.

At its new location, Fort Simpson would eventually become the focus of European influence in Tsimshian society. However, in its early years, the trading post seems to have been accommodated within the traditional seasonal cycle. Tsimshian families would arrive at the post in the spring to conduct their trading simultaneously with the eulachon fishery, after which they would depart. Gradually, indigenous traders would begin to visit the fort at other times of the year. Fall and winter visits are noted in the journal of the fort's chief factor, Peter Ogden, in 1834. During the summer months, however, neither Tsimshian nor Tlingit traders visited the fort (Dean 1994:54). In 1836 Nishoot, leader of the Gitzaxhlaahl, died of smallpox and was buried at the fort with military honours (Marsden and Galois 1995:178). In that same year, Nts'iitskwoodat, a wife of the Gispaklo'ots leader Ligeex, died of smallpox and was also buried at the fort (1995:177). By January 1837 Tsimshian families were camping at the fort until early spring, when they left for the Nass River eulachon fishery. They would stop again on their return but quickly depart, presumably for their interior habitation sites. Sometime during the 1830s thirty to fifty traditional post-and-beam houses were constructed around the fort by households from all the Skeena River village groups. During the summer of 1837 the first recorded feast was held at Fort Simpson, although little is known of it from documentary sources other than that the Europeans observed drunkenness in its participants (Dean 1994:60). By the winter of 1838 trading increased for a feast that was to be held at Metlakhatla, indicating that most of the Tsimshian population remained in their traditional winter villages. That spring, many Tsimshian returned early from the eulachon fishery and encamped at the fort. Interestingly, they refused to trade until the American brigs arrived, effectively putting the trading post under siege (1994:63). By 1839 a resident indigenous population had permanently settled at the fort. In November 1840 HBC documents record ten canoes full of Tsimshian arriving at the fort to make their winter residence there (1994:75).

Gradually, the seasonal cycle of residential movement changed. Although a component of Tsimshian society remained in permanent residence at the fort, and a few traders would arrive in the summer months, the general trend was towards settling at the fort during the winter instead of occupying the traditional winter villages at Metlakhatla. This pattern changed again as more and more people began to live permanently at Fort Simpson. By 1850, out of an estimated Tsimshian population of 8,500, 1,049 were permanent residents of the fort (Duff 1965:19). By October 1857, when William Duncan, an Anglican missionary, arrived, the population at the fort had risen to 2,325 people living in 140 houses (Garfield 1939:333; Murray 1985:36). This would have meant that an average household contained seventeen people.

The focus of trade between the HBC and the Tsimshian during the early years of the fort remained commodity furs. In 1835 the fort acquired less than 1,500 pelts. By 1838 this had risen to just under 3,500 (Dean 1994:62). Two additional trading spheres developed. The earlier Tsimshian practice of trading for valuables and wealth continued. The most sought-after items remained metals, molasses, tobacco, cloth, and ornaments. In addition, a demand for firearms, munitions, and alcohol developed. Traditional trade between different indigenous groups remained a component of the activities at the fort, although one outside of the purview of Europeans. The trade of slaves between groups is especially mentioned by HBC employee John Work, who recognized the value of this market as something that attracted indigenous traders to the fort (1994:65).

Another trading sphere developed around the exchange of foodstuffs. In some cases, HBC staff acquired food supplies such as potatoes, halibut, salted and fresh venison and salmon, and eulachon oil from indigenous families (1994:54). Less trade in foodstuffs occurred in the opposite direction, with the exception of molasses, as the indigenous people frequently found European food repulsive.

Thus, in the first decades after the establishment of Fort Simpson, we can characterize Tsimshian society as undergoing gradual changes in three areas. Each of these changes is evidence of a political and economic expansion of Tsimshian society from a ramage-type system of ranked villages to a regional polity headed by a paramount chief. First, increased trade in commodity furs, established with the sea otter trade, continued with a shift to land-based pelts. The nature of this development is not obvious from European documents. Aemilius Simpson, for example, reported in 1830 that indigenous traders were concealing from him the nature and locations of the interior-to-coast trade routes (Dean 1994:49). Since Europeans did not themselves trap or seek out trappers from whom to purchase pelts, the fur trade continued largely at the behest of indigenous suppliers. The one-sided nature of the exchange was possible in part because the Europeans did not supply necessities. Food, clothing, shelter, and transportation were all available through traditional indigenous sources. The most sought-after items offered by the HBC were luxuries: tobacco, alcohol, arms, and items of wealth. As a result, the HBC trading post remained, for much of its first fifteen years of operation, a way station at which indigenous traders would stop to convert a resource commodity (furs) into wealth.

The second area for which documentary evidence records changes in Tsimshian society is in the settlement pattern. Again, these are gradual shifts from a traditional pattern, in which winters were spent at villages on the coast, spring included a trip to the Nass River for eulachon and trade, and summer months were spent in the interior collecting subsistence resources. The first change was an incorporation of American trading vessels into the springtime trade at the Nass River. When the HBC came to construct its first fort on the northern Northwest Coast in 1831, it chose this same location. After the fort moved in 1834 it became a stopping point between trips to and from the Nass River. Gradually, the Tsimshian began to use the fort, instead of their traditional winter villages, as the site of winter habitation. Eventually, an indigenous community became permanently settled at the fort. Until this last event, it appears that the Tsimshian simply included the European trading post within their traditional cycle of movement. Even after a permanent community became established, Tsimshian families continued to visit their traditional seasonal resource collection sites.

The third pattern to emerge from the documentary evidence is that the distribution of this wealth within indigenous society appears to have favoured, as was the case with the sea otter trade, a few prominent leaders who acted as wholesalers. Among the most prominent Tsimshian figures in this regard was a man named Ligeex. According to Fisher (1977:31) and Wolf (1982:189) Ligeex was the most influential Tsimshian trader. He oversaw much of the interior fur trade, especially the production coming to the coast from the Skeena, Babine, Bulkley, and Nass watersheds. This considerable amount of trade within Ligeex's jurisdiction apparently gave him sufficient authority to, at times, restrict access to the HBC fort to his allies.

Later Developments

Garfield (1939:328) states that, by 1856, the traditional village sites in Metlakhatla had been abandoned in favour of Fort Simpson. In many ways, the modern image of colonization as a departure from traditional indigenous norms to those increasingly influenced by European culture was a consequence of events in the second half of the nineteenth century. Up to this point, changes within Tsimshian society appear to be largely a consequence of indigenous accommodations to new modes and possibilities presented by European trade. After this, European influence on Tsimshian social, ideological, and political principles increases.

An important element in this change was the efforts of missionaries such as William Duncan, who arrived in Fort Simpson in 1856. Supporters of the missionary movement believed that the eventual incorporation of indigenous culture into the European sphere was inevitable. They chose to send operatives to accelerate this process, in part to forestall the influence of more destructive facets of European influence such as alcoholism and prostitution (Murray 1985:16). The tenets of the missionary agenda are well known: rejection of indigenous beliefs in favour of Christianity, adoption of European behaviours and material culture, and eventual conversion to European values. The effects on Tsimshian society have been documented (Murray 1985; Usher 1969; Wellcome 1884) and include Duncan's founding, in 1862, of a Christian utopia at Metlakhatla.

What is significant for our purposes is that this effort, coming some sixty years after contact, represents the beginning, in earnest, of the eventual colonization of the Tsimshian. Certainly, there were shifts towards European norms prior to the mass conversions to Christianity of the 1860s. These occurred, however, within the context of a robust Tsimshian culture independent of European influence. By the second half of the nineteenth century, the political and economic fluorescence occasioned by the wealth of the fur trade was fading. The list of destructive influences is familiar: smallpox, alcohol, and prostitution are commonly cited (Dean 1994; Fisher 1977; Murray 1985; Wolf 1982). More influential, perhaps, was the increasing use of European trade for food staples and necessities like shelter, clothing, and fuel. Duncan, for example, effected moral control over the residents of Metlakhatla through his monopoly on trade at the village store. Those who did not behave were not permitted purchases of basic foodstuffs; those who persisted were thrown out of the village. In a report to the missionary society, he wrote, "I deem it necessary that I must for a time be everything to the settlement, and the Indians naturally ... look to me to be everything to them and thus I have placed myself at the head of their trade" (Murray 1985:89).

The growing reliance on European food supplies was a key element in the colonization of the Tsimshian. It shifted the balance of power from indigenous to European traders as the need for cash became widespread. In its wake grew the wage labour economies that would employ indigenous workers: river transport, fishing, canning, logging, forestry, lumber milling, mining, longshoring, packing, railroad construction, construction trades, and a variety of domestic service roles (J. MacDonald 1984:46). Some of these, such as the freighting business between Fort Simpson and the European community of Hazelton at the confluence of the Skeena and Bulkley rivers, were owned by Tsimshian entrepreneurs.

In addition to the influence of missionaries and the cash economy, the influence of European judicial authority increased in the second half of the nineteenth century. On at least thirteen occasions between 1859 and 1888, the British Navy and, after 1871, the Dominion of Canada's Department of Indian Affairs (DIA), embarked on police action against indigenous peoples (1984:43). Indigenous institutions were no longer the highest authority in Tsimshian society. Authority was exercised in a variety of ways. Starting in 1881, the DIA began commissioning surveyors to demarcate Indian reserve lands throughout British Columbia. Allotments were limited to twenty acres per family, the definition of family being strictly European. Many extended families thus found themselves competing with their own relatives for claim to communally held land. When allotments were in dispute, the DIA appointed judicial tribunals of Europeans to adjudicate (Department of Indian Affairs 1881).

That the erosion of Tsimshian authority over ideological, economic, and judicial aspects of their society increased during the latter part of the nineteenth century is not surprising. The inference that remains from the documentary evidence of contact, however, is that, during the first half of this century, such influence was effectively resisted. The Tsimshian maintained control over the changes occurring in their society as a consequence of contact, probably because of the economic autonomy of their subsistence food supply and their dominant position in the fur trade. The ascendancy of leaders such as Ligeex has been cited as a key factor in this resistance (Fisher 1977; Grumet 1975; Wolf 1982).

Dean (1994), however, argues that the authority of Ligeex has been overstated and that his control did not amount to a monopoly over the interior-to-coast fur trade in the region. He acknowledges that Ligeex had an "exclusive" trading relationship with the HBC but argues that this was less a consequence of Ligeex's efforts and more a result of him being the most powerful indigenous leader to survive the smallpox epidemic of 1836 (1994:75). Dean bases his argument on documentary evidence, especially the records and journals of HBC employees. He disputes claims to Ligeex's monopoly by identifying examples of trade at Fort Simpson conducted with indigenous traders other than Ligeex or his allies. Furthermore, he argues that Ligeex was elevated to his status by the HBC staff, who favoured him among all the Tsimshian traders (1994:76). As an example, he cites John Work's description of HBC staff's "relief" at the news of the death of Nishoot and Txagaxs. Both men were powerful indigenous leaders (of the Gitzaxhlaahl and Ginaxangiik local groups, respectively) who had frustrated HBC attempts to trade directly with indigenous traders from the interior. Meanwhile, the HBC had vaccinated Ligeex and his family against the disease. Dean interprets this favouritism as evidence that Ligeex was the most "pliant" of the Tsimshian leaders (1994:76).

Dean argues that Ligeex rose to prominence between 1831 and 1840 only as a beneficiary of HBC trade and that, by 1862, the Gispaklo'ots had stopped trading in furs (1994:44). Specifically, he argues that, "by 1840 there was no sign of confederation of villages under an autocratic Legaic [Ligeex]; rather the villages continued to exert autonomy in matters of trade and 'foreign' relations."

Mitchell (1983a) makes a similar argument. He suggests that the documentary evidence indicates only that the Tsimshian were organized into individual local groups, which are more accurately described as tribes. Mitchell uses Service's (1962) and Sahlins's (1968) distinction between tribe and chiefdom to make this point (1968:57-58). Tribes are characterized by the absence of a regional leadership role (Mitchell 1983a:59). In chiefdoms, there is an "identifiable and continuing office of chief," and the person who occupies this office has authority over lesser leaders in other communities (1968:58).

Mitchell points out that existing HBC records record events only from 1834 to 1842, 1852 to 1853, 1855 to 1859, and 1863 to 1866 at Fort Simpson. Journals for the other years are missing. From these documents, Mitchell argues that, while there is evidence that Ligeex was the most powerful Tsimshian leader, he cannot be characterized as a chief since there is evidence that lower-status Tsimshian leaders, supposedly under Ligeex's control, frequently did not respect his authority. As evidence of this, he cites the following incidents reported in HBC journals:

> July 1, 1837. Haida traders arrive at Fort Simpson, and some Tsimshian traders demanded their goods at arbitrary (and presumably low) rates of exchange. Fearing violence, Ligeex tries to stop the Tsimshians but, "has no influence among them when interfering with their own interests."

May 30, 1838. Five canoes of Tongass traders arrive at Fort Simpson. Some Tsimshian go to meet them and invite them ashore to trade. Other Tsimshian object and open gunfire on the two parties to drive the Tongass away. This incident demonstrates the lack of unity among Tsimshian traders.

June 20, 1838. Waiks, a Stikine leader, returns to Fort Simpson one year after insulting Ligeex by throwing a valuable copper into the ocean as a taunt. At the time Ligeex had vowed revenge, but does nothing at this meeting.

May 26, 1839. Haidas again cause disagreement among the Tsimshian. Traders from Skidegate successfully meet with Tsimshian traders, but are fired upon by other Tsimshian as they leave Fort Simpson.

October 22, 1855. An argument between a Tsimshian and a Haida man results in the destruction of a Haida canoe. The HBC writer concludes that, "The Chiefs nowadays have little or no influence and the bad characters do as they like."

July 5, 1856 and October 30, 1856. Two examples of Gispaklo'ots Tsimshian and other Tsimshian exchanging gunfire. Ligeex is able to settle the matter with the other leaders.

July 3, 1858. Haidas arrive at a camp of Ginadoiks to trade. Both groups are fired upon by Ginaxangiik Tsimshian. They return the gunfire.

November 28, 1863. The leader of the Ginadoiks visits other Tsimshian leaders to invite them to a feast. He is dissuaded by Gispaklo'ots gunfire from continuing. (Mitchell 1983a:62-63)

In addition, Mitchell points out that all Tsimshian leaders were referred to as "chiefs" in the historic documents and that Ligeex is frequently included simply as one of them (1983:60-61). He also shows that, of the thirty-two different reports of fur trading between the Tsimshian and the HBC recorded between 1836 and 1866, seven refer only to Tsimshian in general, ten are described as being between the Gispaklo'ots and the HBC, and only fifteen specifically mention Ligeex. From this evidence, Mitchell argues that Ligeex may have been a powerful chief, perhaps the most powerful of the Tsimshian leaders, but that he was not a paramount chief.

There are, however, two issues that neither Dean nor Mitchell consider sufficiently. The first is that Ligeex consolidated much of his power outside of the purview of the HBC. This means that documentary evidence does not tell the whole story. Even by Mitchell's own calculations, the Gispaklo'ots accounted for over 78 percent of the fur trade at Fort Simpson between 1832 and 1866. The second important issue is that the most powerful individual to become Ligeex (a number of relatives often bear the same name in succession), the one who is arguably a paramount chief, died in 1840, after which the fortunes of the Gispaklo'ots declined. Consider the hypothesis that a paramount chiefdom began to develop in the early nineteenth century and reached its political apogee during the 1820s and 1830s. Much of Mitchell's evidence describes a time after the chiefdom had developed and during its dissolution. Most of the documentary evidence that suggests that Ligeex was a paramount chief comes from before 1841. Consider the following incident reported in Mitchell (1983a:60):

October 28, 1840. A canoe with 4 Indians of Illegaich [Ligeex's] Gang (no other gang of the Chym. [Tsimshian] tribe being allowed to trade there) arrived from the Skeena River.

In another journal reported in Marsden and Galois (1995:178), Ligeex is described as the chief of Fort Simpson who secures a peace treaty between the Tsimshian tribe and the Kaigani Haida:

February 20, 1835. "A young man Son of Elgigh [Ligeex], the Ft. Simpson Chief accompanies us to deliver a message from his father to the Kygarny [Kaigani] Indians relative to making peace between the two tribes, which have had a misunderstanding for some time."

If the documentary evidence from European sources on the significance of specific Tsimshian leaders is inconclusive, then from where does the widely held opinion that Ligeex was paramount in influence among Tsimshian leaders come? For example, Fisher (1977:47) writes:

When the nine Tsimshian tribes moved to Fort Simpson, they all lived in the same place for the first time, and an acceptable order of rank, both for phratries and for individuals, had to be established. Legaic [Ligeex] certainly had initial advantages, but his pre-eminence was the result of a continuing process of social reordering.

Similarly, we find Wolf (1982:189) describing "the Tsimshian under Chief Legaic [Ligeex] at the Hudson Bay Companys [sic] Fort Simpson engrossed [in] trade on the upper Skeena with the Gitskan [Gitksan]." In addition to these historic reconstructions, this view is expressed in ethnographic sources (Garfield 1939; Miller 1997). In part, the stories of Ligeex have filtered into European histories through missionary reports. Missionary accounts of the work of William Duncan (Arctander 1909; Wellcombe 1887) tend to glorify the opposition he faced by portraying Ligeex as a powerful pagan adversary. Paul Legaic's (Ligeex) conversion to Christianity in 1863 was recounted for potential sponsors of the Anglican Missionary Society as a David-and-Goliath tale of the victory of Christian forces over impossible odds. Thus, Ligeex became featured as the most powerful Tsimshian leader of the time.

Duncan, however, did face a strong adversary in Ligeex, and Ligeex's authority at Fort Simpson was not invented. The relocation of Fort Nass on Tsimshian common land to Fort Simpson on Gispaklo'ots land, the predominance of the Gispaklo'ots in fur trading, and the lopsided trading relationship in which the market economy was incorporated within the indigenous wealth economy without undermining the subsistence economy all point to the development of Fort Simpson as a regional centre under indigenous control. Among the Tsimshian, the stories of Ligeex are part of the corpus of information about the arrival of the Europeans that has survived as oral traditions. These stories provide data that supplement documentary and archaeological evidence and provide a more complete picture of events between 1787 and 1840.

Data from Tsimshian Adawx

Tsimshian oral traditions, called adawx, comprise a complex body of texts. Each Tsimshian lineage owned its own adawx, which explained the significant relationships that legitimized its place in the social and geographical landscape (Marsden 1990). They provided each lineage with a record of events, explanations for territorial ownership, descriptions of significant relationships with other lineages (including marriage and trading alliances), and remembrances of key figures in the lineage's past. Since each lineage owned adawx that spoke of events and relationships in the wider society, collectively the adawx are a palimpsest of records on the history of Tsimshian life preserved from multiple perspectives.

The adawx were traditionally preserved and transmitted to be performed at socially sanctioned public events such as feasts. Public performance of these stories helped to transmit them to younger generations and also helped to ensure that an accurate historiography was maintained since any falsehoods committed by the speaker could be challenged. The texts of oral traditions were frequently preserved intact as heirlooms (Marsden 1990; Vansina 1985). The privileges preserved in the adawx, especially title to land, were frequently preserved in other media, such as crest symbols carved in house and ceremonial poles (Garfield 1947:629). In this way, oral traditions differ from oral histories used in ethnoarchaeology (Adams 1983). Oral histories are the remembrances of individuals, prompted by anthropologists, of the traditional way of life, recalled either from experience or from explanations of older relatives.

Sharpe and Tunbridge (1997) argue that oral traditions of Australian Aboriginal cultures from North Queensland have accurately preserved data from 10,000 to 13,000 years ago. They have found descriptions of geological events (volcanoes) in these stories, which are known to have occurred 13,000 years ago (1997:350-351). In addition, the stories describe how the pre-volcanic desert landscape became the modern-day rainforest after the eruptions. These descriptions match current geological reconstructions of the Atherton Tablelands and the creation of Lake Eacham, Lake Barrine, and the Crater between 13,000 and 7,600 years ago. Similarly, Day (1973) has found accurate correlations between Abenaki (Nova Scotia) oral traditions and historic documents dating back to the mid-eighteenth century. Thus, histories constructed from Tsimshian oral traditions (Marsden 1990; Marsden and Galois 1995) represent a valuable source of data on indigenous developments through the contact era. However, they represent a challenging source of information for Western scholars. The stories were preserved for a Tsimshian audience and assume a level of cultural knowledge necessary to make the information they contain sensible. The multiplicity of time frames and perspectives they represent, combined with their culturally specific epistemology, make the adawx a difficult source to use.

In history, we evaluate the authors of documents based on their occupation, nationality, religion, class, and purpose in an effort to compensate for bias in documentary evidence (Wood 1990). A similar familiarity with Tsimshian culture is necessary in order to ground inductions derived from data taken from individual adawx. Consider the following adawx recorded by Beynon in 1916 (MacDonald and Cove 1987:158-159), which appears to describe the arrival of Colnett in the village of Kitkatla in 1787:

> The Kitkatla were of their fishing village at the south end of Banks Island. All were out fishing halibut, and farthest out was a prince of the Tsibassa [Ts'ibassa] household whose name was Sabane, together with his slave. They were so absorbed in their fishing that they had to talk to the fish through the medium of the carvings on their wooden hooks. They failed to see coming towards where they were, a huge being with white wings. When it was close, the slave looked behind, saw it, and called a warning to Sabane, "A huge monster with white wings is coming towards us, and will soon catch us."

The strange men in "strange attire with very white faces and hands and fair hair" invited the Kitkatla on board their ship:

> The strange men took the Kitkatla people to their ship. When they went on board, they saw the blocks through which the ropes were woven and hearing the creaking sound they believed that these were the skulls of these people's captives, and the creaking was the cries of the agony they were still suffering. They were led down into the living quarters of the ship, and here they beheld many White dishes on the table, and in each dish, they saw

what they thought to be maggots (this was rice). Then they noticed a black substance which they believed to be the human rot extracted from dead people. This (molasses) was being poured on the maggots. There was a huge dish filled with tree fungus (sea biscuits); the men ate this and offered some to their Kitkatla guests, who after watching these beings eat, began to eat also.

The captain of the ship gave a navy uniform to Ts'ibassa and parted with the words, "Hail, hail." Ts'ibassa understood this to mean that the captain was now bestowing a name on him. Then these men departed and Ts'ibassa returned to his central village at Laxlan. He said to his people, "I will show to all my fellow chiefs this new fortune of mine. I will assume the name of Hale, and we will term it to mean, Wihaildem-welwenhlna-khlkehl-kanao: The Offspring-of-the-Frogs-Are-Numerous-Where-They-Sit."

Multiple cultural meanings are embedded in this story, in addition to the retelling of an incident. It has many references to the future relationship between Europeans and the Kitkatla, probably through later embellishment. The comedy of Sabane's first encounter with European items and food is both obvious and characteristic of indigenous disdain for European sensibilities. The more sinister descriptions of the ship's block-and-tackle foreshadow later animosity between the two cultures. Most telling, perhaps, is the meaning Ts'ibassa attaches to the European's parting call, which reflects the ever increasing numbers of Europeans in indigenous life.

Vansina (1985:27-32) discusses the relationship between an event, its incorporation within an individual's oral history (defined as a person's remembrances of her/his own life), and its ultimate conversion to an oral tradition (a story that gets passed to the next generation). Inevitably, the stories selected to become part of an oral tradition serve some purpose, such as illustrating a salient fact, legitimizing a specific claim, or explaining why and how a society is ordered as it is. Lagrand (1997) points out that oral traditions are as susceptible to bias as is any historic source. He notes that they reflect the social order of the people who produce them and that their meaning is continually being reinterpreted by succeeding generations. This suggests that oral traditions become inaccurate with time as they gradually become parables for the status quo. However, we can increase our confidence that an oral tradition reasonably accurately represents past events in two ways. First, their accuracy increases if we find multiple versions of the same story from different perspectives (Vansina 1985:31). This is especially true when we find versions of a story from individuals who do not have any stake in the claims the story makes. Second, we are on firmer ground when we try to identify events of the past rather than intentions or cultural meanings (Layton 1989:11). Sabane, for example, may not have thought that European food was maggots and human ichor, but he probably did get invited aboard for a meal. In the following section, I identify three themes from Tsimshian oral traditions of the early contact period taken from an analysis by Marsden and Galois (1995). In the subsequent section, I tell the story of Ligeex during the early contact era, with reference to specific oral traditions. In both cases, the events I discuss are demonstrable from a variety of perspectives within the Tsimshian oral tradition.

Among the Tsimshian, several hundred adawx have been preserved in print from the work of William Beynon and Henry Tate (Beynon 1969; MacDonald and Cove 1987), who collected them for Franz Boas and later for Marius Barbeau and Philip Drucker. Boas (1912), Barbeau (1961), and Lévi-Strauss (1958) were especially interested in the mythological stories of the adawx, and these cosmological fables are well known. However, there is another, larger class of texts that is of interest here. These are stories that purport to relate significant events in the history of any one House. Many refer to the contact period and discuss the changes precipitated by the arrival of the "Whites" (Marsden 1990; Marsden and Galois 1995).

We can identify three major themes of the contact period from Tsimshian adawx. First, the adawx contain many stories describing how Tsimshian local group leaders adapted the economic potential offered by the Europeans to their own advantage. They are portrayed as shrewd traders who responded to the needs of the market which, in this case, was fur. The first major Tsimshian export was sea otter fur, the trade of which boomed from 1787 to 1805 (Halpin and Seguin 1990:281; Marsden and Galois 1995:171). Those leaders who did not own sea otter hunting grounds went to great lengths to secure access to sea otter territory, usually by marriage alliances. When the sea otter market declined shortly after 1805 because of overhunting, Tsimshian leadership scrambled to control the new commodity, land-based furs. The theme here is that indigenous traders were active in controlling trade between Aboriginal producers and European consumers of commodity goods, and in doing so became very wealthy.

Second, Tsimshian leadership was keen to maintain the social status quo, except where they could increase the status for their own local group or lineage. To this end, they restricted access to European traders to those in leadership roles (Drucker 1965:120). This maintained the dual hierarchies of leaders within local groups and of a ranked hierarchy of the local groups. Claims to status were backed up with either the threat of warfare or the potlatching of wealth. The theme here is that Tsimshian leadership translated their wealth into political power through traditional Tsimshian methods. Even after contact, power remained a function of internal Tsimshian politics.

The final significant theme is that the leadership of some local groups was able to gain considerable advantage in status and political power over their peers by applying the wealth derived from European trade to traditional

Tsimshian status mechanisms. The adawx describe the rising power of several local group leaders on the Northwest Coast. Ligeex, leader of the Gispaklo'ots village group, was legend among them. Prior to contact, the Gispaklo'ots, although highly ranked, owned only a modest territory on the Skeena River. By the 1830s Ligeex had controlled access to the entire Tsimshian interior zone, including the summer territories of the other eight local groups. According to the adawx, he was able to do this by building a virtual monopoly over the interior fur trade (Marsden and Galois 1995:175).

Ligeex

The stories of Ligeex represent a significant component of the adawx recorded by Beynon (1969). Ligeex's stratagems to consolidate his power during the early nineteenth century are famous among the Tsimshian, and his claim to be chief over all the Metlakhatla Tsimshian is still considered legitimate. For example, a traditional canoe made by the Gitksan and paddled from Hazelton to Victoria for the 1994 Commonwealth Games had to turn north to Port Simpson to acknowledge Gispaklo'ots's jurisdiction over the lower Skeena before heading south to Victoria (Wayne Ryan, personal communication). The first challenge faced in reconstructing the history of Ligeex during the late eighteenth and early nineteenth centuries is identifying stories that refer to this time. Ligeex is an inherited name among the Gispaklo'ots, and many of the stories refer to different individuals. For example, in the adawx published by MacDonald and Cove (1987:nos. 17, 18, 19, 22, 25, 27, 28, 29, 30, 31, 33, 34, 35, and 57), many different Ligeexes are identifiable. The earliest stories refer to the founding of the name, and William Beynon (1969:no. 106) identifies them as belonging to the "remote past," probably many generations before contact. Others speak of events from late in the contact era. For example, Beynon identifies the Ligeex in two adawx (no. 8 and no. 129) as the same man who tried to murder William Duncan on 20 December 1858. Marsden (1990) has identified a single individual named Ligeex who led the Gispaklo'ots local group from the late eighteenth century until his death in 1840 (see also Marsden and Galois 1995; Coupland et al. 2001).

Prior to the arrival of the Europeans, Ligeex was the leading figure in the most powerful lineage of the strongest local group (the Gispaklo'ots) of the Tsimshian who owned winter villages at Metlakhatla (Marsden and Galois 1995:170). Though the Gispaklo'ots did not own many productive salmon fishing areas (Coupland, Martindale, and Marsden 2001), part of their political status derived from the economic benefits of their trading arrangements with interior groups. They held traditional and exclusive rights as the only lower Skeena Tsimshian group to trade with the Upper Skeena Gitksan and Wet'suwet'en peoples (Marsden and Galois 1995:170). The significant imports from the interior groups were tanned "moose hides" (most likely elk hides – Gibson 1992:230) and marmot skins. Demand for these products was constant as both were important gifts in ceremonial exchanges. These trading privileges permitted the Gispaklo'ots to demand tariffs from other Tsimshian who wished to trade for interior products. This privilege gave the Gispaklo'ots additional income and prestige as coastal groups would have to trade on Ligeex's prerogative or find some other, more circuitous, route for importing interior hides.

For example, in Beynon's (1969) *Adawx* no. 47, the Gispaklo'ots's ancestral land is described as containing no major river other than the Skeena. Coupland, Martindale, and Marsden (2001) note that traditional Gispaklo'ots territory, located on the Skeena River between two small creeks (Dasque and Whitebottom), would have produced less than 1,000 salmon per year given current Department of Fisheries and Oceans escapement estimates. Instead, the Gispaklo'ots claimed the Skeena River itself. In addition to salmon, this claim included privileged access to trade with interior groups above Kitselas Canyon. In *Adawx* no. 47, which Beynon thought referred to a time in the "distant past," we find this description:

> Two tribes claimed the exclusive privilege of trading with the Gitksan of the upper Skeena. These were the Gispakloats [Gispaklo'ots] and the Gitsolaso [Kitselas]; they were often united together in trade as the Gitsolaso tribe, living as it did right on the canyon, were a dangerous foe, and Lagɛx [Ligeex], in order to ally himself with them, he or others closely related to him, would marry into the Gitsolaso royal Houses. Often his nieces would marry there to form closer alliances. So in this way these two tribes made themselves foremost traders among the Tsimshian. They resented any interference in their trading with the Gitsan [Gitksan] of the interior.

In this story the Kitselas ignored Ligeex's claim and continued to fish the Skeena and trade with the Gitksan. In retaliation, the Gispaklo'ots attacked the Giluts'aaw (part of the Kitselas), but in this early story they lost the battle. Ligeex's position became weaker and the Gispaklo'ots dropped their claim of ownership of the Skeena River, although they were able to keep their trading privileges with the Gitksan.

The Gispaklo'ots's ancestral claim to exclusive trading privileges with upper Skeena groups is reiterated in several adawx, such as one reported in 1950 by Agnes Haldane (MacDonald and Cove 1987:213), a Nisga'a from Kincolith. In another story reported by John Tate in 1948 (Beynon 1969, no. 72), the perquisites of this privilege are described: "No other tribe could go up the Skeena without Legyeex's [Ligeex's] consent, and would have to pay tribute to him for having done it."

The Gispaklo'ots also held prerogatives over the spring eulachon fishery at the mouth of the Nass River. Ligeex's House controlled a large part of the trade in eulachon grease, especially with northern groups like the Tsetsaut, but it is unclear whether this derived from ownership of the resource area or from control of the trading relationships (Marsden and Galois 1995:171). Ligeex's trade influence was maintained, in part, by a loose alliance of Eagle Clan Houses, of which Ligeex was one, from Tsimshian, Nisga'a, and Haisla peoples.

The first significant effect of the European arrival in the late 1780s was the fluorescence of the trade in sea otter pelts. Sea otter hunting grounds, which until then had been a marginal resource, quickly became valuable. The Gispaklo'ots, with their interior trading base, did not own any sea otter hunting areas themselves. Two local groups who did were the Ginaxangiik, led by Txagaxs, and the Kitkatla, led by Ts'ibassa (Marsden and Galois 1995:171). Ts'ibassa was a powerful Southern Tsimshian leader, somewhat removed from Ligeex. The Ginaxangiik were Metlakhatla Tsimshian whose interior territory included the Exchamsiks River. Txagaxs's wealth and power increased quickly as a result of the sea otter trade. His House owned hunting grounds and controlled an early trading anchorage at Big Bay.

Ligeex responded to these twin threats to his status by manoeuvring to control some aspect of the sea otter trade (1995:172). He married Maskgaax, daughter of the leading family of the Gitwilgyoots, another Metlakhatla group with extensive sea otter hunting grounds. He also married 'A'maa'tk, the sister of Nisnawa, the leader of the Giluts'aaw who had exclusive trading privileges with the Kasaan Haida, who were themselves benefitting greatly from the sea otter trade. These alliances gave Ligeex access to pelts and trading privileges that allowed him to keep pace with the increasing fortunes of the Ginaxangiik and the Kitkatla.

When the sea otter trade dwindled in the early nineteenth century, the Tsimshian quickly shifted to importing interior furs. This change was of great benefit to Ligeex since it increased the value of his traditional trading alliances and undermined the value of the coastal trade, which had increased the fortunes of his rivals. However, overland trade through posts of the North West Company at Fort St. James and Fort Fraser in the interior was threatening to divert furs eastward. Ligeex acted quickly to consolidate his interior-to-coast dominance and to forestall an eastern overland trade route (Marsden and Galois 1995:172). There are frequent references throughout the adawx of the contact period to Ligeex's exclusive control over the Skeena River fur trade. These represent a critical element in Ligeex's efforts to expand his authority.

Ligeex's claims of privilege are clearest in stories where they are enforced with the military might of the Gispaklo'ots. Consider the story reported by Matthew Johnson, a Gispaklo'ots, in 1928 (Beynon 1969, no. 8), entitled *The Last Raid of Lagex* [Ligeex] *on the (Skeena) Gitksans*, in which Ligeex discovers that the Nisga'a House of Hlidux has been trading with the Gitksan. Marsden (1990:21) argues that this story dates to between 1790 and 1834:

> Lagεx [Ligeex] had the supreme power on the Skeena River starting from the mouth and up to where the Gitksan lived at Kispaiyaks [Kispiox], this right and power was very closely watched by Lagεx, that none should go and trade with the Upper Skeena people. Only himself having this privilege to trade among the Gitksan and the Hagwolgets [Gitksan of Hagwilget Canyon]. Some times Lagεx would make raids and war upon these Gitksan people always taking many captives women and also much wealth.

When Ligeex finds out that the Nisga'a have been trading with the Kitselas and Gitksan, he retaliates by attacking the Upper Skeena villages. Travelling by night, the Gispaklo'ots raiding party arrives at the village of Kispiox:

> When they were close to the village, Lagεx then sat in the middle of his canoe and when they were close by the Kispaiyaks [Kispiox] village they started to sing their paddle song, mentioning in the song a new naxnox [spirit-power] and Lagεx stood up and spread open the new naxnox ... When the Tsimsyans [Tsimshian] arrived they were singing the naxnox of Lagεx. When they arrived, they entered the house of the Kispaiyaks chief and there a reception halait [feast] was given by the Gitksan and when Lagεx danced in the halait, the Gitksan noticed that he had no eagle down [symbolizing peace] in his dancing hat. This caused the Gitksan to be more frightened. While Lagεx was dancing and when all was ready, they attacked and killed many Gitksan and went into other houses killing and capturing women and children. When he (Lagεx) had finished, he razed the village by fire and prepared to go to the next village below and raid this place. Lagεx and all his followers had taken many scalps and heads and taking these in the canoes went down to the Git'anmaks [Gitnemax] village.

The story continues, describing how the Gispaklo'ots raided and destroyed the villages of Gitnemax, Gitsaguecla, Kitwanga, and Kitselas. Only one village escaped the massacre. The people of Kitwancool had been forewarned of the attack and had retreated to their fortress of Kitwanga (for a description of this site and its archaeological excavations, see G. MacDonald 1984). The final lines of the story foreshadow the eventual decline of the Gispaklo'ots: "This was the last raid of Lagεx up the Skeena River. When he went up again it was with the teachings of Mr. Duncan that he went up with."

Johnson's is not the only version of the story. The same tale is told by John Tate (Beynon 1969, no. 89), John Brown (Beynon 1969, no. 95), Jimmy

Williams of Kispiox (MacDonald and Cove 1987:123), and Chief Semidik of Kitwanga (MacDonald and Cove 1987:125).

Ligeex also exerted his authority in other possible interior-to-coast trade routes through a combination of alliance building and warfare. He married Nts'iitskwoodat, niece of the leading Nisga'a House leader, and extended his control over the Nass River trade. Ligeex was already married into the House of Sagwaan, which controlled the trade down Portland Canal, north of the Nass River. These alliances enabled Ligeex to effectively control three of the four main interior-to-coast trade routes. The last, the Stikine River, was controlled by the Tlingit House of Saiks, which had an alliance with Txagaxs of the Ginaxangiik. By 1822, when the united North West Company and Hudson's Bay Company established a trading post at Fort Kilmaurs on Babine Lake, an estimated 75 percent of the furs from this region were being shipped westward to the coast (Marsden and Galois 1995:173).

The rise of the land-based fur trade marked the beginning of the next phase in the development of indigenous responses to European contact. The process of alliance building from the early years of the sea otter trade continued. From alliances based on the trading and marriage ties of a single local group, leaders such as Ligeex and Ts'ibassa branched out along clan lines creating Eagle Clan and Killerwhale Clan alliances, respectively (1995: 171). Increasingly, these alliances drew together Tsimshian local groups. By the early 1820s, Ligeex had regained his former position and was busy expanding his influence. Other Tsimshian groups were eager to marry into his powerful alliance. These included leading members of the Gits'iis and Gitzaxhlaahl local groups, whose leaders adopted a junior sibling relationship to the House of Ligeex (1995:174). Eventually, Ligeex even established marriage alliances with Txagaxs and Ts'ibassa, creating, in essence, a single large indigenous trading cartel about the time the Hudson's Bay Company began its annual visits to the Nass River in the *William and Mary*.

Marsden and Galois's (1995) thesis, that Ligeex developed a regional trading network that extended from the Bella Bella territory in the south to the Nisga'a territory in the north to the Gitksan territory in the east, is based on the comparison of Tsimshian oral traditions and documentary evidence. From the perspective of the oral traditions, however, Ligeex's regional influence was not simply economic. He was the supreme leader of all the Metlakhatla Tsimshian. This theme is repeated in many stories. Consider a story reported by Walter Haldane, a Nisga'a from Kincolith (MacDonald and Cove 1987:103), in which Ligeex is described as, "the head chief of all the Tsimshian."

There are at least four accounts of the pivotal event that catapulted Ligeex from the highest ranked leader into a more powerful position over the Metlakhatla Tsimshian. The story involves a plot by the other local group leaders to murder Ligeex because he had become too powerful. In an adawx

entitled *The Reason Why Lagɛx* [Ligeex] *Is Foremost of All the Chiefs,* Henry
Pierce (Beynon 1969, no. 120) reported the following:

> He [Ligeex] really seemed to have gotten up to be head of all the chiefs and
> this was why all of the different tribes [local groups] were jealous of him
> and the Gispakloats [Gispaklo'ots] tribe. So this was why once, all of the
> tribes made plans that they would kill Lagɛx [Ligeex] and then the Gispakloats
> would go down in prestige as now Lagɛx had too much power and the same
> with the Gispakloats. So while the people were all at the Skeena River then
> was when they made their plans that they would kill Lagɛx during the win-
> ter when all of the people were living at Metlakhatla. Well, one of Lagɛx's
> nieces had married one of the chiefs of the Ginaxangiik and she heard of
> the plans that had been made and what they would do to her uncle and she
> did not warn him at once. Some time, after a long while, then one day
> when her husband had returned from the seal hunting, she said, "I will give
> my uncle some smoked meat." So she went down the beach and boarded
> her canoe and went across to the village of her uncle and landed below the
> house of her uncle who was Lagɛx and then the woman walked up and
> went into her uncle's house giving him the smoked meat and it was then
> that she warned him her uncle of the things that all the Tsimshians had
> planned to destroy him and his tribe. And this was what the woman said,
> "Well, do not be alarmed, all of the other tribes are going to murder you
> and destroy your tribe and humiliate your tribe. And this winter is the time
> set when they will destroy you and then slaughter your tribe. Well this I
> know the other tribes will do."

Ligeex considered this information in consultation with his closest advi-
sors, X̱-uʿp and Ni·sʼawälp. And then X̱-uʿp, who was the head headman,
said, "It is good, chief, that you tell us of this thing. We will first discuss it
and plan what we shall do. I am astounded at the ambitions of these thought-
less people. We will find some way in which to punish them and they will
never do this again."

Ligeex, recognizing this as a pivotal opportunity, announces his plan:

> Well now you shall hear my plans. We will give a big feast and it is then I
> will combat them with wealth, all of the people. I will challenge anyone to
> combat with me and I will use my copper shields. Well if I am defeated with
> my copper shields and then my wealth, I will use and [sic] if I am again
> defeated then I will use my slaves and if I am again defeated, well then we
> will then really have to fight.

Among the complaints that the other local group leaders had of Ligeex
was that he was too proud and that he had composed a paddling song in

which he proclaimed his power over all the Metlakhatla Tsimshian. As Ligeex quietly made plans for his feast, he received more news of the plot to murder him from many of his House who had married into the leading Houses of the other local groups. When all was prepared, he made his pre-emptive strike:

> When everything was ready messengers were sent and Lagɛx said to them, "My paddle song which tells that my chieftainship is greater that anyone is the one which you will sing." So then the messengers set off before the time which the Tsimshians had set when they would kill Lagɛx. And now the Gispakloats messengers lay off shore below each village and there they sang the paddle song, which all of the tribes hated.
>
> And now all of the tribes felt more angered now that they again heard the paddle song of Lagɛx. And then all of the Tsimshian guests arrived at the same time at the house of Lagɛx and when they got there, Lagɛx first danced the reception dance and then sang about the number of copper shields he had and his wealth and his many slaves. And then he said, "If anyone wants to challenge me let him walk out and we will combat in wealth and we will see who is the wealthiest." After he was finished his reception dance then he distributed copper shields to each of the chiefs and caribou skins to each one of the head headsmen who were the spokesmen of each chief. And in this way without warning, Lagɛx elevated himself above all of the Tsimshians and the Tsimshians knew that Lagɛx was victorious as no one arose to challenge Lagɛx.

To commemorate this important event, Ligeex permanently proclaimed his authority over the territory of the Metlakhatla local groups by painting a picture of himself and the valuable crests he owned on a prominent cliff face, where all the Tsimshian would see it:

> Well some of his tribe selected the Skeena and the chiefs turned it down because not all of the different tribes went to the Skeena, and other places was selected by other people and then the chief Lagɛx said, "Now the mouth of the Nass River is where every canoe goes to, when gathering oolichan and it will be a good place to make the picture and Ten Mile Ck. will be a good place to make it" ... They made a picture which was to be the face of Lagɛx and there were three score and fourteen copper shields were drawn and represented how many copper shields he would have used had anyone accepted his challenge.

As a final statement of his new position, Ligeex held another feast at the painting site to which he invited his new equal, Ts'ibassa of the Southern Tsimshian. Representatives from the Nisga'a were also invited.

Lagɛx gave each one of the chiefs each one a copper shield and to each of the headmen he gave caribou skins and Tsibasa [Ts'ibassa] who was the main guest got more. He got three canoes in which sat three slaves in each one of the canoes. Well this was why he done so to Tsibasa because it was with him that he competed with in yaoks [feasts] and they always really tried to outdo each other in everything. Well this was when the brave chief showed that he was foremost amongst the Tsimshians and he was one who really put to shame those that would have murdered him and there was nothing these many tribes could do now that Lagɛx was again victorious and Lagɛx governed the Skeena and the Nass.

The same story was reported by John Tate in 1952 (MacDonald and Cove 1987:62). The implications of Ligeex's triumph were, in Tate's words, "control" over the Skeena and Nass rivers. Ligeex's position was not achieved through a single feast; rather, it was the result of a long process of alliance building. Consider the story *The Supremacy of Legaix* [Ligeex] reported by Henry Pearce and James Pearcy (MacDonald and Cove 1987:106) in 1947. In this adawx, the story of the feast is retold in the context of describing the Gispaklo'ots's conversion to Christianity in the late 1860s. In converting, they abandoned such traditional methods of status building and feasting.

Another theme regarding Ligeex's pre-eminent status as described in the adawx is how his position as leader of the Tsimshian was recognized at public events. A number of stories describing ceremonies and feasts list the order in which local group leaders were either welcomed to the house or introduced to the ceremony. The last person to enter was the first to be introduced, and this was the position of highest rank. In every adawx relating to contact-era ceremonies, Ligeex is listed as the highest ranked guest. Stories such as *The Festivity of Assuming of the Name of Niesyaganɛt, Chief of the Gitsiis* (Beynon 1969, no. 39), *When T'sibésé* [Ts'ibassa], *Chief of the Kitkatlas Gave His Xmɛs Feast* (Beynon 1969, no. 104), *Notes on the Elevations Ceremony of the Chief of the Ginaxangiik Tribe* (Beynon 1969, no. 117), and *When Lagɛx* [Ligeex] *Ridiculed Haimas (Gitlan)* (Beynon 1969, no. 106) all list Ligeex as the highest ranked guest. Beynon (1969: front matter) lists rank orders of ceremonies from four other adawx, and, in each case, the Gispaklo'ots are listed as the highest ranked local group.

Of the stories published by MacDonald and Cove (1987), rank lists are presented in four. In stories such as *The Xmɛs Feast of Legaix* (92-94), *Legaix's Supremacy Challenged* (95-96), *The Last Feast of Legaix* (99-102), and *A Challenge Feast of Tsibasa* [Ts'ibassa] (112-115), the ranking order always lists Ligeex as the foremost chief. Arguably, this need not reflect anything more complex than a ranked society, which Marsden and Galois (1995:170) state existed prior to contact. Some stories no doubt refer to this time. However, two types of lists suggest that Ligeex's status had increased after contact. Stories that report events after the arrival of Europeans but before the arrival of William Duncan in 1856 indicate that, at ceremonies, Ligeex had no peer other than Ts'ibassa. Ts'ibassa was not Metlakhatla Tsimshian. He had consolidated Southern Tsimshian local groups into a powerful regional alliance of Killerwhale Clans, much like Ligeex had done with his Eagle Clan alliance. Consider the story *When T'sibésé* [Ts'ibasaa], *Chief of the Kitkatlas Gave His Xmεs Feast*, reported by Cecilia Venn of Kitkatla:

> It was now time for T'sibésé [Ts'ibasaa] to give his final feast [in the ascension-feast cycle to claim his status] and it was after autumn and all of the people had gathered together at Lax-klen where they would live all winter. And all of the tribe of T'sibésé were all ready that he will give a potlatch and it was then he called his eldest nephew for him to be the leader of the messengers to each one of the Tsimshian tribes.
>
> And Niastk'u-xsɔ́ was the one who led the messengers. Well, it was the Gispaxlo'ots [Gispaklo'ots] people, the tribe of Lagεx [Ligeex], who were the equals of the Gitxatas [Kitkatlas] and they were the foremost guests which was what the Gispaxlo'ots were to the Gitxatas as they were the ones they combated with in wealth.

According to Beynon's (1969) notes, which append this adawx, this was the last feast Ts'ibassa gave prior to converting to Christianity.

In the story *A Challenge Feast of Tsibasa* [Ts'ibassa], Henry Watt (MacDonald and Cove 1987:112) of Kitkatla describes the relationship between Ligeex and Ts'ibassa as a great rivalry. This was different from Ligeex's relationship to other Metlakhatla Tsimshian local group leaders. With the latter, Ligeex's ceremonial combat was serious, whereas with Ts'ibassa, Ligeex's combats are frequently portrayed as being between peers. In one incident, Ts'ibassa invited Ligeex to a feast but replaced the steps up to the door of his house with "revolving steps" down which Ligeex and the Gispaklo'ots guests tumbled. The feast ceremony continued amicably, although it was recognized that Ts'ibassa had won this encounter. The relationship between these two men is significant because it suggests that they had both become so high in status that they had to look outside of their own areas to find equals. Their rapport suggests that they knew that they needed each other to demonstrate their status, in a manner consistent with Renfrew's (1986) model of Peer Polity Interaction.

The second type of list refers to ceremonies that took place in the late nineteenth century, after the Gispaklo'ots had converted to Christianity. Once Paul Legaic [Ligeex] converted to Christianity in 1863, the Gispaklo'ots abandoned their traditional feasting responsibilities. Many stories from this era point out that, although the Gispaklo'ots were once the highest ranked group, they lost all status once they stopped participating in traditional ceremonies. From statements made in a number of adawx, Paul Legaic appears to have been born in 1823 and to have died in 1868 at the age of forty-five. His successor, also Paul Legaic, died in 1890. The second Paul Legaic tried to resuscitate the Gispaklo'ots's traditional standing by sponsoring the necessary cycle of four ascension feasts, culminating in the final Xmes "Partaking-of-the-Red" feast, probably held in 1879. This event is told in *The Xmɛs Feast of Legaix* [Ligeex] (MacDonald and Cove 1987:92-94) and *The Last Feast of Legaix* [Ligeex] (1987:95-98). In both stories, the Gispaklo'ots spent four years preparing and gave away a tremendous amount of wealth to reclaim their position. This is "Chief Legɛx's Potlatch" described in Garfield (1939:201-204). The success of their efforts is not clear. According to Henry Pearce and James Pearcy (MacDonald and Cove 1987:106), the feast did not resolve all claims against Ligeex, especially from the Kitkatla and Gitando.

In summary, the Tsimshian adawx describe events during the period after the arrival of Europeans but prior to the establishment of the Hudson's Bay Company trading post at Fort Nass in 1831. These stories indicate that, by organizing a regional network of exchange relationships, at times through violent means, Ligeex was able to catapult the Gispaklo'ots into a pre-eminent position among the Metlakhatla Tsimshian. This position was consolidated at a specific feast in which Ligeex challenged and defeated all the other local group leaders combined. His victory was immortalized in rock paintings, one of which remains visible today. By the time the HBC had arrived, Ligeex's status was rivalled only by Ts'ibassa of the neighbouring Kitkatla.

Stories such as these are powerful evidence of Ligeex's increasing status. However, his influence is most evident in the relationship between the House of Ligeex and the Hudson's Bay Company. In 1832, the first year of operation of Fort Nass (the HBC's first location for their trading post in Tsimshian territory), Ligeex's daughter, Sudaahl, married the fort's clerk and physician, Dr. Kennedy. This marriage was another strategic move by Ligeex to ally himself with a new and powerful force in Tsimshian trade. That year, the HBC staff decided that Fort Nass was unsuitable. It lacked direct access to the interior and had little land on which to establish gardens (Marsden and Galois 1995:176). In addition, Sudaahl complained to her new husband that the winters were too cold (Beynon 1969). Explorations of the Nass River convinced the HBC staff that it did not offer direct access to the interior. Instead, they speculated that the major interior access route was the Skeena River and considered moving the fort to what was later to become Port Essington. Eventually, a new location, thirty kilometres west of Fort Nass, was selected. The new post at Fort Simpson was now further away from the interior and the Nass River and only marginally closer to the Skeena River. It was, however, located on or near a Gispaklo'ots traditional camping place at Laxhlgu'alaams, "Place-of-Wild-Roses."

Ligeex's influence on the decision to locate the new fort is unknown. However, he certainly benefitted from the move as he now had control over access to traditional Gispaklo'ots land and the fort it contained (Marsden and Galois 1995:177). This privilege included exacting compulsory gifts from all indigenous traders seeking to do business at the fort. The HBC also benefitted from the alliance as Ligeex was able to redirect trade from American merchant vessels to the fort, particularly with his Haida allies. The mutually beneficial relationship that developed between the Gispaklo'ots leadership and the HBC was manifest in the development of Fort Simpson as a regional centre. In addition to Gispaklo'ots allies, such as Nishoot of the Gitzaxhlaahl, Senaxaat of the Haida, the Tongas Tlingit, and Ligeex's Nisga'a affinal relatives, their competitors began using the fort.

Among these were Haida groups with whom the Gispaklo'ots had a long-standing feud. The history of this conflict is recounted in *The War of the Gispaxloats* [Gispaklo'ots] *and the Haida* told by John Tate in 1954 (MacDonald and Cove 1987:225-233). The feud originated long before contact but remained unresolved when the Haida came to the HBC post at Fort Simpson to trade. This incident may be the same as the one reported by Mitchell (1983a:63) from HBC journals, which occurred on 1 July 1837. In the HBC account, "the Chimsyans [Tsimshian] to whose camp they foolishly went, felt disposed to take their goods from them and give them just what they chose in return. Legegh [Ligeex] done all he could to prevent any disturbance but like all the rest of the chiefs he has no influence among them when interfering with their own interest." The story from Tate is more detailed and describes how Ligeex's niece was insulted by the Haida after haggling over the exchange of eulachon oil for halibut. Ligeex reacted swiftly, attacking the Haida in a gun battle that lasted through the day and into the night. A hiatus in the dispute was eventually negotiated by the HBC's Dr. Kennedy, who negotiated through his wife, one of Ligeex's daughters. During the truce, the Haida sued for peace. Ligeex consented and invited the Haida chief to his house for a feast. At the feast, the Haida presented the Gispaklo'ots with copper shields and trade blankets. In case their gifts were too modest, the Haida chief left behind a number of his family members and killed the woman who had originally argued with Ligeex's niece.

It may have appeared to the staff of the HBC fort that the day and a half of fighting amounted to nothing more than intermittent squabbles. Had they asked Ligeex to put a stop to it, it is not likely that he would have explained the intricacies of the feud and what was at stake. It is also probable that the HBC staff were unaware of the ultimate resolution to the conflict.

However, from the perspective of the adawx, the story is a clear example of the extent of Ligeex's authority at this time. The Haida could trade at Fort Simpson only with Ligeex's permission and were willing to go to great lengths to appease the Gispaklo'ots.

Other Tsimshian leaders were also vying for advantage during the early years of the HBC post at Fort Simpson. Txagaxs of the Ginaxangiik, for example, worked to maintain his ties with the Russian American Company out of his anchorage at Big Bay. But by 1836 the Ginaxangiik were trading substantial numbers of furs at Fort Simpson. Ts'ibassa of the Kitkatla had risen to a stature comparable to Ligeex, with his focus on American traders anchoring at harbours in Southern Tsimshian territory. He also used the indigenous trade in guns and slaves to extend his trading sphere northward without violating Ligeex's trading privileges in furs. However, by 1837 he too was drawn to Fort Simpson and moved his main winter village into the northern reaches of his territory, about eighty kilometres south of the fort. Similarly, the HBC's rivals at the Russian American Company were also making regular stops at the fort. Gradually, Fort Simpson became the nexus of European-Aboriginal trade and a regional community centre overshadowing the fractured collection of winter villages at Metlakhatla.

When Ligeex died in 1840, Tsimshian society was suffering the losses of smallpox epidemics, the first of which occurred in 1836 (Dean 1994). His wife Nts'iitskwoodat, his ally Nishoot, his rivals Txagaxs and Ts'ibassa, and his chosen heir had all died from the disease. His successor, the young Paul Legaic, could not hold the alliance together, and the fluorescence of indigenous responses to European influence waned.

Discussion: The Tsimshian Paramount Chiefdom

The persistent belief in ethnographic literature that the Tsimshian were a rare example of a paramount chiefdom based on a hunting and gathering economy likely has its roots in historical fact. The evidence from archaeological data, European documents, and indigenous oral traditions suggests that this was a postcontact development that began in the late eighteenth century and dissipated after AD 1840. The contradictions evident in ethnographic sources are most likely the result of inaccuracies in the use of the indigenous oral record by Western anthropologists who assumed that descriptions of dynamic and changing events of the late pre- and early postcontact era referred to a stable traditional precontact society. Instead, Tsimshian society through the contact era developed as a result of multiple influences in a pattern more complex than previously assumed, and probably in a more complex manner than described here. However, we can identify a suite of themes that characterizes this period and that can be interpreted as evidence of the development of a postcontact paramount chiefdom.

We can define a paramount chiefdom as a regional polity in which the hierarchically ranked structure of the lineage (the ramage) is mirrored in the structure of both the relationships between lineages within villages and the relationships between the villages within the region. The development towards a hierarchically structured regional ramage is seen in an increase in authority over territory, an expansion of economic control over commodities, and increased differentiation in the wealth economy.

There is solid archaeological evidence that a regional level of spatial organization developed among the Tsimshian during the contact era. This pattern is visible archaeologically as a postcontact shift in settlement patterns from a precontact system of coastal winter villages and interior summer house sites to a postcontact settlement hierarchy involving a coastal regional centre at Port Simpson and interior villages and camps. I have argued that this represents an increase in regionalization and hierarchy in settlement organization.

Similarly, historical documents indicate that indigenous leaders were acting as redistributors for commodity furs and that these roles were being filled by the traditional Tsimshian elite. The consolidation of economic power occurred among Coast Tsimshian speakers under the leadership of Ligeex. A second, similar development occurred among Southern Tsimshian speakers under the leadership of Ts'ibassa. Documentary sources and indigenous adawx present divergent yet complementary narratives of the early encounters between Europeans and Tsimshian. Both indicate that, in the first half of the nineteenth century, Tsimshian leaders consolidated power derived from the fur trade into larger trading networks. Ligeex, in particular, with his affinal, clan-based alliance, his paternal relationship to other noble lineages, his emerging role as a redistributor of trade goods and wealth, and his supremacy at the developing regional centre of Fort Simpson, is identifiable in a role different from his earlier one as the leader of the most powerful lineage in the highest ranked local group.

I describe Ligeex's ascension to regional, or paramount, chieftainship as "incipient" because, though the trend was towards this development, it was fully achieved only for a short time and not transferred beyond one generation. During the years from 1825 to 1840, Ligeex had achieved much of the status of a paramount chief. He exerted control over most of the indigenous trading sphere through his alliance network. He was gradually drawing his indigenous rivals into this network. He exerted substantial influence over the HBC trade by controlling access to the fort and diverting trade to the HBC from the Russian American Company. Finally, some combination of the HBC and the Gispaklo'ots had, in essence, created an indigenous central place at Fort Simpson. These accomplishments have been somewhat obscured by later developments, particularly the well publicized antagonism between Paul Legaic and William Duncan. Most historians (e.g., Fisher 1977; Cole and Darling 1990) do not distinguish between the young Ligeex (Paul), who converted to Christianity in 1863, and the older man, who had effected such change in the Gispaklo'ots's fortunes by combining the wealth of the fur trade with traditional Tsimshian economic principles.

Changes in these three factors (the development of a regional settlement hierarchy, the incorporation of the European trade economy within the traditional Tsimshian subsistence economy, and preservation of the relative status relationships between Tsimshian leaders) imply an entrenchment of social inequality. Using a typological classification model such as that proposed by Wason (1994) or Sahlins (1954) tends to oversimplify reality. However, they provide useful distinctions along a spectrum of political differences. In Wason's terms, the differences in the entrenchment of inequality evident in Tsimshian society before and after contact reflect the development of a chiefdom from a ranked society. In Sahlins's terms, the Tsimshian changed from a two-tier ramage system (household within lineages and lineages within villages) to add a third tier (villages within chiefdom). Regardless of the terminology used, Tsimshian history is more complex than was previously understood. It includes responses by Tsimshian people and their leaders to European influence – responses that transformed their society while preserving their autonomy.

Conclusion

I have attempted to explain the complex data on Tsimshian history during the contact era. It is an effort to reconcile contradictions within Tsimshian ethnographic sources and between archaeological, documentary, and indigenous oral sources. In making such comparisons it becomes evident that history is often more complex than our data allow us to understand. Despite this complexity, comparisons of divergent data sources provide us with a more complete, if less straightforward, view of colonialism. The colonial era is, as all periods of culture change no doubt are, a function of dynamic and contradictory forces. In this case, the efforts of European explorers and traders on the Northwest Coast were well known, but the strategies and effects of indigenous peoples were less well understood in Western versions of history. In this revised view, we can describe the changes within Tsimshian society during the early contact era as a development of political, economic, and status inequality on a regional level, which fits the anthropological definition of the development of a paramount chiefdom.

50 *Andrew R.C. Martindale*

Acknowledgments

This chapter was written while I held a Social Sciences and Humanities Research Council (SSHRC) of Canada post-doctoral fellowship at the Department of Anthropology at McMaster University. I want to thank the department and its chair, Dr. Ann Herring, for their support and encouragement. The archaeological fieldwork at Psacelay was funded in part by a British Columbia Heritage Trust grant. The trust provides financial assistance to support the conservation of our heritage resources and increase public understanding of the complete history of British Columbia. The fieldwork at Ginakangeek was supported by a SSHRC research grant. Fieldwork was, as always, assisted by Mr. Wayne Ryan of Port Simpson, British Columbia. Drafts of this chapter were reviewed by Gary Coupland, R.G. Matson, Aubrey Cannon, Susan Marsden, Leland Donald, and two anonymous reviewers, and I thank them for their generous help and direction. However, all errors and omissions are my sole responsibility.

3
Northwest Coast Wet-Site Artifacts: A Key to Understanding Resource Procurement, Storage, Management, and Exchange

Dale R. Croes

The discovery of seven wooden spears and butchered horse remains from a wet (waterlogged) site on the lakeshore of Schoeningen, Germany, has greatly enhanced archaeologists' view of human cultures of 400,000 years ago (Thieme 1997). With only the stone artifacts, we truly had a different perspective on the food procurement capabilities of these Lower Paleolithic peoples. Now, with the discovery of well-constructed spears used in direct animal predation, these people can no longer be depicted as opportunistic scavengers.

On the Northwest Coast of North America, some archaeologists have been actively recovering perishable artifacts from wet sites over the past thirty plus years, revealing many new prehistoric cultural dimensions concerning thousands of years of cultural evolution. Across all substantially excavated Northwest Coast wet sites, more than 90 percent of the prehistoric material culture recovered is of wood and fibre; only 5 percent to 10 percent is stone, bone, and shell (Croes 1976, 1992a, 1992b, 1995, 1997). With Northwest Coast ethnohistoric records of a rich wood and fibre material culture, these percentages are not necessarily surprising; however, because they come from prehistoric sites dating as early as 6,000 years ago, they contribute whole new perspectives for understanding the earliest of Northwest Coast traditions (Croes 1997, 2001, 2002). This chapter explores how prehistoric Northwest Coast wet sites have revealed important new information concerning the early technologies used in wild food procurement, storage, management, and exchange.

Often using the Direct Historical Approach (DHA), Don Mitchell (1971a, 1990) has analyzed the available stone, bone, and shell artifacts from Northwest Coast shell middens in order to consider functional characterizations of prehistoric "subsistence, technology and social organization." I explore Mitchell's areas of research further by adding a possibly "fresher" array of wood and fibre artifacts to the existing data. I also narrow the category of "technology" by looking at aspects of wood and fibre technologies involved in resource procurement and food storage. When considering the category of "social organization," I limit the discussion to perishable artifacts potentially reflecting management of resources in a stratified society and systems of exchange between prehistoric communities.

Procurement Technologies
As with stone, bone, and shell artifacts, probably the most direct functional analysis of perishable procurement artifacts involves a review of them. In considering the Locarno Beach culture type on the Northwest Coast (c. 3200-2400 BP), Mitchell (1990:341) summarizes the stone, bone, and shell procurement artifacts as reflecting: "toggling harpoons; lance, spear, or knife blades; points for arrows or darts; line or net sinkers; and bone points suitable for a variety of fishing devices." With wood and fibre artifacts from sites dating from this time period, one can often view the complete fishing devices, arrows or darts, harpoons, and even digging or prying devices for plant and shellfish collecting. I briefly consider some of these wet-site procurement artifacts.

Fishing Devices
Fish hooks are the most abundant and stylistically distinct procurement artifact class found in Northwest Coast wet sites. More than 1,300 wooden fish hooks in several styles have been recovered to date (Figure 3.1; Croes 1997, 2001). One of the most distinctive and widespread forms is a self-barbed bentwood fish hook with a carved knob end for a leader attachment (see Type B, Figure 3.1). More than 240 have been recorded from at least six Central Coast sites, dating from 1,000 to 3,000 years ago (Figure 3.2; Croes 1997, 2001). This bentwood fish hook type has no bone barb attached and, being entirely wooden, would not even be recognized without waterlogging.

Another late-appearing bentwood hook type (see Type C, with over 700 from the Ozette wet site, Figure 3.1) and a V-shaped wooden shanked form (Type A, with over 200 from the Hoko River wet site, Figure 3.1) do have bone barbs attached; but, if found without the wooden shanks, these bone bipoints are difficult to associate with fish hook types or with other items. Possibly the most significant analytic contribution that these types of wooden fish hooks have made is in demonstrating a correlation between hooks and the kinds of fish being pursued in different sites and time periods (Croes 1995, 1997, 2001). These fish hooks also give us a better understanding of the importance of deep-sea fishing for at least 3,000 years on the Coast.

These three major types of wooden fish hook are distributed quite differently through time and space. Type A, the V-shaped halibut hook so commonly found at the 2,600-to-3,000-year-old Hoko River Central Coast wet site, is thought to have been used there mainly for flatfish/halibut. (See Figure 3.3, for an image of the hook in use.) Type B, the self-barbed bentwood

TYPE A   Construction: Composite; two wooden shanks in V shape
Barb: Attached bone bipoint
Leader: Attached with clove hitch to carved knob (tab) end

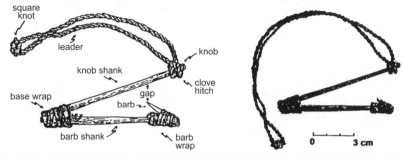

TYPE B   Construction: Bentwood
Barb: Recurved self-barbed
Leader: Attached with clove hitch to carved knob (tab) end

TYPE C   Construction: Bentwood
Barb: Attached bone bipoint
Leader: Attached with clove hitch to
centre of top recurve

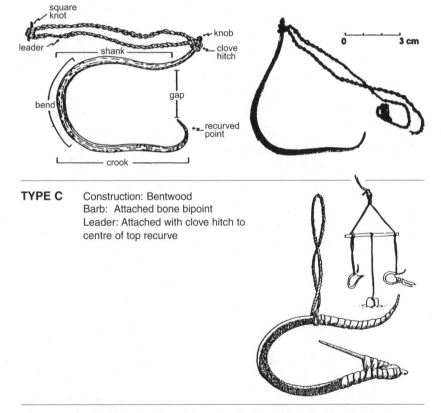

Figure 3.1   Definitions and illustrations of the three major Northwest Coast wet-site fish hook types recovered to date. Types A and B illustrated by Ricky Hoff (1980:163, 266); Type C, Hilary Stewart (1987:89). *Photo profiles are examples from the Hoko River site (Croes 1995)*

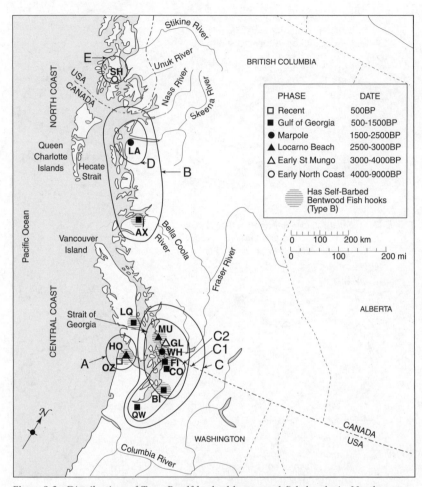

Figure 3.2   Distribution of Type B self-barbed bentwood fish hooks in Northwest Coast wet sites. Encircled A-E regions have basketry style continuity (see Croes 1995:2001b) (modified from base map by Mike Rouillard; see Figure 3.15 for full names of abbreviated site labels).

fish hook, is common to Central Coast wet sites (Figure 3.2), and is thought to have been used for cod fishing at Hoko River. In this southerly Central Coast region, both types disappear by the protohistoric period. On the North Coast, however, both types continue as the main fish hooks for these same fisheries into the ethnographic period (Stewart 1977). The self-barbed bentwood fish hooks of the North Coast are considered to be cod hooks (as at Hoko River). The fact that cod strike so aggressively at their prey resulted in the ancient and ethnographic use of a spring-loaded bentwood hook. In experiments with replicated Hoko River V-shaped hooks, the cod in the Seattle Aquarium would hit them very aggressively and often break them.

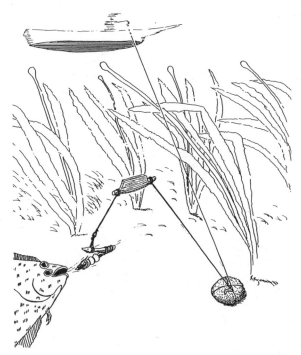

Figure 3.3 Type A fish hook in use to catch bottom fish at 3,000-year-old Hoko River site. *Drawing by Robert Slagle; Croes 1995:102*

These hooks were similar to the broken V-shaped hooks from the site (Croes 1995:104-106), so we concluded that they were not the cod hooks used off the Hoko River for these fish (which are common to the fauna). The more elastic/spring-loaded bentwood hooks served this purpose and continued to be used for cod fishing ethnographically on the North Coast (Croes 1995, 1997, 2001; Stewart 1977:40).

From this temporal and spacial distribution of ancient hook types, and from the earlier conclusion that archaeological phases are actually *economic stages* within the Northwest Coast region (Croes 1992b; Croes and Hackenberger 1988), I have hypothesized that the continuation of these prehistoric fish hook types on the historic North Coast indicates a continuation of the earlier (Locarno Beach/Marpole phase) economic stages, whereas the Central Coast had taken new directions in the Late Phase (Croes 1997, 2001). On the Central Coast Late (Gulf) phase, groups appear to have moved into an economic stage, including an add-on emphasis on sea-mammal hunting (as especially developed in the fur seal and whaling traditions on the West Coast) and increased emphasis on trolling in open waters for fresh salmon and herring. This is seen in the dramatic increase in bone points in assemblages of the Late (Gulf) phase (culture type), or economic stage, with bone

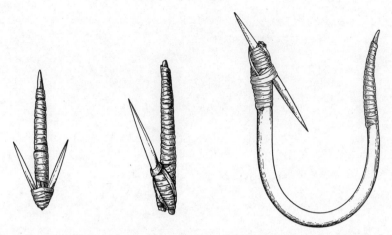

Figure 3.4 Common bone-barbed composite wood-shanked fish hooks from Late Phase Ozette Village wet site (45CA24): double-barbed hooks (*N* = 15), single-barbed hooks (*N* = 57), complete bentwood composite (Type C, *N* = 131) (Draper 1989). *Drawings by Chris Walsh*

bipoints contributing up to 60 percent of the stone, bone, and shell artifacts in sites of this late phase versus 5 percent or less in earlier phases (Mitchell 1971a:47; Croes 1992b:358).

An example of an emphasis on *bone-barbed* fish hooks in the Late (Gulf) phase occurs at the Central Coast wet site of Ozette Village, where the bone-barbed bentwood fish hook (Type C) became the main flatfish/halibut fish hook (*N* = 131 complete examples) and other common bone-barbed fish hooks include composite shank forms attributed to trolling, jigging, and other fishing practices (*N* = 72; Figure 3.4). Perishable fish hook styles can, therefore, be used to test economic hypotheses based on research from archaeological phases defined by stone, bone, and shell artifacts from earlier studies.

Other wet-site fishing devices include nets, wrapped net sinkers, weirs – again, valuable in interpreting procurement of other ranges of fish (Byram 1998; Croes 1995; Moss, Erlandson, and Stuckenrath 1990; Stevenson 1998). Most of these fishing devices are perishable or are recognized because they have fibre components. Nets from wet sites are quite ancient (at least 5,000 years old) and are very diverse in construction (Table 3.1). The common net features have been their string gauge cordage construction and being tied with square knots (which are no-slip knots common to nets made by hand, without a netting needle) (Ashley 1944:64-65).

Arrows/Darts
Another procurement (or possibly defensive weaponry) becoming better understood through wet-site analysis is the whole arrow, or dart. At the

Table 3.1

Definition of nets reported from Northwest Coast wet sites

Wet site	Approximate date	Construction material	Ply direction size	Stretch mesh	Proposed use	Reference
Lanaak, Baranof Island, SE Alaska (49XPA78)	5,000 BP	*Picea sitchensis:* Sitka Spruce Root	None, single strand silament	3.5-5.0 cm	Dip net	Bernick 1999
Hoko River (45CA213) NW Olympic Peninsula	3,000 BP	*Picea sitchensis:* Sitka spruce splint Limbs	None, single strand filament	10 cm	Gill net	Croes 1995
Musqueam Northeast (DhRt4) Fraser Delta	3,000 BP	*Thuja plicata:* Western red cedar Inner bark	Z-ply	15 cm	Gill net	Archer and Bernick 1990
Water Hazard (DgRs30) Fraser Delta	2,000 BP	*Thuja plicata:* Western red cedar Inner bark	S-ply	8.9 cm	Gill net	Stevenson 1989
Qwu?gwes (45TN240) Southern Puget Sound	500 BP	*Thuja plicata:* Western red cedar Inner bark	Z-ply	8.4 cm	Gill net	Croes and Foster 2001
Ozette Village (45CA24) NW Olympic Peninsula	300 BP	*Picea sitchensis:* Sitka spruce root	Z-ply	3.8 cm	Dip net	Croes 1980

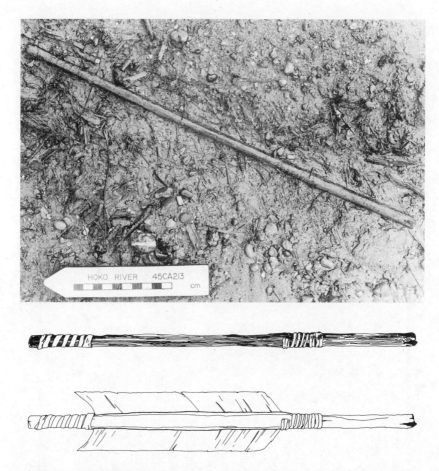

Figure 3.5 Broken Hoko River site projectile shaft, which might have been a light spear armed with a ground slate point (slate points were recovered in the dry-site excavations; see Croes 1995:167-171, 216-217). Note the cherry bark binding that originally might have held feather fletching (lower drawing is a hypothetical reconstruction).

3,000-year-old Hoko River wet site a broken dart shaft was recovered. The base retains two spaced sets of cherry bark binding, no doubt for feather fletching, and has a concave depression at the end, possibly for placement of an atlatl hook or spur (Figure 3.5; Croes 1995:169). Dredging along the Skagit River in Washington produced a remarkable carved atlatl dated at approximately 1700 BP (Fladmark et al. 1987).

   The Ozette Village wet site, with collapsed houses recovered from under a massive clay mudslide dating to about 300 years ago, produced huge numbers of arrow components: 1,534 arrow shafts; 5,189 wooden arrowpoints; and 115 wooden bows (Figure 3.6; Draper 1989:6). With such great numbers,

Figure 3.6 Example of numerous wooden bows and arrows recovered from the Ozette Village wet site. Note that most of the arrows have wooden projectile points.

mainly from two houses, we can assume that these artifacts reflect both resource procurement as well as defensive strategies. Historically, warfare and raids were common, and the fact that there were thousands of arrows in these two-plus houses undoubtedly reflects this concern. Also note that, at the Ozette Village site, *wooden* arrowpoints immensely outnumbered the rare stone ($N = 7$), bone, and shell projectile points (Gleeson 1980a). Without wet-site preservation, their presence would have been unknown to us today.

Harpoons
Antler and bone harpoons are one of the main artifact types researchers have used to define Northwest Coast cultural phases. Toggling harpoons, a major food procurement tool, were made with many types of ground bone, stone, and shell arming points, as were unilaterally and bilaterally barbed harpoons with lineguards and lineholes. A curious situation at the 3,000-year-old Hoko River wet site (a Locarno Beach-phase site) was the lack of bone or antler harpoons, although bone and antler were preserved there (Figure 3.7). Also, it is significant that none of the Hoko River examples are of the female toggling style more commonly associated with the Locarno Beach time period (Borden 1970; Mitchell 1971a, 1982, 1990). Their style is more similar to the unilaterally barbed male harpoons of the very diagnostic Marpole culture type; however, the latter consisted of antler (especially in the early Marpole period) or bone (especially in the late Marpole period), and typically had bilaterally projecting lineguards, though line attachments with unilateral and bilateral notching are reported (Type 2a and 2b, McMurdo 1972; Burley 1980:25; see also illustrated antler or bone male harpoon heads,

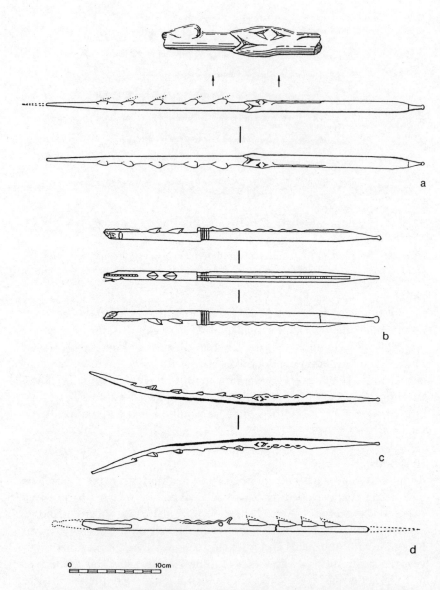

Figure 3.7 Examples of elaborately carved unilaterally barbed wooden projectile points from the Hoko wet site (uppermost drawing is detail of midsection of projectile point below it). Note zoomorphic designs with backbone lineguards and barbs coming out of the mouths of the creatures. *Drawing by Robert Slagle; Croes 1995:167-169*

typical of the middle period as defined by Carlson 1983b:26, 28). In emphasizing these male harpoon heads as a Marpole period marker, Burley (1980:25) states:

> Of all categories of artifacts, that considered most diagnostic of the Marpole culture type is the distinctive unilaterally barbed harpoon. Such a priority is not without its justification. The chronological distribution of unilaterally barbed harpoons, with but a few exceptions, is restricted to the Marpole time period. They are proceded [sic] in the Locarno Beach culture type by single and two piece composite toggling harpoons and are succeeded during the Gulf of Georgia period by two piece composite varieties.

This creates a dilemma in that the dates, stone artifacts, and site features of the Hoko River wet site are characteristic of the Locarno Beach phase, but the site's wooden unilaterally barbed harpoon heads are most similar to the antler and bone harpoon heads of the following Marpole phase. This is an unexpected continuity of style in unilaterally barbed harpoon heads from Locarno Beach to Marpole. Another conclusion that can be made is that most unilaterally barbed harpoons were probably constructed of wood. Or perhaps this reflects changes in materials, from wood to antler to bone, through time in making similar harpoon types. The impetus for this kind of change in material usage may elude us, but with wet sites we can at least *see* the perishable portion of change.

Returning to the Ozette Village site, we see not only composite, valved bone harpoons with bone and shell blades but also the fibre bindings and the harpoon shafts ($N = 124$; some of which are whale-harpoon shafts) and wooden harpoon finger rests from the shaft end of seal harpoons ($N = 22$) (Draper 1989:6). This preservation of sea-mammal-hunting equipment can add greatly to our understanding of the add-on emphasis on sea-mammal hunting over the past 1,000 to 1,500 years on the Central Coast (as discussed above and predicted by computer simulation of economic decision making for this part of the Northwest Coast [see Croes and Hackenberger 1988]).

Digging/Prying Sticks
Northwest Coast wet sites have also yielded perishable implements for foraging and collecting plant foods and shellfish. At Ozette distinct digging and possibly prying sticks were recovered, reflecting the importance of these procurement technologies for the prehistoric Northwest Coast.

Storage Technologies
Because procurement technologies have been better understood through wet-site research, I believe that the problem of when and how long-term

storage affected the development of Northwest Coast complexity can also be addressed with wet-site data. Until now, the debate has centred on faunal analysis, including studying prehistoric butchering techniques that reflect the storage of fish, and using the presence or absence of head bones from halibut and salmon to discern the beginning of intensive fish processing for storage (Croes 1992b; Matson 1992; Matson and Coupland 1995). Wet sites do not produce direct evidence of storage practices, but they do produce the containers used in storage, both bentwood boxes and storage baskets.

Boxes
One of the oldest Northwest Coast collections of kerfed, bentwood boxes or box fragments is from the Lachane wet site in Prince Rupert, British Columbia, dating from at least 2000 BP (GbTo33, $N = 11$ box or box fragments; Inglis 1976). Historically, these boxes had numerous uses (Stewart 1984:86). At the Ozette Village site a huge number of box fragments were recovered ($N = 1,001$; see Draper 1989; Gleeson 1980b). Upon reconstruction, it is estimated that at least fifty-five boxes were in use in the two houses, and the part of the third house, which were uncovered (Mauger 1980:76; Mauger 1982:73). This late protohistoric setting reflects their uses in the house as cooking boxes, water buckets, and elaborate boxes for holding special equipment (Mauger 1982:76). When considering their use as food-storage containers, however, Mauger points out that "Makah informants assert that baskets, rather than boxes, were used for food storage to allow for air circulation" (1982:76).

Baskets
No doubt a more sensitive indicator of food storage would be specific styles of baskets used to hold dried foods, whether fish, shellfish, or berry cakes. As also indicated by my interviews with Makah elders, traditionally dried foods need to be stored in woven baskets (or, more recently, in gunnysacks) high in the house where air and smoke can continue to circulate through them; a closed container, such as a wooden box, encourages mould (Croes 1977:309-321).

At the Ozette Village wet site, the single most common type of basket in the houses is considered a food-storage basket (Figure 3.8, Type OB29, $N = 46$, 19 percent of all basket types; Croes 1977:309-321). This basket type is defined as having an expanding, rounded-cuboidal shape with a twill 2/2-plaited base and body weave, constructed of splint-cedar boughs. These baskets are intermediate to large in size and have a continuous, two-strand cordage-loop handle. Of the forty-six baskets of this type, only thirteen (28 percent) appear to have been in use in House 1 (although many others along the front of the house may have been washed out on the beach by the mudslide); the remaining thirty-three (72 percent) baskets were badly

Figure 3.8 Expanding rounded-cube, twill 2/2, small cedar-splints basket with continuous, one-under, looped-cordage handle. Note colour contrast patterning created by leaving the bark adhering to certain warp elements. *Drawing by Chris Walsh; basket 4/IV/6; OB29; Croes 1977:309-321*

broken and discarded within the outside midden refuse or within the house-floor midden deposit (Figure 3.9). The thirteen complete baskets were found along the house wall areas; only one complete basket, used to hold twelve boiling stones, was found in the central area and was by a cooking hearth in the north-central area of the house (Figure 3.8, Art. 64/IV/41; Croes 1977: 316-317).

I measured the capacity of these twill-plaited, splint-limb baskets, and the other common storage basket type from Ozette, an open-twined, splint-limb or root rounded conical basket, which also has a continuous looped handle (OB38, N = 12, 5 percent of all baskets, Figure 3.10; Croes 1977:321-333) to estimate the amount of dried food that might have been kept in the house. These estimates are not unlike today's estimates of the capacity of the pantry or freezer and were probably used by household managers (probably noble women) to calculate the progress and/or current state of dried foods accumulated or needed to support the household (longhouse) through the winter season.

The actual number of filled baskets probably indicated the amount of dried supplies available and/or needed. These two major basket types (OB29 and OB38) were made of splint-limb materials, open enough in weave for air circulation, and had continuous looped handles to tie in the contents. They ranged in volume from 0.8 cubic decimetres up to thirty-seven cubic

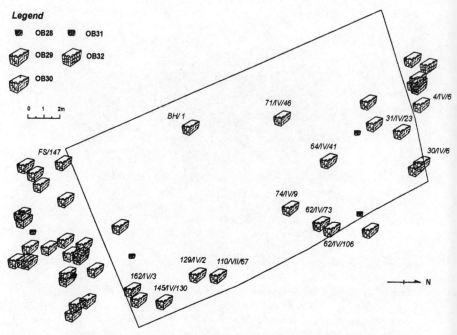

Legend

OB28   OB31

OB29   OB32

OB30

0   1   2m

71/IV/46

BH/1

FS/147

64/IV/41

74/IV/9

62/IV/73

62/IV/106

129/IV/2   110/VII/67

162/IV/3

145/IV/130

31/IV/23

30/IV/6

4/IV/6

N

Figure 3.9   Distribution of large, cedar-splint, twill 2/2 storage baskets recovered from the Ozette House 1 area. Baskets with designated artifact numbers were in use at the time of the mudslide (computer-generated map from Croes 1977:314. Note: Ozette Basket types OB28 and OB32 are defined in Croes 1977; see programming in Croes, Davis, and Irwin 1974).

decimetres (mean = 15.4 cubic decimetres, S = 11.5 cubic decimetres, N = 25; Note: a cubic decimetre equals one litre in liquid measurement). This significant size variation probably reflects their use to store a wide range of foods, including dried berry cakes, shellfish, fish (halibut, salmon, and others), and mammal meats (deer, elk, and others). In Ozette House 1, I would estimate that (projecting as many as forty storage baskets owned by the house) up to 800 cubic decimeters (28 cubic feet) of storage in these designated food-storage baskets was likely.

To see what this represents in terms of stored foods, we can calculate that a butterfly filleted and dried salmon is approximately 30 by 30 by 2.5 centimetres (1 foot by 1 foot by 1 inch) thick and, if wet, represents an approximately 1.8 kilogram (4 pound) salmon (being rather conservative). If this is the case, then twelve stacked fillets would represent 28 cubic decimetres (1 cubic foot), about 22 kilograms (48 pounds) of salmon. If the estimated forty storage baskets in one house represent 800 cubic decimetres (28 cubic feet), then this represents the house capacity to store approximately 610 kilograms (1,344 pounds) of salmon. Again this is a conservative estimate; if the salmon averaged 2.7 kilograms (6 pounds), then this figure would be over 1,000 kilograms (2,000 pounds). In our current cultural setting, about 250 grams (½ pound) of salmon is considered to be one person meal (i.e., a person's serving per meal), so 610 kilograms of stored salmon would be equivalent to 2,688 person meals. With approximately thirty persons in a household estimated for Ozette House 1, this could provide about ninety meals or possibly two months' worth of food. To this would be added sea-mammal-oil products (stored in bladders, skins, or closed boxes), dried shell-fish, and products left hanging on rafters to stay dried. The worst of times for food collection on the Northwest Coast would have been through January and February. As this period approached the managers would have wanted all baskets full to see their households through the winter. If baskets were not filled, increased efforts in other food procurement and drying might have been needed. Of course, during times less lean, the baskets would have been continually replenished as needed or as possible.

Surprisingly, these very common prehistoric storage baskets from Ozette House 1 (type OB29/OB38) are rarely seen in museum collections. In reviewing the entire Makah and West Coast ethnographic basketry collections held at the Smithsonian and at many other museums, I found only two good examples of the most numerous Ozette basket type, the OB29. The Smithsonian examples were both illustrated and described by Otis Mason in his volume *Aboriginal American Basketry: Studies in a Textile Art without Machinery* (1904). In the same museum context, I observed hundreds of open-wrapped pack baskets, reflecting an example of serious bias in museum collecting. One of the more typical baskets likely used in food storage at the Ozette prehistoric site and into the historic period was rarely collected, probably because it was considered *too* "utilitarian."

Otis Mason (1904:420, Plate 152) describes one of the baskets of the Ozette type (OB29) as "an example of twilled weaving from Vancouver island ... It is a large fish basket made from the split root of cedar ... Collected by G.T. Emmons." I examined this basket in 1974, and it appears to be constructed of cedar limb splints. Senior Makah women whom I interviewed also remember this basket type. Nora Barker, Lena McGee Claplanhoo, Isabell Ides, and Meridith Parker all consider this a utility basket for carrying various items. They were used in historic times as suitcases when families were travelling, with the continuous looped handles being crisscross tied over the contents to keep them in. Clothes, blankets, and food were placed in them, tied securely, and put into the canoe for the trip. Meridith Parker, who was particularly well acquainted with the old traditions, thought that in earlier times these baskets held dried fish in storage on high shelves around the walls of the house. Each of these women pointed out that these baskets once were very common and were not considered commercially valuable (personal communications 1974). Meridith Parker, when considering the

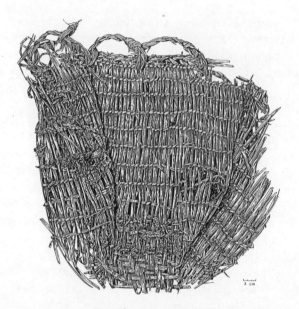

Figure 3.10   Coarsely woven open-twined cedar splints, utility-storage basket with continuous looped handles. Note the cedar bark repairs in body areas and twill 2/2 base weave. *Drawing by Chris Walsh; basket 110/V/13; OB38; Croes 1977:321-333*

open-twined basket type illustrated in Figure 3.10, specifically mentioned that these baskets "stored the dried foods, fish and shellfish, and were kept high on shelving so that the food would stay dry and well preserved" (Croes 1977:332).

The plaited-splint Ozette baskets can be useful in identifying earlier baskets that also might have been used to store dried foods. In addition, baskets of different functional types would be expected to occur in differing frequencies at different types of sites. For example, at the Hoko River fishing camp, the most commonly occurring baskets were not storage baskets but open-wrapped pack baskets (type HO-B1), which represent 74 percent of the baskets recorded (N = 61; Croes 1995:133). A high frequency of pack baskets was common at prehistoric wet-site *fishing camps*, whereas at *major village sites* they would be uncommon; for instance, at Ozette this same type of pack basket accounts for only 4 percent of the baskets, while 19 percent are dried-food storage baskets (Croes 1995:133). At Hoko River, the second most common basket type is the plaited, rounded-rectangular to expanding-rounded-cube, medium to large basket (Functional Set IV, N = 11, 14 percent of all baskets; Croes 1995:134). It very likely served as a food-storage basket, which is consistent with the argument that Hoko River was a halibut-drying camp where both pack baskets (to transport the resources from the beach) and storage baskets (to hold the dried resources) would be needed.

Social Organization

Researchers have attempted to use the archaeological record to determine when complex social stratification emerged on the prehistoric Northwest Coast. They have often looked to the occurrence of head shaping and to the use of labrets as possible reflections of the emergence of differences in status, and they have also explored burials to see when differentials in wealth occur (Ames 1995; Ames and Maschner 1999; Cybulski 1996; Mitchell 1990). I would add that the fairly common recovery of perishable clothing, especially hats, from wet sites may be another indicator of complex social stratification and its evolutionary history. Historically, Northwest Coast social stratification included relatively well defined (through inheritance) nobles, commoners, and slaves. Nobles appear to have emerged as a class of household and territory owners and managers.

Into the historic period, Northwest Coast nobility, as with chiefdoms elsewhere, included persons who inherited their rank. One of the Northwest Coast's main West Coast/Central Coast indicators of nobility was a distinct knob-topped hat, worn by both noblewomen and noblemen (see Mozino 1970:Plate 5). Commoners wore a flat-topped hat (see Mozino 1970:Plate 8). At the protohistoric Ozette Village wet site, three distinct hat types were recorded and considered to be functionally distinct sets: (1) Ozette hat Functional Set I /Types OH1, OH2/: a plain-twined, cedar bark, truncated (flat-topped) conical hat with cedar bark inner layer and headband (Figure 3.11);

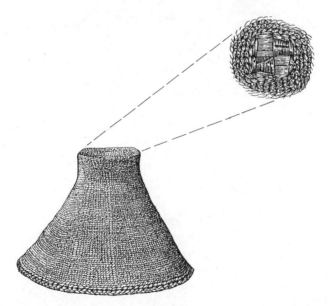

Figure 3.11   Ozette flat-topped, plain-twined, cedar bark hat. Note the checker weave initiating construction of the hat. *Drawing by Chris Walsh; hat 30/IV/44; OH2; Croes 1977:409-417*

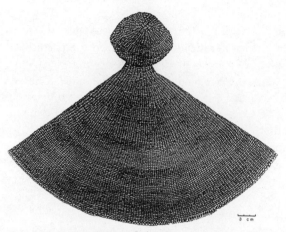

Figure 3.12   Ozette round-knob-topped conical hat. Note the checker weave at the top, the addition of new warp elements creating an expanding conical shape, and the braidlike turned-in brim construction. *Drawing by Madge Gleeson; hat FS/92; OH3; Croes 1977:417-427*

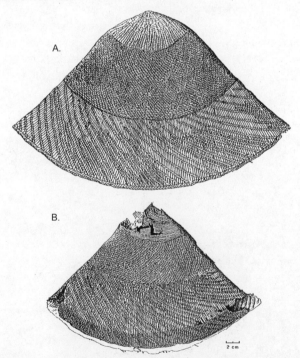

Figure 3.13   Ozette rounded-top conical hats with woven bands of (A, top to bottom) plain twining, diagonal twining, and "skip-stitch" twining; B has been painted (stippled) with a red band around the brim and has black paint on the upper body. *Drawing by Chris Walsh; OH7s; A: 160/tV/1, B: 110/IV/3; Croes 1977: 427-435*

(2) Ozette hat Functional Set II /OH3, OH4, OH5/: a plain-twined, cedar bark, knob-topped conical hat with cedar bark inner layer and headband (Figure 3.12); and (3) Ozette hat Functional Set III /OH6, OH7/: a complex-twined, spruce-root, rounded-top conical hat with an attached cedar bark headband (Figure 3.13) (Croes 1977:409-439).

From ethnohistorical records, it is clear that the flat-topped hats were worn by commoners and that the knob-topped hats were worn by nobles. The earliest actual consideration of hat shapes as a mark of status is given in Jose Mariana Mozino's (1970:15) 1792 account of Nootka Sound: "but more common are two kinds of hats ... the shape of the hat is like a truncated cone, more or less elevated, upon which the nobles superimposed another small one that terminates in a sharp point. Those of the commoners are of a coarser material and have no design." He also provides illustrated plates of a commoner wearing a flat-topped hat and a noble wearing a knob-topped hat (Plates 8 and 5). John Jewitt (1896:57), a captive and slave of Maquinna of Yuquot, Nootka Sound, from 1803 to 1805, distinguished a hat worn by the king as having upon it an ornament in the figure of a small urn. This was undoubtedly a knob-topped hat.

The complex-twined spruce-root hats (Functional Set III) were distinctive in the use of fine spruce-root twining elements, and three of the four had an up-to-the-left twining. The lean of the twining is usually culturally specific (i.e., at Ozette almost all twining is up-to-the-right). This situation is noteworthy since the northern weavers, particularly the Haida and Tlingit, typically twine with a lean up-to-the-left. All the Ozette flat-topped and knob-topped hats are woven with a lean up-to-the-right. Additionally, all of these hats have distinct combinations of plain and diagonal twining as well as a combination of twining techniques called skip-stitch twining that is characteristic of the northern Chilkat Tlingit (Willoughby 1910:4). All these hat characteristics lead me to conclude that this third type of hat is a northern, foreign style (possibly Tlingit or Haida in origin) (Croes 1977:427-435; Croes 2002) and may have indicated the wearer's means. It was possibly worn mainly by West Coast noblewomen, as illustrated ethnohistorically (Gunther 1972:69).

A possible indicator of the longevity of social stratification on the Northwest Coast might be the long-term existence of knob-topped conical hats, as recorded in prehistoric wet sites. At the 3,000-year-old Hoko River wet site, both knob-topped hats and rounded-topped forms were recovered (Figure 3.14; Croes 1995). These hats probably did function as indicators of early status differences, though possibly to a different degree than was the case in later periods (Croes 1995). If the hat forms did reflect some degree of status differentiation, then we can project that control and management of territories by extended-family leaders may have begun to occur by 3,000 years ago. This supposition is consistent with the results of computer

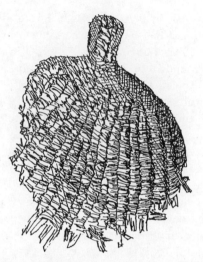

Figure 3.14   Plain-twined, knob-topped hat from the 3,000-year-old Hoko River site (scale 1:1). *Drawing by Robin Pedersen; Croes 1995:134-137*

simulations of economic decision making through time on the West Coast, indicating that the emphasis on and required management of procurement and storage activities, especially the drying of fish, was under way 3,000 years ago at Hoko River (Croes and Hackenberger 1988). Although basketry data were not involved in the simulations, the existence of 3,000-year-old knob-topped hats, possibly indicative of a management role at this time, corresponds to these expectations.

Exchange

As complex societies emerged on the Northwest Coast of North America, and as territories became highly circumscribed and defined, exchange of both rare foods and wealth items became a major form of economic interaction. Members of the nobility, in particular, had to acquire, display, and distribute, through potlatching, large quantities of valuables, and some of this wealth acquisition had to be through long-distance trade. Foreign artifacts are useful indicators of contact or exchange between prehistoric Northwest Coast groups and peoples in other areas. Because bone, stone, and shell artifacts appear to make up a small percentage of the actual material culture (5 percent to 10 percent), as is indicated at all wet sites, perishable artifacts can be the major source of information about prehistoric exchange. Baskets, probably the most abundant and sensitive of perishable artifacts for revealing contact and trade, have proven useful in indicating ethnicity on the Northwest Coast and elsewhere (Bernick 1987, 1989, 1998; Croes 1977, 1980, 1988, 1989a, 1989b, 1992a, 1992b, 1993, 1995, 1997, 2001). Therefore, they can be very useful in determining direction and distance of contacts. Foreign baskets in a site would indicate contact with outsiders, including the acquisition of baskets through trade networks.

The best examples of this kind of exchange are the "foreign" baskets recovered from the large-scale protohistoric Ozette house excavations. Here, styles indicative of historically known types from all possible directions of contact (north, east, and south, excluding the west, or out to sea) have been recorded (Figure 3.15; Croes 1977). And, as mentioned above, the hat types illustrated in Figure 3.13 appear to have been introduced from the north. The four hats from this set were made with spruce root, and three of the four were twined with an unusual twining slant (up-to-the-left), and used the ornamental skip-stitch found mainly among northern Tlingit and Haida groups (Figure 3.13; Croes 1977:427-435). From the east, up the Strait of

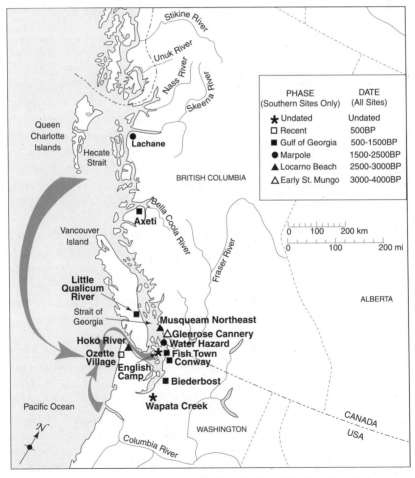

Figure 3.15 Routes of trade to the Ozette site as indicated by "foreign" basketry found at the site.

Figure 3.16   Bowl-shaped coiled basket from Ozette. Note the split-stitch coiling technique and the bundle of sectioned roots as the foundation elements exposed at rim. *Drawing by Chris Walsh; basket 145/IV/133; OB51; Croes 1977:353-365*

Juan de Fuca, came a distinctive late form of Salishan cedar-root coiled basketry, with three complete baskets in use in the house (Type OB51, 52, and 53; see example, Figure 3.16; Croes 1977:353-365). An unusual occurrence of fourteen intentionally cut coiled-basket pieces in the shape of small strips, ribbons, or trapezoidal forms was also recorded (see example, Figure 3.17, Croes 1977:353-365). The cut coiled baskets appear to have been valuable potlatch gifts. At potlatch ceremonies, other things of value, such as blankets and even muskets, were cut up and given out to witnesses as symbols of wealth. Finally, baskets that appear to have been introduced from the south include distinctive forms of small Salishan overlaid-twined, cylindrical baskets (Figure 3.18; N = 4, Type OB54, Croes 1977:365-372), common to the Quinault, Chehalis, Squaxin, and Skokomish. Therefore, in this one village wet site we actually see distinctive and sensitive styles of foreign basketry from the north, east, and south (all possible directions of cultural contacts for the Makah).

Occasionally, I hear the comment that these foreign styles are not necessarily indicative of trade; because women are usually associated with basket weaving on the Northwest Coast, these and other examples might be more indicative of women marrying into the village. Although this scenario is possible, my observations in working with basket weavers throughout this area strongly indicate that women marrying into another village were often obliged to learn the basketry styles of that group (or, more correctly, the family's style within that group). Some of the Makah elders with whom I worked had Salish mothers who married Makahs, and, in each case, the bride was required to learn the Makah family's style of basket weaving. Historically, these styles appear to be jealously guarded by women of particular ethnic communities, and I have observed considerable resistance when

Figure 3.17 Cut trapezoid piece of Ozette coiled basketry. *Drawing by Chris Walsh; basket SB/III/118; Croes 1977:353-365*

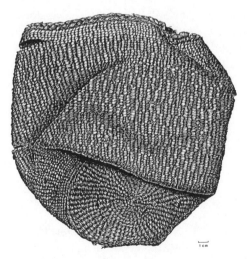

Figure 3.18 Plain-twined, rounded-base cylindrical basket with overlay ornamentation of bear grass from Ozette. Note the spiral-based twining, the row of three-strand twining between the base and the body, and the mock-braid rim construction. *Drawing by Chris Walsh; basket 164/VII/10; OB54; Croes 1977:365-373*

women from one community ask to learn the distinct techniques of those of another community. From these observations, I would venture to say that the prehistoric foreign basketry styles are likely the result of exchanges of basketry between groups rather than of intermarriage.

An earlier wet-site example of a foreign style occurs at the Hoko River wet site – two baskets made with wrap-around-plaiting weaves. This type of basket weave technique is much more common to the contemporary 3,000-year-old Musqueam Northeast site (Gulf of Georgia/Fraser Delta site) (Croes 1995:134-136, Figure 4.50.2). Because this basket is a utilitarian form, perhaps a basket load of goods was traded to the West Coast Hoko River site from a group who put similar emphasis on this distinct wrap-around-plaited basketry, which, so far, has been documented only on the easterly Fraser River Delta for this ancient time period.

Conclusion

This brief survey of Northwest Coast wet-site data reaches beyond previous wet site studies, which define culture-historical sequences and reconstructed past lifeways, in order to begin to examine more theoretical aspects of cultural processes. These include: (1) an examination of changes in procurement strategies through the distribution of fish hook types in time and space; (2) an exploration of food-storage expansion through capacities of perishable boxes and baskets; (3) an analysis of the evolution of complex social stratification through variation in basketry hat types over time and space; and (4) an identification of the direction and intensity of interregional contact and trade (an important aspect of complex societies) through the presence of foreign basketry. These perishable artifacts, once identified as sensitive behavioural markers, can be used to address some of the many cultural-process *why* questions concerning the evolution of Northwest Coast complexity, greatly expanding opportunities to test the many hypotheses brought forward to explain this complexity.

One thing we have learned from Don Mitchell's efforts to elucidate functional information from Northwest Coast artifact collections is to use controlled speculation while approaching and explaining evolutionary characteristics of prehistoric subsistence, technology, and social organization. With Northwest Coast wet-sites data, this path is a little easier to follow but no less tricky.

My aim is to point out some new wet-site dimensions when approaching and exploring the evolution of subsistence strategies, food-storage practices, and management (through social stratification and exchange systems) on the Northwest Coast. Of course, more can be done as additional wet-site data become available to Northwest Coast researchers. As much of Don Mitchell's work shows, we need to continue looking at the data from several new directions in order to come up with better perspectives on cultural evolution and the development of complexity on the Northwest Coast of North America.

Acknowledgments
I would particularly like to thank the conference coordinators and volume editors, R.G. Matson, Gary Coupland, and Quentin Mackie, for their excellent job in producing the CAA symposium in honour of Don Mitchell and compiling this volume. Gary Coupland, assigned to my chapter, provided invaluable and insightful comments. Another version of this chapter has been published as "Northwest Coast Wet Sites: Using Perishables to Reveal Patterns of Resource Procurement, Storage, Management, and Exchange" in a volume entitled *Fleeting Identities: Perishable Material Culture in Archaeological Research*, edited by Penelope B. Drooker (Center for Archaeological Investigations at Southern Illinois University, 2001). Penny Drooker and the editors at SIU have also contributed greatly to earlier revisions of this chapter.

In terms of this chapter, the basis of the data is mainly the Hoko River Archaeological Project research, which is co-sponsored by the Makah Tribal Nation and Washington State University, and has been made possible through the support of the M.J. Murdock Charitable Trust, the National Endowment for the Humanities, US West, and Ray and Jean Auel. Numerous project researchers, Makah community members, field personnel, and students have contributed to data recovery, analysis, and reporting. Though this research owes its existence to these and many previous and current researchers, the summary and conclusions remain my responsibility.

4
The Coast Salish House: Lessons from Shingle Point, Valdes Island, British Columbia

R.G. Matson

The nature and history of the Coast Salish shed-roof house is an important topic in Northwest Coast anthropology. In the early 1990s I became involved in an attempt to compare the archaeological remains of a late prehistoric house with the ethnographic description. To this end, in 1995 and 1996 I directed the excavation of what we inferred to be a shed-roof Salish house at Shingle Point, on Valdes Island, one of the British Columbian Gulf Islands across the Strait of Georgia from the city of Vancouver (Figure 4.1). In this chapter I emphasize the history of the project and the information recovered about this house's physical structure and compare this with information from other houses, both ethnographic and archaeological. In addition to a series of prehistoric houses on Shingle Point, one of which we partially excavated, there appears to be at least two other historic houses, to which I briefly refer.

The Salish Shed-Roof House

The Salish shed-roof house is simultaneously well known and undefined. Here I rely extensively on the description by the dean of Northwest Coast ethnography, Wayne Suttles (1991), whose work has been so helpful in providing an orientation for several generations of archaeologists. Suttles makes clear the many functions of the shed-roof house that are agreed to by most investigators – general purpose, winter dwelling, storage, and location of public ceremonies. The main structural features of this house form are also a point of general agreement. Beyond these general statements, such things as size, number of people per compartment, divisions between compartments, location of different people within the house, and amount of economic specialization are subject to widely varying interpretations. In short, as Fladmark (1973:80) pointed out, the organization of the precontact ethnographic house and household will be determined by archaeology, if it is determined at all. Let us begin with those things that are known, relying extensively on Suttles's 1991 summary but also referring to the archaeological

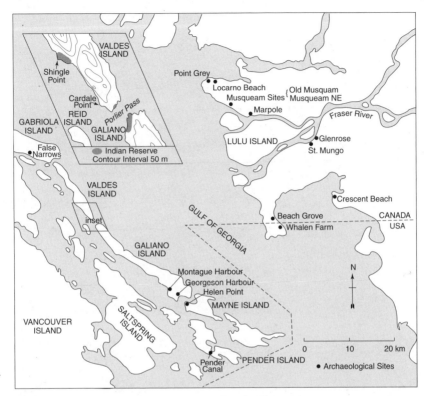

Figure 4.1 Location of Valdes Island and Shingle Point.

information from the structurally very similar Makah and Ozette houses as reported by Mauger (1991) and Samuels (1983, 1991), and the important first-hand description by Boas (1891a). Similar houses may also have been used by the southern Nootkan speakers on the west coast of Vancouver Island; by the time one reaches the more northern area reported by Mackie and Williamson (see Chapter 5, this volume), houses quite different in frame structure are seen, although they may superficially look very similar (Vastokas 1966:57). Mackie and Williamson discuss this in some detail.

In terms of agreed-upon features, the house frame, of parallel lines of vertical rafter support posts and suspended rafter beams, was "permanent," (Suttles 1951:256-261; Suttles 1991; Barnett 1955:35-40), but the cladding of roof and wall planks and their supporting poles were not (Figure 4.2). Typically, a shed-roof house, or portions thereof, would be clad by individually owned roof and wall planks (Barnett 1955:251; Kew, personal communication; Suttles 1951:273-274) in the fall that would be taken apart in the spring as families dispersed to resource-gathering and processing locations. Thus the parallel rows of rafter support posts would represent the

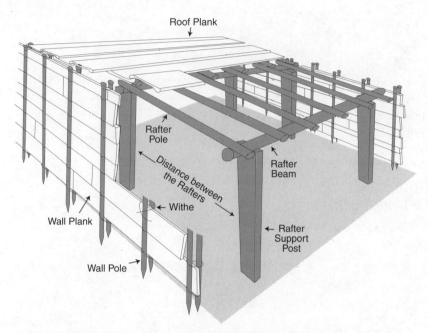

Figure 4.2   Shed-roof house structural elements. Dark elements (rafter support posts and rafter beams) make up the permanent "house frame."

maximum size of the house, not necessarily the usual size fully covered by planks each winter.

Second, the roof and side walls were independent of each other (Boas 1891a; Suttles 1951:257; Suttles 1991). The roof (Figure 4.2) consisted of planks 30 to 45 centimetres wide and long enough to go across the width of the structure laid on top of the rafter poles on top of the rafter beams (Suttles 1951:256, 7; Suttles 1991; Nabokov and Easton 1989:236; Waterman and Greiner 1921). (We have one over 13 metres long at the University of British Columbia.) These planks were usually slightly lipped at the edges (Figures 4.2 and 4.3), so they acted like tiles in that the water ran down them and not off their sides and into the house below. The roof planks rested on cross pieces placed between the rafters. The front (towards the water) side of the house was higher (3 to 4 metres high) than the back, so that the water ran off the ends of the lipped roof planks at the back of the house (Boas 1891a; Suttles 1951:256; Suttles 1991). The walls consisted of shorter (usually 2.5 to 5 metre) planks that were broader (up to 1.4 metres wide according to Suttles [1991] and Barnett [1955:36], but Ozette [Samuels 1991:62-65] and other information indicates they were usually much narrower than this) and were flat on both sides. These were suspended by ties between rows of small, vertical posts (Figure 4.3). Thus, there was no connection between the walls and the roofs (Figures 4.2 and 4.3).

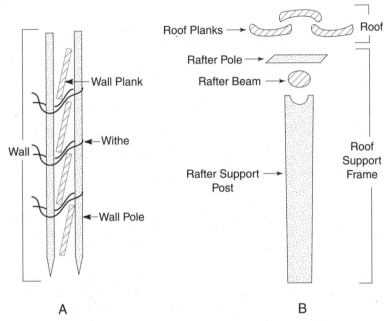

Roof Planks →

Roof

Rafter Pole →

Rafter Beam →

Wall Plank

Withe

Wall

Wall Pole

Rafter Support
Post →

Roof
Support
Frame

A

B

Figure 4.3 Wall and roof details. *A:* Wall details. Note overlapping of wall planks and their suspension between wall poles. *B:* Roof and roof support details. Note the interlocking of roof planks to keep out the rain.

The walls were commonly lined with rush mats (Figure 4.5), which served to seal the cracks between the wall planks (Suttles 1991). These mats were also used as pillows and sleeping mats.

From these "facts," which are agreed to by almost all observers and confirmed by work at Ozette (Samuels 1983, 1991), we move to areas that are relatively agreed to but less clear. First, a bench of some sort is agreed to exist at least against the long front and back walls (Figure 4.4). This was used for storage and sleeping, with items stored both under the bench and on top. Suttles (1991) and Barnett (1955:37-38) indicate that a bench was 60 to 90 centimetres high and 1.2 to 1.8 metres wide, with another, lower bench sometimes existing in front of it. Boas (1891a), however, reports a single, lower bench, about 30 centimetres above the floor, apparently extending along all four walls. Remains from Ozette (Samuels 1991:108, 163) indicate a relatively permanent bench with a special lipped plank at the edge towards the middle of the house that probably usually extended along all four walls but was raised only 23 to 30 centimetres above the floor. These benches, however, were usually not continuous. The Ozette houses, although they had frames, roofs, and walls structurally identical with Salish ones, were not seasonally disarticulated and thus may not be good models for the Salish houses when it comes to the nature of benches.

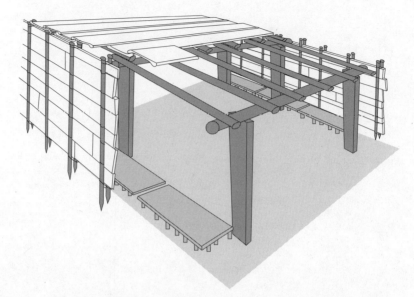

Figure 4.4   Position of benches. Benches are illustrated as being between rafter support posts and exterior wall, along the long walls of the house.

A second feature that is agreed to by most investigators is the presence of at least one hearth between each set of rafters. There is no agreement, though, on the number of hearths or their location. According to some evidence, two usually existed, although a single row running down the centre of the house is also cited (Suttles 1991:215). Suttles (1991) points out that the fire could easily be moved. The hearth(s) and a pair of rafters defined a "compartment" (Boas 1891a:12), which was occupied by a social group analogous to a House or "household" elsewhere on the coast. Boas states that "the fire is near one of the front corners of the compartment, where the house is highest" (1891a:12). Since the high side of the shed-roof is towards the water, Boas is indicating that the hearths are on the water side. The roof planks could easily be shifted by a pole to allow the smoke to escape, permitting the flexibility in location cited by Suttles (1991).

This compartment would typically be occupied by two related nuclear families or a large extended family. Suttles (1951:274) emphasizes the social separateness of the two "halves" of each compartment but admits that this inference applies to no earlier than 1880, when significant economic and social changes had already occurred. Boas (1891a) does not make such a reference. A compartment with a single fire would seem to be de facto a more integrated unit than would one with two, and thus could be fairly interpreted as a single household. I will return to this question of size of household and changes in the nineteenth century later. In some cases, several adjacent "compartments" would belong to the same corporate "house-

Figure 4.5 Paul Kane's painting of shed-roof compartment, *Interior of Lodge with a Family Group*. Note mats against the wall, low bench, and informal nature of hearth. *Courtesy Stark Museum of Art, Orange, Texas*

hold." Depending on the size of the house and the household, the social household may be isometric with the entire shed-roof house.

I found a single representation of a compartment (Figure 4.5) made by Paul Kane, apparently in 1847 near Victoria, British Columbia, of either a Clallam or Songhees shed-roof house. This shows the mats hung on the exterior wall (but only the lower portions of the wall) and a low bench, with other mats and a relatively unstructured hearth. Although this painting adds life to the descriptions reviewed above, and supports such attributes as low benches, relatively narrow wall planks, and casual hearths, it is very much postcontact and other arrangements may well have been used elsewhere. It does, however, show that the compartment is neither an inference only of archaeologists nor a feature of later times.

Although the above features are supported by most accounts, little agreement can be found about additional structural details of Coast Salish houses. Thus, whether one would expect permanent divisions between compartments is moot (Suttles [1991] argues no). Ozette evidence from House 2 (Samuels 1991:108) indicates that some benches may have been perpendicular to the long walls, which could be evidence of some sort of partition, although maybe a very low one. Samuels (personal communication 1999) now thinks that the perpendicular benches were likely placed there by mudslides. One might expect partitions to be absent between compartments that belong to the same multifamily household but to be present between compartments belonging to different households. Boas (1891a) indicates only mat partitions and only in the winter. Hill-Tout (1978:44), another early observer, also argues against permanent partitions. The result of this conflicting information is that the expected existence and nature of any partition is unclear, although it may be that it was just extremely variable.

Another question is whether a specific part of the house, such as the northeast corner, would have the "head of household" (Suttles [1991] again argues no). The size of the compartments and of a "typical" house are also unclear, as are the amount and nature of economic specialization between or within houses. The positioning of the rafter support posts and benches is also not clear, as Boas (1891a) – and Figures 4.2 and 4.3 – places the rafter support posts away from the wall, leaving space for the bench to occur between the post and the wall; however, others put the rafter support posts close to the wall. Ozette (Samuels 1991) is ambiguous on this question, and it may well be that both arrangements were followed. Boas (1891a:12) is almost alone in indicating that, in some places, "shelves hang down from the rafters about seven or eight feet above the floor." It was to investigate these questions, as well as to validate the "agreed-upon" aspects, that we proposed the investigations on Shingle Point.

History of Excavation

The history of the Shingle Point project begins with Grant Myers, a University of British Columbia master's student who was interested in early historic household archaeology. I suggested that he talk with Professor Philip Hobler of Simon Fraser University about his Bella Coola material, and Professor Hobler suggested instead that he look at Shingle Point on Valdes Island, British Columbia (Figure 4.1). Grant did, visiting the site and getting a warm welcome from Chief Thomas of the Lyacksun. As things developed, such a project appeared too large to take on as a master's project, and it became a Social Sciences and Humanities Research Council of Canada project, including Myers's planned dissertation research (which, unfortunately, did not come to fruition).

In 1995 we negotiated an agreement with the then current Lyacksun Band Council, under which we would be able to excavate at Shingle Point if we also sought funding for a full survey of the coastline of Valdes Island, which is the subject of Eric McLay's (1999) master's thesis. In 1995 we excavated six one-by-one-metre units, and Guy Cross (1995) carried out a wide variety of remote sensing investigations, with electromagnetic conductivity apparently being the most useful for the purpose of locating household features.

A previous site record form (Matson and McLay 1996; Matson, Green, and McLay 1999) showed a number of houses, and we have photographs of standing house posts. We did find, though, that the "house depressions" and house posts did not always co-occur, and I will return to the issue of historic houses on Shingle Point towards the end of this chapter (Figure 4.6).

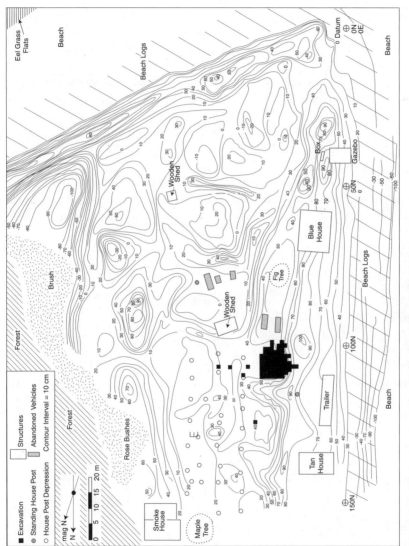

Figure 4.6 Contour map of Shingle Point (DgRv 2), Valdes Island.

Our 1995 test excavations (Matson and McLay 1996) uncovered a well preserved floor in the middle of an area that the remote sensing and ground topography indicated was a structure (Figure 4.6). Unit 108N 21E (Figure 4.7) not only showed a floor close to the surface but also a stratigraphy very different from that of the other units outside of the structure, indicating that we should be able follow out the floor. Further, underneath the floor in Unit 108N 21E was a very different deposit that we inferred resulted from shellfish processing, indicating that we could tell when we went through the floor. Other parts of the site showed, in addition to the shellfish process-ing matrix, layers of water-worn fragmented shell and an apparently natu-rally reworked midden, which should also help us to define the limits of a house structure. Our excavations indicate that the vast majority of the Shingle Point deposits are the result of shellfish procurement and processing, with the winter village activities likely a late, minor activity in terms of volume.

In 1996 we opened up a large area, 76 square metres, slightly more than half the house, and excavated one of two compartments completely (Figure 4.7). The east half of this compartment is the best defined, possibly because

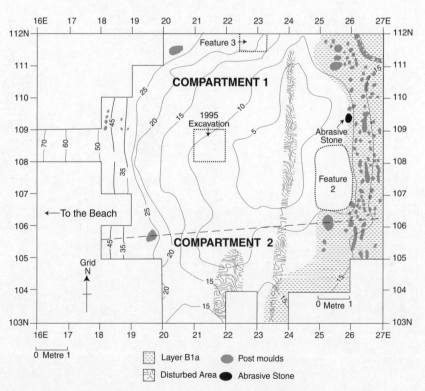

Figure 4.7 Compartment 1; top of floor and bench. Contours in centimetres; reference is to site datum. Layer B1a is water-worn shell.

Table 4.1

Generalized stratigraphy

Layers
Ax	Topsoil
B0x	Archaeological deposits above the floor
B1x	Archaeological deposits outside the floor
C0x	Floor deposits

Interfaces
B0x/C0x	Floor interface deposits
B0d1	Specific layer definitions
B0a	Burned layer, historic, in centre of Compartment 1
B0b	Unburned layer stratigraphically equivalent to B0a
B1a	Light-coloured water-worn shell layer found on east side of excavation
B0d	Layer with finely broken shell fragments found in Compartment 2

the house is delineated by the contrasting and relatively sterile water-worn shell deposits (Layer B1a, Table 4.1) and has less historic disturbance on that side. Unfortunately, the advantage of shallow deposits on top of the floor allowing a large area to be exposed for a relatively modest cost was offset, in this case, by extensive historic disturbance, including a burning episode (Layer B0a) that covered much of the central part of Compartment 1. Most of this historic material appears to date from the early twentieth century, although a few mid-nineteenth-century items were recovered (Matson, Green, and McLay 1999). Thus, the integrity of the deposit over much of the central part of the floor of Compartment 1 is definitely in question, with much more historic than prehistoric material recovered. Because most of the historic material dates around 100 years old, it does not appear that Compartment 1 is an early historic structure but, rather, a prehistoric structure that had its central portion reused in the early twentieth century, perhaps as a dump. This interpretation is supported by the lack of historic items in the best defined parts of Compartment 1, along the east side, and in intact prehistoric layers in the investigated parts of Compartment 2. A radiocarbon assay from Feature 2 (Figure 4.7), along the east side of Compartment 1, resulted in a date of 990 ± 105 radiocarbon years ago (BGS 2262).

Results: Compartment 1
The best structural house information is the size of Compartment 1 and the presence of benches along the east and west sides of the house (Figures 4.7, 4.8, and 4.9). The width of the house is well defined by unmodified water-worn shell on the east (Layer B1a Table 4.1) and the prehistoric cut into the

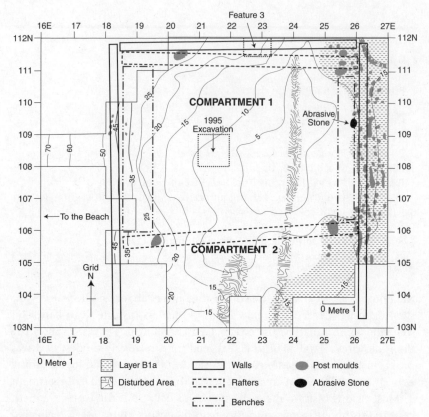

Figure 4.8 Compartment 1, showing inferred locations of rafters, walls, and benches.

beach ridge on the west, with the total distance between the two inferred walls being about 8 metres. On the east we have post moulds in back of the bench area that we interpret as resulting from the pairs of posts from which the wall planks were suspended (Figures 4.7 and 4.8). Unless the posts were left in the soil we would not expect very good post moulds because of the loose nature of the water-worn shell. However, the colour differences that remain are distinct. To the west, several post moulds were recovered outside of the inferred bench area that are likely equivalent (Figures 4.7, 4.8). These west-side post moulds are less distinct in colour but are larger and have a better "outline," as one would expect from a firmer matrix. At one point on the west side we thought we had some actual posts in a location that meant they might be bench supports, although they looked more like decayed remains of vertical planks. Glass at the base of the decayed wood showed this to be a historic intrusion.

In addition to the east and west walls of the house, the benches are also well defined. On the east, the relatively hard-packed living surface we interpreted as a floor quits, and a much less compacted matrix exists about a metre from the edge of the wall, as one would expect of a material that was not being trod upon. Analysis of matrix samples of the inferred floor is quite distinct from other samples (Matson and McLay 1996; Matson, Green, and McLay 1999:83). On the south portion of the bench we found a fascinating deposit, denoted as Feature 2. This appears to be floor debris that was swept under the bench rather than under the rug! On the east the bench area is well defined, and we have evidence for space under the bench being available for temporary waste storage. We also found an abrasive stone in a vertical position, apparently between the back of the bench and the edge of the house (Figure 4.8).

Feature 2 deserves further description. It includes whole shells and broken firecracked rocks not found elsewhere above the floor. Detailed analysis of the mammalian, fish, and bird remains (Matson, Green, and McLay 1999) supports the shellfish analysis carried out by J. Green (Green 1999; Matson, Green, and McLay 1999), which shows that the layers within Feature 2 demonstrate a progression from winter to spring. Thus, Feature 2 appears to be a deposit from a single year, dating approximately 900 calendar years ago, showing a progression from perhaps December through April. The information from this deposit indicates significant differences between the two compartments, as is discussed below.

A final observation about the east side has to do with the house excavation and the wall. The posts that held up the wall are found vertically higher than the bench and floor, indicating that a shallow excavation was made (around 20 centimetres) and that the house floor and bench were placed within this as well as the rafter support post. The wall, though, was placed immediately outside of this excavation, so at least part (around 20 centimetres) of the wall behind the bench consisted of the excavation and not the above-ground plank wall.

The west side of Compartment 1 presents a somewhat different situation (Figure 4.9). First, there appears to be more historic disturbance, as is indicated above. Second, the original ground layer was higher, with the excavation of the house floor being extended into the back of the beach ridge (Figure 4.6). The beach ridge was determined by the excavations of 108N 16E in 1995 (Matson and McLay 1996; Matson, Green, and McLay 1999) to consist largely of shellfish procurement and processing remains rather than refuse from the house. Because of the presence of the beach ridge on the west, there was more excavation needed to level the floor equivalent to that on the east portion of the house. About 70 centimetres difference in elevation exists between the top of the excavation into the beach ridge and the floor in front of the bench (Figure 4.9). The profile illustrated in Figure 4.9, with Layer A1 being the surface disturbed material, the B-series layers above the surfaces interpreted as belonging to the domestic structure, the B0/C0 interface on top of the Layer C- "floor," is that seen generally within

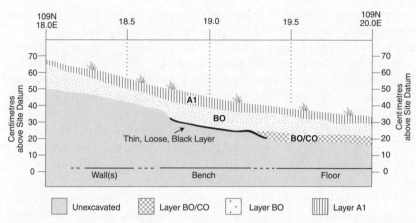

Figure 4.9 Compartment 1; west-side bench. Note the "bench" under the inferred bench location.

the house depression. In Compartment 1, B0x usually had historic material present, but this was not the case in Compartment 2. In the east, the light-coloured, water-worn shell Layer B1a (Figure 4.7) was found underneath a very shallow B0. Elsewhere the layers stratigraphically underneath the surfaces assigned to the house varied in nature but were all dark-coloured cultural layers that did not contrast as strongly as did B1a (Matson and McLay 1996; Matson, Green, and McLay 1999:83).

Apparently, this west-side excavation was not made all the way to the edge of the house at the same level, so a step existed underneath the bench (Figure 4.9). I believe some space existed between the bench and this ledge, based on a thin, loose, black layer that flowed up onto the bench, but I may be mistaken. This space may have been minimal if the height of the bench above the floor was similar to that indicated at Ozette, only 22 to 30 centimetres (Samuels 1991:108). There are some signs that a much lower ledge existed under the bench on the east side as well. This one, though, may be the result of "excavation" of the floor in front of the bench through wear and sweeping. Further excavation higher on the beach ridge revealed layers that may be the result of previous structures that were physically higher and shifted slightly to the west, making the stratigraphy more complicated and less clear than it is on the east. Although the beach ridge was cut into for the house, even in front of the bench it was not excavated down to the same level as is seen on the east, so that there is a gentle slope to the floor from west to east, a total of 25 centimetres at 107N in the 6 metres between the benches.

The lack of storage underneath the west-side bench might be seen as a difference in storage capacity between the west and east sides of Compartment 1. If we remember, however, that Boas (1891a) indicates that, in the higher parts of the house, shelves were hung from the rafters, and that the west side would have been the higher beach side (with the potential to have shelves), this conclusion may be unwarranted.

The north side of the house is poorly defined as the floor ends but neither a ledge, such as is seen on the west, nor obvious bench deposits, such as are found on the east, could be located. A small feature (Feature 3, shown in Figure 4.8), similar in nature to Feature 2, was located on the east end of the north side, which we think was either under the bench or was a small trash deposit immediately outside the house. Historic disturbances may be responsible; indeed, the northwest corner of the house was impossible to find and numerous historic items were located in that area. Only the east portion of the north wall can be said to be reasonably defined at all. The combination of the historic north-south trench through the housepit (see Figures 4.7 and 4.8) along with excavation errors make it hard to demonstrate the exact location of the north wall post fieldwork. Whether a bench existed against this wall is not clear.

In addition to the benches and the east wall, we have pretty good evidence for the rafter support posts, although not as good as I had expected. One post mould is well preserved, two others are possible, and the third corner (the northwest) is badly mashed with no clear prehistoric features. What was unexpected was how the rafter support post moulds were found in higher elevation lobes extending out into the floor (Figure 4.8). Starting the post holes at floor level would just mean that the posts would need to be that much longer. At Shingle Point a deep hole would quickly run into water-saturated deposits as the floor level is the same elevation as are the highest storm-deposited logs on the beaches (Figure 4.6). Also unexpected was how the benches extended behind the posts towards the exterior walls but not in sharp right angles, leaving shallow U-shaped bench areas in the archaeological record, with the ends of the "U"s being the rafter support posts (see the right side of Figure 4.8). This makes sense, though, as the space between the posts and the eastern and western exterior walls would be hard to access.

I could locate nothing similar to this U-shaped pattern either in ethnographic accounts or in other available archaeological reports. In fact, the amount of space between the "rafter support posts" and the exterior walls is ambiguous in the ethnographic accounts reviewed earlier. Some of the Ozette diagrams show something close to a metre, but others show much less (Samuels 1991). Boas's (1891a) discussion has a continuous bench running along the wall, which would require a metre or so of space, and both of his diagrams (Boas 1891a; Figures 4.2 and 4.4) show it. The U-shaped space can be seen as following from this positioning of rafter support posts and walls as well as from the possible existence of some sort of "partitions" between compartments.

The compartment thus uncovered is about 6 metres by 8 metres (Figure 4.8). These dimensions result from the 8 metres being the "width" of the house from west to east, with the distance between rafter support posts being about 6 metres front to back, and 5 metres between pairs of rafters, plus perhaps 1 metre to the north between the rafter and the outside wall. This would be consistent with Boas (1891a). This compartment is thus approximately 50 square metres, which would lead to a "household" of the order of ten to fifteen people, as I explain below.

There are several ways to arrive at the size of the household present in Compartment 1, of which the simplest is to rely on the ethnographic accounts of a family at each side of the compartment (Suttles 1951, 1991). If we assume six people in each family (Cook and Heizer 1968), then that results in a total of twelve individuals. If we assume five, then that gives us ten. Another method of measurement that results in approximately the same figures involves assuming that two hearths are present in each compartment (Suttles 1991), which is supported for most compartments by the evidence from Ozette (Samuels 1983, 1991, 1994), and assuming a nuclear family for each hearth. Another would involve using the floor area of the compartment, utilizing figures developed by other cross-cultural comparisons. Cook and Heizer (1968:93) show a regression line calculated from California Aboriginal data for house sizes and floor areas per person. If we make the assumption that a compartment is equivalent to a house – which I certainly have done elsewhere (Matson 1996) – then the compartment area converts to 540 square feet and a floor area per person of 45 square feet. Dividing the 540 by 45 results in a household size of twelve. Coupland (1988b:254) develops an estimate of 4 square metres per person for ethnographic Tsimshian winter dwellings. The use of this measure results in an estimate of thirteen people for Compartment 1. There are any number of weaknesses in the above estimates, but they all result in relatively similar figures, indicating that it is likely that ten to fifteen people did inhabit Compartment 1, although we would expect no more than half of them to be adults.

In contrast to the relatively abundant structural remains from Compartment 1, the artifactual remains from undisturbed deposits clearly associated with the structure are very limited. The only really substantial "intact" house deposits are those of Feature 2 under the bench on the east side. The only clearly undisturbed prehistoric subsistence remains of any number from Compartment 1 came from this feature, although this limited information is relevant to household archaeology, as is discussed later in this chapter.

Results: Compartment 2
In contrast with Compartment 1, the excavation of Compartment 2 uncovered only fifteen units within intact portions (Figure 4.10), too few to fully

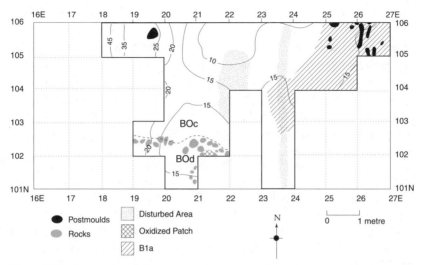

Figure 4.10   Compartment 2.

define it. Another nine units (105N 18 to 26E) lie mainly within Compartment 2, but most of these units show evidence of historic disturbance. (This disturbance means we can say little about any possible partitions between compartments.) Unit 102N 19E to the west, though, indicates that the "ledge under the bench" found in Compartment 1 on the west is either absent or has a different shape there. Unlike the "swept" floor, with early twentieth-century material and burning very close above it (Layer B0a) in Compartment 1, Compartment 2 had neither the burning nor the concentration of historic items close to the prehistoric floor. Instead it had a floor that appeared to be continuous with that found in Compartment 1, upon which a series of prehistoric layers were deposited. Some of these "above-floor" layers were dominated by whole shells (Layer B0c), and other deposits had more broken up shell and looked more like what one would expect for "floor" deposits (Layer B0d). The area excavated was split into two deposits by a row of rocks in Units 102N 19 and 20E, possibly indicating a large hearth (Figure 4.10).

In the spring of 1998 I was confident that Compartment 2 was once part of a shed-roof house but not that these deposits were laid down within a clad house frame (Matson 1998). At first I thought Layers B0c and B0d might be seasonally coeval with Feature 2 but deposited outside the house, which, at that time, might have consisted of only Compartment 1 being clad with planks. Another possibility was that B0c and B0d were deposited within a house of two compartments but not at the same time as the deposits that we recovered from Compartment 1. Analysis of these deposits and comparisons with Feature 2 continued in the spring and summer of 1998 (Green 1999; Matson, Green, and McLay 1999), and, along with a careful evaluation of the fish remains identified by Pacific ID (reported in Matson, Green, and McLay 1999), helped to resolve this situation.

The seasonality of the two compartments' faunal remains for most layers appears to be the same (winter), and these deposits appear to be laid on a floor common to both compartments. This interpretation appears to be true for Layer B0d and the interface layers B0c/C0a and B0c/C0b (Table 4.1), which are close to the surface inferred as the floor, but not for Layer B0c. B0c has very low numbers of herring remains, the only prehistoric layer inside the house to do so, and so likely represents a season after herring spawn (February to early April, Hart 1973). It consists largely of shellfish and so may be mainly the results of shellfish processing that took place sometime after early April. Layer B0c, then, may well be the result of the dumping of shellfish processing debris either after the house was not in use or perhaps when Compartment 2 was not occupied. The question of whether the other winter layers of Compartment 2 were deposited during the same year as Feature 2, though, remains open.

If the deposits found in the two compartments are contemporaneous, then we have two very different housekeeping regimes. One is swept (if sometimes under the bench), and the other appears to be unswept. In Compartment 2 debris from household activities appears to have been strewn on the floor, and the household debris remained. This contrast brings to mind Mozino's (1970:19) comments about "commoner" houses being smelly and full of refuse, in contrast to the equally smelly, but swept, floors of upper-class houses among the Nootkan peoples. Samuels (1999) has offered an interesting explanation for this difference – one without Victorian overtones. He points out that it is upper-class households that would be hosting winter dances and that, if one is barefoot, then one would certainly prefer to dance on a cleanly swept floor rather than on one littered with broken clamshells. If two distinct kin groups/households did share this house, then this factor may explain the differences in the bench areas and in the use of the centre of the compartments.

The line of rocks separating B0d and B0c (Figure 4.10) can be interpreted as separating a large hearth area from the rest of the floor, with the crushed shell (B0d) being the material walked on outside of the hearth and the less fragmented B0c being the untrampled material within the hearth area. Although this explanation is consistent with some lines of evidence, such as patches of oxidized material within the "hearth," it does not appear that the hearth had a consistent location. The seasonality evidence, reviewed above, though, indicates different seasons for Layers B0c and B0d. Although we have no really comparable evidence from Compartment 1, the kind of large hearths surrounded by pebbles seen at Ozette (Samuels 1991) can be rejected for both compartments. Suttles (1991) suggests that hearths could be and were easily moved around, which fits the evidence seen at Shingle

Point. This may be a case where the permanent nature of the houses at Ozette is a misleading guide to the nature of some internal features of the usually seasonally disarticulated – if structurally identical – shed-roof houses of the Coast Salish.

Although we did not locate the same set of features in Compartment 2 that allowed us to measure the size of Compartment 1 with such precision, the surface features indicate a total house size of a width of 8 metres and a length of 12 to 13 metres, which is partially confirmed by excavation. These dimensions agree with what we did find in our excavation of Compartment 2 and leads us to suggest a compartment area of 50 square metres (albeit with less confidence than for Compartment 1).

Comparisons

I have looked at three sources of comparative data, from the Charles and Point houses on the Musqueam reserve, from Ozette (Samuels 1983, 1991, 1994), and from a few other archaeological sites. The Ozette information appears to be the most useful as it is both the most detailed and is clearly prior to AD 1800 and thus not subject to changes as a result of extensive contact with Europeans.

Figure 4.11 plots the existing distance between rafter support posts from Ozette. We have useful measurements from ten compartments and find that the distance between rafters ranges from 4.2 metres to 6 metres, with a median of 4.7 metres (Samuels 1991:201-212). The median is indistinguishable from the 5 metres reported above for Shingle Point. The width of the three

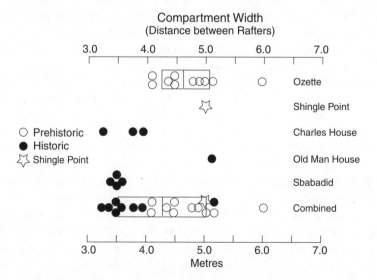

Figure 4.11 Compartment widths. Compartment width is the distance between rafter beams.

Ozette houses ranged from 7 to 11 metres, with the three houses actually measuring from 6.9 metres to 8 metres, 9 metres, and 11 metres, a range that also includes the Shingle Point house but puts it towards the small end (Figure 4.12). All of the Ozette houses are much longer than the one we excavated at Shingle Point, with the smallest, House 2, having three compartments and a length of about 17 metres (Samuels 1983, 1991). I calculate that the areas of the Ozette compartments ranged from 31 to 59 square metres, with a median of 48.3 square metres, again indistinguishable from Shingle Point (Figure 4.13).

At the nearby Dionisio Point site (Mitchell 1971; Grier 1998, and Chapter 7, this volume) a number of house platforms exist. At least two of these are very long, but the smaller ones fit well with multiples of the six-metre distance between rafters seen elsewhere. The width of the platforms in most cases appears to limit the width of the houses to no more than 10 metres, and if one gives one "walkaround" space between the edges of the platforms and the house walls, a width of about 8 metres is likely. Given that only one of these structures has had an extensive excavation, such inferences are only plausible not incontestable. On the other hand, it is another set of data that does not reject the findings based on more definitive investigations.

The Charles House on the Musqueam reserve was a gable-roof house built on a shed-roof frame (Myers N.d.; Ewing 1951). Although it had been extensively modified when described in 1951 (it was torn down in the 1960s), some useful information about the original shed-roof structure is available. In 1951 it consisted of three compartments, and the spacing between rafters ranged from 3.24 metres to 4.0 metres, with a median of 3.8 metres, smaller than those listed above but near in size to the smallest recorded from Ozette. The distance between the rafter support posts ranges from 8.6 metres to 8.8 metres, which results in an estimated original shed-roof house width of about 11 metres, the same as the largest Ozette house. I calculated that the area of the three existing compartments ranges from 42 square metres to 46 square metres, well within the range tabulated above. Interestingly enough, the rafter support posts were very close to the wall along one side but more than 1 metre distant along the other (Ewing 1951). The neighbouring Point House was probably originally part of the same shed-roof house.

The Old Man House (Snyder 1956) also provides some limited information about shed-roof Salish houses. It was a very large house, at least 160 metres long and from 12 metres to 18 metres wide (Figure 4.12). The spacing between rafters averaged 5.2 metres (Figure 4.11), close to that seen at Shingle Point and some of the larger spacings found at Ozette. With that spacing and house width, compartments ranged from about 63 square metres to 94 square metres, with the higher figure 50 percent larger than any other listed above (Figure 4.13).

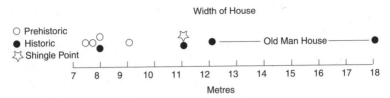

Figure 4.12 Shed-roof house widths.

Historic houses may not represent the prehistoric conditions well: the availability of both iron tools and draft animals greatly changed the economics of large wooden dwellings. Old Man House was likely a "Potlatch House," with the bulk of it not lived in regularly. Snyder (1956) dates the erection of the undisturbed part of the house to 1850 plus or minus five years, well into the historic period. The Charles House was probably built well after that and converted into a gabled structure c. 1890 (Ewing 1951).

Chatters (1981, 1988, 1989) has reported on two very interesting sites with house remains along the Black River, south of Seattle. The best preserved house remains are in Area D of 45KI51, Sbabadid, an early historic house dated by Chatters (1981) to AD 1790-1825, with the later date appearing most likely to me. The total house appears to be 8 metres by 24 metres, with a width similar to many other houses. I measured distances between inferred rafter support post holes to estimate the distances between rafters, which resulted in a median of 3.44 metres, a similar value to that found in the Charles House (Figure 4.11). With a relatively narrow spacing between rafters and an "average" house width, the compartments are relatively small (Figure 4.13), ranging from 27 square metres to 30 square metres. These are equal to the smallest ones at Ozette and are of the size one would expect to find associated with a single nuclear family.

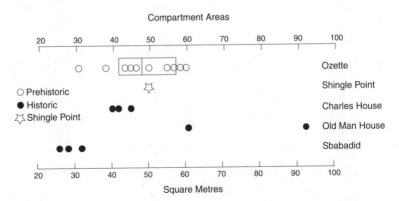

Figure 4.13 Compartment areas. The floor area of compartments defined by rafter beams and outside walls.

The other house remains of interest, investigated by Chatters (1988, 1989), are at the neighbouring site of 45KI59, Tualdad Altu. Here, at cultural Unit I, a house 7.5 metres by 18 metres was radiocarbon dated to AD 400, equivalent to middle Marpole times (Chatters 1988; Matson and Coupland 1995:199-229; Mitchell 1990). No post features were recovered, making a more detailed structural comparison impossible. Chatters (1988), however, infers the presence of a bench surrounding the inside of the structure on the three preserved sides. He also deduces the presence of two households within this house, one large, one small. It is interesting to note that this house is three times the size of the compartment excavated at Shingle Point, so a house of three compartments with one household consisting of two compartments and one of one compartment would fit the pattern he reports.

At both these sites Chatters (1981, 1988, 1989) found evidence indicating the presence of economic differentiation within these houses. These conclusions support the better known ones from Ozette (Samuels 1983, 1991; Wessen 1988; Huelsbeck 1989, 1994a), showing that economic specialization, or at least economic differentiation, may be a regular feature within these structures.

At Shingle Point, the most distinct difference between the two compartments – in addition to those previously described in features and layers – is the abundance of the highly valued green sea urchin *(Stronglyocentrotus droebachiensis)* in Compartment 1 and its near absence in Compartment 2. Green (1999; Matson, Green, and McLay 1999) has shown that this shellfish is an excellent indicator of seasonality, being used (November/December)

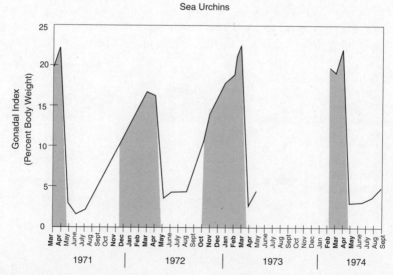

Figure 4.14 Seasonal fluctuation in green sea urchin gonadal weight (after Himmelman 1978)

before herring spawn and ending (March) while herring is still abundant in Feature 2. This interpretation is based on the seasonal increase of the edible portion of the sea urchin, the gonadal material, which disappears upon spawning, usually in late March (Himmelman 1978) (see Figure 4.14).

Green (1999; Matson, Green, and McLay 1999) has shown that the sea urchin is more abundant in the lower layers of Feature 2 (C02 and C03) than in the uppermost Layer C01 (Figure 4.15). This pattern is in agreement

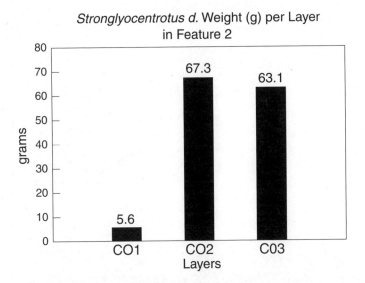

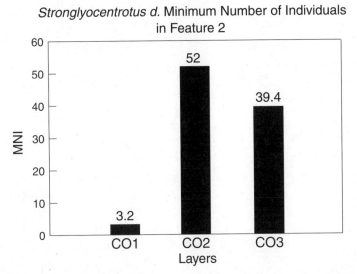

Figure 4.15 Feature 2, sea urchin abundance by layers. Top, by weight; bottom, by MNI.

with the Feature 2 layers representing the time from November/December, the beginning of the sea urchin season, until April, after the sea urchins have spawned. The same pattern appears if one uses the weight of the sea urchin fragments or the Minimum Numbers of Individuals (MNI) measure developed by Green (Figure 4.15). If this interpretation is correct, then herring

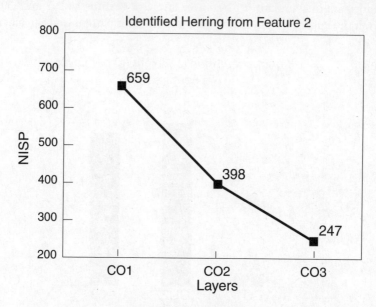

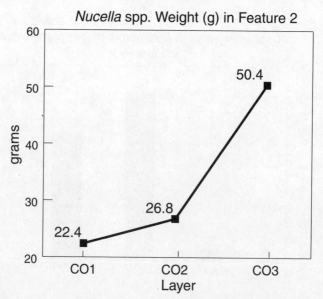

Figure 4.16   Feature 2, herring and whelk abundance by layers.
Top, Pacific herring by NISP; bottom, whelks (*Nucella* spp.) by weight.

remains should be lower in the earlier layers and higher when the sea urchin layers start to decline. Further, large whelks (*Nucella* spp.) are most easily obtained in number when they congregate for mating in the middle of the winter. They, then, should have an abundance that parallels that of sea urchin, and Green has demonstrated that both whelk and herring have the expected patterns (Figure 4.16). Multiple lines of evidence, then, support the hypothesis that the layers within Feature 2 represent a single winter to early spring occupational duration, from November/December through April.

The abundance of sea urchin in Compartment 1 is not replicated in Compartment 2 (Figure 4.17) either by weight or MNI. This lack is not surprising in Layer B0c, which is thought to have been deposited after the herring season. The other layers, though, have the same seasonal indicators as are found in Compartment 2. So the sea urchin's absence in Compartment 2

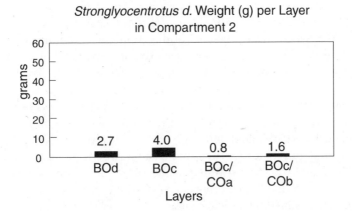

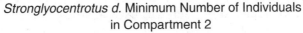

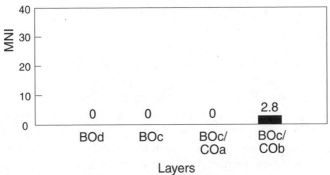

Figure 4.17 Compartment 2, sea urchin abundance by layers. Top, by weight; bottom, by MNI. In both cases the same scale is used as in Figure 4.15.

cannot easily be ascribed to differences in seasonality. Sea urchin is not available adjacent to Shingle Point, with the closest known source being Porlier Pass, some seven kilometres to the south (Figure 4.1). A village site exists in Porlier Pass on the Valdes Island side, and another exists at Dionisio Point (Mitchell 1971; Grier 1998, and Chapter 7, this volume) on the Galiano Island side. Yet another village site is located at Cardale Point (DgRv 1), controlling access to Porlier Pass via the west side of Valdes Island (Figure 4.1). Thus, sea urchin is the kind of highly valued resource that may well not have been accessible to all Shingle Point inhabitants but might be available through connections with other communities. Some compartments/households (higher class?) may have had these connections while others (lower class?) may not.

Other Shingle Point Houses

I earlier mentioned the presence of historic period large houses at Shingle Point that were confused with the row of rectangular depressions such as the one that we excavated. Because of this confusion it is difficult to know how many houses such as the one we excavated existed, but remains of three are now evident. In Figure 4.6 these can be seen to the north of the one we excavated. The one immediately north is of the same width but about 50 percent longer, for a length of 19 metres. The results of a single one-by-one-metre unit excavated within this feature, though, did not reveal any evidence of a floor, although post moulds were present. The next house feature to the north is one that is only partially present, but it is at least the size of the one excavated. Earlier sketch maps show five depressions, with a possibility of six, but the areas where they are indicated have been much modified by more recent activities, so we were unable to identify any surface remains. Thus, a minimum of three houses existed and are assumed to be prehistoric, and it is likely that five and maybe even six existed.

The total of prehistoric house depressions that was present in the 1960s is unclear because of confusion with later historic structures. One of these now consists of three rows of small circular depressions that excavation confirmed (Matson, Green, and McLay 1999) were post moulds (Figure 4.6). Two posts from this structure were still standing in the early 1970s, and one of these posts still exists, although flat on the ground. This structure was probably a gabled house since the middle row of post depressions does not correspond well with the two outside rows, which do line up. The outer rows of posts are 17 metres apart, giving the minimum width of the structure. The three rows are now 55 metres long and may well have extended further to the south, where later house construction may have destroyed evidence of this structure. An entrance is probably located approximately half way down the west side, as is evidenced by the close pair of post moulds.

This was a truly large house, at least 55 metres by 17 metres, with spacing between rafters (or at least support posts) of about 7 metres. Identification of the depressions as post moulds was confirmed by excavation in 1995 (Matson and McLay 1996) and as "historic" by other excavation units within the house area that year (Matson, Green, and McLay 1999; Figure 4.6). Curiously, we can find no documentary or informant confirmation of the existence of this structure, despite a relatively detailed description of the community present at Shingle Point in 1879 (Sproat 1879).

The final historic house structure appears to have been relatively square and is associated with a large depression, now partially occupied with a shed. A single standing post is all that remains of the structure (Figure 4.6). We do have informant testimony that this house existed in ruins around 1940. If it filled the depression, then its size was approximately 18 metres by 20 metres. The single surviving house post is in a position that also indicates a size of this order.

Before moving on, mention should be made of another structure, often thought by visitors to be the remains of a domestic structure. This is a boat house located north of the edge of the contour map. Standing poles still exist. In the late nineteenth and early twentieth centuries the Lyacksun had a very successful boat-building operation and the boat house was part of that activity.

The presence of these two large, but not shed-roof, houses gives an indication of the changes that contact brought to the Northwest Coast peoples. It is clear that contact allowed much freeing up of the constraints that existed previously. Gibson (1992:270-272) argues that, at first, the fur trade strengthened the role of traditional leaders but then later allowed untitled individuals to gain power and prestige. Would this not lead to a reduction in average size of households, according to the logic presented elsewhere (Matson 1996)? I believe the later Shingle Point houses and the information cited by Gibson caution us not to rely too heavily on the measurements and information from early historic times as being necessarily good descriptions of prehistory. Thus, based on testimony taken seventy years later, Suttles's (1951) description of the use of a shed-roof house in the 1880s, in which the two halves of each compartment represent different households, need not be taken to reliably indicate how these were used earlier, particularly given the expectation that household size appeared to decrease in historic times. I find it interesting that Suttles does not refer to separate nuclear family households occupying each half of the compartment in his later summary of the shed-roof house (Suttles 1991).

Conclusion

What can we conclude about shed-roof houses? And what have we learned from Shingle Point? One obvious conclusion is that sometimes when you get what you want – in this case, a floor easy to define and close to the surface – you may not like some of the consequences: in this case, the very abundant historical disturbance at Shingle Point, concentrated in Layer B0a in Compartment 1. If one is going to go beyond the "Pompeii Premise" in associating remains recovered within a house with the activities carried out within it (i.e., equating the "systemic" context with the "archaeological" context), then one needs to have a clear rationale for doing so. In our case, despite the widespread historic Layer B0a in Compartment 1, Feature 2, by dint of its location, nature, and seasonal progression, gives us that kind of association in this compartment. Our changing interpretations of the layers within Compartment 2 demonstrate that this kind of tight relationship between archaeological layers and household activities is not possible there. The interface deposits – B0c/C0a, B0c/C0b, B0d1 – those lying directly on the living surface interpreted as the house floor in Compartment 2, though, do appear to have the same seasonality as Feature 2. And their location on the "floor" does allow them to be interpreted similarly. The issue of associating particular archaeological deposits with activities carried out by part of the community inhabiting a house is not easy – even at Ozette – and will undoubtedly be the focus of a great deal of effort in the near future.

At Shingle Point the size of one compartment, the distance between rafters, and the size of the house are well defined. The compartment size of 50 square metres is also seen frequently at Ozette, which indicates that this may be a basic unit, equivalent to two nuclear families or a single, large extended family household. I note that the earliest Northwest Coast plank house village, the Paul Mason site, appears to have houses that average close to this value (Coupland 1988b) – as do most of the structures at the more recent McNichol Creek site at Prince Rupert, British Columbia (Coupland, Colten, and Case 1993, and Chapter 6, this volume). Martindale (Chapter 2, this volume) reports on houses of this size for the Tsimshian Protocontact (Table 2.1). In contrast, the historic houses of Old Man House, Charles House, and Sbabadid range well above or below this value. It may be (Matson and Coupland 1995:306) that this areal unit of approximately 50 square metres is a more essential structural component of social organization than we have previously recognized.

The nature of benches on at least two sides of the Shingle Point house has been clarified. They are present against at least the long walls and are likely to have been relatively low. The lack of a clear permanent hearth in either compartment demonstrates a distinct difference from what was found at Ozette. A more casual hearth, one that can be moved around, is more in accord with what was found in Compartment 1, although the later historic activities limit the reliability of this inference. The Kane portrait (Figure 4.5) looks to be a good model for what we found.

When we first uncovered the shallow U shape (Figure 4.7), with the rafter support post moulds being located on extensions of higher surfaces out into the house floor, this was unexpected. However, now it can be seen to be consistent with the model put forward by Boas (1891a), with the benches extending behind the rafter support posts and clearly present at Shingle Point (being most distinctive along the east wall) (Figures 4.7 and 4.8). At Shingle Point, because of its very low elevation above sea level, the rafter support posts were excavated into surfaces that were higher than the floor of the house. It will be interesting to see if this positioning is found by others and whether the spaces in back of the rafter support posts are used differently than are the rest of the bench areas along the walls.

Along the east side of Compartment 1 the multiple small post moulds support the ethnographic descriptions of the walls consisting of planks being supported between pairs of slender posts. The multiple moulds also indicate that the walls were reconstructed several times, also in accord with the ethnographic descriptions of frequent seasonal disarticulation of shed-roof houses. Our observations that these post moulds appear to be in three rows in some areas indicate that the walls were not always relocated in the exact same location, another source of variation in this structure.

If the deposits found in the two compartments are contemporaneous, then we have two very different house-keeping regimes; one is swept, while the other appears to be unswept and lived on. This pattern brings to mind both Mozino's (1970:19) comments about "commoner" houses being smelly and full of refuse and Samuels's (1999) more recent explanation that swept floors were a prerequisite for the dancing associated with winter ceremonies. The differences between the compartments in terms of associated deposits certainly indicate the presence of different households (if they were contemporaneously occupied), as do the differences along the west edge with regard to how the floor was extended into the beach ridge.

Others (Chatters 1981, 1988, 1989; Samuels 1983, 1991; Wessen 1988, 1994) have found evidence of economic differentiation and differences in access to resources both between and within houses. At this time, the only clear similar evidence at Shingle Point we can point to is an abundance of green sea urchin in Compartment 1 and almost none in Compartment 2. Before leaving subsistence, I would be remiss if I did not comment on the very limited salmon remains recovered at Shingle Point. If salmon is the basis of the Northwest Coast ethnographic pattern, then Shingle Point is a notable exception that remains to be explained.

In summary, although a lot remains to be learned about shed-roof houses, it is clear that household archaeology can reveal at least some information. I think it is significant that many Northwest Coast archaeologists (Ames 1996; Ames et al. 1992; in addition to those cited above) are now concerned with such things as investigating prehistoric household organization, in effect fulfilling Fladmark's (1973) prediction that archaeology will become the only way to test ethnographic models about the precontact (and early contact) situation and, I would further contend, to develop new understandings of the past.

Acknowledgments

The Shingle Point investigations received the support of the Social Sciences and Humanities Research Council of Canada and the Lyacksun Band. Chief Richard Thomas, Barbara Thomas, and Frank Norris were instrumental in seeing this research proceed, and many other Lyacksun members participated in one way or the other. I thank them for their hospitality and generosity.

Eric McLay assisted in the field in 1995 and 1996, and he helped direct the many students and others that took part in the project. He also directed the survey of Valdes Island. I appreciate the degree of responsibility shown by the excellent students in the field in 1996 and those who carried out laboratory analysis later. In particular, Eric McLay in 1995-96 and Joanne Green, Shannon Cameron, and Martha Graham in 1997-98 analyzed most of the shellfish. A good part of this chapter derives from analyses carried out by Joanne Green. Many thanks to all of you.

As noted in this chapter, the Shingle Point investigations developed from explorations initiated by Grant Myers on the advice of Philip Hobler of Simon Fraser University and were aided by advice from J.E.M. Kew. Associate Dean of Arts D. Paterson provided an important transportation link – a skiff much admired by Gulf Islanders. This particular contribution has been improved because of suggestions made by David Pokotylo, Michael Blake, Gary Coupland, and Quentin Mackie. Susan Matson provided editorial comment and the illustrations. Although many have helped along the way, any responsibility for errors remains with me.

5
Nuu-chah-nulth Houses: Structural Remains and Cultural Depressions on Southwest Vancouver Island

Alexander P. Mackie and Laurie Williamson

During the late summer and fall of 1984 we directed the Ohiaht Ethno-archaeological Project, an inventory of archaeological and ethnogeographic information pertaining to a part of the traditional territories of the Huu-ay-aht First Nations.[1] This chapter presents information about house features found during the survey. These house features provide contexts for evaluating the ethnographic and ethnohistoric descriptions of Nuu-chah-nulth and Makah[2] houses, and add to previous discussions of gable- versus shed-roof house styles. The diversity of houses found in a relatively small study area should be of interest to archaeologists who are currently excavating houses in other parts of the Northwest Coast.

Background

The inventory was confined to a coastal strip about fifty-eight kilometres in length near Bamfield and parts of the nearby Deer Group Islands in Barkley Sound (Figure 5.1). This area has a very diverse range of environments. In the Bamfield area are found closed bays and lagoons protected from wind and waves and having long, flat, intertidal zones of poorly sorted sediments. At the outer reaches of the Deer Group are high cliffs pounded by waves in all but the best weather. Between these extremes are numerous low rock headlands and small bays with varying degrees of exposure to wind and waves. It is common for the bays to have a gently sloping beach of finer sediments and an adjacent flat upland suitable for use and habitation.

Where shorelines were accessible, the study was concentrated in a strip averaging about 100 metres wide but ranging up to about 500 metres in-land. Oakfield soil probes were used to locate cultural sediments and to define site boundaries, a necessary tool to get below the humus, sometimes more than a metre thick and dense with tough roots. Foot survey occurred in all areas where boat landings could be made and in many other less accessible areas. Some of the study area was too rugged to survey on foot,

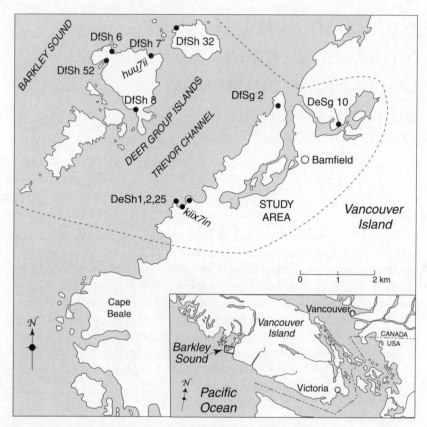

Figure 5.1   Southwest Barkley Sound, showing the 1984 study area.

being characterized by steep cliffs capped with a nearly impenetrable salal understory. These areas were examined by boat only.

The survey area overlaps the territories of at least two of the local groups that amalgamated to form the present-day Huu-ay-aht First Nations (St. Claire 1991:63-65; N.d.). The territory boundaries for these local groups are uncertain, but we think that the study area includes a large part of the *kiixẒin7atẖ*[3] territory and a smaller proportion of the *HuuẒii7atẖ* local group territory.

The Ohiaht Ethnoarchaeological Project recorded 116 sites, including fifty-six shell middens, of which eleven have features associated with houses (Figure 5.1). This chapter is largely concerned with house features from some of these sites, with a particular emphasis on the villages of *kiix7in* and *huuẒii*.

Huu-ay-aht Archaeological Houses

House features are visible on the surface and include house depressions or platforms, a pronounced backridge or wooden structural remains (see Table

Table 5.1

Huu-ay-aht middens and surface features ordered by site length

Site number	Number of depressions	Number of house structures	Backridge size (length × width)	Midden size (length × width)
DfSh 7	10 or 12	n/a	300 × 1.5 to 2 m	305 × 110 m
DfSh 8	– [a]	– [a]	80 × 1 m (approx.)	285 × 40 m
DfSh 6	1[a]	n/a	17 × 0.50 m	270 × 50 m
DeSg 5	– [b]	n/a	175 × 1 to 2.5 m	200 × 55 m
DfSh 152	1[a]	n/a	n/a	195 × 30 m
DeSh 1	11	8	25 × 0.3 m (approx.)	175 × 37 m
DeSg 10	1[c]	n/a	n/a	170 × 25 m
DfSh 32	2	2 or 3	50 × 0.8 m	100 × 50 m
DfSg 2	1	– [a]	– [a]	90 × 35 m
DeSh 25	2 or 3	3	25 × 0.3 m	75 × 28 m
DeSh 2[d]	4 or 6	n/a	not available	50 × 35 m
Total	33 or 38	13 or 14		

a Disturbed
b Vegetation too thick to clearly discern backridge
c Very faint
d Defensive site
n/a Not applicable at this site

5.1).[4] Eight sites have one or more houses with at least two measurable dimensions (Table 5.2) and it is these sites and houses that are useful to this discussion. Three of these sites have structural remains surviving from the post-and-beam big houses. The Euro-Canadian style frame houses that were found at a number of sites are not included in this chapter.

Huu-ay-aht Cultural Depressions
Nine sites were recorded, which have between them thirty-three to thirty-eight cultural depressions.[5] Thirty-one house depressions are sufficiently well defined that both length and width can be measured. Most of these houses are located at two sites, both of which are the naming place for a local group: one is called *huuẔii* (DfSh7) and has ten or twelve depressions; the other is *kiix7in* (DeSh 1) and has eleven depressions, eight of which also contain structural remains. Our discussion concentrates on these two sites, but the data from other locations are in our tables and figures.

Cultural Depressions at huuẔii
The village of *huuẔii* (DfSh 7) is the place from which the *HuuẔii7atḥ* local group derives its name. Relatively little information was related to us about traditional use of this site, suggesting use was discontinued earlier than at some of the other village sites in the study area. The ten to twelve house

Table 5.2

Measurements of Huu-ay-aht house depressions and structures

| House ID | | House depressions | | | House structures | | | Max. height (m) | Avg. height (m) | House volume (m³) |
Site no.	House no.	Length (m)	Width (m)	Area (m²)	Length (m)	Width (m)	Area (m²)			
DfSh 7	1	35	17.5	612.5						
DfSh 7	2	32.5	11	357.5						
DfSh 7	3	30	?							
DfSh 7	4	30	?							
DfSh 7	5	22.5	10	225						
DfSh 7	6	21	17.5	367.5						
DfSh 7	7	22	11	242						
DfSh 7	8	16	7	112						
DfSh 7	9	17	8	136						
DfSh 7	10c	14	8	112						
DfSh 7	10d	27.5	10	275						
DfSh 6	1	16.5	10.5	173.3						
DfSh 152	1	17	5.5	93.5						
DfSh 32	1	19	15.5	294.5	20.5	15.5	318			
DfSh 32	2	17	11	187	16.5	11	182			
DfSg 2	1	5.5	?							
DeSh 25	1	17.5	17	297.5	15	10	150			
DeSh 25	2				17.5	8.5	149			
DeSh 25	3				?	7.5				
DeSg 23	1	10?	5?	50?						

DeSh 1	1	14	12	168	15	10.5	158	3.6	3	473
DeSh 1	2	22	11	242	22	9.5	209	5.1	4	836
DeSh 1	3	22.5	13.5	303.8	25	12	300	3.4	3	900
DeSh 1	4	22	17	374	20	19.5	390	4.5	3.5	1365
DeSh 1	5	18	10.5	189	17	10	170	2.5	2.5	425
DeSh 1	6	11.5	11	126.5	15	10.5	158	4.1	3.5	551
DeSh 1	7	15	10	150	14.5	10	145	4.5	4	580
DeSh 1	8	16	13.5	216	15.5	12	186	4.9	4	744
DeSh 1	9	10	7	70						
DeSh 1	10	12.5	8	100						
DeSh 1	11	12.5	10	125						
DeSh 2	1	13.5	7	94.5						
DeSh 2	2	14	4.5	63						
DeSh 2	3	8	7.5	60						
DeSh 2	4	10.5	7	73.5						
DeSh 2	5	6.5	5	32.5						
Number	36	34	31	31	12	13	12	8	8	8
Maximum		35.00	17.50	613	25.00	19.50	390	5.10	4.00	1365
Minimum		5.50	4.50	33	14.5	7.5	145	2.5	2.5	425
Average		17.60	10.29	191	17.79	11.27	209	4.08	3.44	734
Standard deviation		7.25	3.77	126	3.35	3.13	81	0.87	0.56	306

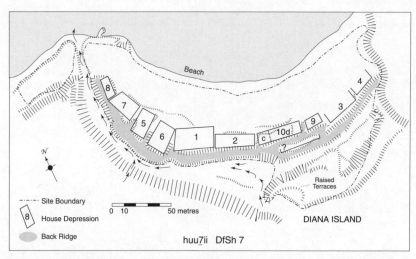

Figure 5.2   Site map of *huuZii* (DfSh 7) as recorded in 1984.

depressions are well removed from the current beach (Figure 5.2). The zone between the house fronts and the beach is about 30 metres wide and has thin and discontinuous cultural deposits. This zone is generally 4.5 metres above mean sea level (masl)[6] or higher, whereas recently occupied sites such as *kiix7in* have a similar, but very narrow, strip in front of the houses, which is about 3.0 metres in elevation. At this village it is likely that some of the zone between the houses and the modern beach results from lowering sea levels, probably a result of tectonic uplift currently under way in the area (Hutchinson 1992:36, 37). It is possible that this zone developed over as much as 1,000 or 1,500 years, although more probably it is less than this.

There is evidence that part of the village was moved or reconstructed closer to the beach. There is a segment of older backridge located further inland than the main ridge. This appears to result from rebuilding one or more houses (house marked "?" on Figure 5.2). A minimum date for the last use of this site comes from a forester who visited the site with us during 1984. He estimated that the over-mature hemlock forest growing on the house depressions would take at least 150 to 200 years to develop.

The houses at this site are recognized by their extremely flat floors, the pronounced backridge (which ranges between 1.25 metres and 3 metres higher elevation than the house floors), and the narrow ridges sloping down from the backridge between the houses. Most houses have their long dimension parallel to the beach. Some of these terminate at a clear front edge where the house floor has been prepared by filling or built up during occupation.

Cultural Depressions at kiix7in

The house depressions at *kiix7in* are recognizable by flat areas located variously between a partial and intermittent backridge, front floor edges raised by filling or use, some small ridges between houses, and other relatively faint evidence (Figure 5.3). The maximum elevation difference from house floor onto backridge is 1 metre and occurs at only one house; most ridge features are only 0.30 metres to 0.40 metres higher than adjacent house floors, some are less. Without the structural remains, it would have been impossible to make confident identifications of some houses from the surficial traces alone. For instance, the structures for two houses (numbers 6 and 7) are within an apparently single platform; without knowledge of the structures, it is likely that the subtle indicators of the rear corners of these houses would have been missed in the field. Another house (3) has no front edge or backridge and might have been identified as a gap between houses. Each end of the village has flat areas without structural remains but with sufficient surficial evidence to identify one house (11) at the west end and two houses (9, 10) at the east end. The latter two houses could readily be considered as one but are distinguished by subtle variations in the back edge and surface elevations. The possibly more recent foundation posts for a frame house or smokehouse are located entirely within the House 9 depression.

Huu-ay-aht Structural Remains

The structural remains found at three sites in Huu-ay-aht territory are the most significant aspect of the data we recorded (Tables 5.2 and Tables 5.4 to 5.19). A village on Helby Island (DfSh 32) has three remnant post-and-beam houses. These are too fragmentary to provide a confident reconstruction of the house styles and, in any case, were not recorded in the same detail as were those found at *kiix7in*.

Another site (DeSh 25) is on a small flat area and separated from other sites nearby with abrupt fingers of higher ground. It possibly has its own Huu-ay-aht name but might well be considered part of *kiix7in*, which is in the same bay and behind the same beach. Here the condition of the structural remains also precludes a confident reconstruction of the houses. They were not recorded in enough detail to present in this chapter. It is of interest that these structural remains are from at least three houses but that two of these house frames are located within a single depression, while the other house has no associated midden features that would be called a house (Table 5.2). Without the structural remains, we would have recorded this site as having one fairly large house.

Houses at kiix7in

The village of *kiix7in* (DeSh 1) is the best preserved Nuu-chah-nulth village found to date. The Huu-ay-aht First Nations have successfully applied to have this village commemorated as a National Historic Site. Included in the agenda paper are some data presented here (Huu-ay-aht First Nations 2000).

The date of construction of these houses is not known, but all are likely to have been built before the 1850s. Its use as a village was probably discontinued during the 1880s or 1890s, when the occupants moved to other locations better suited to changing needs. A census at this site in 1874 records people living in ten houses (Blenkinsop N.d.:8). A sketch of the village made by Alfred Carmichael (N.d.), probably in the 1890s, shows ten houses and provides some information on the owners of each house. He also indicates another four houses further east along the beach, probably at the location of DeSh 25.

At *kiix7in* there are numerous house frame elements surviving from eight houses, and, remarkably, many of the house posts are still standing, with some still supporting beams (Figure 5.3). In 1984 we recorded the dimensions of each post, and the elevations (masl) of the post locations.[7] Of the forty-five posts at this site, we were able to record the dimensions of forty-three (Table 5.3). Many of these dimensions are incomplete in that the posts are sometimes partially or largely encased in a nursing tree, are broken, or have their ends eroded. There are also forty-five major structural beams present at the site, most lying on the ground but some entirely or partially supported on posts. Beams were mapped to scale (1:500), and their dimensions have been derived from the original field map. This same process was also used for deriving house dimensions, which are measured from the mapped locations of posts. Therefore, beam and overall horizontal measurements are not as precise as are those for posts and vertical house dimensions. The dimensions and elevations of each element are provided in the detailed house tables as central to the discussion of reconstructed house

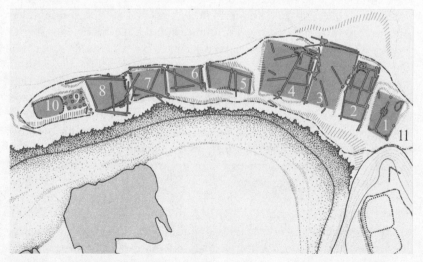

Figure 5.3 Site map of *kiix7in* (DeSh 1) from illustration prepared for travelling exhibit by Lori Graves, 1985.

Table 5.3

Summary statistics of *kiix7in* post measurements and beam diameters, DeSh 1

	Number	Maximum	Minimum	Average	StDev[e]
Posts *(N = 45)*					
Length (m)	18	3.70	2.13	2.81	0.48
Diameter[a] (m)	23	0.75	0.40	0.56	0.11
Beam diameters					
First beam[b] (m)	23	0.75	0.40	0.56	0.11
Second beam[c] (m)	28	0.70	0.40	0.51	0.08
Third beam[d] (m)	8	0.60	0.30	0.50	0.09
Elevations					
Base of post (masl)	33	6.50	4.00	4.90	0.68
Top of post (masl)	18	8.66	6.93	7.63	0.51
Top of all beams (masl)	18	9.46	7.63	8.71	0.55
Height above ground –					
top of structure (m)	18	4.88	2.83	3.89	0.67

Notes: Measurements derived from incomplete elements are not included.
a   Top of post if tapered.
b   Resting on top of post (a), diameters estimated from map, photos, and associated posts.
c   Resting on top of first beam (b), diameters estimated from map, photos, and associated posts.
d   Resting on top of second beam (c), diameters estimated from map, photos, and associated posts.
e   Standard Deviation.

form. Detailed dimensions and elevations of Nuu-chah-nulth houses are not available from any other source that we could find.

With this information we have reconstructed the house frames for many of the houses. Lori Graves's reconstruction (Figure 5.4) was drawn for an exhibit that was part of the project. It shows the reconstructed houses as they may have looked during the mid- to late 1800s (see Huu-ay-aht First Nations 2000 for another reconstruction). It can be seen that the houses are generally aligned with the short side to the beach. This is probably due to the very limited amount of suitable land for houses in this area. Where the bench on which the houses are constructed is broad, the houses are longer rectangles; where the bench is narrow, the houses are more nearly square.

There are three gable-roof houses, four shed-roof houses, and one house has gable-roof construction for the rear two-thirds and a shed-roof for the front one-third, with eave beams that run the length of the house. To the far left in Figure 5.4 is a small building. The evidence for this structure (located in House 9) comprises twelve short posts, about 0.30 metres high, arranged in a grid of four posts to a side. These are likely to be the remnant

Figure 5.4 Reconstruction of *kiix7in* from drawing prepared for travelling exhibit by Lori Graves, 1985.

foundations of a frame structure, perhaps a smokehouse or possibly a seasonal dwelling erected after the village moved to other locations.

Gable-Roof Houses   Gable-roof houses at this site have considerable variety but generally conform to the range of such houses described for Nuu-chah-nulth groups.

House 1:

Table 5.4

House 1 summary description, *kiix7in*, DeSh 1

Roof style	Gable
House length	15.0 m, perpendicular to beach
House width	10.5 m, parallel to beach
House area	158 m²
Height of gable	
Front	9.46 masl; 3.36 m above ground,
Rear	9.36 masl; 3.61 m above ground
Height of other walls	
West	(8:64) to (8.55) masl; (2.05) to (2.54) m above ground,
East	(8.37) masl; (3.02) m above ground
Direction of roof pitch	Gable oriented north-south with 0.10 m drop front to back
Degree of roof pitch	(0.90) m in 5.25 m

Note: Measurements in ( ) are of incomplete elements.

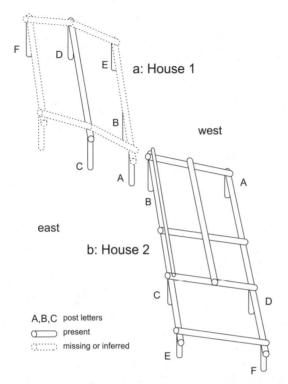

Figure 5.5 kiix7in reconstructed frames of Houses 1 and 2. *From sketch by A.P. Mackie, 1985*

House 1 has a gable 15 metres long oriented at right angles to the beach (Tables 5.4 and 5.5). The house is 10.5 metres wide. The top of the gable measures 3.36 metres above the ground at the front of the house and is very nearly level, with only 0.10 metres change in elevation to the rear of the house. The sides of the house are more than 2.5 metres and 3 metres high (Figure 5.5a).

House 1 has a clearly defined house floor with ridges on all four sides. Midden has built up along much of the front of the house, where it abuts the base of Execution Rock so that the entire house floor is lower than surrounding deposits. The entrance to this house is most likely to have been on the east half of the house front, where there is little change in elevation from the outside to the inside. There is a shallow depression (about 0.25 metres deep and 3 metres in diameter) evident in the centre of the house floor. It now lies under the fallen central beam. There is a low mound (2.5 metres by 4 metres) on the southwest corner of the house floor. It is not known if these are features associated with use of the house. The house depression is 12 metres across the rear corners, and the front is 9.5 metres.

Table 5.5

House 1 structural details, *kiix7in*, DeSh 1

Post ID	Posts (m) Height	Diameter[a]	Beam diameters (m) First beam[b]	Second beam[b]	Third beam[b]	Elevations (masl) Base of post	Top of post	Top of structure at post location	Height above ground[c]	Post location within house
A	(1.65)	0.40	0.40	0.40		6.50	(8.15)	(8.55)	(2.05)	Front – West
	x-section = ½ round, standing, flat face towards house front (against outside), rotted off									
B	(1.75)	0.40	0.40	0.40		6.45	(8.20)	(8.60)	(2.15)	West – Centre
	x-section = ½ round, standing, flat face towards house front (perpendicular to outside wall)									
C	2.56	(0.43)	0.40	0.40		6.10	8.66	9.46	3.36	Front – Centre
	x-section = round, standing, top is flared at least facing into house, possibly flared outwards all around at top									
D	2.81	0.42	0.40	0.40		5.75	8.56	9.36	3.61	Rear – Centre
	x-section = round, standing, rotting, flared outwards all around upper 0.70 m, flared portion has flat sides with rounded corners towards front of house, round (unfinished?) surface to rear									
E	(2.14)	(0.41)	0.40			(6.10)	(8.24)	(8.64)	(2.54)	Rear – West
	x-section = probably nearly round with flattened surface facing back of house (against outside edge), lying down, rotten, broken, possibly split lengthways but not deliberately									
F	(2.62)	(0.34)	0.40			(5.75)	(8.37)	(8.77)	(3.02)	Rear – East
	x-section = round, lying down, broken, possibly split lengthways but not deliberately									

Notes: Measurements in ( ) are of incomplete elements.

a Top diameter if tapered

b In all structure detail tables the first beam is the one resting directly on top of posts, the second beam rests on top of the second beam: thus there can be three beams resting one on another on top of any one post, all adding to the height of the house and influencing the pitch of the roof

c Height of main structural elements (m)

House 2:

Table 5.6

House 2 summary description, *kiix7in*, DeSh 1

Roof style	Gable at rear, shed at front. Rear gable higher due to lower topography
House length	22 m whole house, perpendicular to beach, gable portion 15 m, shed 7 m
House width	9.5 m, parallel to beach
House area	209 m²
Height of highest wall/gable	
Gable, front (north)	(8.72) masl; 3.97 m above ground
Gable, rear (south)	9.68 masl; 5.15 m above ground
Shed, west wall	(9.21) masl; 4.00 m and (4.01) m front
Height of other walls	
Gable, west wall	9.20 and (8.13) masl; 4.6 m and (3.33) m above ground
Gable, east wall	9.15 and 8.13 masl; 4.70 m, 3.33 m above ground
Shed, east wall	9.00 masl, 4.00 m above ground
Direction of roof pitch	
Gable	oriented N-S with 0.96 m drop or less in elevation towards front (north)
Shed	slopes down to east
Degree of roof pitch	
Gable	Rear: 0.48 m and 0.53 m in 4.75 m
Shed	(0.21 m) in 9.5 m

Notes: Measurements in ( ) are of incomplete elements.

House 2 is the best preserved house at *kiix7in* in that it has some beams totally suspended between house posts (Figures 5.6 and 5.7). This house has a gable for the rear 15 metres and a shed roof for the front 7 metres; it is 22 metres long and 9.5 metres wide (Table 5.6 and Figure 5.5). The highest point of the gable is more than 5 metres above the ground, while the highest point of the shed is 4 metres above ground. The side walls range from 4 metres to 3.33 metres high. The shed-roof slopes down to the east.

Some of the posts are flared near the top (Figure 5.8 and Table 5.7). Along the rear east side there survives a secondary rafter pole (Figure 5.9), probably for supporting roof planks on the east side of the house.

The rear and sides of the house are demarcated by ridges of midden that taper to nothing at the front of the house. There is not a noticeable front edge to the house floor. A small area (5 metres by 2.5 metres) of the southeast corner is 0.15 metres to 0.25 metres lower than the rest of the house floor, and this lower area is clearly demarcated by an abrupt edge. Behind this corner of the house, the midden drops sharply another 0.25 metres

Figure 5.6
kiix7in House 2, frame details, SE corner of house looking at House Post B. *Photo by K. Bernick, 1984*

Figure 5.7
kiix7in House 2, frame details, gable beam resting on central cross beam. *Photo by A.P. Mackie, 1984*

before it tapers out into a lower wet area that is behind this corner and extends behind all of House 3. We believe that the drop in the house floor is more likely to be related to filling the lower wet area than that it is a deliberate feature constructed at the rear of the house. The depression can be measured as 11 metres wide across the front and 9.5 metres across the back.

Figure 5.8
kiix7in House 2, detail, east
side of house looking at Post C.
Photo by A.P. Mackie, 1984

Figure 5.9
kiix7in House 2, frame details
showing secondary rafter poles,
east side of house near rear.
Photo by A.P. Mackie, 1984

Table 5.7

House 2 structural details, *kíix7in*, DeSh 1

Post ID	Posts (m) Height	Posts (m) Diameter[a]	Beam diameters (m) First beam	Beam diameters (m) Second beam	Beam diameters (m) Third beam	Elevations (masl) Base of post	Elevations (masl) Top of post	Elevations (masl) Top of structure at post location	Elevations (masl) Height above ground[b]	Post location within house
A	3.40	0.75	0.70	0.50		4.60	8.00	9.20	4.60	Rear – West
	x-section = ½ round, standing, nursing hemlock, rotting badly									
B	3.50	0.72	0.70	0.50		4.45	7.95	9.15	4.70	Rear – East
	x-section = ½ round, standing, still holding beam, top grooved to hold beam, adzed surface has vertical pattern (Figure 5.6)									
C	2.13	0.57	0.70	0.50		4.80	6.93	8.13	3.33	East – Centre
	x-section = 'round, standing, rough finish outside (E) surface, still holding long beam (N-S) and also a x-beam (E-W), flared outwards all around for top 0.67 m, top grooved to hold beam (groove is rotting), leans out badly; long beam broken at top, supported above ground to top of 2B, rest leaning to ground at base of 2E (Figure 5.8)									
D	(2.40)	(0.45)	0.70	0.50		(4.70)	(7.10)	(8.30)	(3.60)	West – Centre
	x-section = round (?), leaning, rotting, broken, 1 rock embedded in top perhaps for holding beam in place?									
E	2.80	0.55	0.70	0.50		5.00	7.80	9.00	4.00	Front – East
	x-section = round, very like 2C, standing, leaning, flared outward all around top 0.70 m, possibly had a grooved top for the beam, rough finish on outside surfaces									

							Front – West
F	(2.81)	(0.47)	0.70	0.50	5.20 (8.01)	(9.21)	(4.01)

x-section = unknown, lying down, rotted, no design visible, perhaps due to condition

Gable, rear	(3.45)	0.70	0.50	0.50	(7.98)	(9.68)	(5.15)

Rear gable is long gable beam resting on x-beams that are above posts 2A and 2B. In the middle of the gable, the gable beam is supported by another x-beam that rests on the long side beams with no posts beneath (Figure 5.7).

Gable, front	(2.27)	0.70	0.50	0.50	(7.02)	(8.72)	(3.97)

Centre of house is front gable end between 2D and 2C, long gable beam (N-S) supported on middle of front x-beam (E-W), shed roof sloping to east exists at front of house (2F, 2E, 2D, 2C)

Notes: Measurements in ( ) are of incomplete elements.
a Top diameter if tapered
b Height of main structural elements (m)

House 3:

Table 5.8

House 3 summary description, *kiix7in*, DeSh 1

Roof style	Probably gable
House length	25 m, perpendicular to beach
House width	12 m, parallel to beach
House area	300 m²
Height of highest wall/gable	
Gable, front	Greater than 8.09 masl; (3.39) m above ground
Height of other walls	
West	Greater than 6.63 masl; (1.93) m above ground
East	Front to rear: 7.8 m, 7.63 m, (7.45) m, (7.17) masl; (2.83) m, (2.8) m, (2.97) m, and 2.83 m above ground
Direction of roof pitch	Gable oriented north-south, possible drop in pitch from front to back
Degree of roof pitch	More than 1.29 m in 6m

Notes: Measurements in ( ) are of incomplete elements.

House 3 is the least well preserved house at *kiix7in*. It is oriented perpendicular to the beach and is 25 metres long and 12 metres wide (Table 5.8). Most of the house posts are to be found encased within spruces that nursed

Figure 5.10
kiix7in House 3, detail, Post A, illustrating degree to which this house has its posts grown over by nursing trees. *Photo by A.P. Mackie, 1984*

on top of the posts and have since nearly hidden them (Figure 5.10 and Table 5.9). One spruce tree is located where one would expect a house post, but there is no outward sign of the post. This was probably a gable-roofed house, given the central post in the front face of the house (Figure 5.11a).

The house floor is very flat but poorly defined. It is about 0.20 metres to 0.30 metres lower than the floor of House 2, and 0.10 metres to 0.40 metres higher than the floor of House 4 to its east. There are no clear indicators of the front or rear edges of the floor. In fact, the edge of the shell midden does not extend as far back as the rear structural elements of the house. The side ridges of the adjacent houses define the sides of this house. The narrowest space between these ridges is 12 metres and occurs at the front. In the absence of structural remains at this site, this location might have been described as a possible house platform or as an open space within the village.

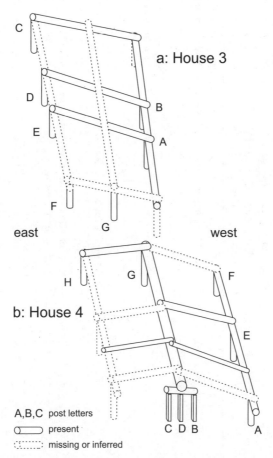

Figure 5.11   kiix7in reconstructed frames of Houses 3 and 4. From sketch by A.P. Mackie, 1985

Table 5.9

House 3 structural details, *kiix7in*, DeSh 1

Post ID	Posts (m)		Beam diameters (m)			Elevations (masl)			Height above ground[b]	Post location within house
	Height	Diameter[a]	First beam	Second beam	Third beam	Base of post	Top of post	Top of structure at post location		
A	(1.93)	(0.54)				(4.70)	(6.63)	(6.63)	(1.93)	West – Centre Front
B						(4.60)	(4.60)	(4.60)		West – Centre Rear
C	(2.37)	(0.50)	0.60			(4.20)	(6.57)	(7.17)	(2.97)	Rear – East
D	(2.20)	0.60	0.60			(4.65)	(6.85)	(7.45)	(2.80)	East – Centre, Rear
E	2.23	0.62	0.60			4.80	7.03	7.63	2.83	East – Centre, Front

A. *x-section = unknown, encased in 1.35 m diameter spruce, only 1 side is showing, crumbling, compressing, no visible decoration or adzing (Figure 5.10)*

B. *x-section = unknown, completely encased in a 1.53 m diameter spruce, only a tiny patch of wood shows through buttresses of spruce*

C. *x-section = probably ½ round, flat surface towards back (against outside wall), lying down, rotted*

D. *x-section = unknown, standing, nursing a hemlock, 30% encased by the hemlock "roots," which are 1.25m in diameter at middle height of post, compressing it. Has vertical and even decorative adzing. Pieces are fragmenting off the post.*

E. *x-section = round with flat surface, flat side facing outwards against outside of house, nursing a small hemlock, leaning, possible L at back, metal "straps" stuck in to the surface of the post that faces inside house (strap = 12.5 x 2.5 cm), stained holes at 1.55 m HAG, which may have held the straps, square nail near the base of the post.*

F	2.55	0.49	0.60		4.65	7.20	7.80	3.15	Front – East

x-section = ½ round, flat surface facing beach (against outside wall of house), several nails in post, at least one of which is square, at 1.70 m HAG is a cluster of 4 nails, partially nursing a large spruce, very rotten, eroded, leaning.

G	(2.19)	(0.48)	0.60	0.60	4.70	(6.89)	(8.09)	(3.39)	Front – Centre

x-section = probably ½ round with flat surface to beach (against outside wall of house), rotted on ground, broken off 0.15 m above ground surface, almost rotted away, probably the front support, which would have held a cross beam and a central long gable beam immediately above.

Notes: Measurements in ( ) are of incomplete elements.
a Top diameter if tapered
b Height of main structural elements (m)

And the rear of the house floor would not have been included within the site boundary. This house seems to have fallen out of use early enough in the history of this site that midden could not accumulate sufficiently to create a clear outline of the house.

House 4:

Table 5.10

House 4 summary description, *kiix7in*, DeSh 1

Roof style	Gable
House length	20.0 m, perpendicular to beach
House width	19.5 m; parallel to beach
House area	390 m²
Height of highest wall/gable	
Gable, front	8.69 masl; 4.54 m above ground
Gable, rear	8.80 masl; 4.40 m above ground
Height of other walls	
West	Greater than 7.45 to 7.15 masl; (3.00) m, (2.95) m above ground
East	Greater than 7.76 masl; (3.76) m above ground
Direction of roof pitch	Gable oriented north-south, 0.11 m drop in elevation from front to rear
Degree of roof pitch	
Rear, east	1.14 m or less in 9.75 m
Front, west	1.54 m or less in 9.75 m

Note: Measurements in ( ) are of incomplete elements.

House 4, the large, gable-ended house that belonged to Chief Tli:shin, is depicted in Figure 5.4 as being only half in use. This is based on the presence and condition of structural elements that are consistently absent or less well preserved on the east side of the house, implying one-half of the house fell out of use earlier than the other. This house is 19.5 metres across the gable end and 20 metres along the gable, which is oriented perpendicular to the beach (Table 5.10). When only the east half was in use the house would have measured about 10 metres by 20 metres.

The gable beam is 0.70 metres in diameter and rested at the rear on a single post (Figure 5.11b), while at the front it was supported on a short perpendicular beam resting on three posts. This beam was decorated with a relief carving facing towards the beach but is too heavily eroded to discern the type of figure. It is round in cross section and still held on two posts (which have rectangular cross sections) to form a sort of archway, while a third central post has fallen out of the arch (Figure 5.12 and Table 5.11).

Figure 5.12 kiix7in House 4, showing arch that formerly supported front end of gable beam, middle support post fallen away, Post B to left, Post C to right. *Photo by A.P. Mackie, 1984*

The top of the main structural elements is 4.54 metres above the ground at the front gable end and 0.14 metres lower at the rear. It is at least 3 metres to 3.75 metres above ground at the sides. The eave beams are about 0.50 metres diameter, and each is supported at either end (the house corners) with one supplementary post in the middle of the west side. A possible post hole suggests similar support on the east side. There is no evidence for supporting posts in the middle of the gable beam, which is supported solely at either end.

The entire area of the house floor is lower than surrounding edges. It appears the ground may have been cut down along the west edge, and a ridge has built up at the rear west corner of the house and along its east and front edges. The rear east side abuts the toe of the main slope. The depression outer edges could be measured at 23 metres by 18.5 metres.

kiix7in *Gable-Roof Houses Summary* Houses at *kiix7in* typically lack central support posts for their gable beam. Some lack central support of the eave

Table 5.11

House 4 structural details, *kiix7in*, DeSh 1

| Post ID | Posts (m) | | Beam diameters (m) | | | Elevations (masl) | | | | Post location within house |
	Height	Diameter[a]	First beam	Second beam	Third beam	Base of post	Top of post	Top of structure at post location	Height above ground[b]	
A	(2.50)	(0.44)	0.50			4.15	(6.65)	(7.15)	(3.00)	Front – West
	x-section = round, standing, leaning, rotted and eroded, probably ca. 0.50 m diameter originally, no decoration visible									
B	3.15	0.58	0.39	0.50	0.50	4.15	7.30	8.69	4.54	Front – Centre West
	x-section = rectangular, 0.21 m N-S x 0.58 m E-W, main support beam for "archway," which holds gable, well finished, rotting, standing with slight lean, holds x-beam (E-W), which connects to 4C with 4D underneath centre and main gable on top of x-beam above 4D. Top is grooved 0.10 m deep to hold x-beam, top also slightly flared N-S.									
C	2.95	0.58	0.44	0.50	0.50	4.20	7.15	8.59	4.39	Front – Centre East
	x-section = rectangular, 0.21 m N-S x 0.58 m E-W, eastern "arch support," holds beam connected to 2B									
D	(2.96)	0.59	0.49	0.50	0.50	4.17	(7.13)	(8.62)	(4.45)	Front – Centre Middle
	x-section = rectangular, 0.18 m N-S x 0.59 m E-W, lying on side, slightly above ground, support for middle of x-beam of arch, which is slightly more rotted on the middle underside surface than elsewhere on beam. Square nails at top; 2.96 m long, but 3.02 m gap from base of post to under surface of x-beam, middle of bottom of post located 1.32 m from 4B and 1.40 m from 4C. X-beam is 0.49 m diameter, 3.15 m long, circular x-section, possibly with notched ends to sit on posts, centre front of beam facing beach is an eroded (beyond recognition) carving 0.60 m long, which is raised 0.10 m to 0.15 m from the surface of the beam.									

E	(1.90)	(0.45)	0.45	4.80	(6.70)	(7.15)	(2.35)	West – Centre

x-section = unknown, lying under two beams, rotted, cannot see the detail

F	(2.50)		0.45	4.50	(7.00)	(7.45)	(2.95)	Rear – West

x-section = perhaps was flat?, encased in roots, barely raised off ground, dug a crater when it fell

G	3.70	0.70	0.70	4.40	8.10	8.80	4.40	Rear – Centre

x-section = round, leaning, rotting, eroding, top probably grooved for the beam, bottom diameter is 0.70m, top diameter is 0.65 m, support post for rear end of long gable beam. It seems that the east ½ of this house (split along the gable) went out of use significantly before the west ½, which overall is in much better condition with greater survival of significant elements, especially beams.

H	(3.35)	0.41	0.41	(4.00)	(7.35)	(7.76)	(3.76)	Rear – East

x-section = may have been ½ round, with flat surface towards back of house (against outside wall), fallen, under and in a root, more rotten, no details are clear

Notes: Measurements in ( ) are of incomplete elements.

a Top diameter if tapered

b Height of main structural elements (m)

beams, others have one or two additional posts that sometimes look as if they were added later, perhaps after the eave beams had sagged to an unacceptable degree. The style of the House 4 frame is the same as a big house at Yuquot, which is depicted in Drucker (1951:68), and also the idealized drawing of a Wakashan style house presented by Mauger (1991:129). With the exception of House 4, all gable-roof houses at this site have the ends of the gable beam supported on the middle of rafter beams, resulting in a very low pitch roof. This is the pattern described by Sproat, who seems to have visited *kiix7in*, probably on more than one occasion, during the early 1860s (Sproat 1987:32, 36). Mauger (1991:136) provides a drawing of a reconstructed house frame based on Sproat's description, which is very similar to such houses at *kiix7in*.

Shed-Roof Houses at kiix7in   Shed-roof houses at this site are not typical of those found in Makah and Salish territories. Mauger (1991) and Matson (Chapter 4, this volume) have illustrated the typical frame for shed-roof houses as having a series of posts evenly spaced down the long sides, with connecting rafter beams across the width of the house. At *kiix7in* the shed-roof houses typically have main structural beams around all sides of the house, resting on four corner posts, some with additional posts near the middle of their long sides. These additional posts tend to show signs that they have been added later, perhaps after these long beams have sagged.

House 5:

Table 5.12

House 5 summary description, *kiix7in*, DeSh 1

Roof style	Shed, two diagonally opposite corners missing
House length	17 m, parallel to beach
House width	10 m, perpendicular to beach
House area	170 m²
Height of highest wall/gable	More than 7.22 masl; (2.40) m above ground
Height of other walls	More than 7.10 masl; (2.22) m above ground
Direction of roof pitch	Cannot say
Degree of roof pitch	Unknown

Notes: Measurements in ( ) are of incomplete elements.

The configuration of beams provides the basis for defining House 5 as a shed-roof house. However, there are only two posts surviving at opposite corners, so the pitch of the roof cannot be determined (Tables 5.12 and 5.13). The main rear beam is 18 metres long and appears to overhang the west post by about 1 metre. The double gable beams are 10 metres long; this measurement has been used for house width. However, the east end seems to be about 11 metres wide and the west end about 8 metres wide. Overall the house is described as 17 metres long parallel to the beach and 10 metres wide (see Figure 5.13a).

The house floor has very little variation in elevation and is lower than surrounding edges except at the front, which drops away onto the beach and is probably eroded. The rear west corner is near the midpoint of House 4, and consequently a small triangular flat area exists between these houses and the main rear slope. The depression for this house is not very square, which corresponds with the structural remains. An eccentric shaped area such as this could be considered a dubious house depression in the absence of structural remains.

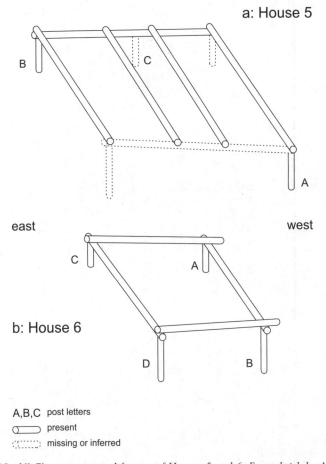

a: House 5

B

C

A

east   west

C

A

b: House 6

D   B

A,B,C post letters

⊂⊃ present

⟨⟩ missing or inferred

Figure 5.13 kiix7in reconstructed frames of Houses 5 and 6. *From sketch by A.P. Mackie, 1985*

Table 5.13

House 5 structural details, *kiix7in*, DeSh 1

| Post ID | Posts (m) | | Beam diameters (m) | | | Elevations (masl) | | | | Post location within house |
	Height	Diameter[a]	First beam	Second beam	Third beam	Base of post	Top of post	Top of structure at post location	Height above ground[b]	
A	(2.00)	(0.35)	0.40			4.70	(6.70)	(7.10)	(2.40)	Front – West
	x-section = round (?), probably a post, rotted, fallen, incomplete									
B	(1.77)	(0.44)	0.45			5.00	(6.77)	(7.22)	(2.22)	Rear – East
	x-section = probably ½ round, with flat surface towards rear of house, (against outside wall), post on ground, rotten, fallen down slope towards the water, house collapsed onto beach, now missing front beam (washed away?)									
C										Rear – Centre
	Probably a rear centre post swallowed entirely within nursing spruce tree; no way to measure any dimensions. Located between two gable beams that are resting on the rear beam. May have been a minor secondary post to support the rear beam.									

Notes: Measurements in ( ) are of incomplete elements.
a Top diameter if tapered
b Height of main structural elements (m)

House 6:

Table 5.14

House 6 summary description, *kiix7in*, DeSh 1	
Roof style	Shed, incomplete post lengths
House length	15 m, parallel to beach
House width	10.5 m, perpendicular to beach
House area	158 m²
Height of highest wall/gable	
Front, east	Greater than 8.65 masl; (4.05) m above ground
Rear, east	Greater than (8.11) masl; (2.71) m above ground
Height of other walls	
Front, west	(8.65) masl; (4.05) m above ground
Rear, west	Greater than 7.70 masl; (2.30) m above ground
Direction of roof pitch	Most likely slopes down to south (rear), partially down to west side
Degree of roof pitch	± 0.95 m in 10.5 m

Note: Measurements in ( ) are of incomplete elements.

House 6 has a shed roof that appears to slope downwards towards the rear, with a secondary slope to the west. It is generally 15 metres long parallel to the beach-front and 10.5 metres wide (Table 5.14). However, the back of the house between the posts is 14 metres long, and the front is around 15 metres long. The main rear beam is 16 metres long so must have had considerable overhang. The west side of the house is around 9.5 metres wide and the east side is around 11.5 metres wide. It was more than 4 metres high at the front (Figure 5.13b). It is uncertain as to whether the front east corner post belongs to this house or House 7 (Table 5.15). It was recorded with House 6 during fieldwork, but analysis of house dimensions and geometry would suggest that it is actually the front west corner of House 7.

There are very subtle variations in the cut edges at the backs of the floor platforms for Houses 6 and 7. In the absence of house frames, these could readily be interpreted as one house measuring 28 metres by 10 metres. As it is, this house depression/platform is measured at about 11.5 metres by 11 metres, which differs from the structural remains because the posts are located outside the cut platform area on higher edges. The rear of this house runs parallel to the base of the slope. The front of the house drops away to the beach and shows no signs of erosion.

Table 5.15

House 6 structural details, *kiix7in*, DeSh 1

Post ID	Posts (m)		Beam diameters (m)			Elevations (masl)				Post location within house
	Height	Diameter[a]	First beam	Second beam	Third beam	Base of post	Top of post	Top of structure at post location	Height above ground[b]	
A	(1.10)	(0.40)	0.70	0.50		5.40	(6.50)	(7.70)	(2.30)	Rear – West
	x-section = probably round, maybe slightly flattened one surface facing the rear against outside wall, leaning, broken (?), rotten, nursing small spruce.									
B	(3.05)	(0.56)	0.50	0.50		(4.60)	(7.65)	(8.65)	(4.05)	Front – West
	x-section = round (?), probably a post, possibly a side (?) or recessed corner post? Hole in ground at inland end of post, depression as if ripped out of ground when it fell over. Post now on ground, rotting, nursing a bush at edge.									
C	(1.51)	(0.33)	0.70	0.50		5.40	(6.91)	(8.11)	(2.71)	Rear – East
	x-section = probably round, eroding badly, probably bigger diameter, rotted but may be original height (not likely?), this house had very thick front and rear beams.									
D	3.12	0.44	0.44	0.40		4.00	7.12	7.96	3.96	Front – East
	x-section = round, standing, leaning, nursing a small spruce and salal, eroding, almost certainly is actually the front W post of House 7 as there is only one surviving corner post at this location for both of these houses which are located very close together. Depression/platform features indicate these to be two houses.									

Notes: Measurements in ( ) are of incomplete elements.
a Top diameter if tapered
b Height of main structural elements (m)

House 7:

Table 5.16

___

House 7 summary description, *kiix7in*, DeSh 1

Roof style	Shed
House length	14.5 m, parallel to beach
House width	10.0 m, perpendicular to beach
House area	145 m²
Height of highest wall/ gable, east	8.77 and (8.47) masl; 3.47 m and (4.54) m (front) above ground
Height of other walls, west	8.19 to 7.96 masl; 3.04 to 3.96 m (front) above ground
Direction of roof pitch	Down to west (side)
Degree of roof pitch	0.59 m in 14.5 m at rear; 0.78 m or more in 14.5 m at front

___

Notes: Measurements in ( ) are of incomplete elements.

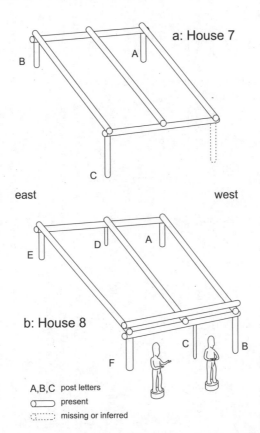

Figure 5.14 *kiix7in* reconstructed frames of Houses 7 and 8. *From sketch by A.P. Mackie, 1985*

Table 5.17

House 7 structural details, *kiix7in*, DeSh 1

Post ID	Posts (m)		Beam diameters (m)			Elevations (masl)				Post location within house
	Height	Diameter[a]	First beam	Second beam	Third beam	Base of post	Top of post	Top of structure at post location	Height above ground[b]	
A	2.23	0.41	0.41	0.40		5.15	7.38	8.19	3.04	Rear – West
	x-section = round, 1.67m long section broken off 0.56m above ground, rotted, eroded									
B	2.50	0.57	0.57	0.40		5.30	7.80	8.77	3.47	Rear – East
	x-section = round, standing, rotting, but condition still okay; vertical adzing is even and well done on sides facing into house, crude axe (?) finish against outside corner									
C	(3.57)	0.57	0.57	0.40		4.20	(7.77)	(8.74)	(4.54)	Front – East
	x-section = round, rotting, detail eroded, this post fell inwards when the house collapsed, gouging a hole in the ground. Hence the height of beam might be too long if much of underground portion of beam now exposed, and depression largely filled in									
6D	3.12	0.44	0.44	0.40		4.00	7.12	7.96	3.96	Front – West
	Recorded also on Table 5.15 (see that entry for additional detail) reflecting organization of field notes. In many respects, this is more likely to be part of House 7 than of House 6									

Notes: Measurements in ( ) are of incomplete elements.
a Top diameter if tapered
b Height of main structural elements (m)

House 7 has a roof pitched downwards to the west. It is 14.5 metres long parallel to the beach at the rear of the house, and 15.5 metres at the front, both measurements taken between the posts (Table 5.16). The front beam is 16 metres long. Across the house width, the east and centre beams are 10 metres long and the house might be measured as 9 metres on the east side and 11 metres on the west side. It was more than 4.5 metres high at its highest point (Table 5.17). Across the length of the house, the roof drops between 0.59 metres and 0.78 metres (Figure 5.14a).

The depression or platform of this house seems to have been cut at the rear into the toe of the adjacent slope and perhaps also along the east boundary with House 8, which has a floor 0.10 metres to 0.20 metres higher than does this house. At the rear east corner there is a ridge between the houses. The west edge is poorly defined. The front of the house appears to be partially eroded. The dimensions of the platform are slightly larger than the structure, which is related in part to uncertainties along the west edge. The rear posts are set in the base of the slope at about 0.5 metres above the house floor.

House 8:

Table 5.18

House 8 summary description, *kiix7in*, DeSh 1

Roof style	Shed
House length	15.5 m, parallel to beach
House width	12 m, perpendicular to beach
House area	185 m²
Height of highest wall/ gable, front	9.22 to 9.08 masl; 4.88 to 4.82 m above ground
Height of other walls, rear	8.88 to 8.79 masl; 3.39 to 3.48 m above ground inside
Direction of roof pitch	Down to south (rear)
Degree of roof pitch	0.34 m in 12 m on east side; 0.29 m in 12 m on west side

---

House 8 has a unique double rafter beam in the front. The extra beam serves to raise the front height of the building, but, perhaps more important, it provides just enough elevation to change the roof pitch so that it drains off the back of the house (Table 5.18). This roof was very nearly flat as the elevation of the roof drops between 0.29 metres and 0.34 metres from front to back across the twelve-metre average width of the house. The house is 15.5 metres in average length parallel to the beach (Figure 5.14b). However, the rear posts are 16 metres apart, and the rear beam is 17 metres long. The front posts are 15 metres apart, and the front beams are about the same length. The east posts are 12.5 metres apart, and the west posts are 11.5 metres apart. The central posts are 13 metres apart (wide), while the east and central beams are 13.5 metres long, and the west beam is 12 metres long.

Bradbury photographed this house sometime not long before 1911 (Figure 5.15) to show the welcome figures in front of it. These two figures now welcome visitors at the main entrance of the Royal British Columbia Museum in Victoria. There is no doubt that these figures were located in front of this house. Not only is the double front rafter beam unique but we can also see, at the far right of the photograph, the small diameter central post, which is positioned off centre from the beam that runs front to back at the centre of the house (Figure 5.15 and Table 5.19). And in Bradbury's photograph the decorative diagonal adzing visible on the corner post behind the male welcome figure can still be seen today (Figure 5.16). The rear posts of this house are fluted at the top (Figure 5.17). Figure 5.18 is taken from the slope behind the house and shows the collapsed house frame and house platform.

The depression/platform has an irregular back edge that, without the house frames for guidance, might lead to the conclusion that two small houses existed here. Overall the house platform has maximum dimensions that are

Figure 5.15   kiix7in House 8 before 1911, note diagonal adzing on post behind male figure. *Photograph attributed to C. Bradbury, PN 4659, courtesy Royal British Columbia Museum*

Figure 5.16 kiix7in House 8, front east corner, Post F showing diagonal adzing also visible in Figure 5.15. *Photo by A.P. Mackie, 1984*

Figure 5.17 kiix7in House 8, rear east corner, Post E, showing fluted adzing found on both rear corner posts, rear beam leaning against top of post. *Photo by A.P. Mackie, 1984*

Figure 5.18 kiix7in House 8 from slope at back of village, showing house frame collapsed onto the house floor. Post E in lower right corner. *Photo by A.P. Mackie, 1984*

Table 5.19

House 8 structural details, *kiix7in*, DeSh 1

Post ID	Posts (m)		Beam diameters (m)			Elevations (masl)				Post location within house
	Height	Diameter[a]	First beam	Second beam	Third beam	Base of post	Top of post	Top of structure at post location	Height above ground[b]	
A	2.29	0.55	0.50	0.60	0.60	5.40	7.69	8.79	3.39	Rear – West
	x-section = round, deeply fluted for top 0.39 m of post, with exception of that part of post located against the outside corner of the house. Matches 8E at other rear corner, rest of post has vertical adzing, rotting on the back side. Detail is beginning to erode, leaning badly.									
B	2.98	0.55	0.70	0.60	0.60	4.20	7.18	9.08	4.88	Front – West
	x-section = round, leaning out of house diagonally, nursing salal, eroded, no detail left except crude finish on northwest side, which would have been against the outside corner of house									
C	(2.60)	(0.31)	0.70	0.60	0.60	4.00	(6.60)	(8.50)	(4.50)	Front – Centre
	x-section = probably round, fallen, thin, eroded, not much of a post, slight depression at base, presumably as secondary support for front beam									
D	(2.40)	(0.30)		0.60		5.70	(8.10)	(8.70)	(3.00)	Rear – Centre
	x-section = round (?), leaning, eroded, rotten, secondary post that took the weight off of a central N-S beam resting on the rear perimeter E-W beam									

E	2.38	0.61	0.50	0.60		5.40	7.78	8.88	3.48	Rear – East
	x-section = round, deeply fluted for top 0.60 m of post, fluting is well detailed and clear on surfaces that face into house only, vertical adzing on inside surface of post, crude finish on outside surfaces, supports one end of the back beam, matches 8A, flutes are 0.05 m wide, supports a large tree too, rotting inside and splitting, top is grooved 0.15 m deep to hold the beam (Figure 5.17).									
F	3.22	0.71	0.60	0.70	0.30	4.40	7.62	9.22	4.82	Front – East
	x-section = round, standing, probably grooved to hold front beam, decorative diagonal (spiral) adzing, rough finish on outside surfaces, axed at base and back side, ledge for plank (?) or vandalism (?), looks like an original feature, leans slightly, rotting inside, but generally okay condition (Figure 5.16).									

Notes: Measurements in ( ) are of incomplete elements.

a Top diameter if tapered.

b Height of main structural elements (m)

slightly larger than the house structure, although some of the west front corner of the house floor may have eroded. The east edge of the house is 0.20 metres to 0.45 metres higher than the adjacent house depression (House 9), so this area may have been filled during construction or accumulated with use.

kiix7in *Shed-Roof House Summary*   The *kiix7in* shed-roof houses do not seem to have frames typical of the more southern and eastern shed-roof houses. All houses described here have both rafter and eave beams; sometimes the eave beams rest directly on posts and hold the rafter beams, but at other times the reverse is true. Some also have beams over the centre of the houses, and most have secondary posts holding up the eave beams where these central rafter beams cross. These secondary posts often appear to be added later to prevent further sagging of the main beams, and they tend to be less robust and not so well finished as the corner posts.

Mauger (1991:171) supports the proposition that shed-roof houses are structurally unrelated to gabled dwellings. He notes that a shed-roof house is not simply half of a gabled structure because the frame that would result if one took half of a gable-roof house away does not resemble that of a shed-roof house. However, some of the shed-roof houses at *kiix7in* could be characterized as halves of gabled houses. Indeed, House 4 was apparently halved along the gable towards the end of its use, resulting in a shed-roof house.

Suttles (1991:220) suggests that "the shed-roof house differed from other types because it served the social, economic, and ceremonial purposes of a different cultural system." He finds that the low gable-roof houses of the Wakashan groups north of Barkley Sound shared many characteristics of the shed-roof house in their external features and internal organization. He notes that their builders were peoples with a "social organization and a ceremonial system more like that of the builders of the shed-roof house than like that of the northern coast" (1991:221). He proposes that the shed-roof house is plausibly an in situ development evolving from a prototypical Northwest Coast plank house, perhaps even from a gable-roof house with fixed wall planks, as found on the North Coast, and changing to its present form in response to changes in the social system, seasonal round, and ceremonial events. He concludes that "archaeological work may eventually show the course of this development, documenting architectural changes from which we might infer social, economic, and ceremonial changes" (1991:221).

We note that the more typical Makah and Salish shed-roof house frame styles do not require as many large pieces of cedar as do the shed-roof and gable-roof houses found at *kiix7in* and further north. Many of the Salish territories are in dryer biogeoclimatic zones where cedar is less common and often distributed in clusters. Also, Swan (1870:4) noted that "the houses of the Makahs are built of boards and planks, split from the cedar. These are principally made by the Indians of Vancouver Island, and procured by barter with them. There is very little cedar about Cape Flattery, and such as is found is small and of inferior quality."

Perhaps the Makah and Salish style of shed-roof house is more likely to occur, or to have developed, in areas where, or at a time when, the procurement of large pieces of cedar would have been more expensive or difficult. It is interesting that Barkley Sound is usually identified as the northern limit of shed-roof house distribution. There is increasing evidence to suggest that southern Wakashan groups displaced, during the last 2,000 years, archaeological culture types that are more commonly associated with Salish territories (Mackie 1992; McMillan 1999:112-121, Chapter 11, this volume; Croes 1995; McMillan and St. Claire 1982). It is possible that the antecedents in the southern areas differ from those of the northern Nuu-chah-nulth groups and influenced more recent house styles in Barkley Sound and Makah territories. It may be that Suttles is right about shed-roof and gable-roof houses having evolved from some common prototype, but perhaps the proto-frame was similar to the varieties of shed-roof house frames that require fewer posts and beams. If such a prototype were to date from the period when cedar was becoming established on the coast, then it more probably started with an economical use of cedar.

Mauger (1991:172) illustrates post-hole patterns to assist excavators to discriminate gable houses from shed houses. At *kiix7in* post holes occur in a variety of patterns, and it would be difficult to define the roof type based on these patterns, principally because some gable beams are resting on other beams and are not supported directly by posts. Mauger's proposed post-hole pattern for the Wakashan or gable-roof house includes a centre post and appears to be derived from ethnohistoric descriptions. His shed-roof house pattern is as found at Ozette. The post-hole patterns from *kiix7in* (Figure 5.19) differ from those predicted by Mauger in that none of the gable-roof houses have any posts within the house, while some but not all have posts beneath the centre of eave beams. And some of these are secondary posts added after support beams sagged, so they tend to be smaller in diameter. These secondary posts are likely to have quite different post holes than those made during construction of the house.

Comparison with Published House Dimensions

It might be expected that house size and form would be more uniform the smaller the study area and the fewer the number of local group territories involved. It is interesting that our results include a considerable range of house size and a great diversity of form. It is also expected that a small study area overlapping with few territories is unlikely to be representative of the range of variation found in the ethnolinguistic area from which the sample

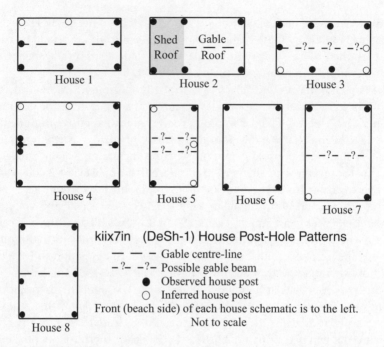

Figure 5.19 Post-hole configurations at *kiix7in* from existing and inferred house posts.

is derived. When we compare the houses from this study area with the ethnohistoric sources, we find that they are consistent with historical descriptions of houses for all Nuu-chah-nulth and Makah territories. Thus, the houses described earlier in this chapter might be considered fairly representative of the range of Nootkan houses.

Ethnohistoric House Descriptions
There are quite a large number of descriptions of Nuu-chah-nulth houses, starting with the drawings and accounts by members of Captain Cook's expedition. Ethnohistoric sources tend to describe the biggest house or houses observed and sometimes provide a range of the biggest and smallest house dimensions; rarely are there multiple dimensions given at one location. We have summarized such observations in Table 5.20, with all measurements converted to metric values. Where a range is given for both length and width, we have applied the larger values to one house, the smaller values to another. Where a range is given for only one dimension, we have made only one entry on Table 5.20, using the largest value in the range combined with the solitary value for the other dimension. The survey of ethnohistoric sources is broadly confined to the more readily accessible published sources and owes much to an earlier summary by Mauger (1978, 1991).

Table 5.20

Ethnographic and ethnohistoric measurements of Nuu-chah-nulth and Makah houses (N = 26); most converted from feet to metres; arranged north to south

Group/Location	Length (m)	Width (m)	Height (m)	House area (m²)	House volume (m³)	Roof type	Source (leading date indicates when observations made)
Friendly Cove, Nootka Sound	30.5		4.3			Flat ("tho somewhat shelving")	1778 Clerke/Beaglehole 1967:1327-1328, cited in Mauger 1991:131
Friendly Cove, Nootka Sound	45.7	9.1		418.1		Shed	1778 King/Beaglehole 1967:1408-1409, cited in Mauger 1991:131-132 for largest houses
Friendly Cove, Nootka Sound	21.3	6.1		130.1		Flat, shelving	1778 King/Beaglehole 1967:1408-1409, cited in Mauger 1991:131-132 for average sized houses
Friendly Cove, Nootka Sound	29.3	16.5	3.7	83.5	1,789.0		1792 *Vancouver* crew member/Meany 1957b:20, cited in Mauger 1991:132-133
Yuquot, Nootka Sound			2.4			Shed, back higher than front	Cook 1784
Yuquot, Nootka Sound	12.2	11.0	3.0	133.8	407.8	gable	1803-05. Jewitt 1967:51-54 in Mauger 1991:133
Yuquot, Nootka Sound	45.7	12.2	4.3	557.4	2,378.6	gable	1803-05. Jewitt 1967:51-54 in Mauger 1991:133
Central and Northern Nootka	12.2	9.1	3.0	111.5	339.8	gabled, two pitched	Drucker 1951:69

▼ *Table 5.20*

Group/Location	Length (m)	Width (m)	Height (m)	House area (m²)	House volume (m³)	Roof type	Source (leading date indicates when observations made)
Central and Northern Nootka	30.5	14.6	3.7	445.9	1,631.1	gabled, two pitched	Drucker 1951:69
Central and Northern Nootka	15.2	6.1		92.9		gabled, two pitched	Drucker 1965:148
Clayoquot Sound			4.6				1785 Alexander Walker (Fisher and Bumstead 1982:47)
Clayoquot Sound			6.1				1788/89. Meares 1790:138-139, in Mauger 1991:134
Opitsit, Meares Is.	24.4	12.2	3.7	297.3	1,087.4	flat	1780s/90s, Boit in Howay 1941:385
Clayoquot Sound	30.5	9.1		278.7		gable	1780s/90s Haswell 1880:714 in Mauger 1991:134
Clayoquot Sound	6.1	9.1		55.7		flat	1780s/90s Haswell 1880:714 in Mauger 1991:134
Cloolthpich, Meares Island	20.1	12.9		259.0			1893. F.A. Devereux survey notes in Arcas 1988:45
Cloolthpich, Meares Island	8.7	5.6		48.8			F.A. Devereux in Arcas 1988:45

Cloolthpich, Meares Island	18.3	9.1		166.5		Gable, two smoke holes for two large fires	before 1920, Matlamatla's house, Peter Webster informant, in Arcas 1988:73
Opitisit, Meares Island	11.0		4.0			gable	Koppert 1930:11
Barkley Sound	24.4	7.6	3.0	185.8	566.3	gable, and shed?	1860s Sproat 1987:248
Barkley Sound	27.4	12.2	3.7	334.5	1,223.3	gable, and shed?	1860s Sproat 1987:248
Cape Flattery	18.3	9.1	4.6	167.2	764.6	shed "least possible inclination"	1860s Swan 1870:5
Makah	15.2	9.1	3.0	139.4	424.8	shed	Mauger 1978:262
Makah	30.5	12.2	6.1	371.6	2,265.3	shed	Mauger 1978:262
Ozette	20.5	12.0		246		shed	Mauger 1978:262
Ozette	17.0	9.5		161.5		shed	Mauger 1978:262
Number	22	22	16	21	11		
Minimum	6.10	5.64	2.44	49	340		
Maximum	45.72	16.46	6.10	557	2,379		
Average	22.9	10.2	4.0	242.2	1,171		
Standard Deviation	10.4	2.7	1.1	146.2	749.7		

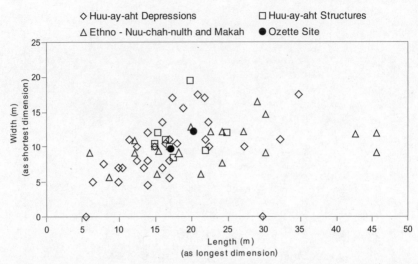

Figure 5.20   Dimensions of ethnohistoric and archaeological houses in Nuu-chah-
nulth and Makah territories. (Data sources: see Tables 5.2 and 5.20).

We have plotted the ethnohistoric accounts and compared them to the
archaeological record (Figure 5.20). This scatter plot shows that the range of
house sizes described by early visitors is consistent with the range of house
sizes recorded in Huu-ay-aht territory. Generally, it is observed that the ethno-
historical accounts tend towards larger houses than those we observed. Their
average length is 23.9 metres (triangles), while the depressions we measured average 17.6 metres (diamonds) and the structures averaged 17.8 metres in length (boxes). Width averages 10.6 metres in the historical accounts,
while in our study the depressions averaged 10.3 metres and the structural
remains averaged 11.3 metres. Height of the reported houses is 3.9 metres
on average, while the average maximum height of measured structures is
3.4 metres. Our data do not include the secondary rafters and roof and wall
planks that are included in most historic observations; these could add more
than 0.5 metres to each dimension of the Huu-ay-aht structures.

That the historical record tends to include longer houses is probably an
artifact of the early observers' interest in the larger houses, with consequent
underrepresentation of the average or smaller houses. This effect may be
compounded by multiple descriptions of some of the most outstanding
houses. In addition, several of the smallest houses in our study area are at
the fortress on Execution Rock (DeSh 2). Fort sites are of a type that are not
recorded in detail in historical documents, but such sites tend to have small
house depressions (cf. Haggarty and Inglis 1985:98-100; Mackie and Wilson

1995:38) dictated, in part, by topography but probably also by the nature and duration of their use.

It is noteworthy that the early accounts by Cook (Beaglehole 1967:317), King (Beaglehole 1967:1408-1409), and Jewitt (1967:51-54) of very large houses do not seem to be exaggerations. They observe, roughly thirty years apart, the biggest house(s) at Friendly Cove, which may be the same structure(s), to be 43 metres (140 feet) and 46 metres (150 feet) long, the roof of which was supported by a single main beam. Houses of this dimension initially seemed unlikely to us, if for no other reason than failure to imagine the logistics of procuring and raising a 150-foot-long cedar beam. However, we see that these reports are similar to a thirty-five-metre long house depression we recorded in the village of *huuZii*. The largest Yuquot houses are 557, 520, and 418 square metres, compared to the big *huuZii* house, which is 612 square metres. The average house floor area for the ethnohistoric houses is 256 square metres, while the Huu-ay-aht house depressions average 191 square metres and the structures 209 square metres.

The similarity of range in sizes between the historical accounts and our house measurements provides some comfort that the early descriptions tend to be reliable, even if skewed towards the more remarkable houses. It should be noted, however, that the early measurements tend to be greater the further north they occur. To what degree this is related to the distribution of gable-roof structures has not been investigated.

The early descriptions of house form are more problematic than are the measurements. Mauger (1991:127-148) has provided a summary of the house types based largely on differences in the style of roof. He notes that "shed-roof dwellings are architecturally closer to Wakashan houses than to any other Northwest Coast house type. These two house types share certain features, particularly withe-slung wall planking and loose roof planks, as well as similar interior arrangements" (1991:148).

The Wakashan roof style is generally comprised of three beams running the length of the house, with the top of the middle, or gable, beam higher than either of the side, or eave, beams. This results in a gable roof, typically of fairly low pitch. The shed-roof houses are characterized by a series of shorter beams spanning two posts across the width of the houses. Such houses have a single pitch "shed" roof. Both roof styles have variations that make them more or less like each other in outward appearance or interior frame construction. For instance, some of the gable-roof houses have very little pitch and may appear flat from the outside. And some of the shed-roof houses have substantial rafter beams perpendicular to and resting on the eave beams. When such rafter beams occur across the middle of the house with plank ends resting on them, they can take on the appearance of a low pitched gable roof (cf. Gibbs's 1855 drawing of Neah Bay [Mauger 1991:41]).

This effect may be even more pronounced if post-and-beam house frames had, at a late date, a frame construction added on top to make a pronounced gable. Comparison of the photographs and surviving post and beams would suggest this to have been the case at *tsuxwkwaada,* a Ditidaht village located between Huu-ay-aht and Makah territories (Sumpter, Fedje, and Sieber 2001).

Mauger finds that Wakashan style gable-roof houses are present throughout the northern and central Nuu-chah-nulth territories and that both are present in Barkley Sound. While he notes some evidence for shed-roof houses as far north as Nootka Sound, he concludes that Barkley Sound marks "the beginning of the transition from Wakashan dwellings to shed-roof houses on the west coast of Vancouver Island. Drucker (1951:178) lists Alberni Canal groups as using the shed-roof house type as well as the Nitinats. In the latter case, this is further verified by contemporary informants" (Mauger 1991:136).

Whymper's illustration, *Ouchucklesit Village, Barclay Sound,* painted during 1864, shows both gable-roof and shed-roof structures (Hayman 1989:192). Our study area is located near the centre of the larger Huu-ay-aht First Nations' territory, which extends into the mouth of Alberni Canal and shares borders with the Ditidaht [Nitinat] and Uchucklesaht First Nations (St. Claire 1991:175.)

Conclusion

The Huu-ay-aht houses that we recorded in 1984 are of a similar range of size and style to those described in the written records. They have a variety of forms that fit with descriptions for Nuu-chah-nulth houses, but the shed-roof houses have a different frame than those found further south and east. The post-hole patterns from these shed-roof houses would be difficult or impossible to distinguish from those of many gable-roof houses, and some would also be difficult to distinguish from the shed-roof house frames described for the Makah and Salish. The data presented here provide an important supplement to the historic and ethnographic record. We hope they will be of interest if someone finds an opportunity to excavate Nuu-chah-nulth house floors, and we think that the significant variety in house size and form occurring in this small area may influence interpretations of the excavations of the necessarily small sample of house floors in the Northwest Coast.

Acknowledgments

The work for this project was funded by the BC Heritage Trust and Employment Canada under program awards made to the Ohiaht Indian Band (now known as the Huu-ay-aht First Nations). Other support was received from the Ohiaht Band and the Archaeology Division of the BC Provincial Museum (now the Royal British Columbia Museum) and private funds of both authors. The work was conducted under Heritage Conservation Act permit 1984-026. The written and oral versions of this chapter are presented in accordance with a 1998 Huu-ay-aht Heritage Investigation Permit.

We would like to extend our thanks to Stella Peters, Lisa Johnson, and Frances Frank of the Huu-ay-aht First Nations, who trained on this project in archaeological field and laboratory methods. However, they were far more than mere trainees: they were an integral part of the project, and its success owes a great deal to their enthusiastic participation. Monty Mitchell of Vancouver was a field supervisor and is responsible for the identification and recording of many of the sites we found. The late Chief Art Peters and Agnes Peters of the Huu-ay-aht provided a great deal of support for the project and helped make us feel welcome in the community. Denis St. Claire worked with many elders and translators from the Huu-ay-aht and nearby First Nations before and during the course of this project, and, while the information they shared has not been incorporated into this chapter, such knowledge comprises the very essence of ethnoarchaeological projects. These elders include: Robert Sport (assisted by Adam Shewish, 1982), Ernie Lauder (1982), William Sport (1983), Ella Jackson (assisted by Agnes Peters, 1984), Bill Happynook (assisted by Lizzie Happynook, 1984), Mary Moses (assisted by Frances Williams, 1984), Alex Williams (1984), John Jacobson (1984), Agnes Peters (1985), and Eunice Joe (assisted by Angie Joe, 1985). Sadly, nearly all have died.

Many others helped throughout the project with equipment, support, or information. These included Huu-ay-aht councillors Larry Johnson and Robert Dennis, Provincial Museum archaeologists James Haggarty and Richard Inglis, Pauline Rafferty of the BC Heritage Trust, and various staff of the Heritage Branch. Volunteers who assisted with fieldwork at the sites discussed in this chapter include Richard Mackie, Quentin Mackie, Steve Lipscomb, and Kathryn Bernick. Alan and Lori Graves helped with exhibit design and report illustrations, while Ole Heggen and Susan Matson prepared many of the final drawings. And others too numerous to list also contributed their efforts. Thanks to all.

This chapter was first part of a symposium in honour of Donald H. Mitchell upon his retirement. We were both students of Professor Mitchell's at the University of Victoria and are indebted to him for a solid founding in the principles and applications of research. From him we learned an appreciation for the importance of ethnographic and ethnohistoric records in the understanding of archaeological materials. Thank you, Don, you prepared us well for careers in archaeology.

Notes

1 Huu-ay-aht First Nations is the name preferred by the Ohiaht Indian Band. There are at least nine other historical and linguistic renderings of this name (St. Claire 1991:25).

2 "Nuu-chah-nulth" is the preferred collective name for those First Nations on the west coast of Vancouver Island that previously were referred to as "Nootkan" and "Westcoast." The Makah are a closely related tribe resident at the northwest tip of Washington State.

3 The practical orthography used here was developed by Randy Bouchard of the BC Indian Language Project (Ellis and Swan 1981:106-108; McMillan and St. Claire 1982:137-138).

4 Unless otherwise stated, the data sources for all tables and figures are Ohiaht Ethnoarchaeological Project field notes and BC Archaeological Site Inventory Forms. DeSh 1 house detail information is from field notes of 13 and 14 September and 19 October 1984.

5 Some house depressions have one or more uncertain edges and could be either part of another house, evidence for more than one house, or partitions within a house (cf. Matson, Chapter 4, this volume), hence the range in numbers.

6 The barnacle line was used as the 0.0 datum from which we took elevations with a hand level at all these sites. This roughly equates to mean sea level. Elevations in any one house are thought to be accurate within ± 10 centimetres and are more usually within ± 5 centimetres.

7 In the summer of 2002, the senior author revisited *kiix7in* as a volunteer with the Huu-ay-aht and Parks Canada. The features at *kiix7in* were recorded with surveying instruments. Preliminary analysis has revealed no substantive differences compared with the 1984 results.

6

Preliminary Analysis of Socioeconomic Organization at the McNichol Creek Site, British Columbia

Gary Coupland, Roger H. Colten, and Rebecca Case

The McNichol Creek site (GcTo 6) is a prehistoric village site on the northern coast of British Columbia, near Prince Rupert. Since 1989 this site has been the focal point of an archaeological research program investigating socioeconomic organization within a prehistoric, complex hunting and gathering society. We wish to understand how the occupants of this village, specifically, and the middle/late prehistoric cultures of the northern Northwest Coast, generally, produced, exchanged, and consumed resources. The period of village occupation of the McNichol Creek site, c. 2000-1500 BP, is a time thought by many to represent the full emergence of the Developed Northwest Coast Pattern (Fladmark 1975; MacDonald and Inglis 1981; Ames 1981, 1994; Matson and Coupland 1995), which included hereditary social inequality and semi-sedentary settlement in large villages with multifamily corporate households. How this vibrant and complex way of life was sustained by societies without farming is one of the critical questions facing Northwest Coast archaeologists today.

Located on the shoreline of the north side of Prince Rupert harbour, the McNichol Creek site is eponymously named for the nearby creek, which empties into the harbour east of the site. Measuring about 100 metres east/west by about 150 metres north/south, the site can be usefully divided into three main areas: back, middle, and front (Figure 6.1). At the back of the site is a deep, concentrated shell midden deposit, which forms a crescent-shaped ridge, rimming the site on the north and west sides. Over 3 metres deep in places, this midden contains a high density of broken shell and other faunal remains, numerous artifacts, and human burials.

Moving south and downslope from the back midden to the middle of the site, we come to the main residential area. This area, which slopes towards the water, contains the remains of fifteen subrectangular house depression features, fourteen of which are arranged in two rows. All but one of these features is oriented towards the beach. The back row contains eight such features (A-H), tightly spaced, side by side (Figure 6.1). In the front row are six house depressions (K-P), including the depression of House O, which was significantly larger than the others (see Coupland 1996). House J is located between the two rows. House K, located at the west end of the front row of house depressions, is separated by about 10 metres from its nearest neighbour in the front row and is the only one oriented parallel to the beach.

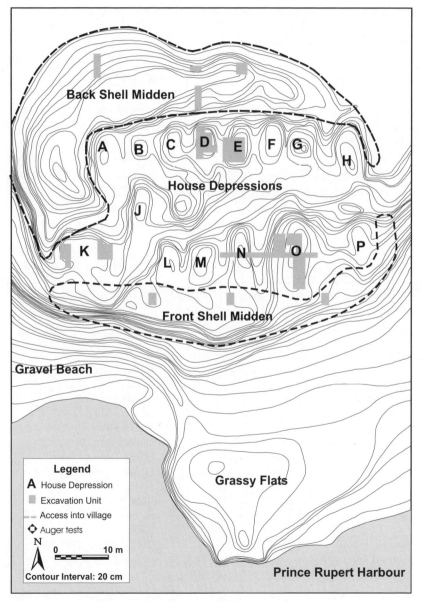

Figure 6.1   The McNichol Creek site.

Immediately in front of the front row of houses, and at the crest of a short, steep slope leading up from the pebble beach and grassy point that front the site, is a long, narrow area with midden deposit. This front midden area may have been used as an exterior activity area. It contains scattered shell deposits – some concentrated, some diffuse – other faunal remains, artifacts, and at least one human burial. After four major field seasons (1990, 1996, 1997, 1999), each of these areas – the back midden, house depressions, and front midden – has received some excavation, with considerable attention paid to the house depressions.

We have seventeen radiocarbon age estimates from the McNichol Creek site (Table 6.1). Four dates from the back midden and one from the front midden are all consistent with the proposed period of village occupation of the site. The twelve dates from the house features have a much greater time range, from c. 800 to 2600 BP, which may result from more intensive trampling and mixing within house floor deposits. Six of the twelve house feature dates, from Houses D, E, and O, do fall within the proposed period of village occupation. In terms of the local cultural sequence for the Prince Rupert area (MacDonald and Inglis 1981), the village occupation at McNichol Creek would appear to be transitional between the middle and late periods. Most scholars would agree that rank society, a hallmark of Northwest Coast

Table 6.1

Radiocarbon age estimates for the McNichol Creek site

Lab sample	Sample material	Age (years BP)	Context
Isotrace 7021	charcoal	810 ± 60	House O, floor fill
Isotrace 7019	charcoal	930 ± 80	House E, hearth
Isotrace 7022	charcoal	1060 ± 50	House O, hearth
Isotrace 7018	charcoal	1350 ± 70	House E, hearth
WSU 4400	shell	1490 ± 105[a]	Back midden, top shell layer
Isotrace 7025	charcoal	1510 ± 60	Front midden, (SM7)
Teledyne 18687	charcoal	1570 ± 80	House O, hearth
Teledyne 16452	charcoal	1580 ± 80	House D, front hearth
Teledyne 16451	charcoal	1590 ± 80	House D, back hearth
Isotrace 7024	charcoal	1660 ± 50	House O, hearth
WSU 4399	shell	1660 ± 85[a]	Back midden, top shell layer
Isotrace 7023	charcoal	1670 ± 70	House O, floor fill
Isotrace 6418	charcoal	1720 ± 60	Back midden, (SM5, upper)
Isotrace 6419	charcoal	2070 ± 60	Back midden, (SM5, lower)
Isotrace 7020	charcoal	2220 ± 60	House E, middle area
Isotrace 2352	charcoal	2560 ± 60	House D, pit fill
Teledyne 18689	charcoal	2590 ± 90	House N, floor fill

a   Age estimates on shell corrected for reservoir effect.

culture, was already firmly developed in the region by this time, and some (e.g., MacDonald and Inglis 1981) would argue that the local ethnographic cultural pattern was more or less in place.

This chapter is a preliminary study. We report some of the results of excavations at the McNichol Creek site, including artifactual, faunal, and stratigraphic data. We compare these data from the three different site contexts mentioned above in an effort to delineate socioeconomic organization within the village. First, we compare the two external midden areas (back midden and front midden). Both areas are external or open spaces within the village. What sorts of activities were conducted in these spaces, and is there any difference between them? Next, we examine archaeological remains from the house features for evidence of socioeconomic differentiation among households. We compare faunal remains from Houses D and O, and artifacts from Houses D, E, and O.[1] Then, we take a closer look at House O, examining spatial patterning of artifactual and faunal remains from within a single dwelling. Finally, we compare the remains from the external middens – open, public, or common spaces – to those from within the houses' enclosed or private spaces.

Outside the Houses

What kinds of activities were conducted outdoors, in public, common spaces at McNichol Creek? And were these activities in any way different from those conducted indoors? Recent research has shown that concerns for privacy may be incorporated in aspects of site architecture and may be an important factor in organizing socioeconomic activities in large communities (Dohm 1992, 1996). We anticipate that some activities (such as secondary refuse disposal) would have been conducted entirely outside the houses, at least outside occupied houses, while other activities (such as food processing, manufacturing, and social or ritual activities such as feasting and burials) could have been conducted either inside or outside the houses. Were there designated external areas for certain kinds of activities? Or was outside space used in an unorganized, unsystematic manner?

The two main external areas at McNichol Creek are the front and back middens. The back midden has been sampled in four different areas that provide good spatial coverage. This broad areal coverage is important because, as Lyman (1991), Stein (1991) and others have shown, cultural deposition in refuse middens is not always homogeneous. One cannot expect that a sample drawn from only one area of the midden will accurately represent the entire midden. About 30 cubic metres of deposit has been excavated from the back midden. Likewise, the front midden has been tested in three different areas across the front of the site; however, only about 8 cubic metres of deposit has been excavated (see Figure 6.1 for location of excavations).

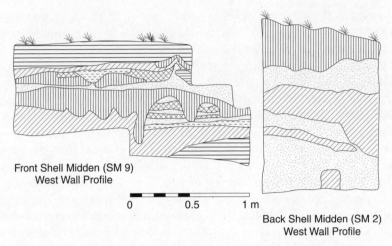

Front Shell Midden (SM 9)
West Wall Profile

0   0.5   1 m

Back Shell Midden (SM 2)
West Wall Profile

Figure 6.2   Stratigraphic profiles of front and back shell middens.

Stratigraphically, the front and back middens are not at all alike (Figure 6.2). The back midden deposit was quite homogeneous, a concentrated shell matrix with few stratigraphic breaks in each of the excavated areas. Most layers were thick (over 1 metre thick in some cases) and covered large areas. In one unit (SM 2; i.e., shell midden excavation unit 2), the shell deposit extended to a depth of over 3 metres. Except for human burials, which were ubiquitous, there were no features in the back midden, no evidence of processing or manufacturing activities. The back midden, thus, appears to have had two main functions: (1) secondary refuse disposal and (2) human burials. With three radiocarbon age estimates ranging from 2070 to 1490 BP, the formation of the back midden appears to relate entirely to the period of village occupation of the site (Table 6.1).

Likewise, the sole front midden date, 1510 BP (Iso 7025), falls within the period of village occupation. But the front midden was much more complex stratigraphically: shell layers intermingled with soil layers. The shell layers, themselves, were quite variable. Some contained high densities of shell, others were diffuse. Some shell layers contained mainly burned shell, while in others the shell was largely unburned. The numerous features in the front midden included small post moulds (drying racks?), hearth spills, and ash lenses. We also encountered one human burial in the front midden (SM9). The three excavation units in the front midden revealed deposits less homogeneous than those in the back midden. SM 7, for example, located just east of the front of House O, contained a much higher density of shell than SM 8 and SM 9. The concentrated shell matrix of SM 7 looked more like that of the back midden. We suggest that a variety of activities were conducted in the front midden area, including processing, manufacturing, inhumation, and primary refuse disposal. That the back midden was used more regularly for refuse disposal than the front midden is supported by the observation that non-shell faunal density (bones) is 38 percent higher in the back (784 elements per cubic metre; Number of Identified Specimens 14,544) than in the front (568 elements per cubic metre; NISP 6,003).

The function of the back midden, as the main disposal area for secondary refuse, may have implications for the very important question of food storage at the site, in particular, salmon storage. In an earlier article, Coupland, Bissell, and King (1993) noted that salmon was, by far, the most abundant and important food resource at McNichol Creek. Subsequent excavations and faunal recovery have not substantially altered this observation. Prince Rupert Harbour is not an important location for salmon fishing, although some creeks and streams that empty into the harbour, including McNichol Creek, do receive small runs. The harbour area was important, however, as the historic winter village location of the Coast Tsimshian local groups (Drucker 1965; Garfield 1951). These groups depended on stored salmon to see them through the winter, and much of this salmon was caught and processed in late summer and fall in the household-owned fishing territories of the lower Skeena watershed (Halpin and Seguin 1990). This ethnographic observation leads to the archaeological hypothesis that much of the salmon consumed at the McNichol Creek site was caught and processed elsewhere, and brought in to the site as a stored resource. To test this hypothesis, we should expect to find lower densities of salmon remains in the main processing area (the front midden) and higher salmon densities in the main refuse disposal area (the back midden). Fish overwhelms all other classes of faunal remains in both external midden areas. Mammals rank second, while birds are represented by only a handful of elements (Figure 6.3). The percentage of fish is slightly higher in the back midden than in the front, but the difference is small – 4.8 percent. Looking specifically at salmon, we see a similar pattern – a slightly higher percentage in the back midden than in the front, but, again, the difference is only 5.2 percent. However, if we compare the front and back middens in terms of the *density* of salmon remains, a somewhat different pattern emerges. In the back midden, salmon density in the excavated deposits is 727 elements per cubic metre (salmon NISP from the back midden is 13,487 elements). In the front midden, salmon density is 473.4 elements per cubic metre (salmon NISP from the front midden is 5,003 elements). The higher density of salmon remains in the back midden provides some support for the model of salmon storage, but we do note that salmon density in the front midden is higher than might be expected.

A second line of evidence for salmon storage is anatomical representation. In all deposits, salmon is strongly represented by caudal vertebrae. Stewart (1998) notes, in her analysis of the back midden sample, that cranial

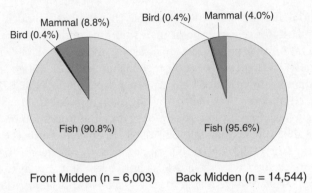

Front Midden (n = 6,003)   Back Midden (n = 14,544)

Figure 6.3   Frequencies of faunal classes in the front and back middens at McNichol Creek.

bones and frontal vertebrae, including the atlas, are vastly underrepresented, which suggests that in many cases heads and connected upper portions of the trunk were removed before the fish were brought into the site – a pattern consistent with processing fish for storage. This line of evidence is contentious because it has often been noted that salmon head bones are fragile and do not preserve in archaeological deposits as well as do the vertebrae (Wigen and Stucki 1988; Butler 1987). The underrepresentation of cranial parts may, therefore, be the result of taphonomic processes rather than cultural ones. However, this reasoning is not accepted by some Northwest Coast zooarchaeologists, who argue that at least some salmon head bones should be expected if the fish were locally caught and processed (G. Calvert and S. Crockford, personal communications 1998), and, in any event, taphonomic processes do not account for the apparent underrepresentation of frontal vertebrae. These two lines of evidence – higher salmon density in the secondary refuse midden and overall underrepresentation of cranial and frontal elements – support the argument that salmon was mainly a stored resource at McNichol Creek, much of it caught and processed elsewhere. Further, we suggest that efforts to quantify salmon remains in primary and secondary refuse deposits may be useful in identifying cases of salmon storage.

Why, then, is salmon density higher than expected in the front midden, the presumed processing area of the site, if salmon were mainly processed off site? We have no conclusive answer to this question at the moment, but one strong possibility exists. McNichol Creek currently receives a small run of pink salmon (*Oncorhynchus gorbuscha*), so some salmon may have been caught locally and processed at the site. As a result, some salmon may have been regularly processed in the front midden, and salmon remains in this area may represent primary refuse.

Before leaving the external midden areas and moving indoors, we offer two observations on the molluscan fauna from the back midden. Harkness

Table 6.2

Shell sizes of littleneck clams (*Protothaca staminea*) measured by three parameters for upper and lower layers from excavation unit SM2, back midden

	Width		Hinge length		Height	
	Lower	Upper	Lower	Upper	Lower	Upper
Mean (mm)	35.4	33.6	40.6	38.5	12.1	11.1
SE	0.21	0.45	0.23	0.49	0.08	0.15
N	592	160	580	153	613	166
t-test	4.26 (99.9%)		3.87 (99.9%)		5.79 (99.9%)	

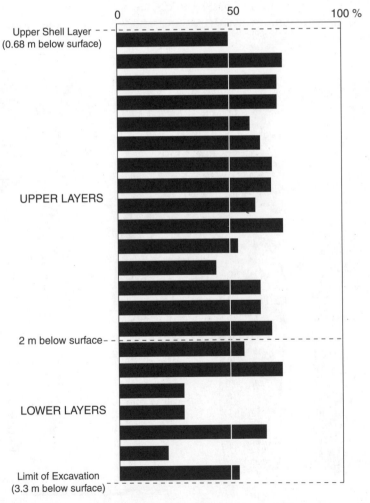

Figure 6.4 Frequencies of mussels (*Mytilus edulis*) by layer from excavation unit SM2, back midden at the McNichol Creek site.

(1997) has analyzed column samples and found that littleneck clams (*Protothaca staminea*), which are more numerous in the midden than any other shellfish, decrease in size from the bottom to the top of the midden (Table 6.2). This decrease is particularly notable in the upper metre of the deposit. He also found that blue mussels (*Mytilus edulis*) increase in frequency in the upper layers (Figure 6.4). Both observations may relate to over-exploitation of local shellfish beds. If clams, especially littlenecks, were the preferred shellfish, then their decrease in size through time may be a function of the depletion of the beds. The increase in mussels may reflect a replacement strategy – mussels-for-clams – but in time, mussels, too, would be depleted. As Croes and Hackenberger (1988) have noted, shellfish, unlike some other Northwest Coast resources, are not intensifiable. Local beds can be depleted through over-harvesting, and this may be one reason for village relocation.

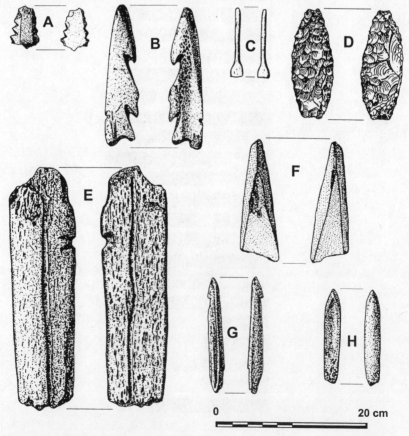

Figure 6.5   Artifacts from the back shell midden (*A-F*) and the front shell midden (*G, H*) at McNichol Creek.

In addition to the abundant faunal remains, nearly 100 artifacts have been recovered from the two external middens. We have recovered seventy artifacts from the back midden and twenty-six from the front midden (Figure 6.5). The density of artifacts per cubic metre of excavated deposit is slightly higher in the front (3.25) than in the back (2.6). What this may say about refuse disposal and processing is unclear. What is clear is that bone tools greatly outnumber stone in both middens (twenty-three to three in the front, fifty to nineteen in the back). The ratios of bone to stone in the house depressions, on the other hand, favour stone, which suggests longer use or greater recycling of stone than bone.

Inside the Houses
Excavations have thus far been conducted in four house depressions: D, E, K, and O. We have concentrated on House O, the largest, where 36 cubic metres of deposit have been excavated over two field seasons. By contrast, we have excavated 15 cubic metres from House D, 16 cubic metres from House E, and 17.5 cubic metres from House K.

House O stands out from the others in a number of ways (Figure 6.6). First, it is estimated to have had over 100 square metres of floor space, while the others averaged about 60 square metres. To put this difference in perspective, House O is roughly equal in size to the two-compartment house at the Shingle Point site reported by Matson (Chapter 4, this volume), while the smaller houses at McNichol Creek are about the size of a single compartment. House O also has some unique features, including a clay floor covering most of the central area of the house depression. To our knowledge, this is the only excavated house with a clay floor on the North Coast, although clay floors have been reported from a few sites along the South Coast (Ames et al. 1992; Erlandson, Moss, and Tveskov 1998).

House O also has a very large central hearth. This feature was partially uncovered in our 1996 excavation of the house and was fully exposed in 1997. It measures 4.5 metres long by 2 metres wide. While we have excavated other hearth features, both interior and exterior, at McNichol Creek, none compares to the size of the House O hearth. Following Brian Hayden's recent work (Hayden 1996; Hayden and Spafford 1993), we suggest that this hearth, given its size and the size of the house in which it was located, may have been a feasting hearth. If, as we believe, House O was residential, private space as opposed to communal, public space, then it seems reasonable to suggest that the kind of ceremony associated with this house and hearth was, in Hayden's terms, competitive feasting. The owner of the house may have hosted such feasts in order to demonstrate and maintain power and influence. Artifacts recovered from House O provide further support for the hypothesis that the owner was an aggrandizer (Figure 6.7 H-N). Among the sixty-five artifacts recovered from this house are a labret (historically a

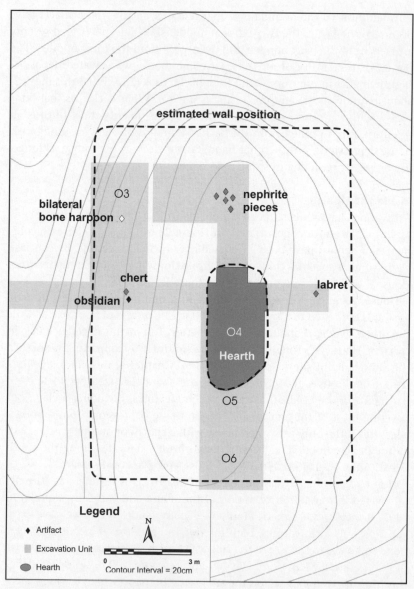

Figure 6.6 House O at McNichol Creek.

symbol of high social status among women on the North Coast) (Figure 6.7 N), five pieces of nephrite (including two adze blades), and flakes of exotic chert and obsidian, which suggest participation in long-distance exchange networks.

The floor plan of House D shows a smaller house with two hearths oriented along the mid-line of the floor (Figure 6.8). Faunal remains were recovered

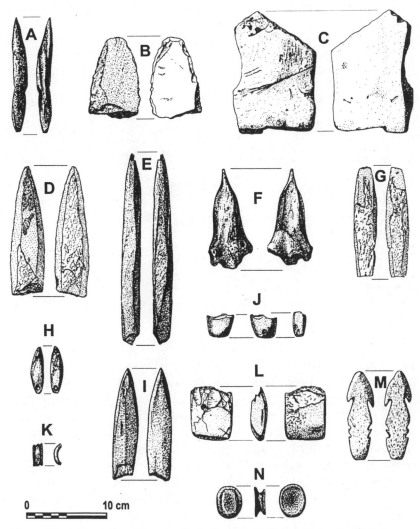

Figure 6.7 Artifacts from House D (*A-C*), House E (*D-G*) and House O (*H-N*) at McNichol Creek.

from both hearths, which suggests they were used for cooking and disposal of bones, in addition to heating. Neither hearth is particularly large, certainly they are much smaller than the feasting hearth of House O. The artifact assemblage of fifty-six items includes three drilled tooth pendants and items of personal adornment (not necessarily related to high social status). One chert flake and one polished nephrite fragment were also recovered.

Excavation of House E revealed one small central hearth (Figure 6.8). A cache of five ground slate points was recovered from just north and west of the hearth, near the back of the house. These include finished and unfinished

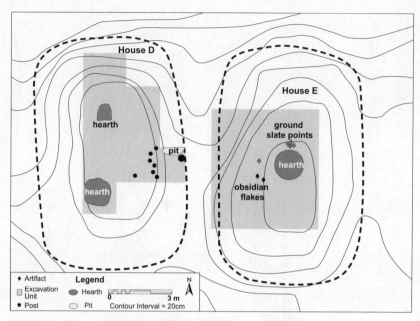

Figure 6.8   Houses D and E at McNichol Creek.

points in what may have been a specialized manufacturing area. The small assemblage of twenty-six artifacts also included two obsidian flakes.

Faunal remains were recovered from all three houses, but so far only remains from Houses D and O have been analyzed. The House D sample, analyzed in its entirety in 1990-91 by Sarah King, contains 3,370 bones (including unidentifiable fragments), while the House O sample, analyzed by Roger Colten, contains 7,370 bones from four two-by-two-metre units: O3, near the back corner of the house, and O4, O5, and O6, near the front of the house and the front of the large hearth. Comparison of the faunal remains from Houses D and O shows some interesting trends. In both houses, fish and mammals predominate; bird remains are poorly represented (less than 1 percent).

In House D, fish account for about 75 percent of the material and mammals for about 25 percent (Figure 6.9). Of the identified elements, salmon rank first, not surprisingly, with 81.7 percent of NISP. Pacific herring rank second at 12.6 percent, followed by domestic dog and coast deer at just under 2 percent each.

In House O, mammals account for about 67 percent of the material, fish for about 33 percent. Here, the representation of mammals is much higher than in House D. In fact, House O is the only analyzed context from the site where mammal remains outnumber fish remains. Most of the mammal remains from House O are very tiny fragments. Genus or species level

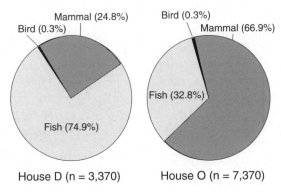

Mammal (24.8%)
Bird (0.3%)
Fish (74.9%)

Bird (0.3%)
Mammal (66.9%)
Fish (32.8%)

House D (n = 3,370)   House O (n = 7,370)

Figure 6.9 Frequencies of faunal classes in Houses D and O at McNichol Creek.

identifications could be made in only a handful of cases (less than 1 percent). In addition, 80 percent of the mammal bones are burned, while only 18 percent of the fish bones and 32 percent of bird bones are burned. This suggests that mammals were processed and their bones discarded in a manner different from fish and birds, and that mammal bones may have been intentionally burned. Several of the large mammal bones also show clear evidence of gnawing, presumably by dogs. It is possible that large mammal bones within houses were consumed or fragmented by dogs. Alternatively, larger bones may have been removed during house-cleaning episodes, leaving only smaller fish bones and fragmented mammal remains behind.

As in House D, salmon, at 90 percent, and herring, at about 7 percent, rank first and second in terms of the more precisely identified remains in House O. The other identified animals, in order of abundance are coast deer, sea otter, dogs or wolves, lynx, beaver, turtle, and harbor seal. Although by no means abundant, the presence of marine mammals in the House O assemblage distinguishes it from other parts of the site. None of the nearly 7,000 previously identified bones from house and midden contexts were from sea mammals. The positively identified remains from House O include a tooth, a cranial bone, and five foot bones from sea otter, and a tooth from a harbor seal.

Inside House O
Ethnographic models of household social organization on the North Coast suggest a spatial gradient in which status declines from the back of the house to the front. Among the Tsimshian, chiefs' quarters were typically at the back of the house, while slaves slept near the front (Garfield 1951; Drucker 1965). The model has been tested archaeologically by some of the authors in this book (e.g., Acheson 1991), and it may account for the distribution of remains in House O. All House O artifacts that may be related to wealth or high social status were recovered from the back half of the house. This

includes the labret, nephrite pieces, a bilateral barbed harpoon (made of sea mammal bone), and obsidian and chert flakes. Although 12 square metres of the front half of the house have been excavated, no wealth or status items were recovered from these units. In fact, artifact density is much higher in the back half of the house than in the front.

We also compared the fauna from the back (O3) and the front excavation units (O4-O6) to try to identify variation within the house (Table 6.3). At this stage of the analysis, results are best considered preliminary because the back of the house sample is derived from only one excavation unit compared to three units in the front. At the moment, it appears that faunal density, like artifact density, is higher in the back of the house (629.8 elements per cubic metre in O3) than in the front (404.3 per cubic metre in O4-O6). However, O4, in the centre of the large hearth, had the highest faunal density (at 760 elements per cubic metre) of any of the four units. Along these lines, we note some other trends: (1) all but one of the twenty-two bird bones were from the back of the house (O3); (2) all identified dog

Table 6.3

The faunal assemblage from House O (NISP)

Taxon	Excavation Units				
	O3	O4	O5	O6	Total
Aves	21	0	1	0	22
Enhydra lutris	1	5	1	0	7
Phoca vitulina	1	0	0	0	1
Lynx canadensis	1	0	0	0	1
marine mammal	2	0	0	0	2
Castor canadensis	0	1	0	0	1
Canis sp.	6	0	0	0	6
Odocoileus sp.	7	2	7	5	21
Cervidae	0	0	1	0	1
Carnivora	2	0	0	0	2
Rodentia	1	0	0	0	1
terrestrial mammal	3	0	0	0	3
large mammal	14	10	1	5	30
medium mammal	7	6	0	5	18
small mammal	7	6	1	0	14
Mammalia	1,204	2,683	763	171	4,821
Onchorhynchus sp.	536	278	341	286	1,441
fish (non-salmon)	58	1	52	3	114
fish	647	46	152	15	860
turtle	0	1	0	0	1
unidentified	1	2	0	0	3
total	2,519	3,041	1,320	490	7,370

Note: Unit O3 is from the back, units O4-O6 are from the front.

bones ($N = 6$) were from the back of the house; (3) salmon density was higher in the back of the house (134 elements per cubic metre) than in the front (75 per cubic metre); and (4) other fish density was higher in the back (176 per cubic metre) than in the front (22.4 per cubic metre). On the other hand, the ten marine mammal bones/teeth were more evenly distributed through the house, with four elements from O3 and six from the front units. The five sea otter foot bones came from O4. Mammal remains (all mammal categories combined) are relatively evenly distributed between the back of the house (314 elements per cubic metre) and the front (306 per cubic metre).

The Middens and Houses Compared

Finally, we compared remains from exterior and interior contexts. Human burials were concentrated in the back midden ($N = 5$), but one burial was also found in the front midden. Both contexts may be considered open, public spaces. No burials were found within the enclosed spaces of houses. Faunal remains overwhelmingly favour fish, especially salmon, in the exterior middens, while the percentage of fish is lower in the houses and is actually lower than mammals in House O. This could relate to taphonomic processes, but we believe it also relates to differences in how fish and mammals were processed, consumed, and discarded. We see no particular trends in artifact functional classes, but we do note that bone tools greatly outnumber stone in the exterior middens, while the reverse is true within the houses. Only House O has roughly equal numbers of stone and bone tools.

Conclusion

This study has provided a number of insights into socioeconomic organization in a middle/late prehistoric Northwest Coast village. Exterior space in the village, public or common space, appears to have been used for a variety of activities. While the large, crescent-shaped back midden was likely designated for refuse disposal and human burial, the front midden bears evidence of these activities and more, including processing and manufacturing. The front midden appears to have been, truly, a common area in the village. Fish remains are abundant in both exterior middens. Those fish that were not caught and processed elsewhere (which we believe is the case for most of the salmon) were probably brought into the front midden area for processing and then discarded in either the back or front midden. Mammals, as we discuss below, appear to have been handled differently.

Important socioeconomic differences seem to have existed among the houses. While there is little to distinguish Houses D and E, which may be interpreted as low-status or at least non-high-status houses, House O is markedly different. The floor area of this house was 40 percent to 50 percent larger than that of other houses in the village. The floor deposit appeared thicker than the other two excavated houses, which may suggest a longer period of occupation for House O, although this is not supported by the radiocarbon dates. The floor itself was unique in that marine clay was brought in and used as a floor covering. House O had a feasting hearth and a higher frequency of wealth or high-status items – including a labret, nephrite, and obsidian – then did the other houses. Each of these observations is consistent with the postulate that House O was a high-status (or perhaps *the* high-status) house in the village – a chief's house, as the senior author has argued elsewhere (Coupland 1999). This hypothesis may be supported by the faunal remains, which clearly distinguish House O from House D. The main difference between these two houses is the higher proportion of mammal remains in House O. Most of the identified mammal remains in House O are from cervids. Dogs and sea mammals, which, so far, are exclusive to House O, are also represented. Among the Tsimshian, hunting, both on land and at sea, has traditionally been considered an activity fit for high-status, or real, people – *smigigyet* (Seguin 1984a:326). Boas (1916:435) states that an ordinary road to wealth was through success in sea hunting or in land hunting. One possibility is that the feasting menu of House O may have favoured fresh cooked meat from mammals (both marine and terrestrial), which might also account for the high percentage of burned mammal bone in the assemblage.

Within House O we find some evidence of a back-to-front status gradient. Wealth or high-status items were found exclusively in the back half of the house, where, historically, the house leader resided. Faunal remains were also denser in the back half of the house and showed more species diversity. The back half also contained most or all of the rare items, including birds, sea mammals, and lynx. Again, this is consistent with people of higher social status being located in the back of the house.

The picture of the prehistoric Northwest Coast village is slowly becoming clearer as the household archaeology approach is adopted by more and more researchers in the area (see, for example, Mackie and Williamson, Chapter 5, this volume; Matson, Chapter 4, this volume; and the symposium on Northwest Coast household archaeology at the 1999 Society for American Archaeology meetings). McNichol Creek, at the dawn of the late prehistoric period on the North Coast, shows some aspects of early ethnographic period village life but not all. For example, use of space within the village was organized according to definite rules, with clear distinctions between open and enclosed spaces. We also see some socioeconomic diversity among the households, especially between House O and the others. Most of the houses, however, are still much smaller than their historic counterparts, which suggests that important changes in household organization, perhaps related to changes in the system of social ranking, occurred during the late prehistoric period. We still have little sense from the archaeological evidence of how social rank was determined at McNichol Creek 1,500 years ago, or of the importance of rank differences in village life. In summary, we are making steady progress towards a better understanding of socioeconomic organization in pre-European contact Northwest Coast villages, but there is still a long way to go.

Note
1 Analyses of faunal remains from House E and faunal and artifact remains from House K were just beginning at the time this chapter was written and are, therefore, not reported here.

7
Dimensions of Regional Interaction in the Prehistoric Gulf of Georgia
Colin Grier

Thirty years ago Donald Mitchell (1971a) argued that the Gulf of Georgia constitutes a distinct region in terms of its natural, ethnographic, and archaeological character (Figure 7.1). Mitchell placed most faith in his conclusions concerning the region's ecological distinctiveness. However, subsequent ethnographic and archaeological research in the Gulf of Georgia has largely corroborated Mitchell's observations, and research has since turned to considering the cultural processes that produced the unique character of Gulf of Georgia societies.

Suttles (1990c:14) has attributed the cultural distinctiveness of the region, at least in part, to the spatial extent and intensity of intraregional social networks in which Gulf of Georgia groups participated. Ethnographically, widespread movements of Gulf of Georgia peoples produced spatially extensive areas of interaction and exchange (Barnett 1955; Mitchell 1971a; Suttles 1998). Groups from various areas of the Gulf of Georgia region travelled significant distances and maintained strong intercommunity ties with affines (individuals related through marriage) throughout the region (Suttles 1987c). An important aspect of these long-distance relations was economic; they worked to redistribute spatially and temporally clumped resources. However, the social and political component of these interactions was also critical. Exclusive affinal relations among high-status individuals from various communities and households formed an important basis for defining a "noble class" within central Coast Salish societies (Suttles 1987b; 1987c).

Archaeological investigations provide some sense of the antiquity of regional interaction and exchange in the Gulf of Georgia (e.g., Brown 1996; Burley 1980). A variety of archaeological materials are widely distributed throughout the region from roughly the Locarno Beach/Middle Pacific period (that is, after 3500 BP), indicating substantial antiquity to the movement of people and goods throughout the region (Burley 1980; Carlson 1994). However, investigating the nature of prehistoric interactions in the

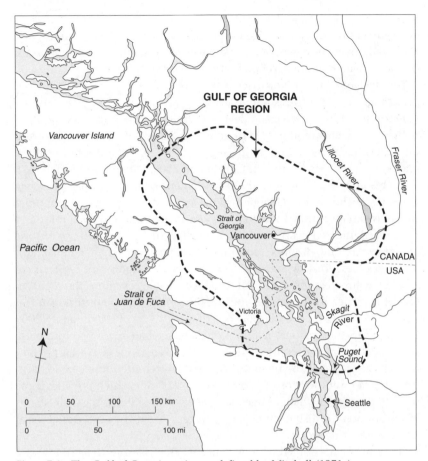

Figure 7.1   The Gulf of Georgia region as defined by Mitchell (1971a).

region is not well served by projecting ethnographically described exchange systems on to these data. There are numerous reasons to be skeptical about this approach, and these are discussed for the Gulf of Georgia region in the next section. The problem for archaeologists is to identify not only the antiquity of exchange and interactions in Gulf of Georgia prehistory but also to employ archaeological data rather than strictly ethnographic models to reconstruct the development and history of regional social networks.

The investigation of how regional exchange systems developed and changed over time has implications that reach beyond the Gulf of Georgia. The existence of regionally distinct cultural expressions within a coast-wide cultural pattern suggests that regional networks may have been important factors that structured the development of the prehistoric cultural landscape. The scale of major changes on the prehistoric Northwest Coast was often coast-wide, where similar developments such as the appearance of large houses and cranial deformation as a marker of status appeared along large areas of the coast within short periods of time. In order to understand these widespread processes of change, we need to view the problem in terms of phenomena that are appropriate to the scale of the events.

The development of Northwest Coast socioeconomic organization can be viewed in light of research elsewhere that suggests that increasing regional interactions preface the development of strong social and political networks (usually accompanied by accelerated flows of material goods) and ultimately hierarchical social forms, regionally integrated economic systems, and polity formation (Graves and Spielmann 2000; Johnson and Earle 1987).

In this chapter, I consider the development of intraregional exchange networks in the Gulf of Georgia region, focusing not on the commodities themselves but on how these networks developed into more complex and regularized interactions through time. I review the situation in the historic period, where long-distance movements and an elite exchange network of social ties (described by Suttles [1987b]) promoted significant regional coherence among central Coast Salish groups. I then examine the archaeological evidence for exchange and interactions in the prehistoric Gulf of Georgia, focusing on the Marpole period (2500-1000 BP). By roughly 2000 BP, it appears that regional relations of exchange had developed into more substantial social and political networks that spread ideas as well as commodities throughout the region. I then present recently obtained archaeological data from the Dionisio Point site (c. 1500 BP), which provides some sense of the way in which a large Marpole-age village site in the Gulf Islands of southwestern British Columbia may have articulated with regional social and economic networks.

These site data, coupled with evidence for the widespread distribution of Marpole iconography in stone sculpture, suggest that the nature of interaction had, by the Marpole period, become more substantive than simple long-distance exchange, facilitating the spread of ideas and cultural practices. Overall, data remain thin and unsynthesized (though see Ames and Maschner 1999:165-174 for a recent discussion), and thus only general statements can be made concerning the nature of prehistoric regional networks. Yet, these data point to the need to investigate generalized exchange networks as the precursor to more formalized networks of social and political relations that ultimately supported social stratification on the later prehistoric and ethnographic Northwest Coast.

Gulf of Georgia Interactions in the Historic Period

Detailed evidence concerning regional interactions in the Gulf of Georgia comes through ethnographic and historical records that document patterns of long-distance movement and exchange following European contact (Suttles 1998). These data indicate that many central Coast Salish groups practised an extensive pattern of seasonal movements within the Gulf of Georgia region, serially exploiting resources that became available throughout the region over the course of a year (Barnett 1955; Mitchell 1971a; Suttles 1990b).

Ethnographies provide useful description of the movements of Hul'qumi'num-speaking groups from southeast Vancouver Island and the southern Gulf Islands (Hul'qumi'num is also referred to as Island Halkomelem, as it is the dialect of the larger Halkomelem language family spoken by groups based in the islands). As part of their seasonal round, which Mitchell (1971a:27) estimates to have covered between 200 and 300 miles (320 to 480 kilometres), island-based Hul'qumi'num groups, including primarily the Cowichan, Nanaimo, and Chemainus, moved in summer from their territory on the west side of the Strait of Georgia to the Lower Fraser River (Figure 7.2) (Barnett 1955; Mitchell 1971a; Rozen 1985; Suttles 1990b, 1998). Large numbers of salmon were obtained during Fraser River spawning periods, and these fish were dried and returned as stores to the islands. Stored salmon provided household subsistence during the sedentary, winter months when local resources were not abundant.

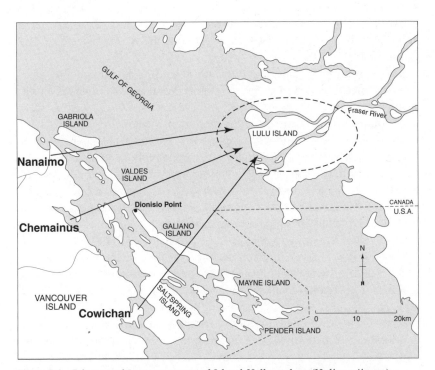

Figure 7.2 Ethnographic movements of Island Halkomelem (Hul'qumi'num) groups across the Strait of Georgia to the Fraser River.

Ethnographic sources indicate that the movement of population to the Fraser River was also substantial. Barnett (1955:22) notes that all the able-bodied Cowichan left for the Fraser River. Hill-Tout (1907) indicates hundreds of Vancouver Island people would catch and dry salmon on the Fraser. At Fort Langley in 1828, McMillan (cited in Duff 1952:25) noted 400 canoes of Cowichan passing by on the Fraser River in just one day. Supporting these accounts of large-scale population movements are records of a number of summer villages in the Fraser Delta area identified as either belonging to or inhabited by island-based Hul'qumi'num peoples (Barnett 1955; Duff 1952; Rozen 1985; Suttles 1998:169). Overall estimates of the number of Nanaimo, Chemainus, and Cowichan that travelled to the Fraser Delta on a yearly basis are as high as 1,500 (Suttles 1998:172). Barnett (1955:22) adds that only a nominal number of Hul'qumi'num people remained behind in the islands to maintain a presence at winter village locations.

While participation in the Fraser fishery was an integral aspect of Hul'qumi'num movements, the aggregation of normally widespread groups on the Fraser River in the summer brought far-flung groups together at various times and places, facilitating trade, marriages, feasting, and exchange (Mitchell and Donald 2001). In the historic period, trade was promoted by the availability of European goods at Fort Langley on the Lower Fraser River beginning in the 1820s (Suttles 1998). Trade at the fort likely broadened existing trade, contact, and alliances between the Aboriginal groups that gathered there (174).

Contact among widespread groups in the context of regional movement and exchange provided an avenue to maintain and expand intercommunity political relations. Suttles (1987b:18-21; 1987c:210-220) has described the ethnographic central Coast Salish noble class as a regionally recognized peer group of elite affines mutually supported by a network of exclusive inter-elite exchange relations. This elite exchange network facilitated exchanges of food, wealth, ritual knowledge, rights of access to resources, and the construction of alliances and marriages. These exchanges promoted regional elite solidarity and the exclusion of lower-class people from access to status resources. This elite exchange system served to reproduce the social stratification evident in ethnographic central Coast Salish societies.

It is clear that regional interactions in the historic period Gulf of Georgia were qualitatively more significant than simple material exchange in commodities. The regional social network of exchange relations was an integral aspect of Coast Salish society. However, the data from which these observations derive have minimal time depth and provide little information on the development of patterns of interaction prior to European contact or how they were affected by changes in population dynamics in the region following European contact.

The historic period pattern of interaction and population movement has been used to interpret archaeological data and suggests that similar patterns of population movement (e.g., Burley 1989) and regional social networks (e.g., Brown 1996) existed as early as 2000 BP. However, caution seems warranted in applying the historic situation to archaeological data. Loss of population resulting from diseases introduced by Europeans may have shifted long-standing territorial relationships and patterns of movement (Suttles 1998:170). Depopulation of areas of the Fraser River Delta may have only recently allowed the establishment of villages on the mainland by Hul'qumi'num groups from the islands.

The draw of European trade goods at Fort Langley may also have significantly altered patterns of movement on the Lower Fraser River. Most island-based groups appear to have included Fort Langley in their summer travels. Whether this location was visited by island groups in the summer prior to the establishment of Fort Langley is unclear. In light of these factors, it is useful to consider archaeological evidence for regional interaction in prehistory, working towards the present rather than back from the present into the past.

Evidence for Regional Interactions in the Prehistoric Gulf of Georgia

The extent and nature of prehistoric regional interaction and exchange within the Gulf of Georgia region is documented primarily through the distribution of various forms of material culture produced within the region as well as the occurrence of extraregional resources in Gulf of Georgia archaeological sites. The earliest evidence for inter- and intraregional exchange is provided by data indicating that significant obsidian exchange networks existed along the coast as early as 6000 BP (Carlson 1994). The distribution of sourced obsidian indicates that material originating in various areas of the Northwest Coast was distributed widely, including within the Gulf of Georgia, by 4000 BP. Nephrite, used extensively in adze blades, is also found widely throughout the region by 2500 BP. Nephrite cannot be attributed to a specific source, though much of this material appears to have originated from the Fraser Canyon roughly 300 kilometres inland (Carlson 1994:337; Galm 1994:294-297).

The widespread distribution of obsidian and nephrite does not directly indicate either that extensive long-distance movement was involved in resource procurement or that highly formalized exchange networks existed to distribute these materials. It does suggest, however, that a significant degree of social connectivity prevailed along the coast and within the Gulf of Georgia.

Obsidian was a practical commodity in that it provided material for the manufacture of chipped tools with sharp cutting edges, and nephrite was used in the important coast woodworking industry. Relatively early evidence of extraregional exchange of materials that were less specifically utilitarian also exists for the Gulf of Georgia. The occurrence of steatite (soapstone) labrets at the Pender Canal site in the Gulf Islands in deposits dating to roughly 3500 BP indicates that soapstone, likely from the Fraser Canyon area (Galm 1994), was moving down the Fraser River by this time.

Exchange in extralocal marine shells, particularly west coast dentalia, became significant by 2500 BP. These materials are found inland some distance, suggesting they may have moved against inland lithic materials such as steatite and nephrite (Burley 1980; Galm 1994). As marine shells generally were non-utilitarian materials, their widespread distribution suggests that trade had come to include prestige or wealth materials that may have been used as a means to mark some form of social differentiation. This is strongly suggested by the occurrence of large numbers of dentalia shell in mortuary contexts after 2500 BP (Burley 1989; Burley and Knusel 1989).

While significant evidence for the exchange of utilitarian and prestige materials is found in the Gulf of Georgia between roughly 4000 and 2500 BP, these archaeological patterns cannot be used to support the interpretation that more than generalized patterns of down-the-line long-distance trade existed. The exchange networks through which materials were distributed appear to have extended well beyond the Gulf of Georgia and provide little indication that the Gulf of Georgia itself had developed into a coherent region of interaction by 2500 BP.

Intraregional exchange relations do appear to become qualitatively different by the Marpole phase. The Marpole phase (2500-1000 BP) is considered by many researchers as the period during which Gulf of Georgia societies developed many of the core cultural institutions that persisted into the historic period (Matson and Coupland 1995:241-242; Mitchell 1971a:52-56). In the Marpole period large plank houses appear, as does evidence for ascribed, hereditary social inequality. The exploitation of salmon was intensified, perhaps to its greatest extent in Northwest Coast prehistory (Burley 1980:55; Matson 1992; Mitchell 1971a:52).

Marpole artifact styles and assemblage patterning are broadly similar across the Gulf of Georgia region, suggesting a level of homogeneity to Marpole phase cultures that may be the product of intraregional social interaction and exchange of material resources (Burley 1980; Matson 1974; Matson and Coupland 1995:211-218). Burley (1979) has noted the occurrence of substantial non-local obsidian in Marpole-phase assemblages throughout the Gulf of Georgia, as well as large quantities of dentalia shell in graves at sites such as False Narrows in the Gulf Islands (Burley 1989), indicating that extralocal goods remained desirable.

However, it is during the Marpole phase that we see the distribution of material culture that appears to reflect the spread of ideas as well as commodities throughout the region. Duff (1956) has investigated the distribution of prehistoric stone sculpture in the Gulf of Georgia region. Most dated examples of this sculpture are Marpole in age (Holm 1990). Duff identifies consistencies in the form and style of sculpted bowls over a large region extending from the Fraser Canyon to Vancouver Island. Given the likely ceremonial function of much of this sculpture, this unity of iconographic style has been used to infer a broad area of shared ideological precepts. The distribution of the sculptural style is also similar to the ethnographic distribution of the Coast Salish language group (Brown 1996; Duff 1956).

Brown (1996) has identified similarities in Marpole earthen burial mound construction that suggest shared cultural practices across the Halkomelem-speaking area at this time. The similarities in construction and design of large earthen mounds from the Lower Fraser Valley, primarily at the Scowlitz site and at Comiaken on southeastern Vancouver Island, indicate that mortuary practices were similar over a broad region. These burial mounds contain high-status burials, implying that the interaction that spread conventions of mound construction occurred primarily among elites. Brown argues that this situation is consistent with the elite exchange model presented initially by Suttles (1987b), in which elites exchange non-local material resources and symbols of power through a system of intervillage marriage alliances.

Examination of the distribution of representation in sculpture and elite mortuary practices indicates that significant exchange of information as well as material resources occurred during the Marpole phase in the Gulf of Georgia region. Both Ames and Maschner (1999:165-174) and Renfrew (1986) have argued that consistency of material culture across regions results in part from the need to have a common yardstick by which concepts such as status and authority may be displayed, perceived, measured, and ordered. Some level of standardization or regularization of cultural notions, and perhaps mechanisms of regional interaction, is thus implied by the widespread distribution of consistent ideological concepts embodied by material culture. These data may be used to posit that, during the Marpole phase, sociopolitical systems, rather than simply exchange systems, were becoming regional in scope.

How such developments were tied to other developments in Marpole societies – the appearance of large plank houses, the use of cranial deformation to mark social status, and the development of large-scale storage economies – remains unclear. Marpole phase societies provide the earliest convincing evidence for ascribed, hereditary status distinctions in the Gulf of Georgia (Burley and Knusel 1989), and the development of an entrenched elite likely occurred in concert with economic intensification and production of a surplus (Hayden 1994). An important question is whether the increasing regional nature of social systems inferred for Marpole societies was tied to the development of a regional surplus economy centred on the Fraser River – an economy in which widespread Gulf of Georgia groups participated.

There is currently little evidence available to address this question, which would require documenting movements of people either directly to the Fraser River or transport of Fraser River salmon to outlying areas. Both processes may be invisible at the resolution archaeological data offer. Below, I consider recently obtained data from the Dionisio Point village site that provide some indication of how groups from the Gulf Islands may have participated in regional interactions in the Marpole phase as well as of how closely these groups were tied to developments along the Fraser River.

Dionisio Point: Evidence for Regional Interaction

Investigations of the nature of prehistoric interaction in the Gulf of Georgia must consider regional distributions of various forms of material culture and resources. Yet it is also useful to explore data from individual sites in detail in order to glean insights into how various areas of the prehistoric Gulf of Georgia were connected to larger regional networks. Data from recent excavations at the Dionisio Pont site provide a means to assess in what ways and to what degree Marpole phase Gulf Island groups participated in social and economic networks outside of their local context.

The Dionisio Point site (DgRv 3) is located on the northern end of Galiano Island. Galiano Island is one of the southern Gulf Islands situated in the Strait of Georgia between Vancouver Island and the British Columbia mainland (Figure 7.3). The site includes five sizable house depressions that contain the remains of plank houses with floor areas that ranged from 200 to 400 square metres (Figure 7.4). While the contemporaneous occupation of all houses has not been directly demonstrated, the site can reasonably be described as a village (Grier 2001). House 2, with thirteen carbon dates derived from a variety of house features, has been securely dated to 1500 BP and was likely occupied for at least a century (Grier 2001:125).

Four of the five house depressions are situated on three prominent terraces. Approximately 2 to 3 metres of elevation separate one terrace from the next. The fifth depression sits by itself on a lower and much less defined terrace area immediately behind the active beach. Terracing to create level platforms to accommodate large houses created a distinctly step-like form from the original gradual slope, and the build-up of ridges of shell midden around the house perimeters (presumably) during occupation of the village site further accentuated the house depression outlines. This considerable architectural investment and significant duration of occupation indicate substantial settlement at this location.

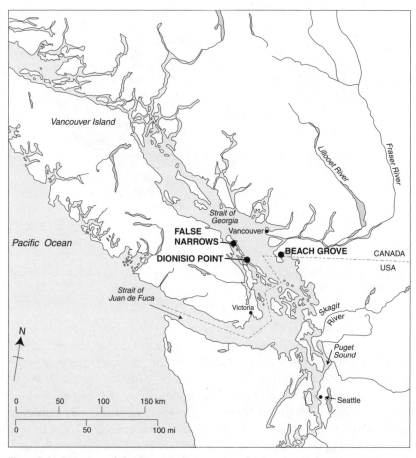

Figure 7.3   Location of the Dionisio Point site and other sites referred to in the text.

Two field seasons of excavation, one in 1997 and the other in 1998, were undertaken at the Dionisio Point site. Excavations sampled two houses, one extensively (House 2) and one modestly (House 5). These excavations produced relatively fine-grained information concerning the spatial and architectural nature of House 2 and recovered artifact and faunal material from its interior. In total, 77 square metres of the roughly 200 square metres of interior space (just under 40 percent of the interior area) in House 2 was excavated down to, and in some cases into, basal non-cultural beach gravel underlying the house occupation deposits.

The faunal assemblage recovered from the House 2 excavations provides some indication that salmon played an important role in the household economy and, coupled with other lines of inference, that this importance

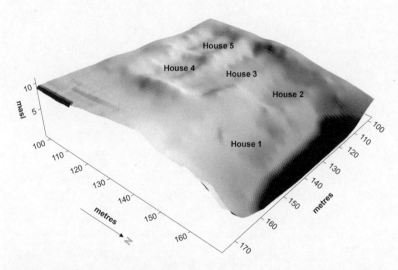

Figure 7.4 Surface map of the Dionisio Point (DgRv 3) site, showing the five house depressions known to exist there.

may be attributed to the consumption of Fraser River salmon resources. An intensive quantitative analysis has not yet been completed for the House 2 faunal assemblage. However, data describing the presence/absence of seven classes of faunal remains in house excavation contexts are available and provide a useful though coarse picture of the relative distribution of seven classes of fauna throughout House 2. Six classes of faunal taxa appear in more than half the forty-four House 2 excavation contexts. These include salmon (31/44), herring (36/44), other fish (36/44, which at Dionisio Point, included primarily rockfish [*Sebastes* spp.] and dogfish [*Squalus acanthias*] but little halibut or other flatfish), bird (26/44), and shell (23/44). Land mammal was particularly widespread among excavation contexts (42/44), while sea mammal was very restricted in its occurrence (3/44). Less quantified observations indicate that salmon vertebrae are relatively common in the contexts in which they appear.

While these data are nominal in scale and should be weighted accordingly, they do indicate that salmon, the only resource that does not occur in significant numbers within a few kilometres of the village site, is generally as abundant (at least in terms of the number of contexts in which it is present) as are local fish, bird, mammal, and shellfish resources. This use of extralocal salmon suggests that at least the one investigated household at Dionisio Point obtained an economically significant resource from a relatively distant location.

A general sense of the season of occupation of the site can be gleaned from the faunal assemblage, which bears on how much emphasis was placed on stored resources. Historically, in the Gulf Islands herring spawned in late winter/early spring (Matson and Coupland 1995:22). The abundance of herring bone in House 2 at Dionisio Point suggests that the residents were at the Dionisio Point village at least during the spring when herring spawned. Spring is also the time during which fresh salmon availability is low in the Strait of Georgia and Fraser River system (Kew 1992:109-111). These observations suggest a winter-through-spring village occupation that relied on stored salmon from fall fishing and subsequently fresh spawning herring in the spring. This pattern is consistent with a variety of ethnographic descriptions of Hul'qumi'num seasonal rounds and sedentary winter-season plankhouse villages in which salmon stores sustained sedentary occupation through the winter (Barnett 1955; Burley 1989; Duff 1952; Suttles 1998).

The substantial architecture that existed at the site can also be seen in light of Ames's (1996:134) argument that the existence of large houses implies significant storage since it would have been difficult, if not impossible, to support large households throughout the winter in most areas of the coast without some form of stored resource. This observation is particularly relevant to residential locations situated away from large salmon-bearing rivers, as was the case with Dionisio Point.

Together these observations support the inference that the occupation at Dionisio Point was focused to a significant degree on salmon fishing and storage, in addition to local resources. However, no lines of evidence point to this salmon as being Fraser River salmon specifically. There are smaller salmon-bearing rivers on the east coast of Vancouver Island, such as the Nanaimo, Cowichan, and Chemainus, that could have been the source of salmon. However, these rivers support fewer species and thus have less abundant and more temporally restricted runs, which ethnographically, were exploited *in conjunction* with Fraser River runs.

It is difficult to evaluate whether the quantity of salmon available in Vancouver Island rivers alone would have provided a basis for a successful storage economy. However, the physical location of the Dionisio Point village, unlike those located directly on these rivers, appears to provide access to both Vancouver Island and mainland salmon-fishing locations. Dionisio Point is roughly the same distance from the north arm of the Fraser River (22 kilometres) as it is from the Nanaimo River (24 kilometres) and the Cowichan River (21 kilometres). To the extent that intensive, surplus economic production was a concern for Marpole groups in the Gulf Islands, the Fraser River would have offered significantly greater returns than would Vancouver Island rivers.

Another line of evidence for the participation of Dionisio Point households in broader Gulf of Georgia interactions comes in the form of symbolic regional culture. Two pecked and ground stone bowls with incised human faces were recovered from the interior of House 2 (Figure 7.5). The

0   5   10 cm

Figure 7.5 Anthropomorphic incised stone bowls from House 2.

two bowls were found upright in their typical use position, suggesting that they were in situ, abandoned either in storage or use context. Why these items were abandoned is not clear; neither was broken or significantly damaged.

The class of portable stone sculpture to which these two bowls belong has been the subject of extensive study, particularly in the seminal work of Wilson Duff (1956). Many of these objects are known to exist throughout the Gulf of Georgia region. Yet few of these objects have been recovered from well documented archaeological contexts (Burley 1980; Duff 1956), and none has previously been recovered from interior house deposits. They are generally believed to be primarily a Marpole-period artifact, though few have been dated directly.

Both bowls conform generally to Duff's Type III Bowls with Human Heads (Duff 1956:22). Duff defined this class of artifact as boulders carved in the shape of a human head, where the whole figure is conceived as a head, with the face covering one side and the depression in the top (1956:69). Two other of these human head bowls have been found in the vicinity of Dionisio Point, one being described only as from Valdes Island (the island north of Galiano) and the other from Cowichan Gap (Porlier Pass), on which the Dionisio Point site is situated.

A human head carved in a style similar to the Dionisio Point bowls but without evidence of a bowl was recovered from the Marpole component (FNII) at False Narrows (Burley 1989:93-95). Duff (1956:71) links Type III human head bowls to the seated human figure bowls that were elaborately carved in soapstone. Focusing on breakage near its bottom, Burley (1989:95) describes the False Narrows head as perhaps having been part of a human seated figure bowl. If true, this would link the human head bowls seen at Dionisio Point very closely with the steatite human figure bowls found along the Lower Fraser River.

Both examples from Dionisio Point are round to oval in overall shape, with a flattened surface on the bottom for stability. Pecked into the top is a shallow depression. In both, the depression is roughly circular in shape and conical in profile but flat-bottomed. On a flattened end of each bowl is a face consisting of two eyes, a nose, and a mouth.

The exact use of incised or carved stone bowls as a class of sculpture remains enigmatic, but most evidence points to a function in ritual. Similar bowls were not in use among historic period Coast Salish groups, though limited ethnographic references to these sculptures unquestionably associate them with ritual, shamanism, spiritual knowledge, and power (Duff 1956:55-59). The actual usable bowl area is certainly too small to have been used in preparing any significant amount of foodstuffs (Drucker 1951:90). However, they would have been suitable for grinding and preparing a modest amount of plant or mineral substances (Duff 1956:55). The stone bowl from the southwest area of House 2 was found to be heavily stained with ochre, with staining occurring within the bowl, on the exterior surface, and on the incised face itself. No sizable pieces of ochre were recovered from the interior or in the immediate vicinity of the bowl, though four pieces of ochre were recovered from excavation units elsewhere in House 2. Ochre preparations and pastes were used ethnographically (and are still used) in many ceremonial and ritual contexts as a body application to provide protection against spiritual entities and pollution. Prehistorically, ochre is found in burials and thus had a role in funerary rites (Burley and Knusel 1989:6).

Most of the finer examples of Marpole sculpture found on the Lower Fraser River, such as the elaborate seated human figure bowls, were manufactured from steatite that originated in the Fraser Canyon. Gulf Islands examples are generally manufactured from locally available sandstone rather than steatite (Duff 1956:48-49), as is the case with the two bowls from Dionisio Point. This suggests local Gulf Islands emulation or adoption of a style of symbolism that had a regional currency, but which Duff argues originated in the Lower Fraser region (1956:71).

These observations suggest that the Dionisio Point House 2 household was drawing upon a Marpole regional ritual-symbolic system and that they had some access to symbolic resources that appear to have been associated most strongly with the Fraser River. Coupled with inferences that large-scale use and storage of salmon was conducted at Dionisio Point, the available evidence suggests that the Dionisio Point household was significantly connected to economic, social, and perhaps political networks that extended beyond their local context.

Archaeological Implications

As Carlson (1994) suggests, addressing the nature of intraregional as opposed to extraregional exchange can be challenging as there are often few materials that can be pinpoint sourced, and many commodities that were traded, particularly on the Northwest Coast, may have been perishable (e.g., subsistence goods). Without specific commodities to track, it is necessary to make inferences concerning the nature of exchange relations through ancillary data and broader inferences concerning social systems. For example, while I have posited that Gulf Island groups as early as the Marpole phase may have obtained and consumed significant levels of Fraser River salmon, there are few direct lines of archaeological evidence that could be used to unambiguously mark the presence of prehistoric island-based Hul'qumi'num populations on the mainland. Consequently, more indirect approaches to the problem are necessary.

One possible avenue to explore is the effect of economic intensification on house size in the Gulf Islands. The household, as a basic social institution in most societies, is linked to social and economic processes that operate at a variety of scales. Household size and composition responds to the broader patterns of economic and social organization (Ashmore and Wilk 1988; Wilk and Rathje 1982). In the prehistoric Gulf of Georgia, as on the Northwest Coast in general, large households provided the labour to carry out complexly organized tasks, including fishing for and drying salmon. Salmon storage economies involved consumption of a large quantity of dried salmon over the winter months, and this delayed consumption would also have required a mechanism to distribute stores to those who contributed labour to production. An important function of most households involves managing the distribution of resources for its members. The distribution of stored salmon resources was thus likely a household issue; in societies on the Northwest Coast, control over subsistence resources generally occurred at this level (Ames 1995, 1996).

If groups from the islands were involved in a regional economy focused on the Fraser River, what effect would this have had on house size and household organization in the Gulf Islands? The Dionisio Point and False Narrows sites indicate that large households existed in the Gulf Islands by the Marpole phase. The development of large households in the Gulf of Georgia region may have been a product of multiple factors. However, if during Marpole times households were assuming a greater role in the distribution and control of stored resources due to a greater reliance on stored salmon, then this would exert upward pressure on household and house size. When delayed consumption of resources occurs (as with stored salmon), this process depends "for [its] operation on sets of ordered, differentiated, jurally-defined relationships through which crucial goods and services are transmitted" (Woodburn 1988:33). Those who produced salmon stores in summer would have expected to be included in the distribution network, and so those involved in production required social ties that ensured access to salmon stores in the winter when they were consumed. The network of production-based relations therefore forms the basis for an appropriate household distribution network. A larger production unit for salmon fishing and processing may have meant larger distribution networks and thus larger households.

Following this logic, we would expect relatively large houses to occur in the Marpole-phase archaeological record of the Gulf Islands only if these groups were involved in substantial surplus production and storage. Two Marpole-age village sites with house depressions from the Gulf Islands – False Narrows on Gabriola Island (Burley 1989; Mitchell 1967) and Dionisio Point (Grier 2001; Mitchell 1971b) – are of mid-Marpole age and are similar in their overall layout, having large house depressions on multiple long benches (Figure 7.4).

Beach Grove, a Marpole-age site in the Fraser Delta area, contained perhaps ten house depressions when first recorded. At present only two of these depressions (numbered 3 and 4 on Figure 7.6) remain relatively intact. A topographic map and measurements of these and several other partial depressions were produced with the aid of a total station EDM in March of 2000. When compared with previous sketch maps that depict areas of the site now lost (e.g., Figure 7.4a in Matson and Coupland [1995:207]), depressions 3 and 4 appear representative of the range of depression sizes that once existed at the site.

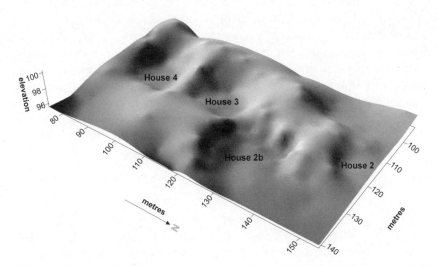

Figure 7.6 Surface map of the remaining depressions at the Beach Grove site (DgRs 1). House numbering follows that used in Figure 7.4a in Matson and Coupland (1995:207), with the exception of 2b, which was not identified as a house depression there. Note that the vertical axis values are not masl values but are relative to the mapping datum, which was arbitrarily set at 100 metres.

A comparison of the similarly aged sites of Dionisio Point in the islands (Figure 7.4) and Beach Grove on the mainland (Figure 7.6), reveals that the Gulf Island houses appear as large or larger. Of the five house depressions at Dionisio Point, four have inside measurements of roughly 20 metres by 10 metres (200 square metres) while the largest is approximately 40 metres by 10 metres (400 square metres). At Beach Grove, the inside diameter of depression 3 measures 13 by 10 metres (roughly 130 square metres) while depression 4 measures 11 metres by 11 metres (121 square metres). The sample of Marpole-age sites with defined house depressions is quite small for the Gulf of Georgia and unfortunately is likely to remain so, preventing widespread comparisons. Nevertheless, houses appear overall to be quite large in the Gulf Islands region in the Marpole period, equivalent to or larger in size than those in the Fraser River area on the mainland, despite expectations that the largest houses should occur in areas with immediate access to abundant resources.

The critical question is whether the development of large houses in the Gulf Islands came about through entirely local processes. My contention here is that large houses did not develop in isolation in the Gulf Islands. There are no salmon rivers in the Gulf Islands that approach the economic potential of the Fraser, and no salmon-bearing rivers in the immediate vicinity of Dionisio Point itself. The Cowichan and Nanaimo rivers on the east coast of Vancouver Island had significant salmon runs, but even when they are considered together the Fraser River still offered a much more reliable, diverse, and abundant source of potential surplus.

If the appearance of large houses reflects the increasing role of households in carrying out processes of intensive production and delayed distribution of stores, then salmon acquisition from the Fraser River was highly influential on household size and organization. This is not to suggest that large households resulted solely from either salmon intensification or economic ties to the Fraser River, but it seems difficult to argue that developments in the Gulf Islands from the Marpole period onward were unconnected to the resources available on the Fraser River.

Conclusion

Existing data, though thin, suggests that by the Marpole phase significant changes had occurred in the kinds of regional interactions that existed earlier in the Gulf of Georgia region. The generalized exchange networks that moved commodities into and through the region prior to 2500 BP appear to have developed into or become embedded in more substantial intraregional relations that spread ideas and symbolic material culture throughout the Gulf of Georgia. This suggests a coherence or unity to the Gulf of Georgia region that is not visible in the earlier archaeological record of the region and that may reflect the development, as Mitchell suggested, of the Gulf of Georgia as a distinct cultural area after roughly 2500 BP.

Suttles (1990b) and Ames and Maschner (1999:165) suggest that there is significant time depth to the regional patterns of inter- and intraregional trade both in the Gulf of Georgia and for other regions along the coast. Clearly, by the Marpole phase interactions within the Gulf of Georgia were qualitatively more substantial than those of simple long-distance exchange. The long-term development of these more substantial Gulf of Georgia interactions appears to be tied temporally to other major developments, such as the appearance of large houses and ascribed inequality both within the region and on the Northwest Coast in general. Careful consideration of the spatial and temporal dynamics of regional interaction systems, and how we may study them archaeologically, will be critical to advancing models for the evolution of coastal societies.

The main limitation to what we can and currently do know is that of data. Acknowledging this reality requires viewing the interpretations provided here as a framework of potentially useful questions rather than specific conclusions. However, avenues that have yet to be explored, such as a broader examination of settlement patterns outside of the Fraser River area, should prove fruitful to pursue. For example, why do large villages such as Dionisio Point and False Narrows occur in the outer, easternmost Gulf Islands during Marpole times? Is this an indication that settlement patterns were oriented with respect to access to the Fraser River? Or are these villages simply the expansion of settlement due to population increases on Vancouver Island? These questions bear directly on how integrated Gulf of Georgia economic and social relations had become at various junctures in prehistory. Thirty years ago Don Mitchell (1971a:29) argued that Gulf of Georgia settlement patterns and economies could be understood with respect to their relationship with economic and cultural developments that centred on the Fraser River. A significant amount of work remains to be done to evaluate how far into prehistory this statement applies.

8

The Cultural Taphonomy of Nuu-chah-nulth Whale Bone Assemblages

Gregory G. Monks

The bones [of whales] received no special treatment. They were simply piled in heaps onto middens and there remained to be discovered and analyzed by scholars.

– Webb 1988:25

Nuu-chah-nulth (Nootkan) whaling has deservedly received much attention in the ethnographic literature of the Northwest Coast. While other groups derived much support for their economic and social systems from abundant salmon runs, the Nuu-chah-nulth derived much of that same support from whales. The cultural importance of whale use and whale hunting to the Nuu-chah-nulth by the time of European contact is well documented (e.g., Drucker 1951; Cavanaugh 1983; Jewitt 1988), but the antiquity of this practice has been investigated only recently (Dewhirst 1980; Calvert 1980; Huelsbeck 1994b; Fiskin 1994; Acheson and Wigen 1996; Monks, McMillan, and St. Claire 2001). Whale bones found in archaeological sites comprise the evidence of Nuu-chah-nulth whale exploitation, but the bones must be transported onto the sites in order for them to become part of the archaeological record. This chapter attempts to discover why whale bones were transported onto sites, why observed modifications to bones were undertaken, and why bones were deposited in specific contexts in sites.

Whales present significant challenges to those who capture them and use their resources. Most people who consider Nuu-chah-nulth whaling focus on the issues of prestige versus subsistence vis-à-vis blubber and whale oil (Dewhirst 1982; Inglis and Haggarty 1983; Cavanaugh 1983); however, whales provide a range of other important resources, such as meat, bone, baleen, sinew, and gut. Bone is the only one of these remains that is found commonly in archaeological sites, and its relationship to the other whale resources and to Nuu-chah-nulth life requires clarification (see also Monks, McMillan, and St. Claire 2001; Monks 2001).

Unlike small and medium-sized animals, but like large terrestrial and marine mammals (Yesner 1995:151), whales cannot be transported in toto onto a site. The best that can be done is to beach the carcass in front of the site, and from there bones and other materials must be carried if there is to be a possibility of their remains being eventually buried in the site. Thus, as with large terrestrial mammals, selection of certain parts for transport requires that decisions be made according to one or more criteria. What are these criteria? To which skeletal elements are they applied? What is/are the benefit(s) that underlies these criteria for these elements? Why bother to transport bones at all if the entire skeleton was frequently available on the beach in front of the site, unlike a distant bison or mammoth kill?

These questions are addressed within the Nuu-chah-nulth region using both ethnographic and archaeological data. In addition, the explanatory potential of utility indices is considered.

The archaeological data to be used in this chapter consist of previously reported material from Ozette (Huelsbeck 1994b; Fiskin 1994) and new material from the Toquaht Archaeological Project (TAP) (Figure 8.1). This project is described in a series of reports (McMillan and St. Claire 1991, 1992, 1994, 1996), and a comprehensive description is found in McMillan (1999:62-75). Five sites spanning the past 4,000 years were excavated as part of the TAP (McMillan 1999:Table 4). The earliest site was Ch'uumat'a (DfSi 4), a major village with direct access to the open ocean. It dates between 4000 ± 140 BP (Beta 98011) and 720 ± 50 BP (Beta 55798), although occupation seems to have been less frequent and/or less dense after c. 2000 BP. Certainly by c. 1200 BP, the site was not much used. This site produced the earliest whale bone, dated to 3480 ± 80 BP (Beta 55800), after which these remains were consistently found throughout the deposits. Occupation seems to have spread to Macoah (DfSi 5) c. 1840 ± 80 BP (Beta 67472) and continued after 580 ± 60 BP (Beta 47310). Very little whale bone was recovered at this site, perhaps not surprisingly considering its distance from the ocean and its reported use as a winter village site. T'ukw'aa (DfSj 23), another open ocean site, emerged as a village (DfSj 23A) c. 1150 ± 90 BP (Beta 55803), and occupation of the adjacent defensive location (DfSj 23B) began c. 780 ± 90 BP (Beta 50030). The youngest date from the village area is 640 ± 60 BP (Beta 67474), but the depth at which the sample was obtained (2 metres below surface) indicates that occupation continued substantially after that date. The most recent date from the defensive location is 150 ± 50 BP (Beta 47313), suggesting a similar late date for the village as well. Whale bones were found throughout the deposits in both the village and the defensive location. Two sites in the George Fraser Islands were tested, DfSj 29 and DfSj 30. Little was produced from the former site, but the latter, possibly a lookout site, revealed a late occupancy from about 440 ± 70 BP (Beta 75887) to at least 260 ± 60 BP (Beta 75888). Few whale remains were recovered, but those few were readily identifiable.

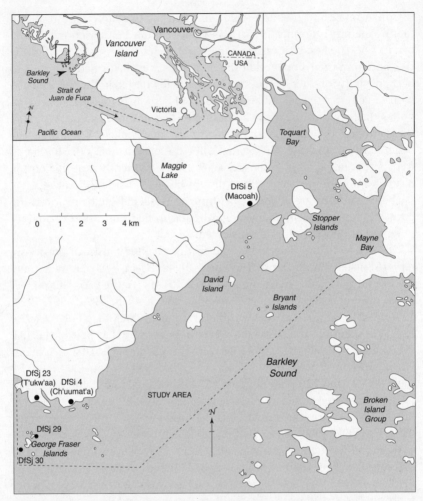

Figure 8.1 Map of the Toquaht Archaeological Project study area.

Data Sources on Whale Bone Utilization

Whales can be thought of as having layered resources, much like layers of an onion, except that each layer contains a set of resources that distinguishes it from the others. The outer layer consists of the skin and blubber inside which is a layer of muscle (meat) and sinew with intramuscular bone (e.g., scapula, vestigial innominates). The next layer contains more meat and connective tissue (sinew, cartilage) and the bulk of the skeletal bone. Finally, viscera and intestinal fat forms the innermost layer/core. Most bone, except for perhaps the forelimb (excluding scapula), is not encountered until after the first layer (skin and blubber) is removed. As the second layer (muscle) is removed, more and more bones become available. Disarticulation of the skeleton, whether partial or complete, produces the bones that may be transported onto the site and provides access to the viscera and intestinal fat (Figure 8.2). The size and weight of the bones alone precludes transporting most of them other than one at a time. Transport of a set of bones, especially with attached blubber and muscle, would be physically difficult, if not impossible, even for a group of men. Sequenced disarticulation by layer and within each layer would have resulted in the most efficient utilization of a whale carcass.

Ethnographic Data

Philip Drucker collected much of the ethnographic material cited below, and later compared to archaeological data, in the late 1930s. By this time, whale stocks had been seriously depleted, disease and warfare had drastically reduced Aboriginal populations, and increasing participation in the Euro-Canadian cash economy had made precontact whaling primarily a thing of memory. The informant testimony received by Drucker consisted of those aspects of precontact whaling that were kept alive in oral history. In most orally transmitted information, however, the important aspects of the event are well preserved, but the mundane aspects of it are blurred or forgotten. With whaling, there is accurate and consistent recollection of how it was done, what the ritual preparations were, who received which piece of blubber for what service, and so on. What was done with the resources apart from blubber and meat, however, is not recalled, except that whalers wanted the skeletons of their kills on the beach in front of their village (Drucker 1950:55). In the remainder of this chapter, the archaeological remains provide new or contradictory information in relation to the ethnographic record, highlighting the effects of selective memory in oral history over a span of around 160 years.

Drucker (1951:39-40, 178-180) states that, once beached, a dead whale was cut up and distributed according to specific rules. The whaler/first harpooner received the choicest piece of blubber, the "saddle," which lies across the back and down the sides of the whale to the ventral pleats, from just in front (4 spans) to just behind (4 spans) the dorsal fin (1951:178). This piece was placed on a rack in front of the whaler's house and was cooked and eaten four days later. The whaler did not eat any of the saddle; instead, it was distributed as a feast. The whaler kept only the tip of the dorsal fin as a trophy (1951:179). "Then portions were given to the whaler's crew, and to his aides and their crews. If men had come to help at towing, they were given pieces. Finally, as the pieces of blubber were cut and laid on the beach, through his speaker the successful hunter gave them away to his tribe, giving in the order of rank, just as in a potlatch" (1951:55). This scenario indicates that, as far as blubber is concerned, all pieces except the saddle were distributed, in the first instance, according to one's role in the hunt. This

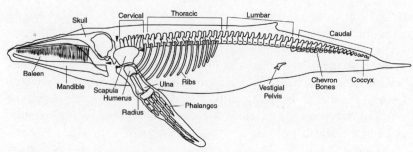

Figure 8.2   Skeleton of a humpback whale (after Kaufman and Forestell 1986), showing primary disarticulation points (arrows).

role, however, was based on social position, so it can be inferred that blubber portions were differentially valued. In the second instance, potlatch rank of non-hunters prevailed for the remaining blubber portions.

In discussing stranded or drift whales, to which a number of chiefs had legitimate claim, Drucker describes for the Kyuquot the priority of rank of claimant and the blubber portion claimed (1951:255). Potlatch seat rank follows the chief's local group affiliation (1951:261, Figure 18):

> The first chief of the confederacy (1) owned both sides of the head; the Tilath chief (12) owned the lower jaw. The Qa'o'ath chief (4) had the right side and the Cawisath chief (3) had the left side of a strip from the blowhole to the saddle in width, from the back to the belly in length. The Tacisath chief (2) owned the right side of the saddle (the same size as described above) and the Qaopincath chief (9) owned the left side of this. One of the Tilath chiefs (21) owned the "right arm"; the informant did not recall who owned the other. Another Tacisath chief (23?), and the A'Licath chief (5) shared right and left halves of a section just behind the saddle. The next section was shared by a Tilath (?) and a Qa'o'ath chief (14). The right side of the tail was owned by a Tilath chief (?); the ownership of the left side (and the belly and tongue also) was not recalled by informants.

Not only does this description provide an indication of how the first layer of the whale was cut up, but it also indicates, in general, the value of each portion of blubber. One might therefore expect that the blubber from a successfully hunted whale would be divided into similar portions, since the saddle remains the same, and that they would be allocated according to their value according to the role played by each harpooner and his crew, then according to the assistance given in towing the dead whale to shore, then according to social rank of those who did not help in the hunt.

The outermost layer (i.e., the skin and blubber) of both hunted and drift whales was thus carefully cut up and allocated according to strict rules.

Figure 8.3   Flensing a whale at Neah Bay. *Photograph by Asahel Curtis; Washington State Historical Society, Tacoma*

Indeed, blubber was cut proportionally so that whales of different sizes always produced the same portions of blubber, albeit of varying size (255). Because blubber and oil were prized resources, their distribution followed and reinforced social organizational positions. The principal whaler (i.e., the one who organized the hunt and who had the right to harpoon first) also had the right (and duty) to distribute the blubber to those who assisted him and to those in his group.

Once the first layer had been removed, the second layer (meat) was exposed (Figure 8.3). Waterman (1967:46) reports that once the blubber had been removed the meat and bones were left on the beach for the birds and other scavengers. Speaking of dead whales that drifted ashore and were claimed by hereditary right, Drucker (1951:39-40) says: "When the blubber had been stripped, and certain choice morsels of meat – the tongue, areas along the lower jaw, the flippers, and the flukes – had been taken by those who owned them, the meat was left for anyone who might want it." Later, he states: "The meat and odd bits of fat belonged to anyone who wanted them" (1951:256). There is an interesting difference between these two sentences in what appears to be meant by "ownership." The first indicates that the whaler left the remainder of the carcass to whoever wanted it, whereas the second states that ownership of the carcass was up for grabs after the blubber had been removed. Which position is correct? This point will be raised again later. Webb (1988:25) asserts, in contrast, that a month was required to render the oil from the blubber (by roasting) and to dry the meat, and that dried whale meat and fish were often served together. He also reports that the Makah considered the meat of minke whales to be excellent food. Meat is therefore an important and highly regarded food, according to Webb, since considerable time was invested in drying it and since it was willingly consumed.

Drucker (1951:40) records that choice morsels of meat were the tongue, areas along the lower jaw, the flippers, and the flukes. These portions, because of their desirability, were also likely to have been distributed according to the recipient's role in the hunt and/or social position. Clearly, the head and the pectoral limbs could be removed at any time after the whale was beached, but the other bones remained concealed until flesh removal occurred. With the removal of meat, progressively more bones became available. First to be exposed would be the scapula, an intramuscular bone, then, with further meat removal, the axial skeletal elements would be exposed. With the skeleton exposed, further meat removal would necessarily involve isolating and disarticulating the rib cage and the spinal column. Indeed, one informant reported that "some old people would go right inside, to get the fat off the guts. When they finished, there wasn't much but bones left" (256).

Decomposition of the visceral contents began almost immediately, and the flesh followed the same path soon afterwards (Waterman 1967:46). This decomposition created both heat and gas. For whales that were killed and beached quickly, this process was less problematic than for drift whales. Gas buildup often caused the carcasses of whales that died or were killed but lost at sea to refloat several days after death, and the heat and bacterial activity in the guts began decomposition of adjacent flesh. Spoilage of thoracic meat might preclude its use from drift whales, although cultural tolerance for decomposed flesh must be considered. Meat in the caudal, and perhaps cranial, areas was less likely to be affected by decomposition because of its distance from the viscera and its contact with cold water. Only whales caught close to the whaler's village were likely to have been sufficiently fresh for most of the meat and intestinal fat to have been used, although older drift whales still could have provided substantial quantities of meat. Also, decomposition of viscera and musculature, in addition to having little reported immediate effect on the blubber and on the oil it contained, would also have little effect on bones or on the oil therein.

The bones themselves appear to have followed several taphonomic paths. One path simply involved leaving the bones on the beach in front of the village. Walker saw the skeletons of eleven whales on the beach in front of a Nuu-chah-nulth village in 1786 (Fisher and Bumstead 1982:47). Another path involved depositing them at specific locations away from habitation sites. St. Claire (1991:140, 157) cites the cases of the Toquaht whaler who attempted to fill the pass between two of the George Fraser Islands with the skeletons of his kills, as well as the Tseshaht whaler who tried to do the same in a pass between Vancouver Island and an offshore islet.

In neither of these paths do bones find their way onto occupation sites, yet archaeological deposits of the area yield whale bone in quantity. The factors affecting the transport of whale bone onto sites are not addressed directly by the ethnographic record, but it does provide some clues. Simply leaving bones on the beach may have been a matter of primary refuse disposal, the creation of a convenient future raw material source, or the social/ symbolic display of whaling prowess. The latter interpretation is supported by the stated intent of whalers to fill passes with the bones of their quarry.

Whale skeletons had symbolic value. They provided evidence of social position (the right to hunt whales) as well as of skill and prestige (successful hunts). Skeletons and individual bones also had utilitarian values, as will be seen below, that are not addressed in the ethnographic literature.

Archaeological Data

Two databases, the Ozette site and the Toquaht Archaeological Project, are now available to show which skeletal elements are present in which frequencies in Nuu-chah-nulth sites. Two-thirds of the Ozette material derives from wide-area excavation of houses dating to the late precontact period, while the other one-third derives from other parts of the site spanning the past 2,500 years. The Toquaht material derives from arbitrarily selected test pits and trenches at four sites spanning the past 4,000 years. The bulk of the Toquaht whale bone assemblage was obtained from two sites, DfSi 4 (Ch'uumat'a) and DfSj 23 A and B (T'ukw'aa village and defensive location). In both cases, the whale bones have been condensed into a single assemblage with the result that comparisons between the two must be seen as broad and preliminary. Since the sizes of the two resulting assemblages are quite different, caution must be exercised in interpreting numeric data.

Table 8.1 presents a summary of Fiskin's (1994:359-377) examination of whale bone from Ozette. The NISP shown in the table differs from the N = 3,204 reported by Huelsbeck (1994b:271, 299) because Fiskin did not provide figures for some elements and because she could not identify to species selected elements (e.g., ribs, vertebrae, and phalanges) that comprised 70 percent of the whale assemblage (see Huelsbeck 1994b:271, Tables 115, 124, 125). Nevertheless, phalanges and some vertebrae are included in Table 8.1 whereas ribs are not. Fiskin sometimes provided indications of quantity, and these have been included in the table as much as possible. While blubber may have been the most sought-after part of the whale, and while meat, internal fat, and viscera may have been left for whoever wanted it, the bones were not always just left on the beach. This table indicates clearly that significant numbers of whale bones were transported onto the site for use in a variety of purposes. Fiskin identifies these purposes as oil extraction, architectural elements, tool manufacture, and symbolic display.

Table 8.1

Ozette whale data, NISP, modifications, and use

Element	NISP	Cut	Chop	Char	Cut brd./chop blk.	Drain	Bank supp.	Art. mfg.	Oil mfg.	Feat.
bulla	22			1				22		
carpals	?									
humerus	39		15	2	3	5	4		15	2
mandible	95		8		33		2	95	6	
max./inter.	?			1	5	23		83	8	
phalange	409	103	111	6	9				29	
radius	58		9		13	minor	minor	5	9	
scapula	115					21				18
skull	5	1	2	2		3			1	2
ulna	35				11	minor	minor	16		
vert. Cd.	?							1		
vert. Cv.	?			2					4	
vert. Lm.	?	yes				yes	yes		yes	
vert. Th.	343	23		6					3	49+
N =	1,121	127	145	20	74	52	6	222	75	71+

Cut = element shows fine, medium, and coarse cut marks
Chop = element chopped with adze-like tool
Char = burning or charring evident on element
Cut brd./chop blk. = element used as a cutting board or as a chopping block
Drain = element used in a drainage feature
Bank supp. = element used in a bank support
Art. mfg. = element used for the manufacture of artifact(s)
Oil mfg. = element used for oil extraction
Feat. = element used in a feature (general)
Source: Fiskin 1994.

Table 8.2 presents corresponding data from the Toquaht Project. In presenting these data, whenever possible an attempt has been made to retain the same broad categories as were used by Fiskin. The element list is, however, more extensive than that from Ozette in terms of the range of identified elements, and some modifications and uses observed in one assemblage could not be observed, or were not interpreted, in the other. The two datasets are thus broadly comparable, but fine comparisons should be considered as tentative due to different excavation and identification procedures. The NISP values in each table indicate the number of discrete skeletal elements in each assemblage (MNE); in other words, fragmentation has been controlled for as much as possible, but since this control is recognized as imperfect, the values presented in the tables should be thought of as minimized NISP. Neither table presents fragment counts that are recognizable parts of the same element. The other values represent numbers of elements exhibiting these modifications or uses. Because one element may exhibit more than one modification and/or use, the numbers in the rows do not equal the total NISP.

Tables 8.1 and 8.2 show that Ozette produced much more whale bone than did the Toquaht Project and that, between the two projects, there are many differences in the elements recovered and their proportions.

- Auditory bullae are found in both assemblages, and they are mainly used in artifact manufacture.
- Humerii comprise small proportions of each assemblage. They are used for chopping blocks/cutting boards and for architectural purposes at Ozette but not in the Toquaht sites; however, they seem to be used for oil production (charred, gouged, chopped) in each case.
- Mandibles are found more than twice as often in the Ozette assemblage than in the Toquaht assemblage. In both assemblages, they are used mainly for chopping blocks/cutting boards, although the poor condition of the Toquaht specimens renders these marks quite indistinct. They were also used for artifact manufacture at Ozette.
- Intermaxillae are reported for Ozette whereas premaxillae are reported for the Toquaht assemblage. There may be some differences in element terminology between Fiskin and Monks based on the reference literature we used. Maxillae and intermaxillae provided raw materials for artifact manufacture (mainly bark shredders) and for drainage channels at Ozette; no uses and few marks were identified on the Toquaht maxillae or premaxillae.
- Phalanges comprise over one-third of the Ozette NISP but only a small proportion of the Toquaht total. Butchering activity accounts for many of the cut marks, especially those on proximal and distal ends, but the

Table 8.2

Toquaht whale data, NISP, modifications, and use

Element	NISP	Fine cut	Coarse cut	Gen. cut	Chop	Gouge	Char	Cutting board	Art. mfg.	Other
bulla	4						1		1	
humerus	5				2	1	1			
hyoid	1	1								
mandible	6			2	2					1
max./premax.	2			1						
nasal	3	1	1	1		1				
phalange	10	1		1	2					2
radius	4			1						
rib	38	3	2	4	5					5
scapula	18	2	1	4	3		1	1		1
skull indet.	16			1			2			
ulna	1	1			1				1	1
vert. epiph.	47	1								
vert. Cd.	13	1				2	1			
vert. Cv.	9	1								
vert. Lm.	6			1			1			
vert. Th.	5			1	1	2				
vert. indet.	9					2				1
N =	197	12	4	17	16	8	7	1	2	11

Source: Monks 1991, Table 3.

chopping noted for the Ozette specimens is likely related to the oil extraction reported for that assemblage.

- Radii are found in low percentages in each assemblage. In each their main modification is chopping, and they are used to some extent as chopping blocks and for oil extraction at Ozette.
- Ribs were not tallied by Fiskin, but Huelsbeck (1994b:Table 124) indicates that ribs comprise (1) 18.67 percent of all elements in a live whale, (2) 11.60 percent of all whale remains in Area A, (3) 19.42 percent of all whale remains in Area B70, and (4) 19.20 percent of all whale bones in other areas of the site. The ribs in the Toquaht assemblage show chopping and a variety of cut marks. For the most part, these marks represent the result of carcass disarticulation rather than subsequent use. One Toquaht rib shows the imprint of a mussel shell harpoon point.
- Scapulae show much cutting and some chopping on their surfaces in the Toquaht assemblage, suggesting initial use as cutting boards, whereas the Ozette scapulae were used in drainage features and in pairs inside houses. One such pair of scapulae was also found in the Toquaht assemblage, and a single scapula was used as a post support, indicating multiple sequential uses.
- Intact skulls are found at Ozette but not at the Toquaht sites, where only cranial elements are found. While little modification of the cranial elements was noted in the Toquaht materials, extensive butchering of Ozette skulls, at least in part for oil extraction, was noted, and they were also used in drainage features.
- Ulnae were used almost exclusively as cutting boards and/or chopping blocks at Ozette, whereas the single specimen recovered in the Toquaht assemblage was chopped in order to remove a blank for artifact manufacture.
- Vertebrae from all parts of the vertebral column are reported at Ozette, although only NISP values for thoracic vertebrae are provided. Otherwise, only vague estimates for the uses to which they were put are given. The same range of vertebrae are present in the Toquaht assemblage, but the proportions differ from what one would expect in a live animal (i.e., 7 [13 percent] cervical, 14 [26 percent] thoracic, 10 [19 percent] lumbar, and 22 [42 percent] caudal in humpbacks). Table 8.2 shows that, in comparison to a live animal, cervical vertebrae are more common archaeologically (21 percent); thoracic vertebrae are quite underrepresented (12 percent); lumbar vertebrae are less common archaeologically (14 percent); and caudal vertebrae are still most common (31 percent) though underrepresented. One vertebral epiphysis exhibited a fine cut mark in the Toquaht assemblage; otherwise, no other epiphyses showed signs of modifications.
- Caudal vertebrae were used in the manufacture of enigmatic objects at Ozette (Fiskin 1994:377), but the Toquaht specimens exhibited the char-

acteristic charring and gouging (Figure 8.4) that suggest they were most likely used for oil extraction. Cervical vertebrae in the Toquaht assemblage show only fine cuts, as if they represent only butchering activity. Ozette cervical vertebrae, on the other hand, show charring, artifact manufacture, and oil extraction. Lumbar vertebrae at Ozette often went through a two-stage use-life. In the first stage, they were brought onto the site and modified for oil extraction. The second stage consisted of architectural use as either drainage features or bank supports. The lumbar vertebrae in the Toquaht assemblage exhibited gouging and charring, both of which suggest oil extraction. Thoracic vertebrae were frequently cut and were used for oil extraction in the Ozette assemblage; similarly, cutting, chopping, and gouging, all suggestive of oil extraction, were observed on these elements in the Toquaht assemblage. The Ozette specimens also served subsequent functions as parts of features, similar to the two-stage use-life of lumbar vertebrae.

Table 8.3 presents a comparative summary of the percentages of the total NISP values for skeletal elements in each archaeological assemblage and the percentage of each skeletal element in a live animal. It must be understood that the frequencies and total NISP values presented here are only for identified bones that exhibit some clear modification or use in one or both assemblages. Some aspects of the data are noteworthy. Skulls appear to be more frequent in the Toquaht assemblage, but fragmentation of these elements clearly inflates the figure. Because a number of them are whole, the percentage of skulls at Ozette may be more reliable. Still, this skeletal part is more common in sites than in live animals. The same is true of mandibles. Figures for vertebrae are difficult to interpret because only thoracic vertebrae were identified at Ozette. In that assemblage, they appear to occur at a much higher frequency than in a live animal, the reverse of the Toquaht situation. In the Toquaht assemblage, cervical vertebrae occur in rough equivalence to their live occurrence, and lumbar and caudal vertebrae occur less frequently than in a live animal. Ribs were not tallied at Ozette, but their occurrence in the Toquaht assemblage is about the same as in a live animal. Scapulae are clearly favoured in both assemblages, suggesting their importance. Humeri are of similar frequency in both assemblages and are more frequent than in a live animal. Ulnae are interesting in that they appear with greater frequency at Ozette than in a live animal, but the situation is reversed in the Toquaht material. Radii are more frequent archaeologically than in live whales, but there is greater emphasis on them at Ozette than at Toquaht. Phalanges are also more frequent at Ozette than in a live animal, but they are relatively underrepresented at Toquaht. In summary, skulls, mandibles, scapulae, humerii and radii are found more frequently in both assemblages than in live whales. Thoracic vertebrae, ulnae,

Table 8.3

Relative frequencies of skeletal elements: Toquaht, Ozette, and live whale data

Element	Toquaht	Ozette	Live
skull	17.86	2.41	0.85
mandible	4.29	8.47	1.69
hyoid	0.00	0.00	0.85
vert. Cv.	6.43	0.00	5.93
vert. Th.	3.57	30.60	11.86
vert. Lb.	4.29	0.00	8.47
vert. Cd.	9.29	0.00	18.64
rib	27.14	0.00	23.73
sternum	0.00	0.00	0.85
scapula	12.86	10.26	1.69
humerus	3.57	3.48	1.69
ulna	0.71	3.12	1.69
radius	2.86	5.17	1.69
phalange	7.14	36.49	18.64
innominate	0.00	0.00	1.69
N =	140[a]	1121	118

a Fifty-six vertebral epiphyses and indeterminate vertebrae removed.
Source: Toquat: author's analysis; Ozette: Fiskin 1994; live: Kaufman and Forestell 1986.

and phalanges are overrepresented at Ozette and underrepresented in the Toquaht material. Ribs were not heavily selected for or against in the Toquaht assemblage, and in neither assemblage were hyoids, sterna, or innominates emphasized.

Which Bones Were Transported onto Sites and Why?

The skull had little blubber or meat on it, yet it fulfilled subsistence, architectural, and probably symbolic functions at Ozette. The previously cited Kyuquot example, in which the first chief of the confederacy owned both sides of the head, also suggests that the skull had a high symbolic value. Choice morsels are reported to have been found along the lower jaw (Drucker 1951:40). Mandibles, then, may have belonged to high-ranking individuals who transported them onto sites. The multiple uses (architectural functions, cutting board/chopping block, artifact manufacture, oil extraction) of these elements at the Toquaht sites and at Ozette indicate their considerable value.

Of all the skeletal areas, the forelimb seems most likely to have been transportable in its entirety. It produced food (including "choice morsels"), bone for oil manufacture, bone for use as tools, bone for the manufacture of tools, bone for architectural use, and, if the scapula was considered as part of the forelimb, bone for features/symbolic use.

Whether the scapula was considered by the Nuu-chah-nulth as part of the forelimb is not known, but the use of scapulae in features inside houses and/or in pairs, as described by Fiskin, indicates that their use was symbolic as well as pragmatic. A scapula would be removed, along with surrounding meat, after blubber was stripped from the area between the head and the saddle. The blubber from this area of a drift whale went to the third and fourth chiefs, so the importance of this body area, as suggested by the blubber distribution and the distinct occurrence of the elements themselves, argues for a non-random claim on this part of the skeleton. At T'ukw'aa village, however, scapulae were used more for cutting boards than for architectural purposes.

There are differences between Ozette and the Toquaht sites with regard to the uses to which skeletal elements were put. At Ozette, skulls were used for drainage, oil production, and possibly as trophies. Maxillaries were used for artifact manufacture and architecture, while mandibles were used for artifact manufacture and as artifacts themselves. Vertebrae appear to have been evenly distributed across most utilitarian functions. Scapulae were used for architectural purposes and in features that, as noted above, may also have had social and/or symbolic significance. Humerii were used for oil extraction and for architectural purposes. Radii and ulnae were used as tools in an unmodified form, and phalanges were used for oil extraction. In the Toquaht sites maxillaries were used in features and, possibly, for oil extraction. Vertebrae and ribs were used for oil extraction, while scapulae were used for artifacts and for architectural purposes. They were also used in features, which suggests the same possible social/symbolic implications as those at Ozette. Humerii appear to have been used for oil extraction, while radii and ulnae were used for oil extraction and architecture and, in one instance, as a raw material source for artifact manufacture.

The absence of skulls from the Toquaht sites is notable. One reason for this could result from sample size, but it could also result from differences in excavation techniques between the two projects. Wide area excavation was used at Ozette whereas test pits were used on the Toquaht project. Chances of finding skulls would thus be significantly reduced for the latter assemblage. Maxillaries were used for architecture in both assemblages, but they were also used for oil extraction at the Toquaht sites. Humerii were used for oil extraction in both assemblages but also for architecture at Ozette. Mandibles seem not to have been used for artifact manufacture at the Toquaht sites, unlike the Ozette mandibles. Vertebrae were used for oil extraction in both cases, but they also served a number of other purposes at Ozette. Scapulae were used for architecture and features in both cases, but they were also used as artifacts by themselves in Toquaht sites. Radii and ulnae were used for cutting boards at Ozette, but in Toquaht sites they were used for oil extraction and as raw material for artifact manufacture.

The evidence presented above indicates that the main skeletal elements and the reasons for transporting them onto sites were:

1 subsistence reasons: bones were brought with attached meat and were used for oil rendering.
2 technological reasons:
   (a) bones were used as artifacts themselves (e.g., cutting boards),
   (b) they were used for architectural purposes (e.g., bank supports, house supports, post supports, and drainage devices), and
   (c) they were used as raw material sources for artifact manufacture.
3 social/ideological reasons: bones (e.g., skulls and perhaps whale scapula features) were used to signify social position and whaling prowess. These uses were likely linked in a number of instances.

Who Was Transporting the Bone?

Drucker (1951:40, 256) reports that, after the blubber and choice morsels had been removed from a carcass, anyone who wanted the meat could take it. This implies that other resources of the carcass (e.g., bones) were also available for anyone who wanted them, but it is clear that many bones were transported onto sites for a number of purposes and under a number of different circumstances. Most bones could not be transported until all of the blubber and most of the meat and sinew had been removed. Did the person with the right to a certain cut of blubber have the right to the meat and bone inside it as well? Or were there different rights for different resources on the carcass?

Huelsbeck (1994b:298) argues that the greater abundance of phalanges in House 1 compared to House 2 at Ozette indicates the relatively higher status of that household head compared to the head of House 2, where more mandibles and vertebrae were found. While one might debate this conclusion, and even argue for the reverse, the point is that bones are thought to have specific social and/or symbolic connotations. The differential distribution of these elements suggests that social rules regarding access to specific elements may have existed. Similarly, scapulae used in features, in pairs or singly with other bones, are also likely to have social and/or symbolic connotations. Even bones left on the beach or used to fill narrow passes indicate that they were used for display. One must wonder why bones would be left for anyone to take if they were, or could be, used in these ways.

In subsistence terms, bones contain large amounts of oil that can be rendered from them. Some bones appear to have been modified for just this purpose, and the rendering or simple "draining" of unmodified bones would also produce oil. Given the economic importance and social prestige of whale oil (Cavanaugh 1983), one wonders again why bones would just be left for anyone to take.

In view of these observations, and in consideration of the technological and architectural uses to which bones could be put, one could reasonably ask several summary questions. Would the bones discussed here be left simply for anyone who wanted them? Would rights be invoked to obtain things like cutting boards (scapula or radius and ulna) or chopping blocks and drainage features (mandibles), or bank supports (humeri)? Would rights be invoked to obtain sources of oil (vertebrae, mandibles) or symbolic materials (skulls, mandibles, scapulae)?

Rather than "no rules," as Drucker states, it is suggested here that there were at least "some rules," if not "strict rules," governing the use of skeletal elements in the pre-ethnographic past. First, because of the uses to which bones could be put, it seems inconsistent, for a culture in which there were highly defined ownership rights, to allow such multipurpose resources to go to whoever wished to take them. On the contrary, one would expect that specific resources from each layer of a whale would be owned. Indeed, the tongue, which possesses no blubber but which is represented in the Toquaht whale bone assemblage by the hyoid, is reported by Drucker (1951:40) to be another "choice morsel." Meat, then, was more or less valued and was unlikely to have simply been left for whoever wanted to take it. Indeed, meat contains 6 percent to 12 percent fat (Brandt 1948:45), making the consumption of fresh meat an additional source of dietary fat that required no rendering. Second, the successful whaler "owned" the whale, in that he distributed the blubber to those who had assisted him. Similarly, it seems to have been his prerogative to take the skeleton and dispose of it where he wished. Thus for a whaler to say that the meat and bones were for whoever wanted them is to say that these resources were not only a gift that the whaler chose to give to the village but also a resource with which he could have chosen to do something else.

The owner of a carcass could have chosen to display the skull by his house, to leave the bones on the beach as a testament to his prowess, or to use the scapulae as features or to give them to be used as such. Oil extraction from bone, for example, could be undertaken as a response to periodic, unpredictable shortages of whales. It could also be seen as an attempt to produce more prestige food, and it could be seen as a source of oil for those of lesser social position who were not recipients of blubber. In all cases, oil extraction is an intensification strategy, and it seems highly unlikely that intensification would involve resources of low value.

The point here is to show just how considerable is the amount of prestige resource that is potentially available in a whale skeleton. The fact that the skeletal elements used at Ozette differ from those used at the Toquaht sites suggests the possibility that "varying rules" were applied as situational needs and wishes arose over time and space. It is also difficult to be sure that only one person (the whale's owner or his designate) conducted all successive uses of elements. For example, did one person have the right to meat from a skeletal element while another had the right to the oil it contained?

Oil Production

The issue of oil production from different parts of a whale bears further consideration. A mature humpback attains an average length of 43 feet to 45 feet (13.1 metres to 13.7 metres) and weighs almost forty tons (c. 36,200 kilograms) (Kaufman and Forestell 1986:19). The skeleton comprises 15 percent of total body weight, or around 5,430 kilograms. The spongy cancellous bone that characterizes all great whales (Mysticetes) contains a fatty marrow that represents approximately one-third of all body oil (Slijper 1962:109; Kaufman and Forestell 1986:27); indeed, the oil content of some bones is so high that they float (Kaufman and Forestell 1986:27). Francis (1990:182) also reports that all parts of whales are impregnated with oil and that the meat and bones contain anywhere from 40 percent to 60 percent of the animal's total oil content. Tønnessen and Jensen (1982:51) report a similar figure of 40 percent to 50 percent of total carcass oil contained in blubber. Dissection and rendering of a blue whale showed that one kilogram of oil could be rendered from either 1.87 kilograms of blubber, 3.08 kilograms of bone, or 8.20 kilograms of meat (Robertson 1954:137-138). Tønnessen and Jensen (1982:250) report that the fat content of a whale's skeleton represents approximately 35 percent of the animal's total fat content, while Slijper (1962:109) records the figure as one-third. Fatty marrow found in bones of the head comprises 80 percent of all fatty marrow found in the skeleton (Kaufman and Forestell 1986:27). These figures complement those of Slijper (1962:109), who equates fat with oil and who reports that marrow in bones of the head contains 84 percent of fat; that thoracic vertebrae and scattered parts of ribs contain red marrow that is composed of 24 percent fat; and that yellow marrow in all other bones contains 32 percent to 68 percent fat. Sechart whaling station, using early-twentieth-century technology, produced 22,000 barrels of oil from around 500 humpback whales, or an average of forty-four barrels per animal (Tønnessen and Jensen 1982:116). Roughly half this quantity would have been contained in blubber, while the other half would have come from meat and bones.

An aggregate calculation of oil extraction using industrial technology showed that, of 1,596 barrels (266 tons) of oil, blubber produced 620 barrels (38.8 percent), meat 515 barrels (32.4 percent), and bone 461 barrels (28.8 percent) (Tønnessen and Jensen 1982:250). Using figures provided in this source, a forty-ton humpback would be expected to produce 4.4 tons of oil from the blubber and tongue, 1.5 tons of oil from meat and viscera, and 2.6 tons of oil from bone. Such an animal would produce 26 barrels of oil from blubber, 8.8 barrels from meat, and 15.4 barrels from bone (Tønnessen and Jensen 1982:250). If one excludes all meat and viscera due to potential spoilage, the blubber and the skeleton of a humpback contain about 4.4 tons (26 barrels) and 2.6 tons (15.4 barrels) of oil, respectively. Further, if one factors out the rendering capability of industrial whaling, there would be no change in the amount of oil available to the Nuu-chah-nulth from blubber. This situation occurs because the blubber would be consumed whether the oil had been extracted from it or not, whereas the amount available from bone would be much reduced. Finally, if 80 percent of bone oil is contained in the head, and if there are 2.6 tons of oil in the skeleton, then 2.1 tons of oil are contained in the cranial skeleton and 0.7 tons in the postcranial skeleton. The latter amount still represents 635 kilograms (1,400 pounds) of oil. Small by percentage, this amount is still considerable in absolute terms and would justify the effort expended to obtain even a portion of it. The reason(s) for taking the whale's head (skull and mandibles) can now be seen in another light. The mandibles together likely contained around 33 percent (1,380 pounds, or 627.5 kilograms), and the skull itself likely contained around 66 percent (2,800 pounds, or 1,280 kilograms) of oil. Heavy gouging of mandibles (Fiskin 1994:Figure 94A; Huelsbeck 1994b:Figure 87) may then come as no surprise. The skull may have had a real symbolic function, and it may have had some meat and bone that could serve utilitarian needs. It was also by far the most productive source of skeletal oil, which would explain Fiskin's (1994:375) observation that those of gray whales at Ozette were "all cut up."

Archaeologically, the criteria are not clear at present for distinguishing between bones that simply have been cut in the disarticulation and consumption stages and those that were purposely prepared for oil extraction. My stance is that any bone that suggests modification for oil extraction should be considered as having been put to that use. In so doing, a rough correction is thought to be made for the omission of bones that were used for oil but that bear no apparent alteration for that purpose. Contemporary informant accounts and ethnographic documentation are lacking on oil extraction, as is controlled experimentation. Nevertheless, as noted above, approximately 30 percent of all body oil is contained in the skeleton. Interestingly, Slijper (1962:109) notes that red marrow predominates in bones in young whales and that most of it is replaced by yellow (fatty) marrow in adulthood. He further notes that the conversion to yellow marrow begins simultaneously in the cervical and caudal vertebrae (and head and forelimbs, presumably) until only the thoracic vertebrae and parts of some ribs contain red marrow. These observations suggest that whalers would select adults so as to maximize fat/oil availability from bones, so archaeological whale bone should consist mainly of adults. Also, the archaeological record should show that processing bones for oil would be less evident on thoracic vertebrae and ribs than on other vertebrae, cranial elements, and forelimbs.

The Toquaht data (Table 8.2) conform more to these expectations than do the Ozette data (Table 8.1), possibly because of local differences in practice or priority and possibly because of the way alterations of whale bones have been perceived and classified. Nevertheless, surface alterations of some bones in the Ozette and Toquaht assemblages indicate that cutting, gouging, and heating may be useful in detecting the elements and extraction techniques that were used to obtain oil from bones (Figure 8.4). Indeed, the earliest evidence of whale use at Ch'uumat'a consists of a gouged and partially charred fifth caudal vertebra of a humpback whale dating to c. 3500 BP (Monks, McMillan, and St. Claire 2001:74). This piece of evidence shows that gouging preceded charring and that this practice is ancient. It may also indicate that bones were used as fuel following the rendering process. Personal observation that oil seeps from whale bones that have not been surficially altered suggests that surface scarification and/or cortical gouging, alone or in conjunction with a roasting process like the one for blubber, would result in considerable oil production. Huelsbeck (1994b:298, 300) also speculates on the extraction of oil from whale bones, despite the lack of ethnographic confirmation of this practice. Quantities of chopped whale bone have been reported at Kupti (McMillan 1969) and have also been noted in the Toquaht material. These fragments may be the results of artifact manufacture, but they may just as easily represent intensification of oil extraction via rendering,

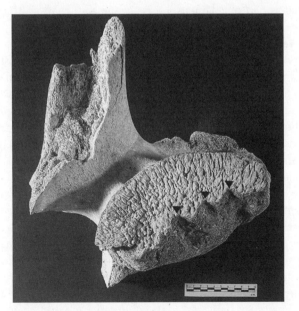

Figure 8.4 Vertebral centrum, showing three gouge marks (arrows) for oil extraction.

especially if they were produced by the chopping and gouging that is evident on a number of element types in both the Ozette and Toquaht assemblages. Such fragments, like the large numbers of whole and modified phalanges at Ozette, may also represent a culinary habit of adding a few oil-bearing bones to a meal.

Blubber, even from drift whales, is said to have lasted well and remained palatable even after it "acquired a high aroma." Indeed, Drucker (1951:40) reports that it "rarely if ever became too rotten to be used." Oil, rendered from blubber or bone, was likely viewed the same way. "There was a tremendous emphasis on fats – oils and greases – in the dietary pattern" (1951:62). All fats were considered delicious, and whale oil was served at meals whenever it was available (1951:63). The sudden massive abundance of food and raw material represented by a whale was accommodated in several ways. One was redistribution within the group (1951:55, 255-256), and another was exchange with other groups (Cavanaugh 1983). Intensification of oil extraction is evident in the archaeological remains, and an additional form of intensification (i.e., storage) is implied. Since blubber and oil are regarded as essential to the diet and as useful regardless of aroma, the extraction of oil from bone as well as from blubber can be regarded as an important adaptive strategy with taphonomic consequences. Storage of surplus elsewhere on the Northwest Coast is seen as a key element in the emergence of social complexity, and the intensification of oil extraction from whale bone should be regarded as part of a similar process in the Nuu-chah-nulth region.

Cultural Taphonomy Proper
The taphonomy considered here deals with the preburial (biostratinomic) portion of the taphonomic pathways followed by whale bones (Lyman 1994:505). At this point, postburial (diagenic) processes are even less well understood than preburial ones. Further, the sampling strategy of the Toquaht Project and the sample size of the whale bone assemblage are unlikely to have produced a reliable representative sample of either living populations or death assemblages (Klein and Cruz-Uribe 1984:3-4) of the major whale species represented archaeologically.

There seems to be a real possibility of complex and variable rules for skeletal element selection and transport. Following transport, a sequence of human uses occurred on the site, including oil extraction, use as artifacts, use as raw material sources for artifact manufacture, use as architectural elements, and use as social and symbolic signs. Some bones likely served several of these functions in sequence. For example, a humerus at Ozette could easily serve as a meat source, then as an oil source, then as an architectural element. Similarly, a scapula could serve as a meat source, then as a cutting board, and then as a feature or architectural element at T'ukw'aa. Or it could serve as a meat source and then as an architectural element or a social/symbolic feature at Ozette. The quantity of unidentifiable bone at the Toquaht sites, at least, may result as much from oil extraction and its attendant damage as to the natural friability of whale bone and the effects of natural decomposition.

Utility Indices

Utility indices have been used in an attempt to understand why whale bones are transported onto archaeological sites. Meat utility indices (MUI) have been calculated for harbor porpoise (*Phocoena phocoena*) (Savelle and Friesen 1996) and bowhead whales (Savelle 1997), and an architectural utility index (AUI) has also been calculated for bowhead whales by McCartney (1979) alone and in cooperation with Savelle (1997:870). Utility indices were therefore enlisted to try to explain the relative abundance of whale bones in the Toquaht assemblage.

The first step in applying such an analysis to the Toquaht assemblage was to see if whale bones existed in the same proportions archaeologically as they do in the whale body. Spearman's rank order correlation coefficient was used because non-parametric measures are robust even if sampling assumptions are not met in the data and because they use ordinal scale data, which are appropriately coarse grained for these initial analyses. In all tests, the 0.05 level of significance was used because it is a standard benchmark against which to evaluate the likelihood of occurrence of individual outcomes. Accordingly, a %MAU (minimum animal units) for humpback whale was compared to %MAU for the Toquaht whale bone assemblage. The result was $r_s = -0.08$, which was not statistically significant. Since H_0 cannot be rejected, this suggests that the bones in the assemblage were selected on some basis other than their proportional availability in the whale body. On what basis, then, were whale bones selected for transport onto the site?

The meat utility index was the first to be considered. First, it was assumed that meat on humpback and grey whales, the predominant species in the Toquaht assemblage, was distributed over the skeleton in much the same way as on a bowhead whale. Second, Savelle's %MUI for bowhead (Savelle 1997:Table 4) was ranked and compared with the ranked %MAU for the combined Toquaht whale assemblage. The rank order correlation coefficient was weak ($r_s = 0.19$) and not significant. An oil utility index (%OUI) was derived from the modern whaling literature on whale bone fat content and from the relationship between fat and oil. Rank order correlation of %MAU and %OUI produced an r_s value of 0.459, but this was less than the required critical value of approximately 0.620 for $N = 11$. An architectural utility index was developed on the basis of the architectural uses of whale bone at Ozette. Rank order correlation of %AUI and %MAU produced an $r_s = 0.16$, which was not significant. A general utility index (GUI) was created by averaging the bowhead %MUI, the Ozette %AUI, and the %OUI to form a

Table 8.4

**Spearman's rank order correlation coefficients
($p \leq 0.05$), selected indices against %MAU,
Toquaht whale data**

Index	Spearman's
%MUI	0.19
%OUI	0.46
%AUI	0.16
%GUI	0.39
%BUI	0.43

%GUI, and this value was ranked and compared with the Toquaht %MAU. The result was a value of $r_s = 0.39$, which was also too low to be significant. Finally, the weight of bone groups (%BUI) in a live animal (e.g., skull, mandibles, ribs, vertebrae) was used as a proxy for general utility. The coefficient was $r_s = 0.43$, again not significant. The results of these analyses are summarized in Table 8.4.

There are a number of ways to interpret these results: (1) I enjoy reporting on failure; (2) it is not possible to explain the transport and use of whale bones through the use of indices; (3) the Toquaht sample size is too small; (4) other avenues of explanation need to be explored. Another way to cast point (1) is to say that finding out what does not work is an aid to discovering what does. The indices as they were constructed do not explain, in a rigid statistical sense, the composition of the Toquaht whale bone assemblage, but they help to do so. The oil utility index approaches most closely the required critical value for the 0.05 significance level, but this benchmark is simply a conventional standard. The critical value for the 0.10 probability level is 0.52, close indeed to the 0.459 obtained by the test. The broad result seems to be that there is a bit more than one chance in ten that the correlation between %OUI and %MAU could occur by chance alone.

Both the oil utility index and the bone weight index look promising for future work and refinement, and they may be related in that larger bones will tend to contain more marrow and hence more oil. Possibly bone density, cortex thickness, or bone shape might prove useful. Another useful line of inquiry would be to develop a theoretical model of architectural utility, as Savelle (1997) did, rather than to rely on an empirically derived model from Ozette. Not much can be done about the sample size from the Toquaht Project, and identifying a larger sample is logistically and financially daunting to say the least. Other explanations besides utility indices should be sought – for example, the natural taphonomic forces, such as weathering and decomposition, or other cultural processes, such as the effects on bone friability of charring, boiling, and roasting, all of which may affect whale bone preservation. Controlled experimentation to explore these effects would assist in revealing the reasons for the composition of whale bone assemblages.

Conclusion

The archaeological and ethnographic data seem, at best, to be complementary pieces of the same picture and, at worst, to be contradictory in many respects. The latter record emphasizes the blubber and oil resources of whales and dismisses the meat and bones (and sinew, baleen, and intestines) as inconsequential. The time elapsed between the collection of ethnographic data and active precontact whaling likely accounts, at least in part, for the lack of information on more mundane aspects of whale carcass utilization and for the discrepancies between the ethnographic and archaeological records. The archaeological record shows that many bones from all parts of whales were brought onto sites, that they were used in a variety of ways, and that there were varying patterns of bone use among Nuu-chah-nulth groups. Oral history accounts support the deliberate use of certain bones, at least for social and/or symbolic purposes.

The patterning evident in the archaeological record suggests that there may have been clear guidelines on the ownership and use of all parts of the whale in the pre-ethnographic past. These guidelines likely varied according to time period, local custom, and prevailing circumstances. The abundance and diversity of resources represented by a whale has, it seems, been either overlooked in the ethnographic literature or forgotten in informant memory. The prestige economy, centred on the hunting of whales and the distribution of blubber and oil, appears to have overshadowed the more mundane and protracted activities involving bones (i.e., meat removal, preservation and consumption, architectural and technological uses, social and symbolic uses, and oil extraction).

The inferences and speculations presented here are based on a small number of whale bone assemblages and must therefore be considered as only preliminary. Further data would add immeasurably to our understanding of the use of whales over time and space by the Nuu-chah-nulth. Detailed re-examination of the Yuquot and Hesquiat assemblages would be a useful first step, yet much time and money is required to take bones to the scattered comparative skeletons in North America. These analyses, and experimental butchering on modern whales, are also required for better understanding of precontact cultural taphonomic processes in Nuu-chah-nulth whale bone assemblages.

Acknowledgments
The Toquaht First Nation, especially Chief Bert Mack, generously gave permission and encouragement to excavate and analyze these data. The Toquaht First Nation, the Nuu-chah-nulth Tribal Council, the British Columbia Heritage Trust, the University of Manitoba Social Sciences and Humanities Council (Research Grants Committee), and the University of Manitoba Department of Anthropology provided financial support. The Royal British Columbia Museum's Mammology Section, the Hawaii Maritime Museum, and the Natural History Museum of Los Angeles County kindly made their research collections available. Project co-directors Alan McMillan and Denis St. Claire invited me to examine the fauna and have been instrumental in facilitating all aspects of this work. R.G. Matson, Gary Coupland, Quentin Mackie, David Pokotylo, and Michael Blake read and commented on the original draft of this manuscript, and their comments greatly improved this chapter. Any errors, misinterpretations, or omissions rest solely with the author. Finally, I wish to thank most sincerely Don Mitchell who, since 1966, has inspired my interest in Northwest Coast archaeology and has patiently assisted me through three degrees, several field seasons, and countless beers and pickled eggs.

9
The Thin Edge: Evidence for Precontact Use and Working of Metal on the Northwest Coast
Steven Acheson

The genesis of this chapter began some years ago with the recovery of a small piece of worked copper from a Haida village site on the southern Queen Charlotte Islands (Acheson 1998) (Figure 9.1). Examination of the metal, using an electron-microprobe, revealed that the object was made of native copper. While not surprising in itself, the piece is noteworthy for its workmanship and for adding to an extensive, diverse, and expanding inventory of precontact metal artifacts from the Northwest Coast. The idea of a well established prehistoric copper complex for the region is not new (see Keddie 1990:18), but it is far from widely recognized. This chapter considers several lines of evidence for the use and working of both copper and iron on the Northwest Coast in order to advance the case for an incipient metallurgical tradition. The discussion includes a detailed description of the object recovered from the southern Queen Charlotte Islands.

The term "metallurgy" refers not only to the ability to extract metals from their ores but also to the art of working metals. The idea of metal working is an important one, if for no other reason than that it affects how we look at cultural form and development. Native copper was utilized by many early civilizations, and it serves to define a major cultural period of the Old World. Terms such as "Copper Age," "Bronze Age," and "Iron Age," which are used to divide and designate prehistoric cultural periods of the Old World, have little chronological value. As we begin to closely examine certain assumptions about cultural development and metallurgy here and elsewhere in the world, the utility of such terms becomes increasingly suspect.

When considering Aboriginal use of metal, two central questions need to be asked: (1) is a metal artifact of indigenous manufacture imported either in raw form or as a finished article? and (2) is the object made without smelting or from smelted, cast, and possibly alloyed metal (after Franklin et al. 1981)? For the purposes of this chapter, several lines of evidence are taken into account to make the case for the existence of an incipient metallurgical tradition on the Northwest Coast prior to historical contact. Beginning

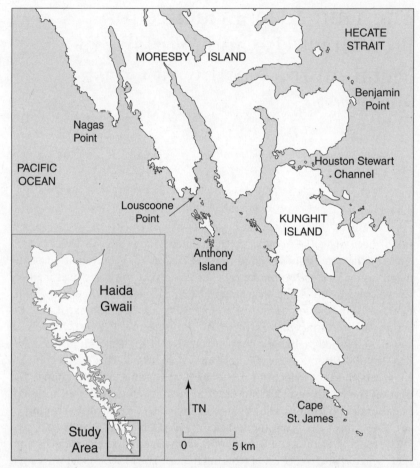

Figure 9.1 Southern Queen Charlotte Islands (Haida Gwaii), showing the location of the Louscoone Point village site.

first with the question of sources for copper and iron, a number of plausible sources are suggested. A discussion of the archaeological and metallurgical evidence for the precontact use and working of iron and copper on the Northwest Coast follows, drawing on a wealth of historical and ethnographic records that document the technical skill and craftsmanship shown in the remarkable pieces of worked copper and iron observed by early traders. I also consider oral history and legends concerning the antiquity and development of metal working on the coast.

Sources for Copper and Iron on the Northwest Coast
By far the most common of the two metals found in an archaeological context on the coast is copper. Copper is widely distributed in nature, occurring

in most soils, ferruginous mineral waters, and ores. Native copper, sometimes termed "malleable copper" or "virgin copper," occurs as a mineral in the upper oxidization zone of copper-bearing deposits, where the deposit has been exposed to atmospheric influences. Because native copper is either a product of chemical reductions from sulphide and oxide ores or is precipitated from solution (reduced from solutions of its salts), it is exceptionally pure. This singular quality is the most distinguishing feature of native copper.

There are a number of minor sources of native copper throughout British Columbia, including a possible source noted by Swan (N.d.) in 1883 on the northwest coast of the Queen Charlotte Islands and another at the western end of Kamloops Lake (Dawson 1879:116 B). Historically, the most important sources of native copper for the Northwest Coast were the Copper River and White River areas of southeast Alaska and southwest Yukon, the traditional territories of the Ahtna and White River Aboriginal peoples. Copper-bearing basalts flank the St. Elias Range, where copper can be found in creek beds as nuggets and slabs ranging in weight from less than half a kilogram to occasionally massive forms of over 900 kilograms (Franklin et al. 1981:5-6).[1]

Use of copper was most prevalent for the Ahtna culture area of southern Alaska. From here, copper was traded onto and down the coast. Native copper used by the Haida was obtained through this trade, as was surmised by James Colnett (N.d.) on visiting the Queen Charlotte Islands in 1787 and later reported by Dawson (1880) and Swan (N.d.). Local residents still recognize the fact that, in the words of Solomon Wilson, a long-time resident and elder of Skidegate, the early copper came from Alaska (personal communication 1974). The other main trade source cited in the literature was the White River First Nations of the Yukon, with the Chilkat Tlingit acting as middlemen (Brooks 1900).

Possible sources of precontact iron is a decidedly more complex question. Iron is the most abundant of the heavy metals, but pure iron occurs naturally only in the form of meteorites. Use of meteoric, as well as telluric,[2] iron is well documented for the Greenland Thule and other areas of the circumpolar region (e.g., Biggild 1953; Holtved 1944), but it is virtually unknown outside the Arctic region. Holmberg (1856) does cite one Aboriginal account collected in 1854 on the Northwest Coast that tells the story of a Chilkat Tlingit woman who made fluted daggers from meteoric iron using a stone anvil.

Numerous authors have made a convincing case for drift iron as a source for this metal on the coast prior to historical contact. De Laguna (1960, 1972; de Laguna et al. 1964) long recognized this possibility in order to account for its presence among the Tlingit prior to contact. Indeed the Tlingit had a term for drift iron that de Laguna (1960:127) transcribes as "gayES." A particularly strong case for drift iron on the coast is made by Gleeson (1980c), with the recovery of a large assemblage of iron tools, including chisels and assorted bladed knives, from precontact levels at Ozette. Gleeson (1981:3) fixed the age of the assemblage at AD 1613 through indirect dating of associated wood pieces using dendrochronology. Spectographic analysis revealed a high carbon steel with the probable source being drift iron, based on apparent similarities between the trace elements curves of the Ozette metal and examples from Japan. Further south again, one other example of iron in a precontact context is reported by Ames (1998) for a Chinookan site on the Lower Columbia River.

Iron was common in Japan by AD 300, and undoubtedly a potential, if sporadic, source was in the form of lost ships being swept by the Japanese current to the Northwest Coast. Keddie (1990:8), summarizing the work of Davis (1872a, 1872b) and Brooks (1876), cites twelve cases where Japanese vessels, or those of neighbouring countries, are known to have come ashore between California and the Aleutian Islands in the years 1617 to 1876. One wreck on the British Columbia coast dates to 1813 and another on Cape Flattery, Washington, occurred in 1834 (Keddie 1990:9). Scant as these occurrences may be, they make the case for shipwrecks being a possible historical source of iron.

Among the Makah, Swan (1870:34-35) remarked on the continuation of the practice of salvaging drift iron until as late as the mid-1800s: "some of them have managed to procure hammers and cold chisels from the various wrecks that have been thrown on the coast from time to time; and the wreck of the steamer Southerner, in 1855, about 30 miles south of Cape Flattery, afforded a rich harvest of old iron and copper, as well as engineers' tools which have been extensively distributed and used among the coast tribes of the vicinity."

Though drift iron is one obvious and plausible source, intercontinental trade with Asian populations has been given little serious attention. De Laguna (1972) recognized the possibility that Aboriginal familiarity with iron likely predated direct contact with Russian traders in the 1700s. Aboriginal knowledge of this metal was indeed acquired through either exposure to drift iron or Aboriginal trade networks extending into Siberia. There are several lines of evidence to support the existence of a precontact Siberian-Alaska trade network (see Whitthoft and Eyman 1969).

Iron may have been present in eastern Siberia by as early as the late Neolithic (first millennium BC). An iron engraving tool recovered at Uelen, Chukchi, dated to between AD 200 and 500 (Levin and Sergeyev 1964), has led to speculation that iron may have penetrated to the Bering Sea region by the first millennium AD through tribes of the lower Lena or Amur regions.[3] According to McCartney (1988:57), the use of metal around the Bering Sea region was so common that Alaskan Neo-Eskimos developed an epi-metallurgical technology about 1,500 to 2,000 years prior to direct Russian contact. Evidence of ancestral Thule cultures in the Bering Strait region using Siberian trade iron by the first few centuries AD includes engraving tools with iron bits from a number of Alaskan sites. Ipiutak sites in Alaska, dated to between AD 300 and 600, have yielded a number of iron tools (Clark 1977; Larsen and Rainey 1948). The subsequent Thule migration across the Canadian Arctic at c. AD 1000 coincides with evidence for the frequent use of native copper among Athapaskans by this time. Metal use became widespread throughout the Arctic and Subarctic by the fourteenth century (Franklin et al. 1981:3). Wrought iron fragments have been recovered from the Yukon coast, along with an assortment of copper artifacts, dating back to AD 1200 (Yorga 1978).

MacDonald's (1996:137) observation regarding the close parallels between northern Northwest Coast groups and Bronze Age China, as regards the use of wooden helmets and visors in armour, is another strand in the idea of a Siberian connection. It is reasonable to expect that, along with the inter-continental movement of goods to the Northwest Coast, came ideas.

Historical documentation offers further tantalizing support to the Siberian connection. As early as 1778, Captain Cook's party observed that the Tlingit of Prince William Sound possessed both copper and iron implements, including iron arrow and lance points, to the extent that: "they never asked for either iron or copper, articles that they seemed to hold in small account, and with which they appeared to be well supplied" (Cook 1967:380). La Perouse (1798:424, 427) observed the same situation among the Haida at Bucareli Bay in 1779. Cook speculated that the iron was acquired through long-distance trade, while copper was either obtained locally or "at most ... passes through few hands to them." Similarly, among the Haida, Colnett (N.d.) found that "none of the small pieces of Copper seemed to be held in any Estimation," suggesting wide availability of this metal for this coastal group at the onset of the maritime fur trade in 1787.

Three iron-bladed tools and an iron adze blade were collected the same year by Captain Cook from the Nuu-chah-nulth on Vancouver Island. Of these, Beaglehole wrote that they were "certainly of their own forming and helving" (Cook 1967:321). Cook considered the source of the metal to be the Russians further west in Alaska but did not rule out the possibility of more remote French or British sources to the east or Spanish sources to the south (Cook and King 1784:2:271).[4] Detailed analysis of two of the three Nuu-chah-nulth knife blades revealed markedly different levels of techno-logical achievement but was inconclusive with regard to their source (Lang and Meeks 1981:103-106).

The enigmatic large coppers of the Northwest Coast epitomize the question of the role of historical trade versus Aboriginal metallurgical knowl-edge and technology. A number of technical studies (Couture and Edwards 1963; Couture 1975; and Jopling 1978) have looked at whether copper artifacts, including a number of coppers from the Northwest Coast, were fashioned from industrial copper sheeting supplied by traders or from native copper. Both Couture's (1975) and Couture and Edwards's (1963) studies used metallographic observations (the structure of solid metals and alloys), electron microprobe analysis (spectroscopy), replicative experiments, and comparisons of thickness and hardness of the material. The studies revealed that, in the case of the copper plaques, all the specimens were fashioned from industrial trade copper sheeting. Jopling (1978) drew the same conclusion in her study of Northwest Coast coppers based on radiography and other tests. Other copper artifacts that were analyzed, including a number of bracelets and copper-wrapped sticks from Prince Rupert, proved to be native copper of considerable antiquity. Couture (1975:8) summarized his findings by remarking that these early pieces were produced by an artisan with considerable metallurgical skill.

The origins of the Northwest Coast copper plaque remain obscure, but whether fashioned from trade or native copper,[5] the extensive use of metal in this manner appears solidly rooted in a long-standing metallurgical tradition. The same can be said for the historical examples of metal daggers on the coast. Daggers of copper, iron, and steel exhibit a level of workmanship many have thought impossible for cultures with no tradition of smithing. There is little doubt that Aboriginal groups throughout the Northwest Coast had access to sources of both copper and iron before contact. And on the matter of Aboriginal metallurgical ability and technique needed to produce these pieces, there is mounting evidence that such skills and knowledge were already centuries old.

Aboriginal Metallurgical Techniques

Franklin et al.'s (1981) detailed work, *An Examination of Prehistoric Copper Technology and Copper Sources in Western Arctic and Subarctic North America*, makes a number of significant observations relevant to the question of Aboriginal metallurgical techniques on the Northwest Coast. A variety of techniques were used among Arctic and Subarctic cultures. In addition to the almost universal practice of "folding" as a way of building up objects from small pieces of native copper, the metal was also annealed and/or hot-worked (see also Whitthoft and Eyman 1969). The widespread occurrence of forging folds and the working of copper at non-ambient temperatures indicates that a shared body of knowledge did indeed exist among northern Aboriginal groups, cross-cutting cultural and temporal boundaries. Franklin et al. go on to suggest that this distinctive northern copper-working technology likely developed in the Beringian area during the first half of the first millennium AD. In keeping with de Laguna's (1972) earlier observation, the authors felt this development was likely due to contact with iron-using populations in Siberia.

De Laguna (1972) has inferred that the Yakutat Tlingit to the south possessed a similar metal-working tradition, which they used to fashion unfinished native copper blanks from the Copper River in Alaska. Examples of this come from the late prehistoric site of Old Town in the Yakutat Bay area of Alaska, which yielded a large assemblage of copper artifacts, including one of the few examples of copper wire (coiled wire beads). The assemblage also included nineteen precontact iron artifacts. According to de Laguna et al. (1964:88-89), the iron was worked in the same manner as was native copper, "by heating it in an open fire and by pounding and grinding it into spearheads, knives and daggers." McIlwraith (1948:253) tells us that the Nuxalk production of large coppers from native copper was similarly achieved by heating the metal in a fire and then beating it into the required shape.[6]

In examining Ozette iron from farther to the south, Gleeson (1980c) considered the question of how it may have been worked. Iron and steel, like copper, can be beaten into useful shapes while cold. Hot-forging and the practice of sudden cooling with water, in turn, enhances the hardness of the metal but at the cost of increasing its brittleness. The invaluable and rather delicate art of tempering the hardened metal by careful and gentle reheating, which will remove its extreme brittleness while retaining most of its hardness, is a process that requires skilful handling.

At the very least, the worked iron at Ozette involved hot hammering to create a serviceable edge, but Gleeson (1980c:53) ruled out the possibility of tempering and annealing, which would have enabled the tools to hold a fine edge. To support this interpretation, Gleeson cited Gibbs's 1877 contention that there was only a limited metal-working ability among the inhabitants at the mouth of the Columbia River. Because smelting was unknown at Ozette, Gleeson (1980c:52) concluded that the practice of tempering was unlikely and that the use of forging was rudimentary at best. Whether the results are evident in the Ozette pieces or not, a survey of the early historical record and metallurgical studies available on early specimens from the Northwest Coast attests to just such abilities.

Returning to the Cook specimens collected from the Nuu-chah-nulth, the analysis of two blades reveals that, while the one piece was simply cold-worked wrought iron, the second one has a laminated structure of iron and steel and was worked extensively using heat as well as cold working. Welding together wrought iron with a piece of steel in this manner was a means to improving the quality of the blade without making it entirely from rarer steel. It is a "purpose-made" cutting tool achieved by reforging, a process not previously thought possible for cultures lacking a knowledge of smelting (Lang and Meeks 1981:103, 106).

Taking the argument for a precontact metallurgical tradition on the Northwest Coast a step further, others have observed that daggers made of native copper were the likely prototype for the later beautifully produced steel

Figure 9.2   Haida iron dagger, collected in 1884 at
Skidegate (48.3 × 9.5 × 1.4 centimetres). The dagger is
concave on the back (not shown) and convex on the
front (shown), with four grooves running the length of
the blade. Top of the blade is covered by a semi-circular
piece of copper. *Courtesy of the Royal British Columbia
Museum, Victoria, British Columbia, cpn 10028*

daggers of the historical period (Figure 9.2) (Vaughan and Holm 1982:64).
The blade form is typically broad and tapered, double-edged, with an abruptly
converging point. The pair of ridges stiffen the blade and converge near the
point to form a wide, shallow flute the length of the blade. Even by today's
standards, to form these ridges is a challenging task for an experienced metal-
smith with a full complement of tools. John Dunn ([1846] cited in Vaughan
and Holm 1982:67) observed in the 1840s the use of files among Northwest
Coast groups to produce "beautifully fluted daggers, some eighteen inches
long, as highly finished as if they had been turned out of a first-rate makers
in London."[7] Indeed, such works were being produced at the beginning of

contact by Aboriginal hands, as Caamano (1938:203) observed among the Kaigani Haida in 1792:

> Everyone carries a sheath knife slung around the neck. This is a well sharp-ened dagger, consisting of a blade some twelve inches long and four in width. The pommel encloses another smaller knife about six inches long and four broad with a rounded point and rather blunt edges, which is used to give the first blows, and for wounding the face ... The hilt, also of iron is leather covered, and is fitted with a thong some seventeen inches long, for securing it to the hand. These knives were so well fashioned and finished, that at first I felt sure they were not of native manufacture, but later I found that the Indians make them themselves quite easily from the iron that they obtain by barter, *heating it in the fire and forging it by beating it with stones in the water.* [emphasis added]

Swan (1870:33-34) noted a comparable skill among the Makah nearly a century later, observing that they employ

> considerable ingenuity in the manufacture of the knives, tools, and weap-ons they use, and are quite expert in forging a piece of iron with no greater heat than that of their ordinary fire, with a large stone for an anvil and a smaller one for a hammer. Their knives ... are made of rasps and files, which they procure at the saw-mills after they have been used in sharpening the mill-saws; or, not uncommonly, they purchase new ones of the traders in Victoria. They are first rudely fashioned with the stone hammer into the required shape, brought to an edge by means of files, and finely sharpened on stones; they are always two-edged, so as to be used as daggers ... As they are experienced in the use of heat, they are able to temper these knives very well. The chisels are made of rasps, or of any kind of steel that can be ob-tained. Sometimes they take an old axe, and, after excessive labor, succeed in filing it in two, so as to make as it were two narrow axes; these are then heated and forged into the required shape, and handles attached.

Concerning the tools of the trade, Swan adds: "Those who have been so fortunate as to obtain iron hammers use them in preference to those made of stone; but they generally use a smooth stone like a cobbler's lap-stone for an anvil. The common hammer is simply a paving stone" (1870:35). Among the Eyak, fine-grained sandstone was reportedly used to sharpen the edges of these blades (Birket-Smith and de Laguna 1938).

In addition to a demonstrated skill in metal working, the Aboriginal com-munity also exhibited an obvious familiarity with the quality and proper-ties of iron from the outset of the maritime fur trade. Iron was eagerly sought at first contact, as the historical record attests, which serves not only as a measure of its rarity but also of the Aboriginal community's familiarity with this metal.[8] At the very outset of historical contact between the Spanish and the Haida in July 1774 at Langara Island, the Haida sought most in their transactions "things made of iron; but they wanted large pieces with a cutting edge, such as swords, wood-knives and the like for on being shown ribands they intimate that these were of trifling value, and when offered barrel hoops they signified that these had no edge" (de la Pena, quoted in Cutter 1969:159-161). By the time of the Spanish expedition of 1779, the Haida at Bucareli Bay possessed iron knives "longer than European bayonets, a weapon, however, not common among them," and lances with iron points reaching sixty centimetres in length and bracelets of iron (la Perouse 1798:424, 427).

To the north, in 1778 Captain Cook (1967:2:379) found that the neighbouring Tlingit of Prince William Sound wanted iron from "eight to ten inches long" and rejected small pieces. "The metals we saw were copper and iron; both of which, particularly the latter, were in such plenty as to constitute the points of the arrows and lances." According to Caamano (1938:205) in 1792 these spears measured "14 to 16 feet in length, with very broad, sharp, iron heads; ... arrows headed with bone or iron barbed points." By 1787, Dixon (1789:243) observed that the variety of iron implements in the possession of the Tlingit "answer their every purpose nearly as well as if they had recourse to a carpenter's tool chest." On the northern Charlottes, "toes [iron adze blades] were almost the only article we bartered ... and taken so very eagerly" (1789:201) at the onset of the maritime fur trade, but attention quickly turned to the quality of the iron. As the availability of iron increased so did the Aboriginal community's discernment about the quality of the metal.[9] At Cumshewa in 1791, Ingraham (1971:129) found that "the least flaw in our chisels or daggers [was] sufficient to condemn them as unfit for their purpose." Similarly, Bishop (1967:71) observed in 1795 how carefully the Tsimshian inspected the iron, remarking that "it was a matter of astonishment to us, to see how readily he would find a Flaw in the Iron." Care of these pieces was also a source of amazement to early maritime traders. Ingraham (1971:151) remarked when trading with the Haida in 1791 that their spears were affixed with iron points, that they were "kept in the best order and are a very formidable weapon indeed. Besides these they all have daggers of iron which in general are from a foot to eighteen inches long ... It is astonishing to see how bright and with how much care they are preserved."

James Colnett (N.d.), who traded extensively on the Queen Charlotte Islands in 1787-88, remarked on the extensive use of copper and iron for personal adornment around the neck, wrists, or suspended from the ears. Copper was in common use for bracelets and neck rings, as well as being used as an inlay on labrets (Dixon 1789:208). Among the Kaigani Haida, in

1792 Caamano (1938:206) observed: "One of their chief ornaments consists of three or four rings, worn around the ankle and wrist, made of copper or iron. These are so extremely heavy as to give the idea of being fetters; especially those that some of the women and most of the men wear round the neck. These are formed on a twisted, hawser-laid, pattern; and are so large as to reach from one shoulder to the other, as well as partly over the breast." Colnett (N.d.) also observed a novel use of copper on which the ethnographic literature is silent: "another method of wearing the copper was beating it out very thin, fixing it round a piece of wood an inch in Diameter & a foot in length Fastend round the neck of their Children & Hung down before them." From Prince Rupert, we have the copper-wrapped sticks, along with an assortment of other copper ornaments, including tubular rolled beads, copper earrings, and a bracelet with a date of 500 BC. The copper tubes were uncovered aligned in double, parallel rows, along with a cache of weapons (a slate dagger and clubs), which suggests to MacDonald (1983:105-106) that the copper pieces may be the remains of a suit of rod armour.

It must follow, considering the range of uses metal was put to, the sheer variety in form, and its wide distribution, that the Aboriginal community possessed a remarkable knowledge of and skill in metal working. Moreover, the archaeological and metallurgical evidence points to this ability as being a long-standing tradition.

Copper Artifact from Louscoone Point

A small fragment of copper wire can now be added to the inventory of precontact Northwest Coast metal artifacts. Recovered from a small Haida settlement at the entrance to Louscoone on the southern part of Moresby Island (Figure 9.1), the object consists of a thin strand of native copper bound and knotted around a small shell fragment (Figure 9.3). A radiocarbon date obtained from an associated feature fixes the age of the piece at between AD 1150 and 1400. Microscopic examination shows the wire to have been made by hammering, a technique not common in Europe after the mid-1600s, while its micro-structure indicates cold working of the metal. There were no non-metallic inclusions visible in the sample, which would indicate whether the metal had been forged or smelted from an ore. The specimen's composition was determined using a Cameca Camebax electron-microprobe to reveal nearly pure copper with only traces of silver and arsenic (C. Salter, Department of Materials, University of Oxford, personal communication 1987). Comparative analysis with four objects made of trade copper held by the British Museum reveals considerably higher levels of impurities than were found in the wire (Figure 9.4, Table 9.1). The piece likely served as a pendant or was possibly affixed to an object such as a mask. An ethnographic example of the use of wire for suspending pendants is documented for the Nuu-chah-nulth. Drucker (1951:54) remarks: "Chiefs

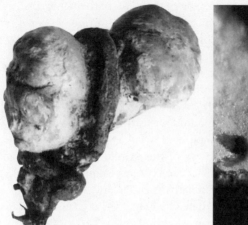

Figure 9.3   Artifact FaTt 9:90: copper wire with shell fragment (magnified view) recovered from the Haida village of *Tc!uuga*, located on Louscoone Point, southern Queen Charlotte Islands. Photomicrograph of strand on right (Leitz microscope 10×50/0.85; Ilford 400ASA).

and sub-chiefs use pieces of copper, brass, rare shell and the like for pendants. These are suspended from the ears and the nose by wire if available, otherwise by cedar twigs ... Any sort of small shell is hung from the ears or the nose by means of a twisted cedar twig."

Conclusion

This selective survey of the archaeological, historical, and ethnographic literature argues both for the presence of a well established metal-working tradition, and of its importance to the Aboriginal community. Copper held mythical and socioeconomic value. The island home of the Haida, for example, rested upon a great supernatural being – "Sacred-One-Standing-and-Moving" – who in turn lay on a copper box (Swanton 1905:12). Intertwined with its obvious functional value, copper served also as a status marker. Items of adornment made of copper were worn only by wealthier higher-ranking Tlingit (de Laguna et al. 1964). Similarly, Drucker (1951:54) observes for the Nuu-chah-nulth (Clayoquot) that "the plebeian or slave who cannot afford metal must be content to make earrings and nose-rings from a smooth, round stick of cedar, spruce, or other wood." Shinkwin's (1979) review of ethnographic sources on the Ahtna reports that copper was an item of wealth and prestige commensurate with its importance as an article of trade. Chiefs possessed large quantities of copper and may have claimed ownership of particular copper-collecting localities.

Copper was also ascribed certain medicinal properties. Among the Nuxalk of the Central Coast, according to McIlwraith (1948:254), large "coppers"

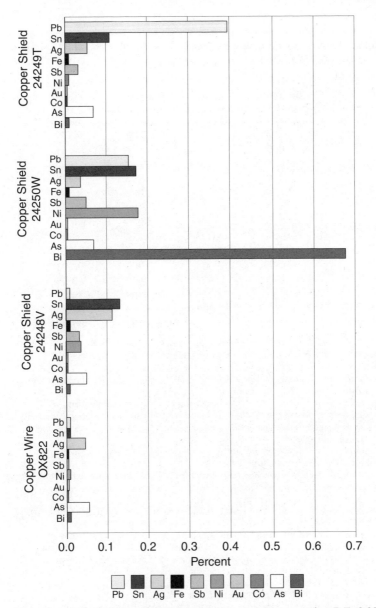

Figure 9.4 Comparison of the chemical composition of copper artifact FaTt 9:90 (Lab No. OX822) and three examples of trade copper.

held curative powers: "If an owner of one [copper] was ill, he used to clear it with a rough stone and water; then he would drink four cupfuls of the liquid which contained minute fragments of metal. In almost every case a speedy recovery followed." McClellan (1975) notes that the Southern

Table 9.1

Chemical composition of copper artifact FaTt 9:90 (lab no. OX822) and four examples of trade copper

BM RL	Plate amulet 23085Q	Copper shield 24249T	Copper shield 24250W	Copper shield 24248V	Copper wire OX822
Cu	92.3	100.00	100.00	100.00	n/a
Pb	0.009	0.393	0.155	0.009	0.01
Sn	8.7	< 0.11	< 0.17	< 0.13	0.009
Ag	0.089	0.053	0.035	0.114	0.046
Fe	0.025	0.011	< 0.008	0.009	0.006
Sb	< 0.03	< 0.03	0.05	< 0.03	0.004
Cd	< 0.0006	< 0.0006	< 0.0008	< 0.0007	n/a
Ni	< 0.004	0.008	0.177	0.034	< 0.01
Au	< 0.004	< 0.004	< 0.005	< 0.004	< 0.005
Co	< 0.004	< 0.004	< 0.005	< 0.004	0.002
As	< 0.05	0.07	0.07	< 0.05	0.056
Mn	< 0.0006	< 0.0006	< 0.0008	< 0.0007	n/a
Bi	0.007	0.007	0.68	< 0.008	< 0.01
Zn	0.054	0.008	< 0.003	< 0.003	0.004

Notes: Samples 23085Q, 24249T, 24250W, and 24248V analyzed by atomic absorption (Craddock, British Museum); sample OX822 (Artifact FaTt 9:90) analyzed by EMPA (Salter, University of Oxford); n/a = not analyzed.

Ag (silver): white, lustrous, malleable ductile metallic element found in the uncombined state in nature as well as in a number of ores.

As (arsenic): semi-metallic element that occurs naturally in various minerals.

Au (gold): yellow, non-rusting, malleable, ductile, high-density metallic element; occurs naturally in the metallic state, never quite pure, but alloyed with silver, copper, platinum or certain other elements.

Bi (bismuth): brittle reddish-white metallic element used mainly as a component of alloys required to have a low melting-point.

Cd (cadmium): bluish metallic element obtained as a by-product of the extraction of zinc from its ores; does not occur in a free state in nature; used in low-melting-point alloys.

Co (cobalt): hard silvery-white metallic element.

Cu (copper): reddish, malleable, ductile metallic element found in a native state as well as in the form of ores.

Fe (iron): one of the most abundant metallic elements; widely distributed throughout the earth's crust in the form of ores and easily reduced; found in its free state only in meteorites.

Mn (manganese): hard grey metallic element essential to the process of steel manufacture.

Ni (nickel): hard silvery-white metallic element widely used in alloys, especially iron, to impart strength and resistance to corrosion.

Pb (lead): easily fusible, soft, grey metallic element.

Sb (antimony): naturally occurring semi-metallic silvery-white element (sulphide); widely used in alloys, especially lead to increase hardness.

Sn (tin): silvery-white malleable metallic element that can occur in a pure state but is more often found as ores; used in a number of important alloys with lead, copper, or antimony.

Zn (zinc): white metallic element used in ancient times as an alloy with copper to make brass.

Tutchone similarly valued the metal for both its technological properties and its ability to ensure good health. The Haida practice of adorning children with wrapped copper, and the numerous copper inclusions with burials on the coast and elsewhere, suggest such linkages.[10]

The widespread distribution of metal artifacts, and the wide range of uses – such as inlay on labrets; tubular beads; an unusual set of copper "dancing images" or figurines recovered from the Queen Charlotte Islands (Deans 1885:15-16) (see Figure 9.5); daggers; spear and arrow points; and wire for suspending pendants – argue convincingly for a well established and sophisticated precontact metal-working tradition on the Northwest Coast and beyond. The growing inventory of sites that have yielded metal artifacts, and their wide geographical range, include such notable interior sites as Chinlac village (Borden 1952), Canoe Creek (Rousseau and Rousseau 1978), the Chase Burial site (Sanger 1968), and the recently uncovered Sheep Creek burials near Williams Lake. On the coast we have the Boardwalk site in Prince Rupert Harbour (MacDonald 1983), Scowlitz on the Fraser River (Blake and Brown 1998), and Ozette on the Washington coast as well as the recently reported Chinookan site on the Lower Columbia River (Ames 1998), to name a few. An even more recent addition comes with the startling 1999 discovery of the frozen body of an Aboriginal who perished some 550 years ago near the divide between coastal and interior northwestern British Columbia. Found with the body was an assortment of artifacts, including a small hand tool equipped with what appears to be an iron blade (A. Mackie, Archaeology Branch, Government of British Columbia, personal communication 1999).[11]

Figure 9.5 Small copper figures collected at Masset in 1883. J. Deans (1885) described them as "dancing images" and believed the pieces were made of native copper obtained from the Ahtna region of Alaska.

As well, the number of examples of precontact metal use may be greatly underrepresented when we consider that many archaeological sites have been assigned as a matter of course to the contact period because of the presence of metal. On closer examination, many of these sites may prove to be older, adding to the evidence for an established metallurgical tradition on the Northwest Coast.

While not a systematic, critical treatment of the topic, the evidence I have gathered points to Northwest Coast groups having possessed a sophisticated knowledge of and skill in working metal prior to contact. Both copper and, to a lesser degree, iron were widely available to precontact populations. Not only do we have a growing inventory of metal artifacts, to which the Louscoone Point example can be added, but the skill shown with the production of some truly remarkable pieces at the outset of contact points to a metallurgical tradition with a long history. It would be difficult to account for the strength and extent of such work as simply a postcontact transferring of skills achieved in one medium, such a woodworking, to metal. Equally telling is the fact the Aboriginal community was fully cognizant of the use and properties of iron at the outset of contact and exhibited considerable acumen when it came to assessing the quality of this metal. If a conclusion can be drawn, then the evidence presented here should serve as "the thin edge of the wedge" to accepting the idea of an incipient precontact metallurgical tradition on the Northwest Coast.

Acknowledgments

Rebecca Wigen and an unknown student lab assistant are credited for having discovered the fragment of copper wire among faunal samples collected at Louscoone Point in 1985. That work was part of a much larger archaeological study of the southern Queen Charlotte Islands funded by the British Columbia Heritage Trust and Petro-Canada Resources, with the support of the Skidegate Band Council of Haida Gwaii. My thanks to Daryl Fedje of Parks Canada for production of the map and to Al Mackie for his practical assistance throughout the preparation of this chapter.

Notes

1 One such slab on display in Whitehorse, Yukon Territory, weighs in excess of 1,130 kilograms.
2 Naturally occurring in the earth's crust.
3 See Keddie (1990:16-18) for a brief review of some of the evidence for the diffusion of metal from Asia.
4 In a study of the protohistorical trade networks of the Skeena River region, George MacDonald (1984:74) made a similar observation, remarking that "metal and trade goods converge[d] on the Northwest coast from three or four directions from the very beginning of the eighteenth century."
5 Keddie (1990:18) has suggested an Asiatic origin for the essential form of the copper among Northwest Coast groups. An intriguing idea, and perhaps the earliest historical record as to the possible function of the copper comes from Colnett (N.d.), who wrote in 1787 that "their [Haida] Copper Breast plate is their under armour, & the wooden stay w: wh is the second case."

6   According to McIlwraith (1948:253), the Nuxalk recognized two forms of copper, making the distinction between native and trade copper. Coppers made of native copper were thicker and heavier and were produced "by heating the metal in a fire, beating it into the required shape." The native form, obtained through trade from northern groups, was considered much more valuable.

7   Some specimens reached lengths of more than 50 centimetres. One example (54 centimetres), collected by Edward Fast in Alaska in 1867-68, has thin copper overlays covering the blade heels, which lead Fast to describe the item as a sword rather than a dagger. The blade form of these early one-piece daggers, with their rounded heels, ogival-shaped silhouette, raised midrib (or flutes) and clipped point is strikingly reminiscent of early European Bronze Age daggers (Vaughan and Holm 1982:67).

8   The trading acumen of the Haida was very quickly recognized by maritime traders, due in large part to the kinds of goods, in addition to the quality of the goods, they sought in trade. Fleurieu (1801:240) made the astute observation in 1791, while trading with the Haida, that the kinds of goods preferred in trade were never "agreeable to the useful."

9   The volume of goods was tremendous. Gray's expedition alone between 1790 and 1792 carried 267 sheets of copper, weighing close to 1,600 kilograms, and 6,755 quarter-pound "chisulls" and other assorted goods (Hoskins N.d.). There were in excess of 450 known expeditions to the Northwest Coast for the period between 1785 and 1825 (Acheson 1998:100).

10 A particularly poignant example is the mummified burials accidentally uncovered at Canoe Creek on British Columbia's interior plateau in 1978. The individuals were buried with an extensive assortment of worked copper. Also associated with one burial was a large iron spear point. Ironically, although the copper could not protect them from smallpox, it did preserve their bodies (and belongings) after death. Copper nitrate and cupric amine produced from chemical reactions with the copper acted as a bacteriocide and fungicide contributing to their remarkable preservation (Rousseau and Rousseau 1978:29-30).

11 Named *Kwaday Dan Sinchi* ("Long-Ago Person Found") by the Champagne and Aishihik First Nation, the body was discovered in the St. Elias Mountains. The tool came with a leather pouch, and attached to the wooden handle is a section of an animal bone or a tooth backing a badly deteriorated fragment of iron. Further analysis is planned to confirm the identification.

Aboriginal Education Department
12772 - 88 Avenue, Surrey BC V3W 3J9
RESOURCE CENTRE

10
A Stitch in Time: Recovering the Antiquity of a Coast Salish Basket Type
Kathryn Bernick

Tracing cultural diversity on the Northwest Coast back through time is constrained by the highly perishable nature of many items of material culture as well as by the dearth of ethnographic information for the early postcontact period. Although the conventional "non-perishable" archaeological record can document cultural change (e.g., McMillan, Chapter 11, this volume), the absence of a ubiquitous culturally sensitive artifact type such as ceramics hinders reconstruction of cultural relations in antiquity. This highlights the contributions of "wet sites" where normally perishable wood and bark artifacts are preserved in anaerobic water-saturated deposits. Wet sites on the Northwest Coast often contain large quantities of basketry (e.g., Croes 1977) – which comprises an artifact type with proven potential to reflect ethnicity and other sociocultural characteristics (see Adovasio 1986 and references therein; Elsasser 1978; Jones 1976; Mason 1988 [1904]; Porter 1990; Petersen 1996).

Basketry resembles ceramics in its capacity to inform reconstructions of the past. James Deetz (1967:45-49) credits additive manufacturing processes, such as making baskets and clay pots, with optimum potential to display variation that represents cultural traditions. He reasons that, because artifact form corresponds to a "mental template" specific to a cultural group, basketry holds considerable promise for reconstructing ethnicity and cultural identity in the archaeological record. This capacity of basketry has been demonstrated for the Great Basin culture area (Adovasio 1986). Similarly enlightening conclusions should be forthcoming for the Northwest Coast when more archaeological basketry collections are recovered. Descriptive studies (e.g., Emmons 1993; Laforet 1984; Nordquist and Nordquist 1983; Paul 1981; Thompson and Marr 1983) as well as statistical analyses (Jones 1976) document that, during the postcontact era, Aboriginal people of the Northwest Coast made baskets in techniques and styles that identify them as the respective products of particular cultural groups. Archaeological

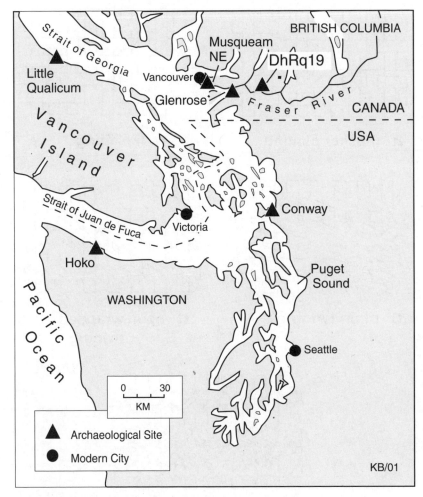

Figure 10.1 Locations of selected wet sites in the Coast Salish region and surrounding area.

specimens display the same degrees of variability (e.g., Bernick 1998b; Croes 1977, 1989b).

This chapter presents an example of how basketry can elucidate questions of cultural attribution in the Coast Salish region of the Northwest Coast. The story concerns a recently found 1,000-year-old archaeological basket and the insight it provides into an enigmatic type of basket made by Coast Salish women in the late twentieth century. Before proceeding with the story, I provide some contextual information about Coast Salish basketry. Figure 10.1 indicates locations of archaeological sites. For definitions of basketry weaves, see Figure 10.2.

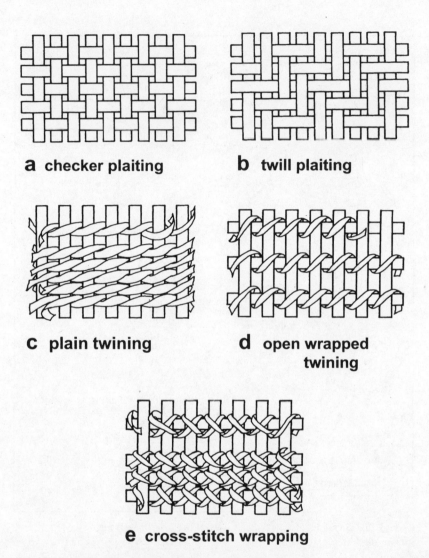

Figure 10.2   Basket weaving techniques mentioned in the text.

I also wish to stipulate that the anomalous archaeological specimen comprises a poor sample of a fragmentary archaeological record. Whether it represents a common method of making baskets in the past cannot be deduced from a single example. Nonetheless, its unique techno-stylistic characteristics call for explanation. Direct dating indicates that it is not modern, and the fragility of its construction and the perishable nature of the material argue against postdepositional relocation from far away. Since the only known analogues are modern specimens from the same region, an explanation that links the ancient and modern technologies seems plausible.

Coast Salish Basketry

My interest in basketry as an indicator of ethnicity and cultural identity began in the early 1980s with an attempt to find parallels for unusual types of baskets from wet sites in the Coast Salish region, particularly the 3,000-year-old Musqueam Northeast (DhRt 4) assemblage that I was analyzing in collaboration with David Archer (Archer and Bernick 1990). I searched the ethnographic and ethno-historical literature for information about woven baskets on the Northwest Coast. I focused on woven (versus coiled) baskets because all archaeological basketry from the Coast Salish region is woven. To my knowledge, no coiled basketry dating from the precontact era has been recovered in the Coast Salish region. I also looked at museum collections but found them of limited use for my purpose due to poor provenance documentation. Museum accession records, which track the source of an acquisition (i.e., the vendor or donor), often lack information that identifies the person who made it or even the place and date of manufacture. For the Northwest Coast as a whole, I concluded that woven basket types from the postcontact era fall into three geographic clusters, which I referred to as "Northern," "Wakashan," and "Southern" basketry areas (Bernick 1987:253-254). This clustering differs from other anthropological subdivisions of the Northwest Coast culture area (see Suttles 1990c:9-12). Notably, the Coast Salish region does not appear as an entity. Moreover, the boundary between my Southern and Wakashan basketry areas cuts across the middle of the region inhabited by Coast Salish peoples. I hasten to emphasize that this geographic pattern in which the Coast Salish are not represented reflects ethnographic and ethno-historical information only about woven baskets.

If we consider the full range of basketry technology as it was practised on the Northwest Coast during the postcontact era – that is, coiling as well as weaving – then the Coast Salish region is clearly distinct. The Coast Salish did and still do make baskets by coiling, and in this respect Coast Salish ethnographic basketry decidedly differs from that of their coastal neighbours, none of whom made coiled baskets. Coiling and weaving are entirely different ways of making baskets (compare Figures 10.2 and 10.3). Coiled baskets are sewn, not woven. The difference is so pronounced that some anthropologists (e.g., Drucker 1963:202) cite coiled basketry as a diagnostic trait defining the Coast Salish. However, apparently the Coast Salish did not make coiled basketry before the contact era (Barnett 1955:124; Haeberlin, Teit, and Roberts 1928:133-136). They adopted coiling from the Interior Salish, at least in part to take advantage of opportunities created by the tourist and collector market. The ethnographic information about Coast Salish basketry was obtained in the late nineteenth century and first half of the twentieth century, as were most museum collections of postcontact Coast Salish baskets. They mainly document coiled basketry and do not reflect the industry as it existed prior to contact-induced influences. Therefore, in the

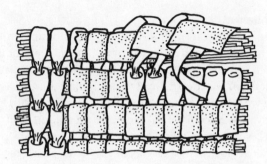

Figure 10.3 Imbricated split-stitch bundle-foundation coiling technique characteristic of Salish basketry.

case of the Coast Salish, tapping the potential of basketry to inform reconstructions of cultural identity in the past requires archaeological evidence.

Although as yet no Coast Salish archaeological basketry is reported from the early postcontact era, there are now seventeen dated collections from the Coast Salish region, ranging in age from 4300 BP to 700 BP (Bernick 1998b:142). Comparisons of techno-stylistic attributes with those of ancient baskets from other parts of the Northwest Coast reveal marked differences. Archaeological data show that in the Coast Salish region basketry was distinctive for at least three millennia (Croes 1977, 1989, 1995:116-132). They also provide evidence of techno-stylistic changes in basketry within that time span – changes that coincide chronologically with the phases and culture types that were identified from other types of evidence (Bernick 1998b).

In terms of basketry, the Coast Salish region is recognizably distinct in modern times and also in antiquity – but due to different aspects of the technology. Since there is a gap in data for the era spanning the time of contact, when Coast Salish basketry technology changed from exclusively woven to predominantly coiled, the respective archaeological and ethnographic records of Coast Salish basket styles do not show continuity. Nonetheless, the observation that techno-stylistic attributes of baskets cluster in a consistent geographic pattern in both pre- and postcontact times seems to me significant. If this region has been inhabited by the same cultural group (Coast Salish) from antiquity through to modern times, then basketry should reflect the continuity.

Evidence of technological continuity in basket styles that links the archaeological and ethnographic records exists elsewhere on the Northwest Coast. For example, in the case of Tsimshian basketry, Dale Croes (1989) finds statistically significant similarities between postcontact museum specimens and the 2,000-year-old assemblage from Lachane (GbTo 33) near Prince Rupert, British Columbia. In southeastern Alaska, even though only a few small collections of archaeological basketry are reported, there is clear evidence that ethnographic Tlingit basketry has very ancient roots. Cylindrical baskets woven in plain twining, which are considered to be typical ethnographic Tlingit manufactures (Emmons 1993; Paul 1981), have parallels in a 6,000-year-old specimen from Prince of Wales Island (Fifield and Putnam 1995) and 5,000-year-old basketry from Baranof Island (Bernick 1999). The technique that Tlingit basket makers call "between weave" (alternating rows of checker plaiting and plain twining) is reported from a 600-year-old site at Yakutat (Davis 1996:516-519).

The evidence of linguistics and oral history indicates cultural continuity in the Coast Salish region linking the pre- and postcontact eras (see McMillan, Chapter 11, this volume). Moreover, the conventional non-perishable archaeological record shows the Coast Salish region as a distinct cultural entity for the past several millennia (Mitchell 1971a, 1990). Evidence for cultural continuity should also be manifested in basketry technology. Basketry is credited as being highly sensitive to cultural preferences and a better indicator of ethnicity than many other classes of archaeological remains (Adovasio 1986; Deetz 1967:46-49; Matson and Coupland 1995:180). As I have previously argued (Bernick 1987), there should be as-yet-unrecognized residual specimens of distinctive types of archaeological woven baskets in the repertoire of Coast Salish basket makers from the past 200 years or so. Coiling is unlikely to have abruptly and completely replaced weaving techniques that were a long-standing cultural tradition.

Alan Hoover (1989) suggests that baskets woven in twill plaiting (Figure 10.2b) from wood splints may represent one such residual type. In the course of seeking analogues for a wood-splint twill-plaited basketry cradle purchased on southeastern Vancouver Island and acquired by the Royal British Columbia Museum in 1988, Hoover found a few examples of similarly constructed postcontact Coast Salish woven baskets. The closest parallels that he discovered were two archaeological specimens from the Puget Sound area of 700 and 1,200 years old. In the following paragraphs I describe another distinctively Coast Salish basket type that spans the pre- and postcontact eras and relate how I came to know about it and to appreciate it.

An Unusual Find

The story begins in September 1993. A private citizen rescued a waterlogged basket from the surface of a muddy beach in the Fraser River estuary in the Vancouver suburb of Coquitlam. The finder correctly surmised that the basket would be of scientific interest. He brought the basket to the attention of an archaeologist he knew, who referred him to me. Although I have come to know about quite a few interesting wet-site finds through similar circumstances, this particular basket genuinely captivated me (Figure 10.4). It is

Figure 10.4   Ancient cross-stitch-wrapped basket from DhRq 19.

woven entirely in a cross-stitch-wrapping technique (Figure 10.2e), which is unlike anything I had remembered seeing before.

The location where the cross-stitch-wrapped basket was found is a re-corded, though uninvestigated, archaeological site, DhRq 19 (Figure 10.1). It features an eroding river-beach component containing perishable arti-facts; that is, ancient objects made of wood and bark. I had known about this water-saturated component since 1990 and had seen other perishable artifacts that were rescued from it – some by collectors, others by archaeolo-gists. In addition to portable artifacts, nub ends of stakes (probably remnants of a fish trap or weir) can be seen protruding from the mud during seasons of low tides when water levels in the Fraser River are low.

The perishable artifacts that have been recovered from DhRq 19 include other unusual specimens in addition to the cross-stitch-wrapped basket. One artifact appears to be the remains of a net weight. It consists of an oval hoop, 18 centimetres long and 8 centimetres wide, a stone weighing 27 grams that originally would have been positioned at the centre of the hoop, and remnants of cherry bark strips that attached the stone to the sides of the hoop. The hoop is fashioned from a withe, probably western red cedar, measuring 5 millimetres in diameter. Additional perishable artifacts recov-ered from the site include braided bundles of twigs, wood-fibre cordage, cedar-bark cordage, fragments of a checker-plaited (Figure 10.2a) cedar-bark basket, and fragments of a checker-plaited cedar-bark mat. There are stone artifacts on the river beach, including fragments of ground slate knife blades.

Most of the perishable artifacts from DhRq 19 that I have seen are unex-pected or unusual forms for the region. Neither hoop-type net weights nor braided twigs are reported from ethnographic or archaeological contexts in this part of the Northwest Coast culture area. Checker-plaited cedar-bark basketry is uncommon in archaeological assemblages from the Coast Salish region, though specimens have been recovered from some Gulf of Georgia culture-type components that are about 1,000 years old (Bernick 1998b).

The cross-stitch-wrapped basket is unique. It is made from slender withes or roots about 4 millimetres in diameter. Microscopic examination of thin sections, which I conducted in September 1993, confirmed the wood species as western red cedar (*Thuja plicata*). My examination included samples of the warp and of each of the two types of weft elements, all of which are western red cedar. (I was unable to determine whether the wood is root or withe; for methods see Bernick 1983:341-348.) The basket was at least 19 centimetres high and had flared sides. Neither the base nor the rim (selvage) has survived. The weave is slightly open and of relatively fine gauge, seventeen warps per 10 centimetres. The warp (i.e., the vertical weaving elements) consists of longitudinally split withes/roots. The weft, which is oriented at a right angle to the warp, consists of two types of elements. One of these is a rigid whole-round element that was placed across the warp on the inside. I refer to it as the rigid, or the passive, weft element. The other type of weft element is flexible and active. It is made of thin, longitudinally split withes/roots. The flexible weft strand attaches the rigid one to the warps by wrapping them at the points of intersection (Figure 10.2e). On the working surface (the outside) each intersection of warp and weft is covered by a cross-stitch (i.e., an X pattern). The non-working surface (the inside) is ridged and is completely covered by the wrapping element (the flexible weft strand), which passes diagonally across the warp-weft intersection and vertically between warps. On the inside the stitch looks like a tilted V. The ridges inside the basket are formed by the naturally rounded shape of the withes (or roots) that comprise the horizontally laid passive weft elements.

Search for Analogues

Ever since I first saw the DhRq 19 cross-stitch-wrapped basket, I have been looking for information and examples that would help place it in cultural context. My first clue came from the spring-summer 1993 catalogue of the Basketry School in Seattle, which offered a "cross stitch cedar" basket-making class. The illustration in the catalogue shows a cross-stitch-wrapped construction that differs from the archaeological specimen in shape and general appearance. It is square with straight sides rather than bowl-shaped, and it has thin cross-stitches that leave most of the warp visible. The instructor told me that she learned to make this type of basket in a class at the Burke Museum of Natural History and Culture in Seattle in 1983 (Phyllis Pearson, personal communication October 1993). She further related that, in the early 1990s at the Seattle Folk Life Festival, she had watched a Lummi woman make a cross-stitch-wrapped basket with a handle and that the woman said her grandmother had made them that way.

At about the same time, Dale Croes (whom I had contacted with an excited "have-you-ever-heard-of-this-type-of-basket?" e-mail message) sent me photographs of a cross-stitch-wrapped basket made in 1990 by Ida Williams of Swinomish. The Swinomish and Lummi are Coast Salish tribes in the Puget Sound region south of the Fraser Delta. Croes (personal communication November 1993) knew of other basket makers in the Puget Sound region who make cross-stitch-wrapped baskets. Subsequently, I found a photograph of a cross-stitch-wrapped basket in June Collins's (1974) ethnographic study of the Upper Skagit Indians, yet another Coast Salish tribe in the Puget Sound region. These modern cross-stitch-wrapped baskets are all woven in the same technique as the archaeological specimen but with materials that give them a different appearance. Instead of cedar withe/root elements, the modern specimens are made using strips of cedar bark for the warp and rigid weft, and coloured raffia for the cross-stitch wrapping. Moreover, because raffia is not indigenous to the Northwest Coast (it is African) and is a popular material for present-day fibre arts and crafts, it marks the modern cross-stitch-wrapped baskets as having non-traditional characteristics. I have seen several small baskets of this type for sale in shops in Victoria and Vancouver. When listed, the basket maker invariably hails from one of the Coast Salish tribes in the Puget Sound region.

Cross-stitch-wrapped baskets appear to be sparsely represented in museum collections. I have seen specimens on display at the Suquamish Museum near Seattle and in the Hastings Mill Museum in Vancouver. The University of British Columbia Museum of Anthropology does not have any. The Burke Museum of Natural History and Culture in Seattle has one cross-stitch-wrapped basket in its collections, but the curators and staff had not recognized it as Coast Salish. It was acquired from a private estate in 1969 and catalogued as "unknown style, contemporary piece; NWC?" (personal observation October 1999). The Royal British Columbia Museum has four cross-stitch-wrapped baskets and another two with the same general appearance but made using a combination of cross-stitch wrapping and wrapped twining (personal observation March 2000). None of the specimens at the Royal British Columbia Museum has documentation that indicates the cultural affiliation of the respective basket maker. One is catalogued as "Coast Salish type" and another as "Puget Sound??." Several were acquired on Vancouver Island, but that is not necessarily where they were made.

Most of the cross-stitch-wrapped baskets that I know about appear to have been made in the twentieth century, some of them in very recent times. Shapes vary from rectangular to cuboid. Many feature geometric designs or horizontal bands produced by using different colours of raffia. In 1998 I

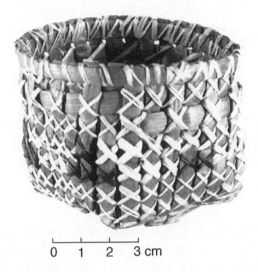

0   1   2   3 cm

Figure 10.5   Modern cross-stitch-wrapped basket; made by Lisa Boome (Upper Skagit). Size: 5 cm high.

had an opportunity to talk about this type of basket with Lisa Boome, a basket maker and member of the Upper Skagit Indian Tribe in Washington state. She grew up in the Fraser Valley and learned to make baskets from her aunt, who is a well known Stó:lö basket maker, and also from an Upper Skagit woman, now deceased. The latter taught her to make cross-stitch-wrapped baskets. Lisa Boome makes them with coloured raffia to effect designs (Figure 10.5), but she told me that the woman who taught her disdained the use of raffia and used cedar bark for the wrapping element.

Antiquity of the Cross-Stitch-Wrapping Technique

In support of my efforts to investigate the cross-stitch-wrapped archaeological specimen, the British Columbia Archaeology Branch funded AMS assays on samples from three DhRq 19 artifacts: the cross-stitch-wrapped basket, a checker-plaited cedar-bark basket fragment, and a checker-plaited cedar-bark mat fragment. The resulting dates (Table 10.1) cluster around 950 BP, which is consistent with the latest precontact culture type in the region (Mitchell 1990). That is exactly what I had expected for the two checker-plaited cedar-bark specimens. There are similar artifacts from 1,000-year-old components at the Conway site (45SK59b) and the Little Qualicum River site (DiSc 1) – both within the Coast Salish region (Bernick 1983; Munsell 1976). I was not sure what to expect for the cross-stitch-wrapped specimen, which is unique in the archaeological repertoire. It looks much more like the wrapped basketry that characterizes 3,000- and 4,000-year-old assemblages from the Fraser Delta than like the wrapped baskets from

Table 10.1

Age estimates for DhRq 19 perishable artifacts

Lab number	Artifact type	Material	Age BP[a]
Beta-73592/CAMS-14133	plaited basket fragment	cedar bark[b]	860 ± 60
Beta 73593/CAMS 14134	cross-stitch-wrapped basket	wood	900 ± 100
Beta-73594/CAMS-14135	plaited mat fragment	cedar bark[b]	1010 ± 60

a Conventional ^{14}C age at 1 sigma (not calibrated to calendar years).
b "Cedar bark" refers to secondary phloem tissue, not true bark.

younger collections. Since nothing is known about the physical or cultural stratigraphy of the DhRq 19 site, and the artifacts were recovered with no contextual information, their relationship to one another was unknown. Although it seemed to me likely that they would be the same age, the possibility that the site contains more than one cultural component could not be ruled out.

Another twist to this story concerns the nature of the cross-stitch-wrapping technique and the differences and similarities in details of construction between the 1,000-year-old specimen from the Fraser estuary and the recent examples from the Puget Sound region. On the Northwest Coast, cross-stitch wrapping occurs in archaeological basketry of various ages as an occasional row or part of a row, for example, to hold the centre of the base while beginning construction (see Bernick 1998a:Figure 1). The cross-stitch-wrapped basket from DhRq 19, as well as most of the modern specimens that I have seen, have basket walls made entirely by cross-stitch wrapping. Some recent baskets have one or more weft rows, usually at the top, woven in checker plaiting that is wrapped with cross-stitches.

From a technological perspective, cross-stitch wrapping is a variant of wrapped twining. Both are produced by laying a passive weft element across and at a right angle to the set of vertical warp elements and wrapping it onto them. But the method of wrapping differs (compare Figures 10.2d and 10.2e). The term "wrapped twining" is somewhat misleading since the active operation involves wrapping rather than twining. However, the term "wrapped twining" has been used in publications about Northwest Coast basketry for a century or more (e.g., Mason 1988:72-74 [1904]). During the postcontact era the close-woven form of wrapped twining has attained widespread recognition as a basketry technique characteristic of the Makah and the Nuu-chah-nulth. The open-weave version – that is, open wrapped twining (Figure 10.2d) – was made throughout the Wakashan region and also in parts of the Coast Salish region.

Wrapped weaves in general appear to be characteristic in the Coast Salish region during some eras, and there are a number of variants documented in archaeological collections. Whereas wrapped weaves predominate in 3,000- and 4,000-year-old assemblages, they are conspicuously absent from 2,000-year-old Marpole-age assemblages (Bernick 1998b). Basketry woven in open wrapped twining, which is the variant of wrapped weave documented for the Coast Salish in British Columbia during postcontact times, occurs in some archaeological sites in the region, including the 4,000-year-old component at Glenrose Cannery (DgRr 6) (Eldridge 1991:36-40) and the 1,000-year-old Little Qualicum River site (DiSc 1) (Bernick 1983:264-282). There are also open-wrapped-twined baskets in the Musqueam Northeast collection (Archer and Bernick 1990:98-109), but these, like a contemporaneous specimen from the Hoko River site (45CA213) (Croes 1995:Figure 4.50), differ in that the weave is "inside out" in comparison to younger specimens, both archaeological and ethnographic.

The method of weaving is exactly the same on the modern and archaeological cross-stitch-wrapped specimens. But they vary in respect to material, shape, and ornamentation, and consequently they differ in appearance. The archaeological cross-stitch-wrapped basket, which is now flattened, would have been bowl-shaped, and there is no evidence of designs or any other decoration (Figure 10.4). All three types of elements are thin cedar withes (or roots). The wrapping strand is essentially the same width as the warp elements so that the Xs cover most of the outer surface of the basket. Furthermore, the tension with which the wrapping was applied has resulted in non-symmetrical Xs.

The modern specimens (Figure 10.5) are made from thin, flat cedar-bark strips for the warp as well as for the passive wefts that lie across the warp on the inside of the basket. The wrapping strands, which are raffia, are much narrower than the cedar-bark strips so that the Xs leave much of the warp visible. The Xs are symmetrical and carefully aligned, serving both structural and decorative functions. Geometric designs are produced by using different colours of raffia. These baskets are rectangular, often cube-shaped with slightly rounded corners. The base is usually twill-plaited (Figure 10.2b). Rectangular twill-plaited bases are characteristic of archaeological baskets from the Coast Salish region, at least for the past 3,000 years.

Although some Coast Salish women who make cross-stitch-wrapped baskets today learned the technique from their mother or another older woman in the tribe, they do not know from whom those women learned it. I sense some uncertainty about the origins and antiquity of the cross-stitch-wrapping technique. The weavers who employ it recognize that it differs significantly from other types of Northwest Coast baskets. Cross-stitch wrapping is not mentioned in descriptions of Coast Salish ethnographic basketry (e.g., Jones 1982; Thompson and Marr 1983) and is not displayed in anthropological museums in the Pacific Northwest. Moreover, raffia, which is indigenous to Africa, clearly is not a traditional Coast Salish basketry material. Popular association of cross-stitching with European and North African embroidery adds to the uncertainty about its antecedents.

The Potential of Basketry

Despite the small sample size, I have no doubt that the modern type of basket made in cross-stitch wrapping from cedar bark and raffia is directly related to the version made from cedar wood fibres in antiquity. The similarity of the distinctive cross-stitch-wrapped weave seems too great to be attributed to coincidence. Cross-stitch wrapping appears to comprise a residual type of ancient woven basket that continues to be made in the Coast Salish region, albeit with changes. These changes are an example of what Leland Donald (Chapter 13, this volume) refers to as a dynamic local development. Donald emphasizes, citing Kroeber (1939), that the very intensity of such reworkings of cultural traits characterizes the Northwest Coast culture area. In this sense, the fortuitous archaeological find contributes to conceptualization of Coast Salish culture history as a process.

Phrased in more usual archaeological language, the DhRq 19 specimen woven in a cross-stitch-wrapping technique provides an example of stylistic continuity in the Coast Salish region from precontact times through to the present day. Although a sample of one is too small to suggest conclusions about the prevalence of this basket type in antiquity, it nonetheless reinforces the premise that basketry has considerable capacity to provide evidence of cultural traditions. I suggest that cross-stitch-wrapped baskets are one type of distinctive Coast Salish artifact reflecting cultural continuity. Wood-splint twill-plaited baskets appear to be another (see Hoover 1989). In both cases, archaeological basketry specimens comprise clues for recovering lost information about ethnographic traits. To realize the full potential of basketry to inform Coast Salish culture history will require discovery and detailed documentation of larger samples and additional archaeological collections.

Another, equally relevant, conclusion concerns implications for present-day Coast Salish basket makers who weave cross-stitch-wrapped baskets. To them, the discovery of an ancient specimen assumes a personal dimension, and the way in which the basket type has changed demonstrates the skill, versatility, and creativity of their ancestors. The archaeological find reassures people like Lisa Boome that the seemingly unusual method of weaving baskets that they learned from their elders was not invented recently or adopted from missionaries and White settlers but, rather, that it is grounded in a cultural tradition that is at least 1,000 years old.

The relationship of basketry to ethnicity and cultural identity is complex and multifaceted. One may look upon the unique archaeological cross-stitch-wrapped basket as evidence that projects either forward in time to enlighten the ethnographic record or backward in time to illustrate the antiquity of a Coast Salish characteristic. The artifact documents a particular cultural trait at a specific time in the past. Simultaneously, it documents the product of a dynamic culture.

Acknowledgments
I am grateful to the institutions and individuals who have facilitated my research of the cross-stitch-wrapped basket, especially Lisa Boome, Dale Croes, Alan Hoover, Joyce Johnson, Martin Oates, Phyllis Pearson, Laura Phillips, Michele Robbins, and Robin Wright. The AMS date estimates are courtesy of the British Columbia Archaeology Branch. My thanks to Glen Joe of the Kwikwetlem First Nation for reviewing the manuscript and to R.G. Matson and Leland Donald for constructive editorial suggestions.

11
Reviewing the Wakashan Migration Hypothesis
Alan D. McMillan

An expansion of Wakashan-speakers from an initial homeland has been suggested by a number of researchers as providing the best explanation for the present distribution of Aboriginal languages on the central and southern coast of British Columbia as well as accounting for a perceived discontinuity in the archaeological record at several locations in this area. The importance accorded migration in archaeological explanations, however, has varied considerably over the past several decades. This chapter examines the fluctuating fortunes of migrationism in archaeological theory, places the Wakashan migration hypothesis in its historic context, and extends the argument to the southern Wakashan.

History of Migration as an Explanation on the Northwest Coast
In the early years of Northwest Coast studies, migrations were commonly invoked to explain the observed distribution of cultural traits. Franz Boas (1905:96) considered the Tsimshian and Salishan groups to be relatively recent migrants from the interior, displacing "an older littoral people." Alfred Kroeber (1923:17) shared this view of the Salish as late arrivals on the coast. In his major synthesis, Kroeber (1939:28) suggested that the basic Northwest Coast cultural pattern had its beginning in the interior as groups adapted first to riverine environments and only later achieved fully maritime lifeways. Later anthropologists built on this idea, judging the Wakashan, particularly the Nuu-chah-nulth of western Vancouver Island, to have the fewest "interior" traits and, therefore, to resemble most closely the original coastal population. The Wakashan were described as "the purest strain of Coast culture" (Drucker 1955a:76) and "the base from which all coast cultures began" (Gunther 1960:270). The Salishan-speaking peoples, on the other hand, continued to be dismissed as recent arrivals from the interior (Drucker 1955a; cf. Suttles 1987d).

A tendency to attribute major changes in the archaeological record to migrations was a characteristic of North American archaeology into the 1950s

(Trigger 1989:194). The prominence of such ideas in the early development of archaeology on the Northwest Coast is particularly evident in the writings of Charles Borden. In his pioneer research along the lower Fraser River he identified what he thought was an early maritime, or "Eskimoid," culture that presumably had spread down the coast from the north (Borden 1950, 1951). Expressing views typical of his time, he considered the Nuuchah-nulth, whom he described as "the Indians who have lived longest on the coast" (Borden 1951:39), to be a surviving remnant of this early maritime population. Subsequent waves of migrants from the interior were repeatedly invoked to explain the changes in more recent artifact assemblages. In advancing his early interpretations, the following comments are typical:

> Great unrest was caused among the Salish. It appears that Salish-speaking groups were jostled out of positions in the Interior ... and migrated toward the Coast, where they adapted themselves to a new life. They did not necessarily settle for long periods of time in one place after arrival on the Coast, but often may have been hustled along to more distant places by new groups coming from the Interior ... It must be the remains of these intrusive Salish and of their descendants which we find in the upper levels of many of the middens along our Southern Coast. (Borden 1950:245)

Although this quote was taken from Borden's early work, prior to the availability of radiocarbon dates, even his later writings strongly feature such terms as "coastal expansion" and "population shifts" as explanations for changes in artifact types (e.g., Borden 1979:966).

By the 1960s, however, migrationist models for cultural change in the archaeological record were increasingly being viewed with distrust (Adams, Van Gerven, and Levy 1978). Such models were attacked on several levels. First, a variety of alternative explanations, not requiring wholesale movements of people, were increasingly applied to the archaeological data. Second, processualist viewpoints that were gaining dominance discouraged all forms of historical explanations in favour of more systemic models of analysis. Existing claims of past migrations were held to be inadequate as they did not attempt to explain why such movements occurred. Migrationism came to be viewed as non-scientific, applied post hoc to account for changes in the distribution of cultural traits. The general dismissal of such explanations as simplistic and impossible to test objectively led to a "retreat from migrationism" that persisted until relatively recently (Adams, Van Gerven, and Levy 1978; Anthony 1990, 1997).

In 1969, in a symposium on current archaeological research at the Northwest Anthropological Conference, Donald Mitchell presented the results of survey work he had been conducting in Johnstone Strait, off northeastern Vancouver Island (Mitchell 1969). In his conclusion, he contrasted the prevailing migrationist models with a continuity approach, emphasizing in situ development, and announced a commitment to such interpretations in his continuing fieldwork. Although Borden, a discussant in this session, denounced what he termed "Mitchell's Midden Manifesto" (Borden 1969:255), the theoretical emphasis had clearly shifted. Migrationism continued to play a role in archaeological interpretations on the Northwest Coast, but its former dominance was greatly eroded.

Following his stated intention, Mitchell employed a continuity approach in his later writings, particularly in his broad syntheses. In an overview of culture history along the Strait of Georgia, for example, he interpreted the available archaeological evidence as demonstrating continuity between each of the major stages, from at least the Charles phase (beginning c. 5500 BP) to the immediate ancestors of the historic Coast Salish in the region. Changes from one stage to the next were interpreted as "indigenous and evolutionary" (Mitchell 1990:352). Other researchers, writing around the same time, have also argued strongly for lengthy cultural continuity in the archaeological record of this region (e.g., Carlson 1983b, 1990, 1996; Carlson and Hobler 1993). The continuity model has clearly dominated in reconstructions of Northwest Coast culture history over the past few decades.

In one area, however, Mitchell has proposed population replacement to account for a perceived discontinuity in the archaeological record. Ironically, this was in the area around Queen Charlotte Strait off northern Vancouver Island, which includes the region where he initially proclaimed his commitment to a continuity model. In two overview articles (Mitchell 1988, 1990), he proposed two distinct cultural periods: an earlier Obsidian culture type, followed by the Queen Charlotte Strait culture type, the latter seen as directly ancestral to the Wakashan peoples speaking the Kwakwala language who occupied this region historically. Archaeological features of the two culture types differ markedly. In the Obsidian culture type a great quantity of obsidian flakes, generally showing evidence of bipolar production, dominate the artifact assemblage. Faunal remains suggest a broad economy, but coast deer were clearly paramount among the mammals represented, with harbor seal a distant second. By contrast, in the subsequent Queen Charlotte Strait culture type, flaked stone implements were all but absent. A wide range of artifact types was recovered in an assemblage dominated by bone tools, particularly small points and bipoints. Faunal remains indicate an emphasis on maritime resources, with harbor seal and sea lion dominating the mammals, and salmon overwhelmingly important among the fish. Mitchell (1988) examined a range of possibilities for this distinct cultural shift but eventually concluded that population replacement, occurring around 2400 BP or shortly after, provided the best explanation.

Linguistic Evidence

Earlier work in linguistics provided much of the framework for this hypothesis. Migrationism had not suffered the same decline in linguistics as it had in archaeology. In fact, it would be hard to account for the scattered distribution of many language families in any other manner. Indigenous oral traditions and more recent historical accounts also offer ample testimony of recurrent past population movements. Archaeologists, despite their earlier "retreat from migrationism," have expressed renewed interest within the past decade or so, although perhaps stressing a more rigorous application (Rouse 1986; Anthony 1990; Chapman and Hamerow 1997). Archaeological claims for population movements are strengthened by congruence with linguistic evidence or historic accounts (Rouse 1986; Renfrew 1987). Renfrew (1992) applauds the renewed interest between archaeology and historical linguistics, noting the possibility of a "synthesis on a grand scale." Attempts to trace movements of indigenous North American language families into their historic homelands, in addition to the Wakashan case discussed here, include the Numic-speakers in the Great Basin (Bettinger and Baumhoff 1982; Madsen and Rhode 1994), the Iroquoians of the eastern Great Lakes (Snow 1995), and the pioneers of Eskimoan stock who settled the Arctic (e.g., Dumond 1998). As there is no direct relationship between the distribution of people, languages, and objects, however, attempts to correlate archaeological remains with historic linguistic groups generally remain inconclusive.

The Wakashan language family contains two major branches, which are rather distantly related (Sapir 1911:15; Thompson and Kinkade 1990:39). The most numerous of the northern Wakashan are the various Kwakwala-speaking groups on northern Vancouver Island and the adjacent mainland. Historically termed the "Southern Kwakiutl," these people today prefer to be known collectively as the Kwakw<u>aka</u>'wakw (literally, "those who speak Kwakwala"). To the north are the closely related Heiltsuk (or Bella Bella) and Ooweekeno on the central British Columbian coast; the language of the Ooweekeno, known as Oweekyala, is considered a major dialect of Heiltsuk by most linguists (e.g., Thompson and Kinkade 1990; Goddard 1996; Campbell 1997), although others give it separate language status (Lincoln and Rath 1980; Rath 1982). The northernmost Wakashan are the Haisla, in close contact with the Tsimshian of the lower Skeena River and adjacent outer coast. The southern Wakashan branch consists of the Nuu-chah-nulth and Ditidaht along western Vancouver Island, along with the closely related Makah of the Olympic Peninsula in Washington state. Figure 11.1 shows the historic distribution of members of the Wakashan family, indicating hypothetical past movements.

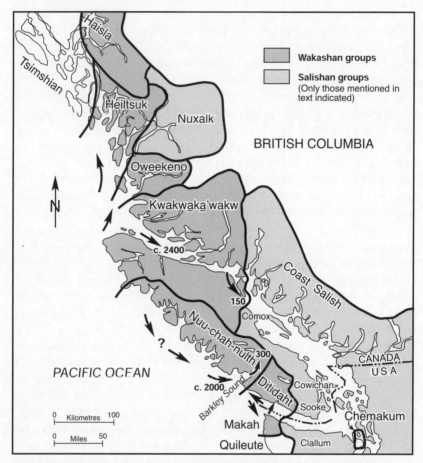

Figure 11.1   Historic distribution of Wakashan groups and their neighbours, showing hypothetical past movements and possible dates (expressed as BP, or "before present").

A number of linguists have suggested that the speakers of proto-Wakashan, ancestral to all members of the family, emerged from a homeland around northern Vancouver Island (Suttles and Elmendorf 1963; Kinkade and Powell 1976; Thompson and Kinkade 1990:47; Foster 1996:81). Edward Sapir (1916), in his pioneering work in historical linguistics, proposed the "centre of gravity" principle, the argument that the deepest cleavage between related languages will mark the original homeland. In the case of the Wakashan family, the greatest divergence occurs just south of Quatsino Sound, on northwestern Vancouver Island, at the boundary between the two branches. In a second principle, Sapir also suggested that, as languages continue to differentiate over time, the original homeland will be marked by the greatest linguistic diversity. This also seems to be met by the Wakashan case as both the Kwakwala and Nuu-chah-nulth languages, on each side of the boundary between the two branches, contain a series of dialects, while the Wakashan languages to the north and south are more uniform.

In an attempt to date the divergence of the two Wakashan branches, Swadesh (1953, 1954) employed detailed comparisons of word lists in a technique known as glottochronology, arriving at an estimate of about 2900 years. Glottochronology, however, rests on a set of highly questionable assumptions, including a constant rate of language change, and has had only limited acceptance. In a review of the Wakashan language family, however, Jacobsen (1979) found Swadesh's estimate to be "plausible." It is also in reasonable accord with the archaeological evidence, preceding by only a few centuries the evidence for cultural replacement in Queen Charlotte Strait noted by Mitchell (1988, 1990).

Despite the problems with glottochronology, some linguists (e.g., Foster 1996) defend its use, particularly considering recent refinements. In the Wakashan case, Embleton (1985) has recalculated the divergence between the two major branches, using a technique that takes into account borrowing and prolonged contact between members of the family. This led her to a considerably earlier estimate of about 5,500 years.

The geographic separation of the Nuxalk (or Bella Coola) from all other Salishan languages has also figured in the arguments for Wakashan expansion. Swadesh (1949:166) proposed that the Nuxalk isolation was due to incursions of "Kwakiutl" (northern Wakashan) along the coast as well as to Chilcotin moving southward in the interior. Suttles and Elmendorf (1963) later suggested that a Wakashan expansion from Vancouver Island had disrupted a continuous distribution of Salishan languages along the mainland coast, separating the Nuxalk from other members of the Salish family. This scenario rests on considering Nuxalk as belonging to the coastal branch of Salishan languages (Swadesh 1950; Suttles and Elmendorf 1963; Suttles 1987d). Newman (1974) and Kinkade (1991), however, note that numerous Nuxalk terms for coastal flora and fauna are borrowings from Heiltsuk, suggesting an interior origin. Present practice is to consider Nuxalk a distinct branch of the Salishan family, separate from both the coastal and interior Salish languages (Kennedy and Bouchard 1990a).

This hypothesis of northern Wakashan expansion was employed by Mitchell (1988, 1990) to account for the discontinuity in the archaeological record he noted in the Queen Charlotte Strait area. His Obsidian culture type was equated with the earlier Salishan populations, while the later Queen Charlotte Strait culture type was associated with the arriving northern Wakashan. Unfortunately, the Obsidian culture type, with five radiocarbon dates clustering between 2900 BP and 2400 BP (Mitchell 1988:253), is followed by an unexplained hiatus as there is no evidence for the poorly dated

Queen Charlotte Strait culture type until c. 1600 BP. This almost certainly reflects a gap in the data rather than abandonment of the area, and Mitchell (1990:353) elsewhere places the Queen Charlotte Strait culture type immediately following the earlier Obsidian. If population replacement is indeed reflected in these changing culture types, then this would date the Wakashan expansion from northern Vancouver Island to c. 2400 BP or the following few centuries. Other archaeologists have also found this model to be useful in explaining their data. Hobler (1990:305), for example, has suggested that archaeological changes discernible in the Bella Coola Valley between c. 4500 and 2000 BP may be attributable to movements of Salishan and Wakashan populations.

Less attention has been paid to movements of the southern Wakashan, the ancestral Nuu-chah-nulth, Ditidaht, and Makah, although insights regarding their past movements may also be derived from historical linguistics. As the groups that became the historic Nuu-chah-nulth moved south along the outer west coast, they left a chain of dialects extending to just south of Barkley Sound. Subsequent southern movements eventually gave rise to the southernmost Wakashan peoples, the Ditidaht and Makah. Lack of internal dialects, as well as close similarity with Nuu-chah-nulth, suggests relatively recent separation as distinct languages. Ditidaht and Makah are particularly close, with a considerable level of intelligibility between them (Bates 1987:54; Arima 1988:23). The divergence of Ditidaht and Makah may have occurred about 1,000 years ago, based on glottochronology (Jacobsen 1979:776).

Prior to the Makah arrival, the northern Olympic Peninsula appears to have been the homeland of Chimakuan peoples. By historic times this language family was reduced to two widely separated members: the Quileute (on the outer coast south of the Makah) and the Chemakum (at the northeast of the peninsula adjoining Puget Sound) (Kinkade and Powell 1976; Elmendorf 1990:438). Lack of any strong differentiation between these two languages suggests that they had been separated in relatively recent times, presumably by the arrival of the Makah. The Clallam Salish also historically held territory between the two Chimakuan groups, although their arrival is thought to have been even later (Kinkade and Powell 1976:97; Foster 1996:82). This scenario is given further strength by the presence in the Makah language of Chimakuan place names for prominent landmarks in Makah territory (Kinkade and Powell 1976). Swadesh (1955:60) estimated a time depth of about 2,100 years between Quileute and Chemakum, although this need not refer directly to the time of Makah arrival. Kinkade and Powell (1976) suggest that the Makah occupation of the Olympic Peninsula began about 1,000 years ago, although evidence for such a date is highly tentative. In a review of the archaeology of the Olympic Peninsula, Wessen (1990:421) cautions that there is no discernible break in the archaeological record as known for the past two millennia or so. Swadesh's glottochronological determination may provide a more realistic estimate than Kinkade and Powell's suggested date.

Among the Ditidaht, extant oral traditions of population movements describe a relatively late arrival in their historic territory. According to one such tradition, the Ditidaht stem from a group of people who lived at Tatoosh Island, off Cape Flattery in historic Makah territory (Bates 1987:293-94; Clamhouse et al. 1991:288). After a battle with the inhabitants of Ozette, the most southerly Makah village, the ancestors of the Ditidaht moved across the Strait of Juan de Fuca and settled around the Jordan River, near the historic boundary with the Salish-speaking Sooke. There they lived for a long time, taking their name from that of the Jordan River (*Diitiida*) (Bouchard and Kennedy 1991:3; Clamhouse et al. 1991:285). Frequent hostilities with their Salish neighbours eventually led them to move further north along the coast, settling in a number of villages around lower Nitinat Lake and the adjacent outer coast. Such detailed recorded traditions of past population movements are unique among the southern Wakashan. If Jacobsen's (1979:776) estimate of 1,000 years for the linguistic separation of Ditidaht and Makah is accurate, then this may roughly date the Ditidaht movement back to Vancouver Island.

Archaeological Evidence

If this linguistic information accurately reflects past population movements along the west coast of Vancouver Island, can evidence of this migration be detected in the archaeological record? Although far from conclusive, recent archaeological research around Barkley Sound suggests that it can. The archaeological evidence for the west coast is limited, however, as few excavation projects of any size have been conducted in Nuu-chah-nulth and Ditidaht sites of the necessary age to detect such culture change.

Our view of Nuu-chah-nulth culture history has been drawn primarily from the major village site of Yuquot (DjSp 1) in northern Nuu-chah-nulth territory at the entrance to Nootka Sound. Until recently, this was the location of the only large-scale excavation on western Vancouver Island providing a lengthy and continuous cultural sequence, extending back over 4,000 years. Dewhirst (1978, 1980) has argued for cultural continuity throughout this time, interpreting any changes in the archaeological record as increasing adaptation to the outer coast environment over time. The West Coast culture type, proposed by Mitchell (1990) in his archaeological overview, was defined almost entirely on Yuquot and the nearby Hesquiat Harbour sites. This culture type was presented as a stable and relatively unchanging continuum leading directly to the historic Nuu-chah-nulth groups. From earliest times at Yuquot the artifact types were considered to be recognizable in terms of historic Nuu-chah-nulth material culture.

Evidence of population replacement, however, may occur to the south in the area around Barkley Sound. The argument is strongest from the Shoemaker Bay site (DhSe 2) at the end of the long Alberni Inlet from Barkley Sound (McMillan and St. Claire 1982). Throughout the time period represented by these deposits, extending back as much as 4,000 years, the entire cultural sequence was tied to the Strait of Georgia and was markedly dissimilar to the West Coast culture type as known from Yuquot. This was particularly evident in the artifact assemblage from the earliest component, Shoemaker Bay I, which contained chipped stone tools, including stemmed and leaf-shaped projectile points and knives; ground stone points, including large faceted examples; and quartz crystal and obsidian microblades and microflakes. All are characteristic of the Locarno Beach culture type in the Strait of Georgia (Mitchell 1990:341; Mitchell 1998a:468; Matson and Coupland 1995:156), with which they are contemporaneous. In contrast, ground stone artifacts are relatively rare, and those of chipped stone are nearly absent from West Coast assemblages (Mitchell 1990:356). Shoemaker Bay I also contained a burial covered with boulders, resembling cairn burials known from Locarno Beach sites (Matson and Coupland 1995:161). The later component, Shoemaker Bay II, most closely resembles the contemporaneous Strait of Georgia culture type in that region, although several artifact types indicate ties to West Coast sites (McMillan and St. Claire 1982; Mitchell 1990:357).

This archaeological evidence for an earlier Strait of Georgia-related occupation was supported by strong ethnographic traditions and linguistic evidence for late Nuu-chah-nulth arrival in the Alberni Valley, displacing and absorbing earlier Salishan populations. The Nuu-chah-nulth arrival and occupation of this area is well documented in the oral traditions and ethnographic accounts (Sproat 1868:179; Boas 1891b:584; Carmichael 1922:51-64; Drucker 1951:5; St. Claire 1991:30, 79-81). Although the earlier residents were acculturated into Nuu-chah-nulth language and traditions, certain Salishan names and speech patterns persisted (Sapir 1913:77; Sapir 1915:19). In the late nineteenth century several middle-aged informants told Boas (1891b:584) that their grandfathers had spoken a Salishan language (the Nanaimo dialect of Halkomelem). This and other chronological clues suggest a very late Nuu-chah-nulth arrival, possibly only in the eighteenth century. This reinforces the archaeological view of the West Coast culture type as an outer coast adaptation, only in very late times extending to the far inner reaches of the west coast.

More recently, similar claims came from archaeological work at Little Beach (DfSj 100), an outer coast site at Ucluelet on the western edge of Barkley Sound. Shell midden deposits on a raised beach terrace are dated between 4000 BP and 3000 BP, with an overlying darker layer dating to 2500 BP, after which the site was apparently abandoned (Arcas Consulting Archeologists

1991). Only a small sample of artifacts was recovered during the brief salvage excavation, but these include such diagnostic items as a leaf-shaped chipped stone projectile point, a crudely chipped cobble tool, a thick ground slate point fragment, and a fragment of what appears to be a large flanged labret. Numerous midden inhumations, including cairn burials, were also encountered. Again, such traits differ markedly from those known from the lower levels at Yuquot, instead resembling Shoemaker Bay I and the contemporaneous Locarno Beach culture in the Strait of Georgia. While this led the excavators to postulate a cultural stage preceding the Nuu-chah-nulth in this area, the small excavated sample precluded any definitive statement.

Large-scale archaeological research was initiated in this area by the Toquaht Archaeological Project (McMillan and St. Claire 1991, 1992; McMillan 1999). In four field seasons between 1991 and 1996 we surveyed the shoreline of traditional Toquaht territory in western Barkley Sound and excavated at five sites. The most extensive excavations took place at two nearby ethnographic villages, T'ukw'aa (DfSj 23) and Ch'uumat'a (DfSi 4), both at the western edge of Barkley Sound near Ucluelet (see Figure 8.1). The large artifact sample from T'ukw'aa, the largest village, can be assigned to the West Coast culture type (McMillan and St. Claire 1992). It is characterized particularly by abundant small bone points of various types, along with a scarcity of stone artifacts other than abrasive stones, and a near-absence of chipped stone. This artifact assemblage differs markedly from Little Beach despite the close proximity of the two sites, a fact attributable to temporal differences as the dated deposits at T'ukw'aa are restricted to the last 1,200 years.

In a search for older materials, the Toquaht Project began work at the village site of Ch'uumat'a, slightly further into Barkley Sound (Figure 11.2). The front, brush-covered portion of the site was occupied into early historic times, with basal dates between 1000 BP and 2500 BP. Older portions of the site exist in the back forested area, where 4 metres of shell midden deposit date to as much as 4,000 years at the base. The 1996 excavation concentrated on this area, extending an earlier test unit into a two-metre-wide trench, reaching the clay and sand at the base of the cultural deposits for 7 metres of its length. A series of consistent radiocarbon dates provided a chronology for the trench deposits from c. 700 to 4000 BP (McMillan and St. Claire 1996; McMillan 1998).

Most of the Ch'uumat'a trench deposits are roughly contemporaneous with Locarno Beach in the Strait of Georgia, as well as with Little Beach and Shoemaker Bay I. Several cairn burials, dated to about 2500 BP, are among the common features linking Ch'uumat'a with these sites and the Strait of Georgia. Chipped stone artifacts include one stemmed and one leaf-shaped projectile point, several chipped schist knives, and two small pebbles showing bipolar retouch, classified as pièces esquillées (Figure 11.3). A considerable

Figure 11.2   Village site of Ch'uumat'a (DfSi 4). The open area at the front of the site was occupied into early historic times; older midden deposits extend into the forest behind. A cleared canoe run is visible on the beach.

number of flakes, some of which show evidence of retouch, were also found. Ground stone implements include small rectangular celts and a large faceted point fragment. All are characteristic traits of Locarno Beach assemblages in the Strait of Georgia (Mitchell 1990, 1998a; Matson and Coupland 1995) yet are absent from the West Coast culture type as presently known. Chipped stone artifacts comprise 10.6 percent of the artifact total from Ch'uumat'a deposits predating 2000 BP, a significant figure considering their virtual absence from contemporaneous levels at Yuquot. However, this is substantially below the frequency seen in Strait of Georgia sites, where chipped stone artifacts may comprise 30 percent to 55 percent of the totals (Matson and Coupland 1995:Table 6.2).

Some decorative items also suggest ties to the Strait of Georgia. A number of carefully shaped ground stone and bone objects have a general resemblance to Gulf Islands Complex items (or "whatzits") found in Locarno Beach contexts in some Strait of Georgia sites (McMillan 1998). In addition, an incised and drilled schist object (Figure 11.4) was excavated from the deepest level of the site, sitting on charcoal that yielded a date of 4000 BP. One polished face is incised with a design, following the shape of the scalloped edges, which resembles a feather-like or shell-like pattern. Similar fragments of schist and shale, with incised designs and decorative edges, came from equivalent time periods at the Glenrose site on the Fraser River (Matson 1976). Such items have been identified as a characteristic trait of the Charles

Figure 11.3 Chipped stone artifacts from Ch'uumat'a: *a-b*, projectile points; *c*, schist knife; *d-e*, pièces esquillées; *f*, andesite flake; *g-i*, chert flakes; *j*, chert debitage reworked as a possible piercer.

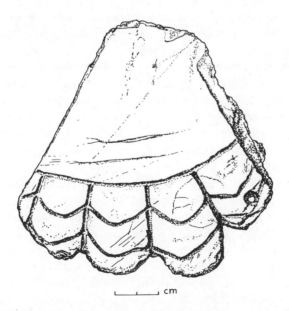

Figure 11.4 Incised and drilled schist object from the base of deposits at Ch'uumat'a.

culture type, which precedes Locarno Beach in the Strait of Georgia (Pratt 1992; Pokotylo 1998).

Although no major discontinuity is evident, the cultural sequence at Ch'uumat'a can be divided at about 2000 BP. The distinctive artifact types indicated here, including all chipped stone, are restricted to the earlier period (see McMillan 1998 for more detailed discussion). Conversely, certain artifacts characteristic of the West Coast culture type, such as stone and bone fish hook shanks, occur only in the later deposits at Ch'uumat'a. If the earlier period of occupation is related to Strait of Georgia cultures, as is suggested here, and the later stage is assigned to the West Coast culture type and is therefore considered ancestral Nuu-chah-nulth, then it can be argued that cultural replacement occurred around two millennia ago. This figure corresponds reasonably closely to Mitchell's estimate for northern Wakashan expansion into the Queen Charlotte Strait area.

Migration Incentives and Mechanisms
Any examination of migration hypotheses should also look at the driving forces that stimulated such population movements. Mitchell (1990:357) speculated for the northern area that the rich salmon fisheries in rivers such as the Nimpkish, plus the important eulachon fisheries in Knight and Kingcome inlets, could have provided the motivation. For the southern Wakashan, whaling likely provided the economic incentive. Arima (1988) and others (Clamhouse et al. 1991:289) have argued that it was development of effective open-ocean technology, including the historically known whaling equipment, that allowed southern Wakashan expansion, ultimately reaching the Olympic Peninsula. Later, desire to control the salmon rivers of the inner coast, along the sounds and inlets, became the primary ethnographic motivation for Nuu-chah-nulth warfare and territorial expansion (Swadesh 1948). New and more intensive methods of warfare may also have enabled Wakashan movement into new territories. Defensive sites on elevated rocky bluffs or islets are common features of Wakashan territory in both the northern and southern areas. Although few have been dated, their widespread occurrence, generally overlooking major village sites or controlling strategic coastal locations, suggests their fundamental importance in Wakashan patterns of settlement and defence.

It is also important to examine the mechanism by which language group distributions change. Terms such as "expansion" and "spread" have been criticized for not distinguishing between migrations of people and diffusion of languages (Adams, Gerven, and Levy 1978:486). Oral histories and ethnographic traditions are replete with specific accounts of past population movements, which also appear to be reflected in much of the linguistic data. In at least several cases, however, Wakashan expansion was accomplished by "linguistic capture" or cultural assimilation of other groups.

The two Nuu-chah-nulth bands in the Alberni Valley today provide a good example of this process. The larger of these bands, the Tseshaht, is a historic amalgamation of a number of formerly autonomous groups, several of which forcefully seized this area for control of its rich salmon fishery in relatively late times (McMillan and St. Claire 1982:14; St. Claire 1991:79-81; McMillan 1999:205-208). Genealogical clues in the ethnographic traditions place this event in the seventeenth or eighteenth century (St. Claire 1998:60-61). Members of the second group, the Hupacasath, trace their ancestry to three formerly Salishan-speaking local groups that occupied the valley prior to the Tseshaht arrival. After an initial period of warfare, during which many of the original occupants were killed, peace was established through intermarriage of chiefly families and the establishment of a new territorial boundary, by which the Tseshaht gained possession of most of the Somass River and its bountiful salmon runs (St. Claire 1998:58-59). Intensive contact and continued intermarriage with the newcomers eventually led to Hupacasath absorption into Nuu-chah-nulth culture. Language replacement in such cases may occur through a process of "elite dominance," a feature of ranked societies, where one group seizes control of political power and economic resources (Renfrew 1992:15).

In a similar case, the southernmost Ditidaht-speakers, the Pacheedaht at Port Renfrew, are known to have spoken the Salish language of their Sooke neighbours in earlier times (Clamhouse et al. 1991:289). Extensive intermarriage and acculturation through contact with the Ditidaht eventually led to the adoption of the Ditidaht language. This apparently occurred relatively recently ("three generations of grandparents ago when there were no Whitemen"), perhaps about the same time as Hupacasath acculturation into Nuu-chah-nulth culture.

Wakashan expansions have continued into recent times. By the mid-nineteenth century, the southernmost Kwakwala-speaking groups had forcefully occupied territory on northeastern Vancouver Island held by the Comox Salish, displacing that group to the south (Taylor and Duff 1956; Kennedy and Bouchard 1990b:441). Earlier access to firearms may have enabled the Wakashan expansion at the expense of their neighbours. As the newcomers took over this territory, around Campbell River and Quadra Island today, they retained the previous Salishan place names (Taylor and Duff 1956:59). Subsequent contact and intermarriage eventually led to extensive acculturation of the Island Comox, with Kwakwala gradually replacing Comox as the ceremonial language (Figure 11.5). Today Comox is simply considered the most southerly Kwakwaka'wakw village (Assu with Inglis 1989:11; Kennedy and Bouchard 1990b:441).

Among the southern Wakashan, groups of Ditidaht continued to move inland, one reaching Cowichan Lake by the mid-nineteenth century. In subsequent decades they established a village and intermingled with the

Figure 11.5   Dance house and totem pole at the modern Comox reserve on Vancouver Island. The painting and carving reflect the Kwakwa̱ka'wakw affiliation today.

Cowichan Salish (Jenness N.d.). In addition, in recent times intermarriage between the Pacheedaht and their Sooke Salish neighbours has led to inroads of the Ditidaht language among the latter group (Bates 1987:128).

Conclusion

These late Wakashan expansions provide glimpses into a process that began at least two millennia earlier. A perceived discontinuity around that time in the archaeological record of both the northern and southern Wakashan regions has been interpreted as evidence of these early movements. The earlier assemblages show ties, particularly in the relatively abundant chipped stone artifacts, to the contemporaneous Locarno Beach culture type in the Strait of Georgia, while the later materials have been seen as directly ancestral to the historic Wakashan. Only at Yuquot, located closer to the suggested Wakashan homeland of northern Vancouver Island, do we find an apparent continuity throughout the archaeological deposits, with an artifact assemblage markedly dissimilar to that of the Strait of Georgia.

Assessing this idea of a distinct Wakashan core area will require further research at sites of the requisite age on northern Vancouver Island, such as at Kyuquot or Quatsino Sound. Relatively few excavated and dated assemblages are known for the Wakashan area, and cultural constructs (such as the Obsidian culture type) are poorly understood. Although Mitchell

(1998b:700) has argued that cultural replacement in Queen Charlotte Strait provides the best explanation of the archaeological data, he also urges caution, stating that "too little work has been done in this region to make definitive statements about its culture history." Oral traditions, however, make it clear that cultural dislocations did occur, with both population movements and cultural assimilation of neighbouring peoples contributing to Wakashan linguistic expansion.

12
Location-Allocation Modelling of Shell Midden Distribution on the West Coast of Vancouver Island
Quentin Mackie

Predictive modelling of archaeological site location is now commonplace on the Northwest Coast and elsewhere. Most approaches use combinations of local environmental variables to divide the landscape into zones that have varying degrees of potential for archaeological sites. These zones may then be investigated to see if the kind and amount of archaeological materials within them meet expectations. Or, if there is a statistically useful sample of known site locations (and, crucially, non-site locations), then a more refined approach can be taken, in which environmental variables associated with known sites are subjected to multivariate analysis and a model can be built that seeks to explain (and thus predict) site location. In this approach, a validation sample of known sites and non-sites is held back and used to test the model. This sort of sophisticated archaeological predictive modelling is exemplified by work in Tebenkof Bay, Alaska (Maschner and Stein 1995), in which the authors demonstrated some success at explaining why some places in the coastal environment had shell midden sites and others did not. A model built through logistic regression and log-linear analysis produced the (rather non-surprising) result that variables such as solar exposure, climatic exposure, upland slope, and presence of fresh water were strong determinants of site location. In effect, these models attempt to recover the decision-making set that led people to site their activity in certain localities: they conducted activity in well-drained, sunny, sheltered places where one can land a canoe and have access to fresh water. One might thus hypothesize that the increasing quantity and/or quality of these determinant variables might positively correlate with site size: the nicer the place, the more time is spent there. However, these variables were completely independent of site size: "The intensity of occupation by Native Tlingit inhabitants was completely independent of these [environmental] factors ... we still have no understanding of the variables that influenced how long, or at least with what intensity, a site will be occupied" (1995:932).

One variable not included in the Tebenkof Bay study was the location of other archaeological sites, despite the probability that the presence of one site increases the likelihood of more sites being nearby. Naturally, a model that depended on known site locations would be of little use in a predictive modelling exercise. However, known site locations are themselves evidence for the social geography of the landscape and can be included in modelling-based settlement archaeology. In this chapter I discuss possible determinants of site size on the Northwest Coast, arguing that the spatial relationships between known site locations can explain certain aspects of site size. Application of a spatial interaction model to places and routes across a regional landscape produces a clear result but one that defies explanation in straight-forward decision-making terms. Before discussing the implementation of this model, I outline the study area and offer some orienting assumptions.

Study Area and Orienting Assumptions

The study area (Figure 12.1) is located on the west coast of Vancouver Island and includes the coastline between the southern boundary of Kyuquot

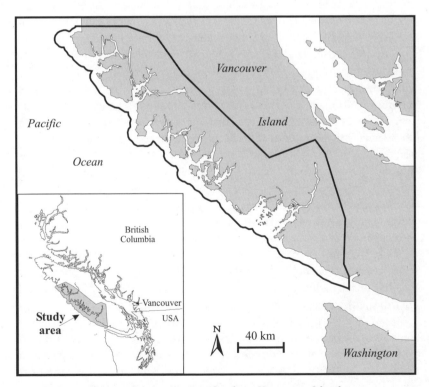

Figure 12.1   Study area, Kyuquot to Port Renfrew, Vancouver Island.

Channel and Port Renfrew, which is the area with the most complete archaeological coverage. This area measures approximately 240 kilometres by 80 kilometres in its maximum extents, although it contains considerably more linear kilometres of coastline. Site data current as of August 1994 were used, comprising 1,069 archaeological sites, of which 576 are shell middens. In order to limit the time frame as much as possible in a large region with little archaeological excavation, sea-level change has been used to establish site contemporaneity. Sea level for the west coast of Vancouver Island has been investigated by Friele (1991), who found that a still-stand approximately 2,000 years ago of 2 metres above modern sea level was followed by a period of dropping sea levels to the present day. All sites in this study are at least partially on the modern shoreline, with occupation at less than 2 metres elevation, and are therefore assumed to have been occupied during, though not necessarily exclusively during, the past 2,000 years. While this is an imperfect means of determining contemporaneity of site occupation, it does eliminate some sites known to have been long-abandoned, such as the Little Beach site (Arcas Associates 1992). Thus, the site record is believed to represent a reasonably knowable map of place, route, and intensity of use in the study area during the past 2,000 years.

Shell middens are a complex site type with a number of behavioural correlates. Nevertheless, all such sites to some extent represent "general activity," in the sense that the shell deposits are by-products of resource consumption and procurement activities, but the deposition of such shells is not an end in itself. Rather, shells accumulate as a by-product of other activities, and this makes them fundamentally different from features such as fishtraps or house platforms with their connotations of intentionality. No one ever set out to create a shell midden, yet they are a worldwide phenomenon. The British Columbia site record process recognizes this by assigning "general activity" as the primary "functional" category for shell middens, followed by more precise assignation (resource procurement, habitation, etc.) if possible. In this study, despite whatever functional assignments may have been made, all shell middens are considered comparable as records of general human activity in the world. Following Ingold's (1993:169) definition of a building as "any durable structure in the landscape whose form arises and is sustained within the current of human activity," the archaeological landscape of the study area is referred to as a built environment.

The size (area) of shell middens can be determined with unusual ease and some accuracy because of the distinctive matrix. In agreement with Maschner and Stein (1995), I argue that the size of the shell midden is a rough indication of the intensity of use of the place in question. While there might be some sites in which shells build up unusually quickly, and others where

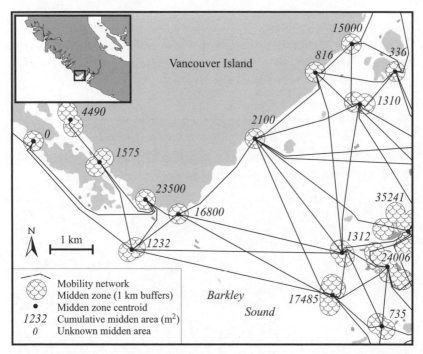

Figure 12.2 Detail of creation of site network. Shaded circles are site buffers that define midden zones; dot represents the centroid of those zones, which is used as the node for network creation.

they accumulate rather slowly, this effect is assumed to even out over time and to have no inherent spatial patterning inconsistent with the current study. To further reduce the idiosyncrasies of any one site, each site was buffered by a radius of 500 metres. Any sites that had intersecting buffers were lumped together into "midden zones" for the purposes of analysis. Each midden zone is represented by the centroid of the polygon formed by the intersecting buffers and does not necessarily fall on the coastline or even on land. Site areas for all such clustered middens were summed to form a midden zone area (Figure 12.2). It was felt that this procedure would also reduce meaningless micro-distinction of sites based on small intervening areas in which no midden was present. In this manner, the site sample was reduced from 576 individual sites to 238 midden zones. Many midden zones contain only a single site.

Western Vancouver Island is a rugged fjordland archipelago. The land, which is generally steep and heavily vegetated by temperate rainforest, is very difficult and slow to traverse on foot. While the marine environment varies greatly in aspect and exposure, watercraft will almost always be the most efficient means of transportation. The opposition in ease of travel between marine and terrestrial environments means that, with some reservations, the basic transportation structure of this (and perhaps any) fjordland archipelago can be known simply from examination of the gross geography. In essence, as argued elsewhere (Mackie 1998, 2001), this type

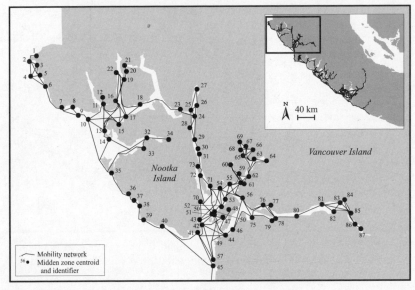

Figure 12.3   North end of the site network.

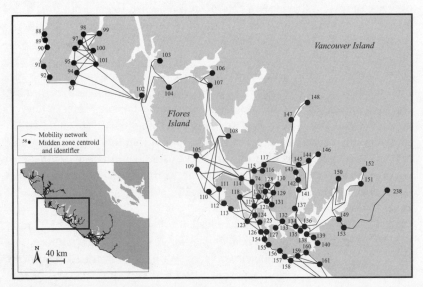

Figure 12.4   Central area of the site network.

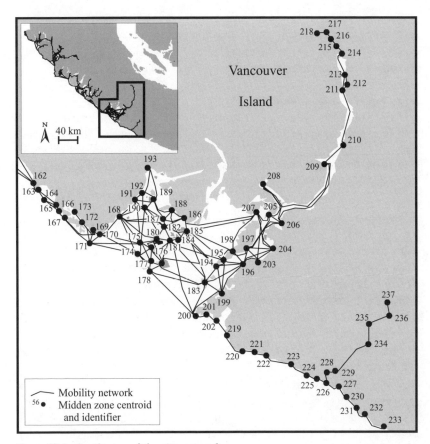

Figure 12.5 South area of the site network.

of landform has extreme directional constraints relative to terrestrial landforms or to less steep archipelagos. Accepting that the basic transportation structure is knowable, then one has the unusual opportunity (at least for an archaeologist of the precontact period) to define confidently not only site location but also the likeliest routes between sites. By imposing a network of shortest-path water distances between sites, a schematic transportation network, a "road map" of the archipelago, is defined (Figure 12.2 shows a detail of construction of the network; Figures 12.3 through 12.5 show the whole study area). Thus, this study includes the following initial assumptions:

- Low-elevation shell middens in this area are roughly contemporaneous.
- Shell middens are mainly produced by general activity, the intensity of use of which is proportional to their size.
- Sites can be meaningfully joined together by shortest-path distances across water to represent a transportation network.

As a system of points and lines, this network has the mathematical character of a graph and is therefore open to analysis of spatial relations based on graph theoretic and matrix mathematical approaches. One such approach is the network implementation of the location-allocation model.

Location-Allocation Modelling

Location-allocation is a type of spatial interaction analysis. Spatial interaction methods minimally deal with at least pairs of points or areas in space between which there is posited to be some sort of flow of people, goods, or information (Bailey 1994), although the precise nature of that interaction need not be specified. The most commonly used general spatial interaction analyses are the family of gravity models (Haynes and Fotheringham 1984). These were widely used in geography and archaeology on an intuitive, "even metaphysical" (Tobler and Wineburg 1971:40), basis before being theoretically justified as the general solution to an entropy maximization problem (Bailey 1994:34-35). In the gravity model, interaction between pairs of points or places is proportional to both their relative sizes and their relative distance apart. It is important to realize that size and distance do not necessarily have to be physical mass or linear distance but, rather, can refer to population, capital, goods, cognitive (perceived) distance, distance expressed as travel time, or even frequency of place names on tablets (Tobler and Wineburg 1971).

Location-allocation modelling was developed to help solve site selection problems in the public and private economic sector for facilities such as retail outlets, schools, fire stations, and medical facilities; namely, in situations where an organization needs to obtain the most efficient distribution of a system of facilities according to various (market or non-market) criteria. For example, rules can be applied, such as: no child should live more than two kilometres from a school; no house should be more than five minutes' travel from a fire hall; or hamburger outlets should be optimally sited with reference to intensity of lunch-time traffic. The unique aspect of location-allocation is the ability to solve the problem for *all* facilities in the system at the *same* time (despite using pair-wise comparisons), thus incorporating the *inter*dependence of central places with each other into the solution. For example, the location of one school or one fire hall necessarily affects the potential location of all others. Take the example of the school. To optimally site a school in relation to children, one might set the criteria that the collective distance travelled by all children should be minimized. In these terms, the most central place in the city is that place to which, if all the children went to a school sited there, their total summed travel distances from home to school would be the smallest possible number. Location-allocation differs from conventional notions of centrality when the decision is made to build two or more schools. Logically, the second most central place in the city is right across the street from the most central place. However, only a very foolish school administrator would build both schools on the same intersection; rather, they would seek to place the schools optimally in relation to both the students and to each other. If two schools were to be built, neither would be in the single most central location relative to the students, but they would be in complementary places. If they were both built in the same place there would be no benefit to students living close to the central place, nor would there be any benefit to those living far away. An interdependent placing of the schools imposes an additional cost on centrally located students but more than balances this with a benefit to those who are peripheral. Equally, three schools, four schools, and so on should be placed so that if all students travel to one or another school, then the schools are located and students are assigned to them such that the total travel distance is minimized. This is the essence of interdependent versus independent centrality. While it is clearly not always possible to meet this ideal, location-allocation is a widely used tool for such complex problems of supply, demand, and public facility location.

Thus, in location-allocation modelling, a set of points or places is assigned to a centre or to a set of interdependent centres in a way that optimizes some external criterion, such as collective minimization of total distance travelled to a central location. The process is described in more detail below, in which reference is to the simplest model, the p-median, used in this analysis.

Terminology Used in Location-Allocation Analysis

An *origin* node is a node on the network that contains the potential for interaction with a centre. This node might be a household with a quantified desire to purchase hamburgers or it could be a certain number of school-age children; or it might be a more abstractly defined notion, such as a place with "potential for interaction" (ESRI 1995). The centre, then, can be a school, restaurant, fire hall, or any other place with potential to satisfy demand. In this case study, the clustered shell midden sites ("midden zones") are the origin nodes. As records of general human activity, they are witnesses to actual interaction. In the location-allocation model, their only attribute of interest is their location on the network.

A *candidate* node is a node on the network deemed suitable for the possible location of a centre (see below). In retail or other contemporary implementations, external criteria such as zoning laws, unsuitable infrastructure, and other logistics will rule out some locations. Thus, of many vacant lots in a city, one subset may be considered suitable for locating a school, while another (perhaps different) subset may be suitable for a sewage plant. An implementation free of external criteria is used in this study: all origin nodes (midden zones) are also candidates for designation as a centre. In most applications in prehistoric contexts there will be little or no a priori knowledge of what culturally specific external criteria might apply.

A *centre* node is either a fixed candidate (such as a pre-existent school) or a mobile candidate chosen because it optimizes the objective function. In the case of a single-centre solution in the p-median model, the candidate node that minimizes the total distance travelled across the network will be selected. In the case of a two-centre solution, the chosen candidates will be those that together minimize this objective function and so forth. It has been seen that centres influence each other's location and that centrality is thus measured *relatively*.

The *objective function* summarizes the goal of the formula used by the location-allocation model. It incorporates the objective (such as to minimize distance or to maximize coverage) and any constraints. For example, the objective function of the p-median model, used throughout this study, is to minimize the total distance between all origin nodes and the central places to which they are assigned (Hillsman 1984). Put another way, it is to determine the location of a designated number, p, of centres, such that the total distance between origin nodes and these centres is minimized (ESRI 1995). All origin nodes must be assigned to a centre. This process can be visualized as a method of calculating all the possible paths between all the origin nodes and then finding the unique combination of centres that together minimize collective distance travelled across the network. The result is similar to k-means clustering: it is partitive spatial clustering of cases based on a single attribute (distance), with re-optimization at each stage. The central places are directly analogous to the centroids of k-means clusters in their attribute space. As with most clustering analyses, the procedure is iterative: there is no a priori knowledge of what constitutes a meaningful number of clusters (and, indeed, there may be more than one such number).

Related location-allocation approaches, such as the maximal-covering model, have seen occasional use in archaeology (e.g., Bell and Church 1985; Bell et al. 1988; Bell and Church 1987; Steponaitis 1978). These all require a priori constraints (e.g., non-linear distance effects or ascribed catchment radii) as inputs; in a prehistoric archaeological application these constraints will necessarily involve tenuous argument. For example, it is by no means clear what sorts of distance decay effects might have influenced Aboriginal "cost-benefit" calculations on the Northwest Coast: these should be a topic of investigation not assumptions in a model. While the p-median model is certainly not assumption-free, it is based on much more general principles of least effort and entropy maximization rather than on case-specific constraints imposed by the investigator. Mathematically, all location-allocation models ultimately devolve to the p-median model (Hillsman 1984:307). Nevertheless, they have quite different assumptions, require different input knowledge sets, and produce markedly different solutions. Formulae and discussion of the *p*-median model are found in Chapter 6 of Mackie (2001).

Summary of the Application

To recapitulate, the network of sites and routes defines the basic intersite topology. All shell midden zones have the same potential to be chosen as a central place, and any number of sites can be assigned to any given central place. The application therefore is concerned neither with differential "demand" across the network nor with the capacity of central places to meet that "demand." Both of these factors are assumed to be constant and non-constraining. The application only finds subsets of the midden zones that are centrally located, using as a definition of centrality the quantifiable measure of the total distance-minimizing properties of the location – a measure that, furthermore, includes optimization relative to other central places.

Midden surface area within the midden zones does not enter the calculation of centrality. Cumulative midden area within zones, as a measure of intensity of general activity, can therefore be held as a dependent variable, against which the solution sets can be compared to see if there is a relationship between a location-allocation solution set of interdependent centres and the intensity of the use of these central places. In this way the purely descriptive location-allocation model can enter into a hypothesis-testing mode using statistical tests of association.

The spatial relationships between sites within the study area can be represented as a network, which provides a quantified, schematic representation of the structure of some aspects of prehistoric general activity. Location-allocation is a potentially useful procedure for partitioning the region-wide general activity into any number of subregions, based on travel distance. These partitions consist of a subset of the midden zones. One midden zone in each partition is identified as a central place, based on its interdependent centrality. As there is no prior reason to assume that any given number of central places within the study area is the "right number," the application was run iteratively for different numbers of central places. In this application, an iteration is a solution for a given number of centres. The model was run for one central place through twenty-five central places producing twenty-five solution sets, each containing a corresponding number of central midden zones. Each iteration is independent of the previous one, and therefore each solution set is optimal for the number of centres it contains.

Results

Running the location-allocation model iteratively for one through twenty-five central places results in twenty-five separate solution sets. Solution Set 1 contains a single midden zone as a central place, Set 2 contains two midden zones as central places, and so on. Distance minimization is reoptimized at each iteration, so there is no necessary retention of midden zones from one set to the next. Solution Sets 1, 3, 5, and 9 are shown in Figures 12.6 through 12.9. The results (Table 12.1, Figure 12.10) show that from Solution Sets 3 through 10 the averaged sizes of the midden zones chosen as central places is quite large. Applying a difference-of-means test to these iterations shows that midden zones in the bracket of Solution Sets 5 through 9 are larger than would be expected by chance alone (Figure 12.11).[1] From Set 10 onwards, the solution set midden zones are not, on average, different than

Table 12.1

Results of tests of significance by solution set and of distances travelled

Solution set	MZ area (m²)	Average distance "travelled" (km)	p
1	46,376	78.32	**0.03**
2	6,816	41.12	0.84
3	22,014	27.92	0.18
4	21,637	22.04	0.14
5	30,174	18.46	**0.01**
6	26,445	15.23	**0.01**
7	26,709	13.84	**0.01**
8	23,484	12.52	**0.02**
9	27,743	11.92	**0.00**
10	18,300	11.43	0.10
11	16,766	10.56	0.16
12	15,408	10.03	0.22
13	14,872	9.65	0.25
14	13,810	9.05	0.25
15	13,097	8.86	0.31
16	11,855	8.45	0.45
17	5,712	7.95	0.53
18	5,420	7.62	0.46
19	5,604	7.50	0.47
20	5,504	7.18	0.43
21	6,508	6.95	0.60
22	6,711	6.65	0.62
23	8,252	6.51	0.96
24	8,563	6.27	0.97
25	5,759	6.10	0.95

Notes: MZ Area refers to the arithmetic mean size of the midden zones in the solution set. Thus, Solution Set 10 has 10 midden zones sets of diverse sizes, with an average size of 18,300 m² for the nodal midden zones.

MZ = midden zone

p = two-tailed probability from t-test (values in **bold** are statistically significant at 0.05 level)

might be expected by random selection from the population of 238 midden zones in the study. By way of comparison, Figure 12.12 shows the results of a simulated procedure of drawing random iterative samples from the study population: note the wavering, insignificant variation about the mean.

The solution sets can therefore be divided into three groups based on Figure 12.11: Solution Sets 1 through 4, 5 through 9, and 10 through 25. The breaks between these are referred to as the lower and upper thresholds of significance, respectively; while Solution Sets 5 through 9 are referred to as falling within a bracket of significance. The following discussion concerns the iterations below and above the lower and upper thresholds (Sets 1 through 4 and 10 through 25), and then those that fall within the bracket of significance itself (Sets 5 through 9).

Solution Sets 1 through 4
The statistical significance of Solution Set 1 probably reflects the number of large sites in Clayoquot Sound, which happens to be in the middle of the study area. This impression of chance is supported by the consideration

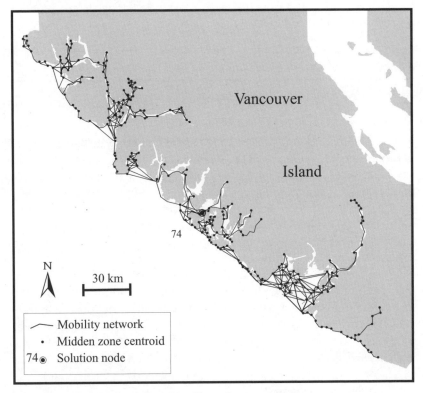

Figure 12.6 Solution set for one interdependent central place.

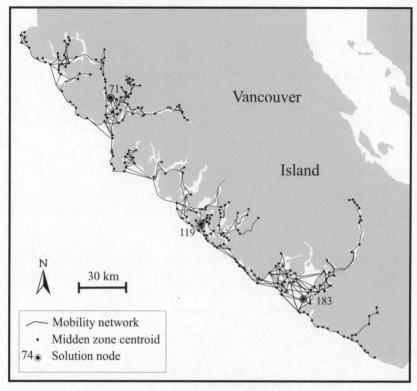

Figure 12.7   Solution set for three interdependent central places.

that the site in question, Midden Zone 74 (the important Kelsemaht village of Cloolthpitch [Drucker 1951] on Meares Island) is never again selected in any solution set. Solution Set 2 is also composed of two zones (171 and 42) that are never again selected, but these sites are only of average size, suggesting they bear no relationship to interdependent network centrality across the archipelago. With Solution Set 3, all three central nodes are greater than 14,000 square metres and are in the top 18 percent of all sites with known areas. While not statistically significant, this is suggestive that the threshold from Solution Set 5 downwards should not be taken overly literally and that the threshold could, perhaps should, be set at Solution Set 3. Nonetheless, strict interpretation of the statistical test enforces the conclusion that, with the frankly anomalous exception of Solution Set 1, interdependent centrality is not related to midden zone size below five partitions of the study area.

Solution Sets 10 through 25
After Solution Set 9, the model has passed through the group of solution

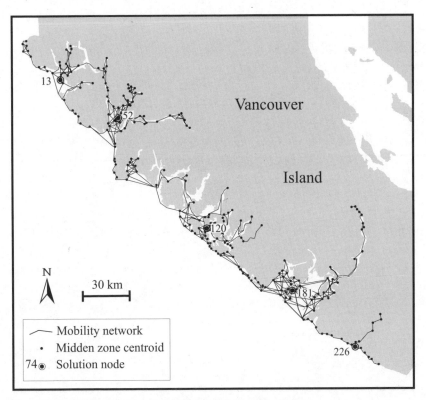

Figure 12.8 Solution set for five interdependent central places.

sets that are significantly correlated with midden zone area. Zones that are added to the solution sets with each iteration after Set 9 tend to be no larger than expected. The possible meanings of the bracket of significant solution sets itself is discussed further below; at this point discussion is limited to why there might be a "threshold" beyond which iterations of the model lose their significance. A number of possibilities present themselves.

First, it is important to dispel any impression that all big sites are picked and that, after the threshold is passed, there are no further large sites left to pick and thus the model is forced to pick solution sets with smaller and smaller sites. Of the 238 midden zones, 198 are *never* picked in *any* solution set, including those ranked first, third, and fifth by size. While this dispels the notion that all large zones are picked, it also indicates that factors other than interdependent centrality also affect intensity of use. It is not my in-tention to conclude that only interdependent centrality affects site size: many other factors must be involved.

Second, it is very unlikely that underlying data problems prevent the se-lection of a larger number of significant solution sets. In order for this to be

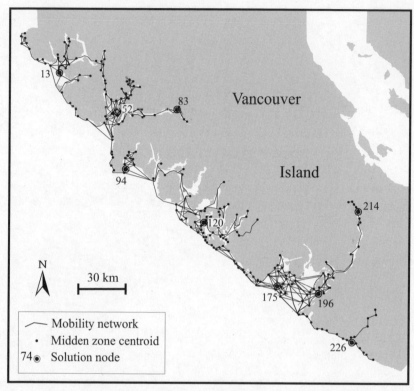

Figure 12.9   Solution set for nine interdependent central places.

the cause of the decline in statistical significance, incompleteness of the data would have to be systematic. In other words, one would have to argue that there was an underlying pattern present beyond Solution Set 9 but that this pattern was obscured because of systematic data skew. The main potential sources of data skew include simple measurement error, the use of differing criteria by different archaeologists in recording the size of sites, and incomplete coverage of the study area (Mackie 2001). While these factors are acknowledged to influence the study area dataset, there is no reason to believe the sample is *systematically* skewed in a way that would produce a false result of the sort encountered. Indeed, the identification of this real and replicable result from a large and heterogeneously derived dataset is in itself an indication that these data, for all their faults, are not skewed.

Third, it is possible that, above the upper threshold of significance, microenvironmental variables become relatively more important determinants of intensity of site use than does site network centrality. For example, local environmental factors such as proximity to fresh water, presence of suitable beaches for canoe landing, and exposure to prevailing winds are known to be important ethnographically (Drucker 1951; Arima 1983) and have been shown to be important for archaeological predictive modelling in the similar environment of Southeast Alaska (Maschner and Stein 1995; Maschner 1997). Similarly, singular strategic resources may be important determinants of site location. Marshall (1993:100-146) describes a number

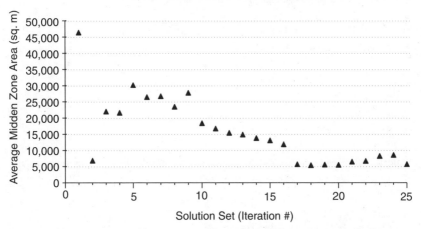

Figure 12.10   Results of twenty-five iterations of the location-allocation model, based on Table 12.1. Each symbol represents the averaged area of the "solution nodes" midden zones selected within each solution set.

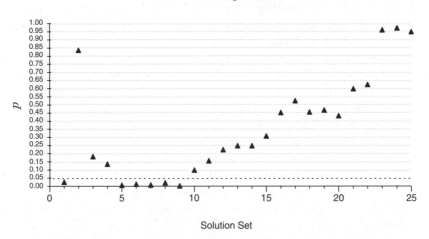

Figure 12.11   Plotted tests of significance of size of solution set "nodes" midden zones. Calculated using Student's t-test, values given in Table 12.1. All sets where $p < 0.05$ (lowest dashed line) are statistically significant.

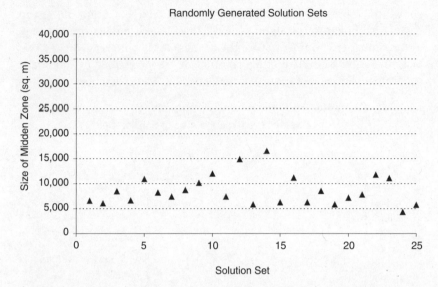

Figure 12.12 Results of twenty-five iterated solution sets chosen at random. Each symbol represents the averaged areas of the midden zones selected within each solution set. Note the lack of patterning compared to Figure 12.10.

of relatively local environmental and social factors with inferred importance for site size in Nootka Sound. Proximity to defensive sites, salmon streams, sheltered waterways, and other localized "tethering" resources may increase intensity of local general purpose activity, as may "jostling" for position on the outer coast. It is possible that after a certain spatial size threshold is crossed, interdependent network centrality (as identified in the p-median model) may matter less for site location than more local factors. The problem with this explanation is that it implies that conscious decision-making behaviour produced the pattern observed in Solution Sets 5 through 9. As this pattern consists of sets of *interdependent* centres, then it follows that decision makers would have needed both an apprehension of the study area as a whole *and* sufficient social control to collectively intensify behaviour at those optimal places. It is worth noting again that the location-allocation model did not have any environmental or cultural variables as an input, only relative site location on a schematized transportation network.

Fourth, the annual round may mask the effect at a local scale. It is well known (e.g., Drucker 1951:36-51; Mitchell and Donald 1988) that, ethnographically at least, indigenous people in this area made at least two seasonal moves.[2] At the broad scale this might not influence the result because fewer solution sets than ethnographically documented local indigenous groups or polities are being selected. Once this point is passed, then each local group will have two or more foci of intensity of use (a winter one and a summer one), and the model will be projected onto a binary space of discontinuous occupation.[3] In other words, emphasis on shell middens as *general* activity occupation sites may mask some other patterns that would be reflected in more specific site typology. On the other hand, the emphasis in this study is on general activity across a large region taken as a whole: it is impossible to explain all aspects of human activity in a single study and probably undesirable to try.

Fifth, there might be a historical connection to places that, over time, became non-optimal. Significant components of the built environment may be at locations that were once optimal relative to other sites but, after millennia of environmental and human history, become suboptimal. It is unlikely that slight differences in relative optimality would cause the abandonment of these sites. This scenario has appeal for explaining the lack of significance at the narrower scales as it does not call for a simple underlying environmental determinism of site location but, rather, allows for historical process.

Finally, it must be noted that all or some of the five explanations above may be acting in combination to produce the lower threshold of significance. As Marshall (1993:119) notes, some large Nootka Sound sites are in especially favourable *local* conditions while "others definitely [are] not, suggesting factors other than physical terrain were directing the selection of [large] site locations."

In summary, it seems probable that, for reasons that cannot be wholly explained at present, the relationship between site size and p-median centrality does not hold after the archipelago is partitioned into more than nine interdependent regions. Yet, within the brackets of Solution Sets 5 through 9, the relationship *does* hold. This pattern is real, and, regardless of uncertainty in determination and description of its upper and lower thresholds, the meaning of the observed pattern must be discussed.

Solution Sets 5 through 9: Towards an Explanation

Some reasons for the bracket of significant relationship between midden zone size and p-median network centrality are discussed below.

First, as above, one may suspect that data problems or anomalies are causing the effect to be more apparent than real. This seems exceptionally unlikely as any skewing would have to be very strongly patterned in order to produce the observed pattern of selected large central midden zones. There is no obvious way in which the data, although incomplete in the ways previously noted, could contain such a skewing pattern, especially as the result holds for a study area that as a whole has never previously been subject to a single archaeological analysis and whose site-survey data is unlikely to contain either a single or a systematic skewing factor. (The data themselves would, in effect, need to be "interdependently biased.")

Second, the most obvious reason for the observed pattern would be that people were deliberately, consciously optimizing their movements across the study area as a whole and, thereby, creating large sites at central places. While superficially attractive, this explanation is implausible because it would imply that there had been long-standing, centralized, political control over the whole study area that recognized the location-allocation type of inter-dependent network centrality and that intensified at central places accordingly. Or, at least it would imply that the archipelagian landscape of the study area was apprehended in toto[4] and that distance minimization solutions were then calculated and acted upon. Similarly, each of the central places and their satellites could be interpreted as having some sort of direct political or ethnolinguistic correlates, which would lead to the question: how did they manage to arrange themselves so optimally across the land-scape? All of these scenarios are implausible for ethnographic reasons (what polities? what motivations to minimize distance for the collective good?) and because there is no supporting archaeological evidence that points to such a social or perceptual unity. These scenarios would also necessarily imply that the lower threshold is the result of "centrality no longer being important to decision making," which shifts the burden of explanation elsewhere without solving it. The optimizing explanation takes the objective function of the model much too literally: behavioural convergence on "distance minimization" is easily totalized as being intentionally produced. The observed, significant pattern of midden zone sizes is best considered, in the absence of a total social phenomenon that controls the optimization of the objective function, to be a simple measure of interdependent centrality within a holistic network. As discussed below, the procedure used to generate the pattern is a single-attribute *descriptive* clustering solution that should not be used to generate rule-based behavioural explanations.

Another option is that these large, central midden zones represent home bases in a logistically organized mobility system. This possibility fails scrutiny because of the interdependency dilemma. If these home bases are situated relative to resources (as is central to the home-base concept), then it follows that the resources themselves must be arranged in a mutually inter-dependent way across this large study area. There is no plausible way by which such diverse resources as anadromous fish, herring, halibut, sea mammals, shellfish, and birds could be thus arranged, singly or collectively. Further, the resources themselves do not enter the model: all that enters are individual site locations and their relative connections. As discussed above, there is reason to believe that specific single site locations are influenced by the local environmental (not resource) variables identified in Tebenkof Bay. Therefore, base camp sites might be central relative to resources, such sites might indeed be larger than average and contribute to a settlement hierarchy, but it is difficult to equate the behaviour and constraints underlying local logistical mobility with regional interdependent centrality. Nonetheless, different inputs and assumptions might enable a different, more conventional application of location-allocation to home-base theory. It is, after all, a spatial economic model stressing rationality and resource supply and, therefore, is congruent with the notion of home bases.

Finally, in the presence of a real pattern of optimal mobility patterning, and in the absence of a plausible, rational, decision-making scheme to account for that patterning, one is led to consider that this pattern was generated *non-deliberately*. The following discussion proposes a mechanism consistent with the location-allocation model by which some sites could become large. It does not seek to explain the entire site hierarchy.

Having rejected the above explanations, it is difficult to know what to make of the result. A start on this is to recognize that the patterning of shell middens and their respective sizes is not itself a planned product; rather, it is an interrupted process, a long-term indigenous historical trajectory both rudely and arbitrarily interrupted by the arrival of Europeans, with settlement and subsistence changes in their wake. Had Europeans not arrived for another millennium, a quite different picture of relative settlement size and location might have developed, even without major restructuring of the indigenous culture and economy. Since the built environment can be seen as the "work in progress" of actors who may or may not have been intentionally optimizing their behaviour by either scale-specific criteria or through habit, it is apt to consider the fallacy of the rule in anthropological explanation. Barrett (1994) notes that, in the "fallacy of the rule," the anthropologist or "learned questioner" and the informant share a similar thought process, although their derived constructs will, of course, differ:

a) behaviour is observed, or reflected upon,
b) a rule is concocted that fits the behaviour,
c) the mistaken assumption is made that the rule that fits the behaviour actually guides the behaviour,
d) the conclusion is reached that the behaviour is caused by the rule.

In archaeology, this is made manifest through the description of a spatial pattern, the fitting of a descriptive spatial rule to that pattern, and the false conclusion that the pattern is generated by the rule. Thinking of the regional settlement dynamics as an unfolding process rather than as a static product does not incline one to look for goal-directed decision-making explanations.

One alternative to such explanations can be found in Pierre Bourdieu's (1977, 1990) theory of practice. Bourdieu's concept of habitus is inconsistent with normative views of "culture." People are not wholly guided either by rules or by norms towards which they strive; rather, Bourdieu claims that people are generally aware of such rules only when they stop to dwell upon them (for example, when prompted by anthropological questioning). The vast majority of their lives are situated in the habitus, a non-discursive domain of structured dispositions to action, in which people are guided more by their *sense* of (right and wrong) behaviour than any *code* of such behaviour. The concept of habitus has been extended to include spatial and material implications by Gosden (1994:119), with his proposed "landscape of habit":

> *Habitus*, then, is a general, concerted but unconscious harmonization of social life, a second nature. *Habitus* is not so much a state of mind, but a state of body. The human body is the nexus of the *habitus*, which organizes movements through space and time through forms of deportment and movement. As Bourdieu (1990b:69) puts it, "Arms and legs are full of numb imperatives ... what is learned in the body is not something one has, but something one is ..." Bodily movement is also channelled through the material world, during which time dispositions are enforced and reinforced.

By "material world," it is clear Gosden means both the built and the unbuilt environments; therefore habitus is not just an abstract behavioural domain of structured dispositions but must have spatial implications as well. The landscape of action is inseparable from the landscape of consciousness (Trigger 1995) and vice versa, and one can be approached through understanding of the other. The clearest way to approach these implications is through the concept of the *social field*.[5] Gosden, for example, discusses the spatial implications of the unconscious routinization of behaviour. The implications of the scalar thresholds identified in this study are consistent with Gosden's (1994:119) definition of a field: "a field is a geometric space in which points are connected by a series of relationships, in which the *whole is greater than the sum of the parts*" (emphasis added). If we accept this holistic definition of social relations within such a field, then it becomes easier to understand how collective centrality-optimization can be an *emergent* property of a landscape of habit. The proximal mechanism of how this emergence occurs is discussed in a later section.

To this point, the lower and upper thresholds have not been defined as real-world distances. However, by plotting the solution sets in order versus the objective function of collective distance minimization it is possible to now put a spatial definition on the landscape of habit. As Figure 12.13 shows, Solution Sets 5 through 9 (the bracket of significance) correspond to average "distances travelled" of nineteen through twelve kilometres, respectively. In other words, at partitions above and below this spatial threshold, collective distance minimization no longer appears a significant element in determining where people intensify their general activity.

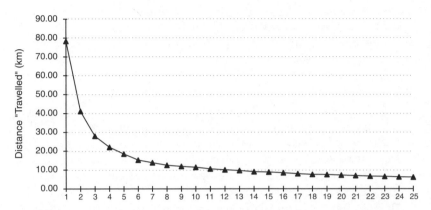

Figure 12.13 Plot illustration optimization of the *p*-median model's objective function (minimization of total distance travelled) through twenty-five iterations. Based on Table 12.1.

However, it is perhaps misleading to take the objective function of the location-allocation model too literally. Recollection that the model has its roots in a retail geographical landscape of rational actors and centralized calculation of cost-benefit by CEOs cautions one against applying a decision-making set too closely tied to the objective function. At no time in the prehistory of the study area were all routes and sites simultaneously traversed. So, rather than seeing it as a synchronic decision or even bodily realization, it is preferable to view it as a long-term expression of "muscular consciousness" that leaves congealed behaviour in the form of discarded shell. As discussed below, the spatial implications of the centrality thresholds will allow archaeologists to discover "emically" relevant spatial units rather than impose them.

General Discussion

Having followed Ingold's (1992, 1993) exhortation to leave "culture out of the equation," at least temporarily, we are left with a subtle model of dispositions towards practical behaviour played out within the newly defined scalar thresholds of a landscape of habit. As Jorge Rocha (1996:21) implies, social science has been subject to a tautology of rationality in which models of behaviour had intentionality as a silent input rather than as a question or as a topic of investigation: "the economist only allows maximization to be rational, thereby inserting a tautology into his argument: the individual is seeking to satisfy his satisfaction." Rocha proposes a fivefold typology of goal-directed social action:

1   Teleological Action: the actor pursues an end or achieves a certain desired state of affairs by choosing the most congruent means and applying them in the most efficient manner possible. In social science this is mainly modelled through simple optimizing theory and, as such, underpins much processual archaeology.

2   Strategic Action: the actor takes the action of other actors into account. This is mainly modelled in archaeology through game-theoretic models (e.g., Shennan 1993) and human evolutionary ecology. These models were specifically designed to counterbalance the individual-actor of classical and neoclassical economics (Rocha 1996:19).

3   Norm-regulated Action: actors work together to achieve ends, guided by a set of common goals. In archaeology, this is the foundation of normative culture-historical accounts.

4   Dramatic Action: actors participate in a series of interactions in which each is a public or spectator for the others, and the goal is achieving a desired impression on the other actors. In archaeology, this can be seen in performative analyses of power and gender.

5   Communicative Action: actors collectively create texts of meaning mediated through language but constrained both by shared norms and imperfect individual perception of phenomena. In archaeology, this is probably best seen through the "landscape-as-text" metaphor.

Rocha's analysis of the decision-making "black box" is instructive yet incomplete. Archaeology, with its grasp of immense time and space, must confront another sort of action, which I consider to be responsible for the observed pattern of midden zone sizes described above.

We have seen that Maschner and Stein (1995) could not explain variation in "intensity of use" (as measured by shell midden area) via correlation with microenvironmental variables at the subregional scale. What sorts of explanations are left to account for efficiencies that are not rationally directed? Ingold (1996) approaches this problem in his critique of optimal foraging theory (OFT). After rejecting the precepts of OFT, Ingold proposes a "received strategic framework," a construct essentially indistinguishable from Bourdieu's habitus. There is frequent confusion between an individual's capacity for rational choices of different kinds and the conception of rational choice as a modus operandi: reality and the optimizing metaphor may have their uses, but when fused the consequence is to impose the fallacy of the rule. As Ingold notes, one must ask whether the choices of action are real choices. If they are, then they cannot be bound by past selective pressure; if they are not, then there is no actual choice and so actors are prisoners of enculturation. Ingold (1996:33) then echoes Bourdieu by proposing a "predisposition" to action as a middle ground to explain optimizing in non-teleological terms. Indeed, as Bourdieu (1977; 1990:12) notes, the generative predictor of social practice is better conceived of as an opus operatum than as a modus operandi: the former is uncertain, contingent, and fuzzy, while the latter is axiomatic, rigid, and post hoc.

For example, Donald and Mitchell (1994:115) suggest that "there was a cultural response to this variation [in salmon distribution and density]. Territories grouped streams together in a way that not only reduced the variation in resources." In their example, the descriptive grammar of salmon escapements is used to generate cultural projects of risk-buffering resource stabilization. While they show that group populations and boundaries are sensitive to salmon escapements – and their work is rightly considered a landmark of cultural ecology – these responses can be seen and explained as relatively straightforward feedback-driven tuning to environmental variables. The relationship between local group population and resources that Donald and Mitchell identify looks at factors internal to predefined territories and then compares these to each other. Their measures of population are at the group level, whereas this study looks at the intensity of use of certain places in a region *not* pre-divided into territories. One would need to demonstrate that the salmon resources themselves bore some relationship to wide-regional interdependent centrality for their results to be in any explanatory conflict with the ones here: both approaches can happily coexist. Salmon escapements *are* something that can be known through the senses and knowledge of them *can* be built up over centuries. Interdependent centrality is not such an empirical variable. Indeed, it would be specious to discuss "knowledge" of something so wholly and inextricably linked to a top-down geographic model, which poses an abstract question with no obvious behavioural, cultural, or other solution. Were it not that it had an empirical relationship to site size, it might even be considered to be not only an abstract question but an asinine one. The fact that such centrality apparently mattered to people over the very long term *despite* their lack of discursive knowledge of it poses the explanatory paradox this chapter is addressing.

We can now glimpse an underlying truth about Marx's famous dictum: "man makes himself, but not in circumstances of his own choosing." Indeed, a similar point was made more clearly by Sartre: "what is essential is not that human beings are made, but that they make that which made them" (Sartre quoted in Rowntree 1986). The importance of the built environment as a structurer of disposition is precisely that it is *not* always the result of a plan and is, therefore, one of the unchosen circumstances within which "man makes himself." And, since the built environment as a "work in progress" is archaeologically accessible, it cannot easily be ignored, as Barrett (1994) demonstrated in his Neolithic case study. By eliminating or minimizing teleological action the fallacy of the rule is avoided, both in space and over time. For example, some of the arguments in Matson and Coupland (1995) concerning the "achievement of complexity" on the Northwest Coast can now be seen as assertions of long-term, teleological optimizing behaviour targeted towards the ethnographic present.

It is also worthwhile considering built environments from other living domains and how they arise from unintentional harmonic action. "Stigmergy" refers to the "guidance of work performed by social insects through evidences of work previously accomplished" (Wilson 1975:186). In effect, stigmergy is equivalent to a kind of communication that Wilson (1975:186) characterizes as an "increase in signal duration." Take the example of termites: when initially building a nest, termites randomly drop small balls of saliva-laden earth. Subsequently, a termite encountering such a ball is more likely to drop another one close by. Piling behaviour is thus reinforced through these two dispositions (random dropping and prompted dropping) until a certain threshold of height is reached, when other termite habits start to join these together into a nest. Termite nests are not just macro-spitballs: they have an internal structure that produces warmth-cold-moisture differentiations for specialized purposes, and the structure as a whole creates a draft for ventilation. Thus, a stochastic process plus a response to an environmental inscription allows order to emerge by structuring habits: the more order emerges from chaos, the more that order is reinforced. As Hoffmeyer (1997:938) puts it, "no direct interaction is necessary between the animals, since co-ordination is assured solely through the artefacts resulting from their behaviour." In other words, termites practise cooperation without communication, apart from the communication medium of the material residue of their action and their predisposed reaction to that material. It would be a gross simplification to assert that this is equivalent to a "termite landscape of habit," yet both entomologists and archaeologists share a totalizing perspective on the material products of action in the world. It is difficult, but one must be open to the possibility that, *at certain scales*, human behaviour can produce optimal solutions that *look like* the product of intentionality but are no more so than a termite nest is the result of intelligence or communication. As Ward (1998:32) comments, ant success at foraging stems not from intelligence but from "using the world as a prompt" – a built environment of paths and places inscribed by pheromones. Just as an entomologist must learn to see the order of the termite nest as an emergent property of inculcated dispositions within a built environment rather than one of collective termite design-intelligence, so must the archaeologist learn to see that, at certain scales, order in the archaeological landscape can result from the durable products of inculcated predispositions, as demonstrated in this study. Instead, the built environment becomes a form of information storage and a medium of communication that can also act as an amplifier of such information – Schwartz's (1978:229) concept of "exthesis." Thinking of the built environment as including unconscious, but real, communication within and across generations prevents one from imposing the fallacy of the rule as there is no way to retrodict process from product. Thus, to Rochas's typological list of social action I would add a sixth item:

6   Unintentional Harmonic Action: actors have their dispositions to action structured by the habitus, with neither complete determination nor complete free will. Therefore, the built environment is not wholly ordered by efficiency-directed rational decision-making sets, but efficiencies and *apparent* rationality can be part of a process of emergent complexity, coordinated through the durable communication medium of material cultural. To elaborate upon Bourdieu, the structured *dispositions* of the habitus lead to a structured *deposition*, which itself acts as a *structuring* deposition.

Conclusion

The location-allocation model works top-down and sees the spatial pattern as a whole, dividing it for the *collective* minimization of distance "travelled." It is therefore difficult to interpret the pattern as the result of calculated practice, whether manifested as a simple "principle of least effort" or as the result of "Central Place Theory" within ethnolinguistic territories. Further, Maschner and Stein (1995) show that one can predict site location using local environmental variables but not site size.

In order to understand the results presented above, we must treat the built environment (spatial patterning of sites) not as a *planned product* but as an *interrupted process*. Since it is not a planned product, and yet is a real pattern, it must be an *unplanned* product. And as such, it can be interpreted as an emergent property of the long-term, unintentionally harmonic behaviour of individuals within a "landscape of habit," analogous to either stigmergenic communication or a spatio-temporal expression of the habitus.

In this way, the stage is set for a return to traditional Northwest Coast ecological culture history, but with a gain in knowledge and perspective. Some patterns and processes unfold over longer terms and spaces than ethnography can capture and result from non-discursive behaviour. Much of archaeology is the by-product of unintentional activity, and shell middens, perhaps above all, capture and record "general activity."

One tangible by-product of this research is the realization that, if a settlement hierarchy was considered to be an indicator of social complexity, then the patterning observed in this study would, *by itself*, give the false impression of social complexity. For example, I suggest that the unexpected shell midden settlement hierarchy in Tierra del Fuego (Yesner 1990), whose traditional inhabitants, the Yamana (Yahgan), exemplify "simple" hunters and gatherers, may have been produced by unintentional harmonic action. Studies of the formative periods of Northwest Coast prehistory will need to be aware of this potential illusion, while studies of the later periods will have to account for the "noise" this may bring to settlement patterns caused by more conventional cultural forces. Another by-product of this study is that one can now promote a novel way of selecting archaeological sites to excavate: robustly central large sites might well have a unique archaeological signature reflecting their positions at the persistent crossroads of the archipelago.

Thus we arrive at another tangible benefit of this attempt to create a humanistic human ecology: the *discovery*, rather than the *imposition*, of a scale of habitual action that can be transposed into the identification of more meaningful archaeological units of spatial analysis. The advantages of a fjordland maritime case study are now clearly apparent: the "knowability" of environmental constraint is the entry point into understanding the practice of mobility.[6] Having a point of entry in this case study is what allows specific conclusions to be drawn. Ultimately, the ability to identify a scale in which habitual action makes both a significant and recognizable contribution to the archaeological signature is a significant advance in archaeological spatial analysis. As Schwartz (1978:223) notes, "Size is a continuous variable, but we want scale to sort itself out into levels with differing organizational and experiential implications. We should be looking for a series of levels or break points in scale, although of course we do not expect abrupt breaks, beyond the lower end of the size dimension."

It is fair to say that these results satisfy Schwartz's expectations.[7] Indeed, this case study points the way beyond using networks as metaphors for social spaces and shows how networks can be made operational in an environment of non-Cartesian social geography. By allowing the investigation of the scalar principles of intentional behaviour, it will become possible to model and test proposals such as Gamble's (1995, 1998) regarding Local Hominid Networks and Social Landscapes. Key components of these are differences in planning and anticipatory behaviour, which come with the weighty baggage of intentionality and imposed scalar thresholds. It is intriguing to see that Gamble (1995:256) categorizes material from a thirty-to-eighty-kilometre radius around a site as "exotic" raw material: this compares well to the approximately nineteen-to-seventy-eight-kilometre "average distances travelled" (conceived as radii of the objective function) of Solution Sets 1 through 4 in this study. Therefore, the investigation of the scale of habitual action may be useful in finding or confirming the size of relevant spatial units of analysis. In other words, this study provides a method by which archaeologists may be able to *discover* their units of spatial analysis rather than *impose* them, and it offers attendant benefits for the confidence of interpretation through a combination of social theory, sociobiology, and ethnography.

Hence, this study reaffirms the importance of theory – especially interdisciplinary theory – in guiding archaeological questions and interpreting anomalous results. Without theory from quantitative geography and inspiration from Martin Wobst's locational analyses, there would be no spatial pattern to discuss. Without the aid of social theory developed in archaeological and sociological contexts it would have been even more difficult to fit an explanation to the observed pattern. By simultaneously considering both the "knowability" of the archaeological record and the universality of certain aspects of human existence, this study demonstrates one way of moving beyond the rhetoric of postprocessual archaeology. The middle ground in archaeological theory is here manifested as the alliance of social theory to quantitative geography – the production of demonstrable, testable results and their alliance to humanistic explanations. This is truly a *humanistic human ecology*. In particular, the use of the habitus as a bridging argument, similar to "middle range" theory (although not as empirically grounded), offers one path out of the theoretical canyon between what Patty Jo Watson (1991:170) has termed the "methodless soul" of postprocessualist archaeology and the "soulless method" of processualist archaeologies.

Acknowledgments
Donald H. Mitchell taught me at the undergraduate level, supervised my master's thesis, and was a key reason I was attracted to archaeology to the extent that I now occupy his former office. I hope he enjoys this chapter, which I dedicate to him, although it may well break his dictum that if a project isn't worth doing, then it isn't worth doing well! I am also grateful to Professor Clive Gamble, Dr. Yvonne Marshall, and Dr. David Wheatley of Southampton University, to the Social Sciences and Humanities Research Council of Canada, and to the Association of Commonwealth Universities. I also thank Rosaline Canessa and Kristin Ackerson, students in Anthropology 449 and 540, and Joanne Richardson, who copyedited this book.

Notes
1 Student's t-test was used. Midden zone area values were converted to base-10 logarithms, normalizing a log-normal distribution and allowing the use of a parametric test (Shennan 1988).
2 Although McMillan (1996:26) notes that some groups may have been dependent on local resources year-round.
3 There is also the possibility/probability (Haggarty and Inglis 1983) of more than two annual moves, and for regional variations in the number of moves. But the more mobile the population the less the expected skewing effect of annual-round activity in that general activity becomes more dispersed across the landscape and less systematically biased at the scale of the significant solution sets.

4 It could not have been the sum of smaller apprehended parts – a collection of canoe-eye views – because there would be no way to calculate the complexities of interdependent centrality.

5 This concept is tied to network analysis through the work of Wobst (1974, 1976) and, especially, Lesser (1961).

6 More subtle renderings of this model could include local environmental conditions such as wind, tide, and size of landform, probably incorporated via dynamic-segmentation of the network and through constraints on the nodes to facilitate interaction.

7 What is interesting, and perhaps unexpected, is that the focus on tracks and paths keeps interpretation away from simplistic imputation of bounded social units. Rather, the effect of "fuzzy" scalar breaks is to eliminate the possibility of finding such units without considerable external sources of evidence.

13
The Northwest Coast as a Study Area: Natural, Prehistoric, and Ethnographic Issues
Leland Donald

Nowadays the culture area concept is often regarded as rather old-fashioned, its usefulness and time long past, what remaining value it has being as a way of organizing ethnographic data for teaching purposes. I suggest that the idea of the culture area has more life left in it than is typically thought. My focus is on the application of the concept to a single area, the Northwest Coast of North America, but some comments have wider applicability.

Most of those doing research on the north Pacific coast of North America use the term Northwest Coast when situating their work, whether their concerns are very localized or more broadly regional (see, for example, the chapters in this book). Usually they invoke the name Northwest Coast without paying much attention to the larger possibilities and challenges the term may raise. I consider some of those possibilities and challenges here.

As A.L. Kroeber points out in *Cultural and Natural Areas of Native North America*, the culture area concept developed out of early attempts at geographic and environmental groupings of cultures in opposition to groupings based on nineteenth-century evolutionary schemes. Yet for Kroeber at least, culture areas are in some sense historical phenomena, hence his interest in "culture climaxes." Culture areas are regions of the most intense interactions between peoples, and, in some sense, never fully worked out by Kroeber, they share historical traditions and developments that allow us to group cultures together in terms of their overall similarity and in contrast to other blocks of cultures.

Well before Kroeber, the particular distinctiveness of the Northwest Coast among Native American cultures was recognized, although, in his classic paper "American Culture and the Northwest Coast" (1923), he analyzed this distinctiveness as well as anyone has done. Here, I use Kroeber's 1939 formulation of the boundaries of the Northwest Coast as the basis for my discussion, as they fit closely with most previous and subsequent mappings and are widely accepted (see Figure 13.1).

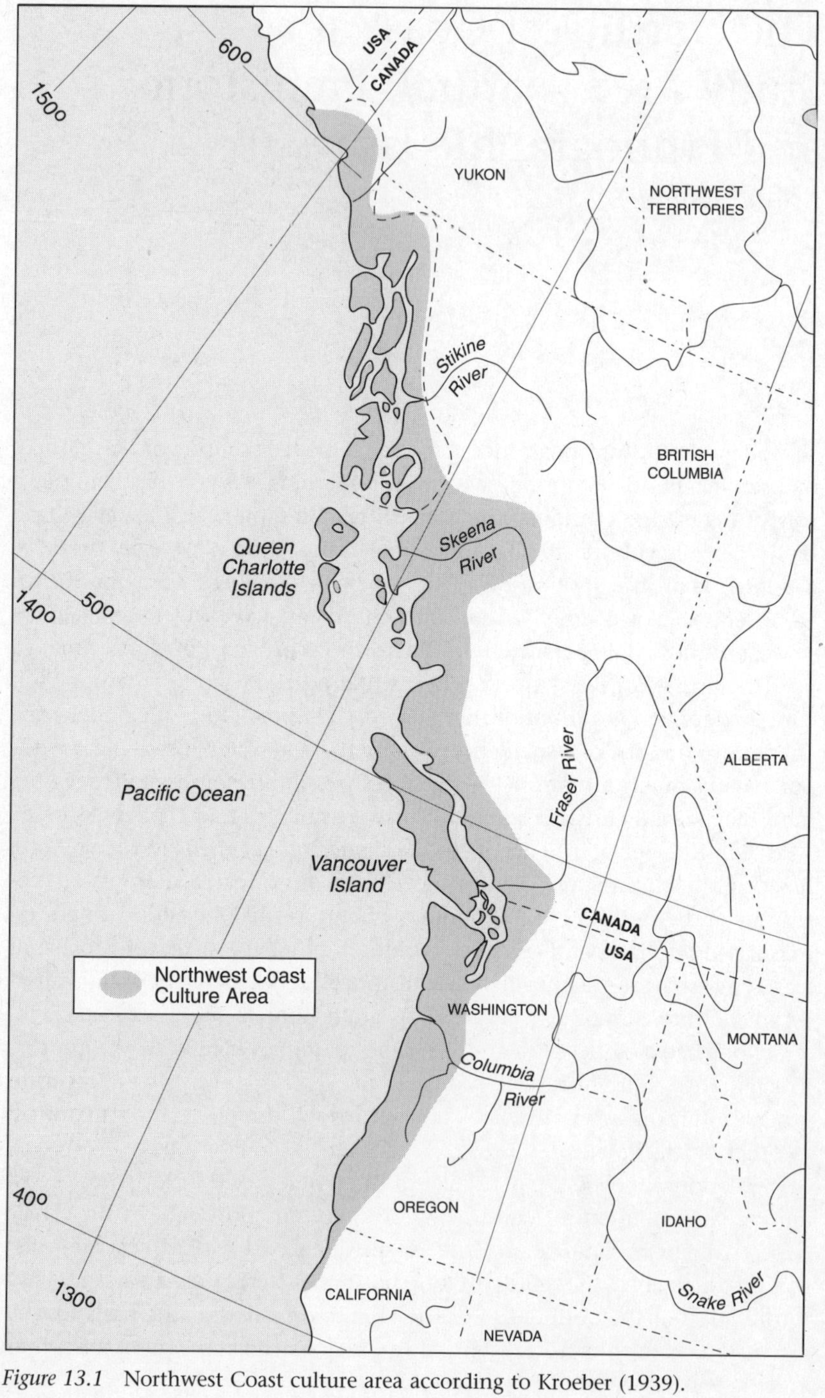

Figure 13.1   Northwest Coast culture area according to Kroeber (1939).

Although the culture area concept has most often been used in a synchronic way to group and classify ethnographic cultures, I propose we use it more dynamically – to explore both prehistoric and postcontact materials. Culture areas are thought of as changing over both time and space. The challenge is to use the concept to help us plot, describe, and finally explain and understand both culture history and culture processes.

I begin with a section that highlights some of the environmental characteristics of the region upon which the Aboriginal peoples built their cultures and which both contributed to and constrained what they could do. Next comes a section on the ethnographic Northwest Coast culture area. This is partly descriptive, to orient the discussion, but I pay some attention to dynamics and change with respect to selected features of these cultures. This is intended to suggest how ethnography and prehistory must play an integrated role in our regional researches. Finally, I turn to issues raised when we attempt to delimit the boundaries of the Northwest Coast. Most of my attention is directed to the questions and topics raised by attempts to satisfactorily construct the southern and northern boundaries.

In raising and attempting to resolve such questions, I am not merely engaging in an exercise in classification. Following Kroeber's lead, I assume that culture areas are (or ought to be) natural taxonomic units that reflect the culture history of a region, that represent zones of relatively intensive contact and sharing, and that have a meaningful common historical and developmental background. Kroeber's efforts to identify culture climaxes are an attempt at a historical and developmental interpretation and not merely a ranking of cultures.

The Natural Environment

Overview
The rainy Western Hemlock Forest Biome lies along the north Pacific coast of North America. This "hemlock-wapiti-deer-red cedar-Sitka spruce" biome begins in the vicinity of Kodiak Island, Alaska, and extends south in a coastal band to the vicinity of San Francisco Bay, California, a distance of over 3,800 kilometres. At its two extremes this biome is only a few kilometres wide, but at its widest extent (near the British Columbia/Washington border) it is over 300 kilometres wide. The most striking feature of the biome is the mature dominant trees of several species. Some of these frequently reach 40 metres to 60 metres in height and nearly 5 metres in diameter (western hemlock, Sitka spruce, Douglas fir, western red cedar), with the geographically restricted redwood achieving heights of over 90 metres. The biome has three major subdivisions: hemlock-cedar forest on the western slopes of the Cascade Range from northwestern California up to about fifty-one

degrees north latitude in British Columbia; hemlock-spruce forest on the western slopes of the coastal mountains from about fifty-one degrees north latitude to Kodiak Island; and redwood forest on somewhat localized slopes and pockets near the coast from southwestern Oregon south to the vicinity of Monterey Bay, California. There are pockets of other plant communities within this general area due to local variations in altitude and rainfall, but these forests of great trees dominate. The biome is supported by generally high rainfall (125 centimetres to 250 centimetres), low hours of sunshine, and fairly long frost-free periods. (For a good discussion of the biome and its variants see Shelford 1963:211-234.)

For its Aboriginal inhabitants this set of variables supplied a fairly rich set of plant resources and significant mammalian food resources (especially deer and elk), but the most important food resources of the region came from the rivers and the sea – as fish, sea mammals, marine invertebrates, and birds. Although land resources were not unimportant and were certainly used, the principal subsistence orientation of the area's Aboriginal peoples was to the exploitation of river and sea.

There is not space here for a detailed analysis of the north Pacific coast environment and its resources from the Aboriginal perspective, but I will offer a brief discussion of two key resources: western red cedar and salmon. These are singled out because one is the most important plant resource and the other is the most important animal resource for most Aboriginal communities. I argue that, although many other resources were certainly important to the region's indigenous cultures, between them red cedar and salmon formed the environmental base upon which classic Northwest Coast culture was built.

Cedar

The western red cedar (*Thuja plicata*) is not a true cedar but a cypress. It is common throughout most of the hemlock forest biome, but its relative abundance varies considerably on a local basis. It can grow to a very large size (up to 70 metres high and 4.3 metres in diameter) and has a number of characteristics that made it of great value to Aboriginal peoples throughout its range. Wherever available, red cedar was the principal wood for making dugout canoes (which reached nearly 20 metres in length in some groups), house posts and planks, storage and cooking boxes, and ceremonial gear, including carved poles. The bark and roots were also used for basket and mat making. (For fuller discussions of indigenous uses of cedar, see Turner 1979:74-90; and Stewart 1984.) Given traditional Northwest Coast technologies, red cedar logs are easier to work than most other types of logs. This is true whether one considers dugout canoe manufacture or the splitting off of large planks for house construction. Cedar also resists rot well and thus the labour involved in manufacturing cedar products is well invested.

Western red cedar has not been important in the Pacific coastal forests since "time immemorial." Paleobotanical evidence suggests that between 10,000 BP and 6000 BP cedar was rare throughout most of the northern and central parts of its recent range. Beginning about 6000 BP it began to become more common, reaching its recent co-dominant status with western hemlock about 2500 BP. Archaeological evidence for the central and northern parts of the culture area suggests that large-scale plank houses and large dugout canoes began to develop about 3500 BP and that the full woodworking technology for handling large logs was well developed by about 2500 BP. In other words, Northwest Coast wood-working technology developed as the importance of red cedar in the region's forests increased. (See Hebda and Mathewes 1984 for a succinct review of the paleobotanical and archaeological evidence.)

The recent range of western red cedar is not perfectly coterminous with the Northwest Coast culture area as usually defined (see Figure 13.2).[1] In the north, it is found up to about fifty-seven degrees north latitude, while Tlingit territory continues up to about sixty degrees north latitude. Given this, it is not surprising that large Haida (red cedar) canoes were an important item in Tlingit/Haida trade. To the east there are important stands of red cedar in the western Rocky Mountains, well outside the culture area. And in the south, the red cedar continues to grow down into northwestern California until almost forty degrees north latitude.

Salmon
The anadromous Pacific salmon enters streams on both sides of the north Pacific Ocean to spawn. Five species of Pacific salmon spawn in North American streams, ranging from the Mackenzie River on the Arctic coast to Monterey, California (see Figure 13.2). Each of the five species has a different range, and when these ranges overlap (which is much of the time) a particular stream may be used by any number of the potential spawning species. Thousands, even hundreds of thousands, of fish may return to a particular stream to spawn. The great salmon rivers of western North America are tremendously productive, and even streams with quite modest runs relative to the great salmon rivers were important food sources for Aboriginal communities. For most Northwest Coast groups salmon was the single most important food resource. This should not be taken to mean, however, that other foods were not important or even vital for most groups' survival.

At the northern and southern extremes of each species' range most of the runs are less important and less predictable. Overall the chum (*Oncorhynchus keta*) is the most important north Pacific salmon, contributing as much as

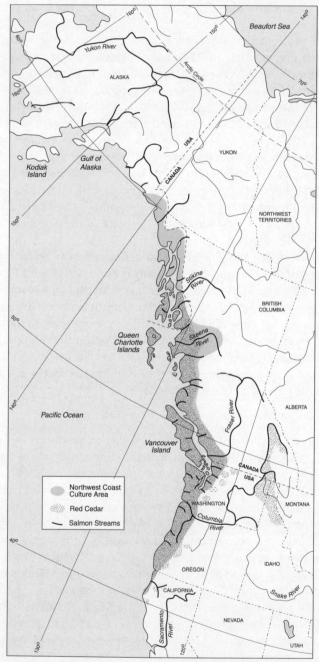

Figure 13.2   Range of the western red cedar and the major
Pacific salmon rivers on the north Pacific coast of North
America (for western red cedar: Little 1971; for Pacific salmon:
Aro and Shepard 1967, Groot and Margolis 1991).

50 percent of the annual biomass of the seven species of Pacific salmon (Salo 1991:233). The other species may be quite important in particular streams; for example, the millions of sockeye (*O. nerka*) that run into the Bristol Bay, Alaska, watershed or the Fraser River drainage of British Columbia. As can be seen from Table 13.1, however, major runs of the four most important species do not extend far south of the Columbia River system.[2]

On the Oregon coast only three species of Pacific salmon (chinook, chum, and coho) regularly run into rivers and streams from the Necanicum River south to the Coquille River, while on the remainder of the Oregon coast and the northwestern California coast only two species regularly run (chinook and coho) (Atkinson, Rose, and Duncan 1967:80-84). Only four river systems in this part of the coast appear to have even moderately important salmon runs: coho into the Nehalam River, Alsea River, and Ten Mile Lakes systems; and chum into the Klamath River system. Many other streams did, of course, have small runs of one or more species, which could be of considerable importance to a local population. My general impression, however, is that, south of the Columbia River system, salmon, although not insignificant, were not present in the kind of numbers that are found in the Columbia and north. Salmon were present in sufficient numbers to be important to particular indigenous communities but were rarely so numerous as to form the basis of the subsistence economy, as was the case for many communities from the Columbia River north.[3]

In contrast with the south, although the runs of the various salmon species north of their most intense spawning ranges decline, there are still many important, even major, salmon streams along the Alaskan coast north and

Table 13.1

North American overall ranges and ranges of major runs of Pacific salmon

Species	Overall range	Range of major runs
Sockeye (*O. nerka*)	Kotzebue Sound, Alaska, to Sacramento River, California	Kuskokwim River, Alaska, to Columbia River
Pink (*O. gorbuscha*)	east of Point Barrow, Alaska, to San Lorenzo River, California	Norton Sound, Alaska, to Puget Sound, Washington
Chum (*O. keta*)	Mackenzie River, NWT, to San Lorenzo River, California	Kotzebue Sound, Alaska, to Tillamook Bay, Oregon
Chinook (*O. tshawytscha*)	Kotzebue Sound, Alaska, to central California	[run size correlates strongly with stream size, not lattitude]
Coho (*O. kisutch*)	Point Hope, Alaska, to San Lorenzo River, California	Bristol Bay, Alaska, to Rogue River, Oregon

Source: Groot and Margolis 1991.

northwest of what is usually considered the northernmost extent of the
Northwest Coast culture area.

Salmon return to their natal streams to spawn on a seasonal basis. This
return is usually some time in the fall months, and the local timing is fairly
predictable. The size of the annual runs of each species into a stream also
varies from year to year. The degree of variation tends to be greater at the
extremes of each species' range, so that Oregon and California coastal streams
will show considerably more variation over the years than streams in the
central and northern parts of the culture area (Puget Sound north to the
Alaska panhandle). A partial exception to this rule is chinook, whose run
size tends to correlate with stream size even at the extremes of its range
(Healey 1991:316).

As is the case for red cedar, salmon were not a dominant part of north
Pacific coast environments since time immemorial. During the period from
14,000 BP until 10,000 BP salmon were not a significant species in the rivers
of coastal Alaska and British Columbia and were also probably less important further south as well. This is because in the earlier part of this period
most rivers were blocked by glacial ice and were unavailable for spawning.
In the latter part of this period the ice retreated, but the glacially fed rivers
were very unstable. Shifting sea levels also contributed to stream instability.
These highly unstable conditions led to drastic channel changes and other
conditions not conducive to successful salmon spawning.[4]

By about 10,000 years ago, sea level and river conditions had become
more stable. Although this was truer in the southern part of the area than
further north, salmon probably began to establish spawning populations in
coastal streams. There is, for example, good evidence for large salmon runs
in the Columbia River by at least 7700 BP (see Cressman et al.'s [1960] report on the Five Mile Rapids site at The Dalles). Although the evidence for
the entire coast is somewhat spotty, it suggests that, from 10,000 BP to about
6500 BP salmon became increasingly well established along coastal streams
and thus were increasingly available for exploitation by the region's human
population. After 5000 BP, the pace of human exploitation of salmon picks
up considerably, suggesting that the historic abundance of salmon was probably present.

As with western red cedar, the recent range of the five species of Pacific
salmon is not coterminous with the Northwest Coast culture area as usually
delimited. There are a few salmon streams in California south of the most
southerly drawn boundaries of the culture area. More important, there are
many very productive salmon streams in Alaska in territories traditionally
occupied by Eskimo and Athapaskan speakers whose cultures are not considered a part of the Northwest Coast culture area. Some of the major rivers
of the north Pacific coast of North America have drainages well into the
interior, to the east of the usual boundary of the culture area. Yet these river

systems support spawning salmon in much of their drainage areas. The Columbia, Fraser, and Yukon systems are the most important examples of this (see Figure 13.2).

Historical Summary

The pattern of development for these two key Northwest Coast resources was very similar: until after 10,000 BP, neither was important, at least not in the northern and central part of what became the Northwest Coast culture area of the early contact period. Indeed, red cedar became important well after this time period. The pattern of colonization of the coast by both species was also similar: both spread from south to north. Only when both red cedar and the various species of Pacific salmon were flourishing did classic Northwest Coast culture fully develop.

The Ethnographic Northwest Coast Culture Area

Summary of Characteristic Traits of the Culture Area

The communities usually considered a part of the Northwest Coast culture area as it existed around the time of first European contact were not culturally uniform. No one culture trait or small set of traits characterizes all of these cultures, nor is any trait exclusive to the culture area. Nevertheless, it is not difficult to describe a distinctive set of characteristics that typifies Northwest Coast cultures and that, as a collection, sets them off from neighbouring cultures and from the rest of traditional Aboriginal North America more generally.

Overall one can identify a marine and riverine orientation that encompassed not only subsistence practices but ideology and outlook. Subsistence activities emphasized fishing and marine mammal hunting, although there was also considerable gathering of shellfish, other marine invertebrates, and plant foods. The peoples of the culture area employed a highly developed wood-working technology whose most spectacular products were large plank houses, very large dugout canoes, and various carved and painted wooden art objects, some of which can only be described as monumental sculpture.

There was an emphasis on property, both tangible and noncorporeal, with the control of all types of wealth as the principal criterion of social importance and success. Both kinship groups and individuals held various types of property, and individual and kin group ranking were important. In addition, there was a tripartite system of social stratification that included a lower stratum of hereditary slaves who originated as war captives. In spite of the presence of an elaborate system of ownership and social stratification (which included slavery) there was no intercommunity political organization, and even individual communities were often not political units. Significant political office was absent.[5]

Although Northwest Coast peoples lacked agriculture and employed what is usually described as a "hunting-and-gathering" technology, this technology provided a highly sophisticated adaptation to the rich maritime and riverine environment that they exploited. The best recent estimate suggests a population for the region of as much as 150,000 at the time of first European contact (Boyd 1990:136). This would give an approximate density of over forty persons per 100 square kilometres, which is higher than the density for many other parts of Aboriginal North America, including some whose populations practised agriculture.

Aboriginal North America is usually divided into about nine or ten culture areas. Edward Sapir (1949:427), ever the "lumper" in matters of classification, suggested in 1916 that "an historical analysis of North American culture would quite probably reduce the present culture areas to two or three fundamental ones, say a Mexican culture area, a Northwest Coast culture area, and a large Central area of which the Pueblo and Eskimo areas are the most specialized developments."

Although Kroeber (1923:2, 8) never reduced the number of North American culture areas to anything approaching Sapir's three, he did maintain, as Sapir implies, that the Northwest Coast culture area was the most distinctive of the Aboriginal culture areas of North America, suggesting that those elements it shared with most other North American culture areas (such as the dog, the bow, the firedrill, woven basketry, shamanism, and life crisis rites for individuals [especially for adolescent girls]) were a common inheritance from the earliest populations to settle in North American via the Siberia/Alaska land bridge route. He observed that it shared few, if any, of the traits that had diffused from Middle America to most other culture areas on the continent and that the area had a number of aspects that seem to have been local innovations and that had diffused to only a modest degree into closely neighbouring culture areas. In the same discussion, Kroeber also made the important point that traits absent from the Northwest Coast but common elsewhere in North America were as significant as were those that were present. For example, he observes that

> the Northwest is substantially without officials, chiefs, government, or political authority. This may seem a strange statement about a culture in which a class of chiefs or nobles is recognized as distinct from commoners. Yet the very breadth of this class of chiefs argues that it is something different, in the main, from a group of officials constituting part of a political mechanism. The concept of such a mechanism is what seems to be foreign to the Northwestern culture. It knows privileges and honors, but not office; a status of influence, but no constituted authority. (1923:9)

He then went on to observe that

what counts among these people is possession; possession of property, of inherited or acquired use, of privilege, of ritual. Enough of such possessions, jealously maintained, give honor and influence and command. Custom law operates to guard and increase the possessions, prestige, and power of the wealthy. (1923:9)

Finally, Kroeber added historical implications to his suggestion of the distinctive character of the culture area, hypothesizing that there was "an active cultural focal center lying within the Northwest area and rather rigorously limited to it" (1923:14), and arguing that the large number of traits and customs specific to the Northwest Coast were the result of local innovations or unusually thorough transformations of borrowings.

Definitions/Mappings of the Northwest Coast Culture Area

The distinctiveness of the indigenous cultures of the north Pacific coast of North America has been recognized by anthropologists since Otis Mason (1896) published the first overall classification of North American Aboriginal groups based on the geographical clustering of cultural features. Since Mason, every attempt to deal with the entire North American continent or with the north Pacific coast of North America has recognized some version of the Northwest Coast culture area. Although the exact definition of the area has varied, all classifications known to me include (from north to south) the Tlingit to the Salish-speaking peoples of the greater Puget Sound area. Most discussions continue the area south to the mouth of the Columbia and include the Chinookan speakers around it.[6]

The most influential treatment of the North American culture areas has been Kroeber's in *Cultural and Natural Areas of Native North America* (1939). Kroeber appears to present a taxonomy of Aboriginal American cultures, but it is not a systematic or consistent one. Nowhere in *Cultural and Natural Areas of Native North America* does he discuss the hierarchical aspect of the classification that underlies his presentation. At the beginning of his discussion of specific culture areas he speaks of "eighty or so areas" being aggregated into six groups (or "grand areas" as they are labelled on his Map 6). Most of these six major groups (including the Northwest Coast) are "believed to represent a substantial unit of historical development, or of a prevailingly characteristic current of culture" (1939:20). All of these major groups (culture areas in most subsequent discussions) are divided into areas (subareas in most subsequent discussions), and some of these areas are divided into subareas. I follow most writers subsequent to Kroeber and write of the Northwest Coast as a "culture area" and of Kroeber's areas within the Northwest Coast as "subareas."

Kroeber's Northwest Coast culture area ranges south from the Tlingit in Alaska, largely along the coast, until it reaches the Hupa and Wiyot in northwestern California. Kroeber recognized seven subareas within the larger area. Five of these subareas make up the agreed upon core of the culture area: Tlingit south to Lower Columbia Chinookans. The southernmost of these five regions, the Lower Columbia, also includes the Upper Columbia Chinookans (Wasco-Wishram), whom some have placed in the Plateau culture area, and the northernmost Oregon coast groups – the Tillamook, Alseans, Siuslawans, and Coosans.

Kroeber's other two Northwest Coast subareas are the Willamette Valley, essentially the relatively poorly known Kalapuyans, and the Lower Klamath, which includes "Northwestern California with Rogue and upper and middle Umpqua drainage in Oregon," featuring the Yurok, Karok, and Hupa. In other schemes these have been excluded or included, in whole or in part, from the Northwest Coast equally often.

I have used Kroeber's delineation of the Northwest Coast for my maps, and it forms the basis of my discussion of the culture area. However, I do not accept all of Kroeber's ideas about what to include or exclude from this culture area.

Some Typical Traits

Slave Killing at Funerals of Titleholders

The practice of true slavery is one of the important traits that distinguishes traditional Northwest Coast cultures from almost all other traditional Native American cultures. By true slavery I refer to a situation in which war captives became permanently low-status stigmatized individuals without kin ties or any rights in their new communities. They were the property of their owners, who controlled their labour and could exchange them for other property or kill them at will. The offspring of slaves were slaves, and escaped slaves remained stigmatized even if they were able to return to their home communities. This contrasts with the situation in most of Native North America, where surviving captives often gradually obtained improved status and where their children were regarded as free.[7]

Slaves were found in every Northwest Coast community from the northern Tlingit (Yakutat Bay) south to the Lower Columbia Chinookans and the Tillamook. For the Oregon coast peoples south of the Tillamook, the data on slavery are very sparse, however it seems probable that true slavery was practised by the Alseans, Siuslawans, and Coosans but not by the southwestern Oregon Athapaskans (see Barnett 1937 and the relevant group chapters in Suttles 1990a). The northern California peoples considered by Kroeber to belong to the Northwest Coast culture area had a status usually labelled "slave" in English, but the available material, which is fairly rich for the Yurok, indicates that this was a status involving debt servitude and not true slavery: "slave" status was not inherited and control over the person and even the labour of the "slave" was not complete (this is best illustrated in the accounts in Spott and Kroeber 1942, especially pages 149-153).

In the Plateau culture area, which in Kroeber's scheme borders the Northwest Coast from the Bella Coola south to the Lower Columbia Chinookans, we find again that "slavery" is reported for a number of Plateau peoples who are neighbours or near neighbours of Northwest Coast peoples. However, the sparse data available strongly suggest that this status was generally a temporary one that was rarely, if ever, inherited and does not represent true slavery of the fully developed Northwest Coast type: even if a captive did not eventually become a low-status free person, his or her children did (see Donald 1996 for the Interior Salish). An exception to the preceding statement is the Upper Chinookans (Wasco-Wishram) who certainly did practise Northwest Coast style slavery (Boyd 1996:89-91, 111-112; Spier and Sapir 1931:221-224).

North of the Plateau culture area, the Subarctic (Mackenzie-Yukon region) and then the Arctic culture areas border the Northwest Coast. Several of the peoples along the boundary with the Northwest Coast did practise true slavery: the data are clear for the Eyak and, perhaps, the Southern Tutchone. The Southern Tutchone are unusual among Athapaskans in having true slavery, but Legros's (1985) material is very suggestive for this people, who interacted frequently with the Tlingit. The Inland Tlingit, a heavily "Tlingitized" Athapaskan group, also appears to have practised something very much like Northwest Coast slavery (McClellan 1975): some captives became slaves in the Northwest Coast sense, but others did make the transition from low-status captive to low-status free person, much as captives among the Interior Salish peoples briefly mentioned above. Further west of the Eyak, along the Pacific coast of Alaska, the Pacific Eskimo (Chugach, Koniag) and the Aleut also practised slavery in a manner very similar to that of the Northwest Coast peoples (Birket-Smith 1953; Jordan 1994; Lantis 1970).

One common custom among Northwest Coast slave owners was the killing of a slave in association with the death of a titleholder (kin group leader or close relative), usually as a part of funeral rites. The slave (or slaves) killed usually belonged to the deceased man or woman, but sometimes slaves were purchased for the occasion. Figure 13.3 shows the distribution of this trait. From the northernmost communities in the culture area (Yakutat Tlingit) south to the mouth of the Columbia River the practice is reported for virtually all communities for which there is good information. Only for one people, the Twana, is the ritual slave killing denied. The data on slavery (and most other topics) are very sparse for most of the groups between the Twana and the Chinookan speakers of the Lower Columbia, and the sources are silent on the subject of ritual slave killings for these groups – hence the question mark on the map.

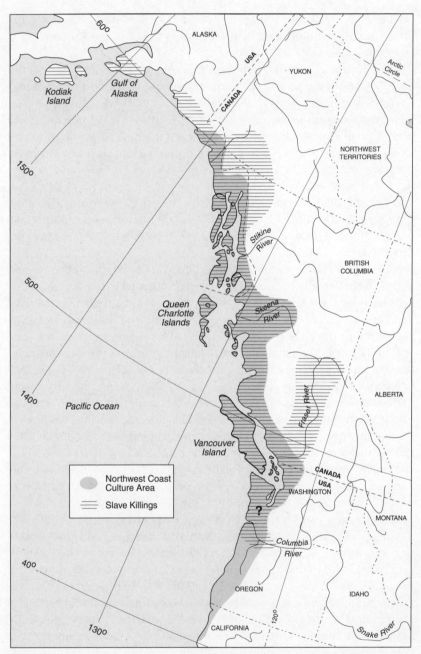

Figure 13.3   Distribution of ritual slave killings at the death of a titleholder (Donald 1997).

South of the Lower Columbia Chinookans, no evidence that slaves were ritually killed among any of the slaveholding Oregon coast groups is known to me. What little is said in the sources about this topic (Barnett 1937:194) supports the interpretation that slave killing at funerals did not occur. There is no evidence for ritual slave killing among the northern California groups that Kroeber included in the Northwest Coast (see, for example, his silence on the subject in his notes comparing Yurok and Twana practices, in Elmendorf's [1960:343-347] Twana monograph).

Upriver from the Lower Columbia Chinookans, their linguistic confreres, the Wasco-Wishram, practised Northwest Coast style slavery as noted above and also killed slaves at titleholder funerals (Boyd 1996:111-112). Among other Plateau groups, captives are reported as having been killed occasionally at the funerals of important people among the Upper Nlakapamux (Upper Thompson), Secwepemc (Shuswap), and Stl'atl'imx (Lillooet) (Donald 1996:81). Further north and west of the Northwest Coast, all five of the peoples reported above as practising slavery (Eyak, Southern Tutchone, Inland Tlingit, Pacific Eskimo, and Aleut) are also reported as killing slaves at the funerals of leaders and other important persons.

The distribution of ritual slave killing both within the Northwest Coast and just outside it is very similar to the distribution of true slavery. Where both traits are definitely or probably missing is largely in the southern part of Kroeber's Northwest Coast, south of the Columbia River.

Head Deformations and Labrets
Cranial deformation of infants was a widespread practice in the culture area. The infant's head was bound, often with the use of flat boards, to cause the cranial bones to grow into the desired shape, producing one or another variety of what were often known in the local languages as "flatheads" (see Boas [1921:657-680] for a detailed description of the process of producing the desired head shape among the Kwakwaka'wakw; for a modern discussion by a physical anthropologist see Cybulski [1975]). Boas (1891:647-648) identified three major styles of cranial deformation, which he labelled with the names of ethnic groups he thought practised a particular style in its most extreme form. These were the "Koskimo," the "Cowichan," and the "Chinook" styles. Not all Northwest Coast peoples practised head deformation, so "undeformed "can be considered a fourth major style of head form.

The various styles of cranial deformation were not confined to a single ethnic unit or even language, however; instead, each was practised over a rather wide area. Adherence to the local custom was particularly important for members of the elite. Various scholars (Hajda 1984; Suttles 1990c:13-14) have suggested that the areal distribution of head shapes coincided with subareas of relatively intense social interaction, particularly involving marriages, trade, and ritual cooperation. Hajda makes a good case for the existence of such a social and economic interaction sphere centred on the Lower Columbia River, and a good case can be made for such a sphere among the northernmost peoples of the culture area (see the following paragraph). Other social interaction spheres posited to lie between these two are not as well documented or worked out, but there is some support for the existence of each.

The northernmost groups (Tlingit, Haida, Tsimshian, Haisla) did not practise head deformation. They also formed a social interaction sphere. Not only were they all matrilineal, but their moiety/phratry systems were aligned, which facilitated marriage across ethnolinguistic lines (see Dunn 1984). Such marriages were important to the elites of all these peoples.

South of this block of peoples the practice of head deformation begins. Suttles (1990c:13) has suggested that differences in preferred appearance of the head divided the remainder of the region down to the Columbia River into four blocks: (1) Haihais, Heiltsuk, Nuxalk (Bella Coola), and Oowekeeno; (2) Kwakwaka'wakw, northern and central Nuu-chah-nulth, and northern Coast Salish (Comox and ?); (3) Nitinat, Makah, Quileute, Central Coast Salish, Chemakum, and Puget Sound Salish; (4) Southwestern Salish, Lower Colombian Chinookans, and the northernmost Oregon coast peoples (Tillamook, Alseans, and some Siuslaw). In addition, the fourth block included the northernmost Kalapuyans (in the northern Willamette Valley) and the Upper Chinookans (Suttles 1990c, supplemented by Barnett 1937:173; Boyd 1996:92; Hilton 1990:315; Zenk 1990b:548; Zenk 1990c:573). This was the distribution of preferred styles of cranial deformation around the time of contact, although there was variation within individual ethnolinguistic units as well as within these larger blocks, and it can be difficult to decide how to classify particular examples as to type (see Cybulski 1975). Figure 13.4 plots the five regions as demarcated by style of cranial treatment.

Cranial deformation has been practised in the region for a long time. In the Strait of Georgia area there is evidence for the practice from Marpole times (2400-1400 BP) until the contact period (Cybulski 1991:8). I am not aware of archaeological evidence for head deformation from the other areas where it was practised during early historic times.

Styles of cranial deformation are not the only alterations of the human form that have probable associations with participation in subregional social interaction spheres on the Northwest Coast. Labrets, while primarily objects of adornment, may also have been such social indicators. Where they were worn in historical times on the Northwest Coast they were certainly a marker indicating high social status. Labrets are ornaments that project through a hole or holes pierced through the skin just below the lower lip or, more occasionally, the corners of the mouth (for illustrations

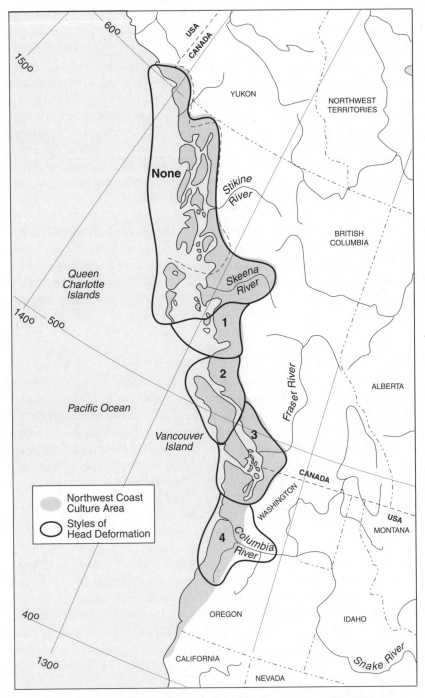

Figure 13.4   Distribution of styles of head deformation (Suttles 1990b; Barnett 1937; Boyd 1996; Hilton 1990; Zenk 1990a, 1990b).

of the various types of labret found on the Northwest Coast and elsewhere see Keddie 1984; most of the distributional information that follows is based on Keddie's paper).

In early contact times on the Northwest Coast labrets were worn by upper-class women among the Tlingit, Haida, Tsimshian, Haisla, Haihais, and Heiltsuk. All of these peoples had matrilineal descent groups. The first four did not practise head deformation, but the Haihais and Heiltsuk did. One interpretation of this is that, as their elite women bore markers indicating membership in two spheres of social and economic interaction, these two peoples were positioning themselves to participate in both.

The wearing of labrets gradually disappeared in the first century of contact, but early in this period labrets were also worn to the northwest of the Northwest Coast along the Alaska coast. Although the immediate neighbours of the northernmost Tlingit, the Eyak, did not wear labrets, a number of Gulf of Alaska peoples did (Chugach and Koniag). Labrets were also worn by the Aleut and by both Yupik and Inupik speakers in coastal western Alaska. Among the Inupik, men rather than women wore labrets. That labrets were social markers relevant to interaction patterns along the Alaska coast as well as on the Northwest Coast is suggested by Keddie's (1981:69) report that some Ingalik men on the lower Yukon wore labrets but that this was confined to those who traded with the Coastal Inupik. Labrets are reported in historic times as far east on the north Alaskan coast as Cape Bathhurst.

The archaeological evidence suggests a more complex situation on the Northwest Coast well before contact. Labrets are not uncommon prehistorically in the Strait of Georgia, the area occupied ethnographically by the Coast Salish, having been found frequently in both Locarno type sites (3200-2400 BP) and Marpole type sites (2400-1500 BP). However, they are not found in Strait of Georgia type sites (post-1400 BP) and they are unknown there in historic times (Mitchell 1990:341, 345).

A few possible labrets have been found archaeologically in territory that was Heiltsuk ethnographically, but they seem to be undated (Keddie 1981: 65). Further north, labrets are much better documented for prehistoric times. Early dates for labrets for the various ethnographically known group territories include, for the Tsimshian, 3000-2500 BP and, for the Haida, c. 2000 BP (Keddie 1981:65-66). There are archaeological labret finds for the Tlingit area that date as early as 4600-3200 BP (Matson and Coupland 1995:132).

Labrets are also found archaeologically along the Alaskan coast. Moving from Cook Inlet west and then north, we find that the sample dates include 2700-1400 BP at Cook Inlet, c. 2000 BP in Prince William Sound, 1400 BP at Yukon Island, 2100-1000 BP on Kodiak Island, 3200-300 BP in the Aleutians (with one early date of c. 4000 BP), 2700-1400 BP in the Inupik-speaking area of the Alaska coast, and pre-600 BP in the Mackenzie Delta (Keddie 1981:67-72).

The archaeological/historical incidence of labrets suggests a fairly continuous distribution along the north Pacific coast of North America from the vicinity of Milbanke Sound in British Columbia north around coastal Alaska with a late, but still prehistoric, spread as far east on the Arctic coast as the Mackenzie delta. The most important exception to this statement is the prehistoric appearance of labrets in the Strait of Georgia area for a period of around 1,600 years, with their disappearance from this area being the immediate archaeological precursor of the historically known Coast Salish cultures. The prehistoric gap between the Strait of Georgia and Milbanke Sound should be confirmed or filled in with closer archaeological scrutiny.

The main purpose of this section is to suggest that certain culturally distinctive practices – head deformation and labrets – may also serve as markers of regions of more intensive social and economic interaction within the larger Northwest Coast culture area. This was almost certainly so in early historic times and may well have been true prehistorically. At least these two culture traits are archaeologically identifiable, and they would allow us to trace changing and developing spheres of interaction and contact.

Change and Dynamics: Some Examples

Dancing Societies

As an example of change and development immediately before and during early contact times I take the ceremonial complex often referred to as the Dancing Societies. These were a set of ranked or graded ritual dramas ("dances") that represented the supernatural experiences of the performer's ancestors. Those being initiated into a particular dance re-enacted (or, better, re-experienced) an ancestor's encounter with a supernatural being.[8]

In their most elaborate form, among the Heiltsuk and their fellow northern Wakashan-speaking neighbours, there were three cycles of dances, hence three Dancing Societies. In late precontact times the centre of creative development for these ceremonies was located among the Heiltsuk. These ceremonial cycles were most fully developed among the Heiltsuk, Ooweekeno, Haihais, and Haisla. The best known of these cycles is the Shamans' Society (this was not an organization of shamans in the classical sense, although some shamans were members), which featured performances by "cannibal" dancers. The Shamans' Society was found among the four Northern Wakashan peoples mentioned above and had spread to the various Kwakwaka'wakw groups whom Boas had named the Southern Kwakiutl. It was also performed among the Nuxalk (Bella Coola) and the Southern Tsimshian groups (Kitasoo, Kitkiata, Kitkatla). Some of the Coast Tsimshian had taken it up in partial form, and important people in some Haida and southern Tlingit communities had the rights to use certain masks, songs, and dances from the ceremonies as part of their crest displays (although

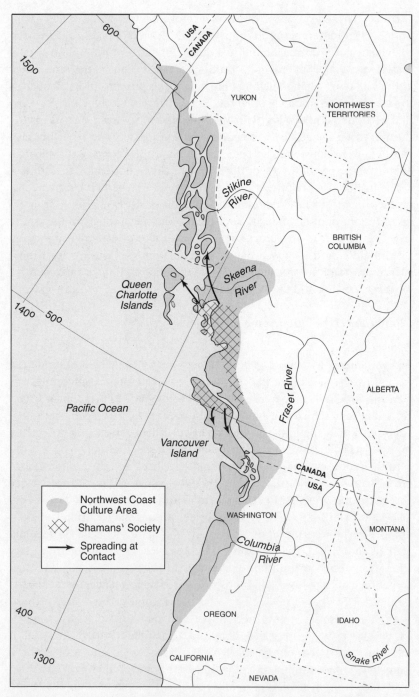

Figure 13.5 Spread of the "Shamans' Society" (Boas 1956; Drucker 1940, 1955, 1965).

they did not perform the full rituals). This was also the case with some Nuu-chah-nulth (Nootka) who obtained the privileges via the Kwakwaka'wakw. In addition, in early contact times some of the northern Coast Salish (Comox, Klahuse, Homalco) used elements from the Dancing Society rituals that are almost certainly Heiltsuk in origin and came to them via the Kwakwaka'wakw.

Although the Shamans' Society probably developed out of very old Wakashan-wide ritual ideas and practices, there seems little doubt that in its ethnographically known form it is Heiltsuk in origin. Oral traditions, linguistic usage (the terminology is often Heiltsuk no matter what the language spoken by the performers and audience), and trait distributions all point this way. Figure 13.5 diagrams the spread of the Shamans' Society and its influence as we are able to reconstruct it. We also know something of how this spread occurred from its creative centre among the Heiltsuk: ritual privileges and paraphernalia and even entire dances were often transferred from one family to another as a part of marriage prestations or as a result of the capture in war of both the regalia and someone with the right to the dances.

Such a spread of trait complexes and practices (involving both ritual and other aspects of culture) from a creative centre to other parts of the culture area must have happened frequently throughout history. The even more widespread appearance of versions and elements of another dancing society (the "Nutlam") of undoubted Wakashan origin, and probably considerably older than the Shamans' Society, suggests that the latter was simply the latest burst of ritual and ceremonial creativity that had begun to spread over parts of the culture area just before contact occurred.

Seated Human Figure Bowls

Reconstructions of older developments depend, of course, largely on archaeological work, and the nature of archaeological evidence will limit what we can reconstruct. However, much could be done with a careful recording of the distribution of the various kinds of evidence that archaeology can produce.

As an example of what was probably a similar kind of spread from a creative centre in prehistoric times, Figure 13.6 shows the distribution of seated human figure stone bowls. These stone sculptures are mostly small (8 centimetres to about 30 centimetres, although one is nearly 55 centimetres tall) seated human forms whose arms and lap together form a small bowl. It is almost impossible to resist an interpretation of ritual use for these sculptures. Stylistically they sometimes seem to prefigure elements of the classic northern style of Northwest Coast art (for illustrations and discussion see Duff 1956 and 1975). Unfortunately most of these finds have not been dated, but some evidence suggests an origin around the mouth of the Fraser River

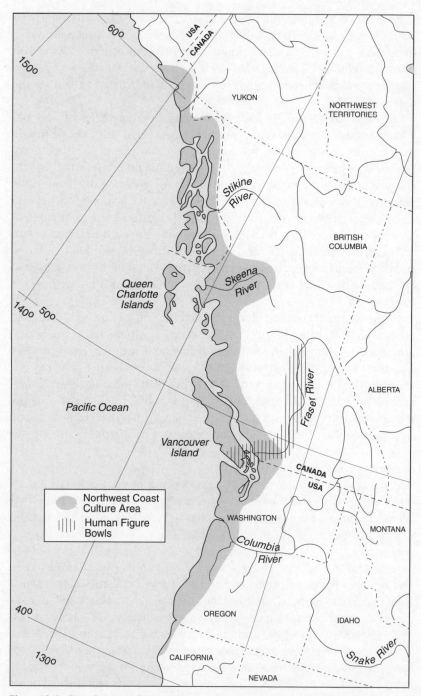

Figure 13.6 Distribution of seated human figure bowls (Duff 1956, 1975).

c. 3000 BP (for the evidence see Mitchell 1990:344, 345. The interpretation is mine).

Boundaries of the Northwest Coast Culture Area

The author of any culture area scheme that is intended to be continent-wide, or to cover even a major portion of a continent, usually aims to be inclusive: all cultures and all parts of the region under consideration should be incorporated in one or another of the culture areas. Taxonomists and taxonomies tend to abhor incompleteness. This makes decisions about boundaries important, and, as Kroeber (1939:5) observed, "the weakest feature of any mapping of culture wholes is also the most conspicuous: the boundaries."

For the Northwest Coast most of the perceived problems relating to determining boundaries have been in the south, especially with groups on the Oregon coast and in northwestern California. The northern boundary has been of interest because of the protohistoric expansion of the Northwest Coast Tlingit at the expense of the Eyak and because of the insistence of some that there are important connections west along the Pacific coast (for example, the late Richard Jordan's [1994] suggestions of Kodiak affinities with the Northwest Coast).

The eastern boundary has not attracted much attention, apparently having been taken as relatively unproblematic, at least in ethnographic terms. Nevertheless, the Plateau and Northwest Coast share one of western North America's major language families – Salishan – suggesting strong ties between the Northwest Coast and the Plateau. There were major blocks of Salishan-speaking peoples in both culture areas in historic times, but Jorgensen's (1969:62-69) *Salish Language and Culture* shows a major cultural split between the interior and coastal Salish in terms of ethnographically known cultural affinities. At times in the prehistoric past, the differences between the Northwest Coast and the Plateau, at least in parts of these culture areas, may not have been so great. The "Old Cordilleran," which appears in locations that fall within what became ethnographically the central Northwest Coast and the Plateau, is a good example, although the date of this complex (8500-5500 BP) is considerable and allows for the rise of differences between the two culture areas from a variety of causes during the period when the ethnographic culture types were developing. Hayden (1992) has interpreted his findings relating to the more recent prehistoric past of part of the Plateau as indicating much greater sociocultural complexity there than the ethnographic record suggests. His interpretations would make some prehistoric Plateau cultures more like those of prehistoric and historic Northwest Coast cultures than is usually thought. However, such issues have not been central to most discussions of the culture area in either its prehistoric or historic manifestations.

My discussion of boundaries focuses first on the problem of delimiting the culture area's southern boundary and then on issues relating to affinities between the Northwest Coast and the cultures along the Pacific coast to its north. My goal in all of this is not to settle any boundary questions, but rather to suggest how considering such problems challenges us to ask questions about prehistoric and historic developments and interactions that will help us better understand both the Northwest Coast itself and culture processes.

The Southern Northwest Coast and Its Boundary

The position of the peoples along the Oregon coast and in northwestern California has always been most puzzling. In part this is because the data for the coastal Oregon groups, whether prehistoric, ethnohistoric, or ethnographic, have been very thin. This has begun to improve on the archaeological side, but the prospects for improvement on the ethnohistoric or ethnographic side seem very modest indeed (see, for example, the comments in Erlandson, Tveskov, and Byram [1998] and the sources cited therein). The material on the northwestern California groups is much richer, but the Oregon coast gap will always impede our understanding of their relations to the Northwest Coast. The primary reason for the weaknesses in the ethnographic and ethnohistoric record is the very early demographic collapse in the Oregon coastal populations due to the impact of disease and other deleterious aspects of Euro-American contact and settlement.

A.L. Kroeber's Southern Northwest Coast

Kroeber's Northwest Coast culture area begins with the Tlingit in Alaska and goes south, largely along the coast, until it reaches the Hupa and Wiyot in northwestern California. Kroeber recognized seven subareas within the larger area. In the context of the southern limits of the culture area, three of these subareas require some notice here: the Lower Columbia, the Willamette Valley, and the Lower Klamath.

Kroeber (1939:30) put the Willamette Valley cultures (Kalapuyans) into the Northwest Coast, even though he recognized they had a distinctive, inland, non-Northwest Coast environment. The editors of the recent *Handbook of North American Indians* follow Kroeber's lead, although, to me, what little we know of Kalapuyan culture makes it appear much more Plateau than Northwest Coast (see Zenk 1990b). As already noted, continental culture area schemes require everyone to be in some area, and Kroeber chose to make the Kalapuyans a distinctive part of the Northwest Coast rather than of the Plateau. This is perhaps because his Plateau is clearly labelled the Columbia-Fraser Plateau, and he took a narrow rather than a broad view of the Plateau culture area. At the same time he assumed a broad rather than a narrow view of the Northwest Coast, as his treatment of the northwestern California groups discussed below indicates.

The Lower Columbia region went from Shoalwater Bay on the Washington coast south to the Umpqua Mountains of south central Oregon and also included the lower reaches of the Columbia River. The cultures in this area were the Lower Chinookan, Chehalis, Tillamook, Alsean, and Siuslaw.

The Lower Klamath area went from the Umpqua River in Oregon south to the Eel River in northwestern California. The cultures in this area included the Coos, Yurok, Wiyot, Karok, the Takelma, the southwest Oregon Athapaskans (Tututni, Upper Coquille, Upper Umpqua, Galice Creek, and Applegate Creek), and many of the northwest California Athapaskans (Tolowa, Hupa, Chiula, and Whilkut).

Kroeber (1939:30) also recognized a "subperipheral transition region ... extending in an arc from the Shasta on the middle Klamath to the Wailaki and Sinkyone on the middle Eel [River]" but included this area in his California culture area. In his 1936 paper, "Culture Area Distributions: III Area and Climax," Kroeber (1936:102) recognized a Northwest California culture area, classifying the Yurok, Hupa, and Karok as the "climax" cultures of the area and including all the other groups as subclimax and margin. The subclimax groups included the Tolowa, who straddle the Oregon/California border and whose linguistic affinities are with the southwest Oregon Athapaskans rather than with the northwest California Athapaskans, the two sets of Athapaskan speakers being separated by the Algonquin-speaking Yurok and the "Northern Hokan"-speaking Karok.[9]

Kroeber does not provide detailed reasons for including his Lower Klamath subarea in the Northwest Coast culture area. Perhaps the most important point he makes is that he regards the redwood forest of northern California as a specialized extension of what he labels the "Northwestern Hygrophytic Coniferous Forest," which he felt was the ecological basis of Northwest Coast culture. In particular, he notes that the "denser and more characteristic part" of the redwood forest is its northern half (to about Cape Mendocino) – the half occupied by the California cultures that he included in his Lower Klamath subarea (Kroeber 1939:28). Finally, in a footnote that takes into account ethnographic work conducted in northwestern California and southwestern Oregon in the mid-1930s by Philip Drucker and Homer Barnett (i.e., after the original manuscript was written), Kroeber notes that the Coos and Suislaw are too culturally similar to put into two separate subareas as he had originally done. However, he is uncertain as to whether they should both be classified as Lower Columbia or as Lower Klamath (1939:30).

In his overview discussion of Northwest Coast subareas, Kroeber notes that his seven subareas form a series of longitudinal belts that are almost parallel to the coast (1930:31). He identifies the climax cultures of the Northwest

Coast with an extreme maritime orientation and places the subareas with the least developed adaptation to water as the furthest removed culturally from the former. Only the Willamette Valley Kalapuyans are less oriented to the water than are the Lower Klamath cultures, who, along with the Lower Columbia and Puget Sound subareas, are described as riverine rather than maritime in adaptation.

Thinking over Kroeber's subarea classification, and the problems he had with it, leads me to the following conclusion: the groups along the Oregon and northern California coasts from the mouth of the Columbia River to the Eel River belong to at least two sets of groups (i.e., at least two subareas). The questions to resolve are: How many sets are there along the Oregon and northern California coasts and which, if any, should be attached to the Northwest Coast? If one or more sets are not classified with the Northwest Coast, then where do such sets belong?

Joseph G. Jorgensen's Southern Northwest Coast
Most North American culture area schemes since Kroeber follow his lead fairly closely, with respect to the Northwest Coast Kroeber's culture areas and his subareas were based on his extensive knowledge of Native American ethnography and were helped along by his intuition and flair. The most extensive work on the ethnological classification of the Aboriginal cultures of western North America since Kroeber's is Jorgensen's *Western Indians* (1980). Based on an objective multivariate methodology, his conclusions about the southern portions of the Northwest Coast culture area closely resemble Kroeber's.

In his efforts to define culture areas for western North American groups based on a sample of 172 groups and 292 variables, Jorgensen (1980:2) found that "the Northwest Coast and California regions posed the largest taxonomic problems: several cultures ambiguously took places between the Northwest Coast and Northern California areas." Indeed, when one carefully examines his two-dimensional smallest space mapping of the similarity coefficients for his 172 western North American Aboriginal groups, these Northern California groups appear closest to his "Northern and Central California" culture area (1980:89). Because of the "unique adaptations to coastal and riverine life in the wet forests and oak woodlands" (1980:92), Jorgensen decided to follow Kroeber, Driver, and Drucker, and so the Northwestern California groups "were considered to compose a southernmost province of the Northwest Coast and were analyzed as such, while ... the avowedly California nature of this subarea [was emphasized]" (1980:92). Those who, like me, are less certain of the clear Northwest Coast affinities of cultures such as the Hupa, Karok, and Yurok will note that, on the dendrogram of the nonmetric tree analysis of the similarities of the 172 groups in his sample, the results place many of the northwestern California groups squarely in the middle of the list of the groups in his "Northern and Central California" culture area and that this culture area is separated from his "Northwest Coast" area by his "Plateau" culture area (1980:94).

In the nonmetric tree dendrogram, in contrast to all other groups in the Northwest Coast culture area, the Oregon coast groups in Jorgensen's sample (Tolowa, Chetco, Tutuni, Galice Creek, Coos, Siuslaw, Alsea, and Tillamook) form a major subcluster. The two-dimensional smallest space mapping confirms that the Oregon coast groups are not closely grouped with the other Northwest Coast groups in Jorgensen's sample: they are about halfway between the other Northwest Coast groups and the Northern and Central California area groups, with a gap between themselves and each of these groups. In my view, Jorgensen's data and his multivariate analysis of them strongly suggest that the Oregon coast cultures cannot be easily and unambiguously placed in either of the major culture areas that lie to their north and south, respectively.

If this conclusion is a reasonable one, then the question remains: Do the southern Oregon coast groups appear to be only very weakly associated with the Northwest Coast culture area because of the poor quality of the available data or because they were in fact part of a peripheral backwater, only weakly influenced by either the Northwest Coast to the north or the local "climax" groups of northwestern California to the south? As implied earlier in this discussion of the southern boundary, the answer to this question must come from archaeology if it is to come at all.

Tying the Southern Oregon Coast to the Northwest Coast Culture Area
After a slow, protracted start, Oregon coastal archaeological research has recently intensified in pace and scope. Much remains to be done, but if the current level of work continues, then culture-historical and many other types of questions about the prehistory of this area will be easier to explore.

In a discussion of the implications of this recent research, cast as an overview of some aspects of "the development of maritime adaptations on the southern Northwest Coast of North America," Erlandson, Tveskov, and Byram (1998:18), who identify the southern Washington, Oregon, and northern California coasts as "southern Northwest Coast," "take issue with the notion that [the Oregon coast] cultures were somehow marginal or peripheral to the 'classic' Northwest Coast cultures to the north." While quarrelling with the marginality view, they acknowledge that, on the basis of current evidence, we cannot assume that elite ranking was present on the southern Oregon coast prehistorically and that an assumption of elite management of resource exploitation is "unfounded" (1998:18). They further suggest that the importance of sea-mammal hunting as a subsistence strategy has been overemphasized in the recent archaeological literature. As well, although fishing weirs were present in the area, they were smaller than those characteristic of the Northwest Coast further north (and of some northern California groups also) and appear to have been used not so much as a major technique for salmon harvesting but as a means of taking a wide range of river estuary fish species (1998:16). They also conclude that the presence of a salmon-based subsistence economy is not demonstrated for the Oregon coast, a conclusion that fits with the regional distribution and varying abundance of salmon described earlier. All of this suggests a less than classic Northwest Coast southern Oregon coast.

Erlandson, Tveskov, and Byram (1998) are interested primarily in "maritime adaptations," and culture-historical issues are not central to their concerns. Can we tie the Oregon coast (and northern California) to the Northwest Coast with more traditional culture-historical kinds of evidence – traits, trade patterns, and so on?

In their discussion of the Developed Northwest Coast Pattern (achieved 2,500 to 1,600 years ago) Matson and Coupland (1995) conclude that the Palmrose site near the mouth of the Columbia River on the Oregon side of that river exhibits many features of their Developed Northwest Coast Pattern at the right time period. They are able to list a number of specific features characteristic of this pattern that are present in the Palmrose site (a stored salmon-based economy, toggling harpoon valves, multifamily planked houses, winter occupation) and even suggest "a Marpole-like emphasis on decorated objects, including a variety of zoomorphic figures" (1995:229).[10] But they also conclude that, "south of the mouth of the Columbia River, no clear equivalent stage could be found along the coast" (1995:229). Matson and Coupland include the Oregon coast and northwestern California as a part of the Northwest Coast culture area, but, as the previous quote indicates, they produce few arguments based on archaeological evidence for doing so.

But there were no doubt ancient contacts between parts of Oregon and the classic Northwest Coast region. Figure 13.7 is based on one of Roy Carlson's (1994:342-343) mappings of the origins of obsidian used in tools on the Northwest Coast. This particular map is for between 2000 BP and 1000 BP. Carlson's maps for earlier time periods show even more distributions of this nature (1994:338-345). Unfortunately, these particular mappings really do no more than tie north central Oregon as a source of obsidian into the Columbia River trade network (which we know flourished prehistorically and historically) and then ties the latter into the larger Northwest Coast. This is because Carlson's research problem, like those of many of us working in this area, is focused on a modern political entity ("trade and exchange in prehistoric British Columbia") and not on a meaningful prehistoric region. Obsidian from the Oregon sources identified by Carlson undoubtedly went in other directions, as well as those indicated on Figure 13.7; however, as far as I know, no one has ever put the obsidian trade picture together for the entire region. As this example suggests, thinking in

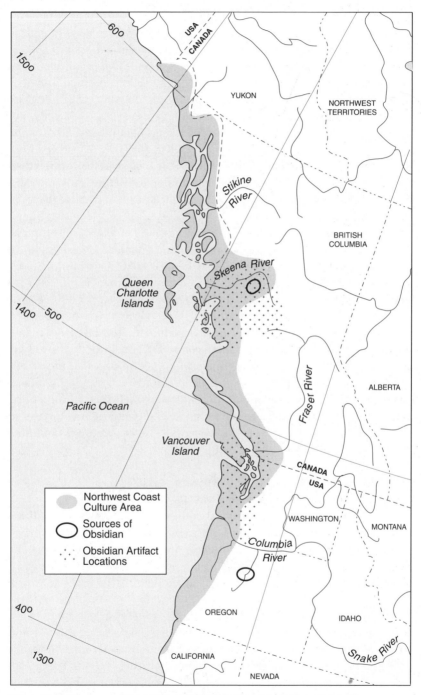

Figure 13.7 Sources and locations of obsidian found in British Columbia archaeological sites dated 2000-1000 BP (Carlson 1994).

culture area terms is more likely to lead us to explore problems in terms of relevant prehistoric areas than is the case when we are constrained by modern political boundaries.

But Carlson's maps do identify one important trade item that went north from Oregon to many classic Northwest Coast locales, and it is likely that some of this obsidian also made its way to the Oregon coast during the same time periods. This ties the two areas together at least indirectly. But what specifically went south? If we turn to ethnography and look at the Yurok, far and away the best described of the Oregon Coast/Northwest California peoples (and Kroeber's own "people," if indeed he had such), then one answer is dentalia. Dentalia were very important to the Yurok as wealth items, probably more important than they were further north, and the usual source identified for Yurok dentalia is the west coast of Vancouver Island, where historically the best known dentalia grounds lay (see, for example, Kroeber 1925:22-23). But, as recent work by Andrew Barton (1994) has shown, individual species of dentalia can rarely be identified in archaeological remains or in finished artifacts, and there are many probable and possible sources of various dentalia species along the Pacific coast, including some in northern California. Yet the Yurok testimony points us north. Here again Barton's recent study is useful, for he documents the Hudson's Bay Company's importation of dentalia into south coastal Oregon in the 1820s and the continuing importation by Euro-American traders of dentalia into northern coastal California until at least the 1850s. Kroeber's Yurok informants could easily have been talking about this trade when they identified the "north" as an important source of dentalia. It is obviously much easier to document postcontact than prehistoric ties between northern California and the core of the Northwest Coast.

The Northern Boundary of the Northwest Coast:
Relationships with Coastal Alaska and Beyond

Nearly everyone's Northwest Coast takes the northern extent of the Tlingit as the boundary of the culture area. The recent *Handbook of North American Indians* includes the Eyak in its Northwest Coast volume. These people, the next group north and west of the Tlingit, were virtually unknown when Kroeber was constructing his culture areas and writing *Cultural and Natural Areas of Native North America*.

Although the Eyak did not have the fully developed Northwest Coast style culture of their Yakutat Tlingit neighbours, they appear to fit about as well into the Northwest Coast pattern as they do into Subarctic or Arctic patterns (the other two culture areas whose boundaries meet at Eyak country). Eyak is a coordinate branch of the Eyak-Athapaskan language family, and in the early eighteenth century Eyak speakers probably occupied a coastal strip from Controller Bay southeast to about the Italio River. During the course of the eighteenth century the southeasternmost parts of this territory (i.e., Yakutat Bay) became Tlingitized. Indeed it seems likely that all of the Eyak would have become Tlingitized were it not for the appearance of the Russians late in that century. The westward spread of the Tlingit along the Alaskan coast had been going on for some time. The Dry Bay Tlingit just south of the Yakutat were Tlingitized Athapaskan speakers, and Tlingit oral tradition suggests that the early Tlingit homeland was the Nass/Skeena area from which they gradually spread north, eventually being pushed out of most of the Nass/Skeena area by the Tsimshian.[11]

The Tlingit were also an important influence to the northeast in what is now the Yukon. Many of the Athapaskan-speaking peoples just east of the coastal mountains adopted versions of some Tlingit cultural practices, and the "Inland Tlingit" were previously Athapaskan speakers who had adopted the Tlingit language and become partially Tlingitized in other ways during the nineteenth century (McClellan 1981:469).

The spread of Tlingit language and culture (particularly into Eyak country) probably represents one of the most important ways in which the various versions of Northwest Coast culture spread throughout prehistory. But the expansion into Eyak country is an eighteenth-century phenomenon and does not create major boundary problem issues for students of the region that are at all comparable to those posed by the Oregon coast groups. The boundary issues in the north are of a different type and relate to the cultural and historical relationships between the Northwest Coast culture area and the cultures and peoples west northwest along the coast of present-day Alaska (as well as to affinities with and influences from the cultures and peoples of Siberia).

Along the north Pacific coast of North America, beginning at about fifty-two degrees north latitude, there are several blocks of peoples: the "Northern Maritime" subarea of Kroeber's Northwest Coast (primarily Tlingit, Haida, and Tsimshian), which he regarded as the "climax" of the ethnographic culture area; the Pacific Eskimo (including Koniag and Chugach); and the Aleuts of the Aleutian Island chain. (I am aware of the coastal Athapaskan-speaking peoples of the Cook Inlet area as well.) All of these peoples based their lives and cultures on a maritime subsistence adaptation, and, as a result, exhibit some broad similarities as well as much local variation, reflecting both regional and local environmental characteristics. Even a casual reading of the ethnography of the north Pacific Rim, however, suggests the presence of the outcome of a long and complex history of both local development and contacts and influences from elsewhere in the region.

Northern Expansion of the Northwest Coast
Before the Russian irruption into the area, insofar as the eighteenth-century Tlingitization of coastal Athapaskan and Eyak speakers added the territory

formerly occupied by these new Tlingit to the Northwest Coast, the Northwest Coast was expanding northward and west along the coast. Although
all of the Eyak might well have been eventually absorbed by the Tlingit
expansion had the Russians not arrived, it is doubtful that the Tlingit could
have successfully spread much further along the coast and maintained their
Northwest Coast style culture relatively intact. Some key elements in the
rich environment that supported the general Northwest Coast adaptation
were missing. The Pacific salmon and various species of marine mammals
were present all along the coast into the Aleutians and beyond, but key
plant resources were not. The northern limit of red cedar is about fifty-
seven degrees north latitude (i.e., about the latitude of present-day Sitka,
Alaska). The ethnographic territory of the Tlingit goes up to about sixty-
degrees north latitude. There are species of large trees present through most
of this northern part of Tlingit territory, but none has the characteristics
that make red cedar so important for canoes and large plank houses. So-
called yellow cedar, for example (Alaska cedar, Nootka cedar, *Chamaecyparis
nootkatensis*), is useful for many smaller items (paddles, chests, adze handles) and its bark is perhaps superior to that of red cedar for weaving clothing and blankets, but it does not so easily split into large planks (Turner
1979:70-71).

More generally, the core environment of the classic Northwest Coast, including most of the Northern maritime subarea, can best be described as
island archipelago. The coastline is well broken by rivers, large streams, and
numerous bays, and islands of all sizes are scattered along the mainland
coast. But from Cross Sound (Cape Spencer) northwest for nearly 500 kilometres northwestward to Prince William Sound, the coastline is broken by
only a few significant streams; there are few bays or harbours and no important islands. This relatively unbroken shore is very different from the archipelago that stretches south as far as southern Vancouver Island and Puget
Sound. Yakutat Bay, nearly the northwestern extent of the historic Tlingit,
is about halfway along this nearly open coast. Of note is the fact that the
immediate Yakutat Bay environment is somewhat like a small-scale archipelago (see the descriptions in de Laguna 1972:21-106).

Koniag and Chugach/Northwest Coast Affinities
Even though it is likely that the historic form of Northwest Coast culture
had just about reached its sustainable limits in the northwest, affinities and
similarities between Northwest Coast culture and that of the nearest Pacific
Eskimo peoples, the Chugach and Koniag, are easy to find. The ethnohistoric
and ethnographic evidence makes it certain that, throughout the eighteenth century, there was considerable interaction between the Chugach,
Koniag, and the northernmost Tlingit via Eyak intermediaries and sometimes more directly as well.

Although trade took place between them, many of the contacts between the Tlingit and the Chugach and Koniag were far from friendly: in fact, they were often violent. The Yakutat did hold slaves of Pacific Eskimo origin either taken in war or obtained in trade with the Eyak. It is less clear that slaves of Tlingit origin were ever taken or held by the Chugach or Koniag.[13] Slaves should not be overlooked as a source of culture contact and transmission. They were certainly an important means for the spread of ritual ideas and practices among Northwest Coast peoples (Donald 1997:177), and it would be surprising if this had not happened in the Tlingit/Eyak/Pacific Eskimo nexus as well.

However ideas and objects were transmitted, there is ample protohistoric and historic evidence for contact and influence. Bill Holm (1988) has been able to trace quite specific Tlingit influences on motifs and other aspects of Pacific Eskimo art. Holm's study is supported by archaeological materials that suggest much of his reconstruction has prehistoric antecedents going back several hundred years. His analysis, in combination with Richard Jordan's (1994) ethnohistoric reconstruction of Koniag social and ritual life, certainly seems to lend credence to his conclusion that "there was considerable interchange of ideas, and the Northwest Coast overlay on Pacific Eskimo culture is obvious" (Holm 1988:281; see also Jordan and Knecht [1995]).

Pacific Eskimo influences on Northwest Coast cultures are less dramatic. Holm is able to document the early contact period presence of some northern Tlingit material culture traits of obvious Pacific Eskimo origin – the sea otter harpoon-arrow, for example (1988:281-282) – but it is hard to find clear and specific traits of probable Pacific Eskimo origin with a more widespread distribution on the Northwest Coast. Holm is probably right in suggesting that influences did go both ways, but influences from the Pacific Eskimo and further west that became important in Northwest Coast cultures probably came earlier than the eighteenth century and will require archaeology to uncover them. The issue of Pacific Eskimo influences on the Northwest Coast and/or vice versa is not a new one for archaeologists, of course. See, for example, Carl Borden's (1962) discussion of hypotheses about "Eskimo" influences on early cultures of the Northwest Coast and his counter-arguments (and evidence) about possible Northwest Coast influences on the Pacific Eskimo.

Broader Regional and Siberian Influences and Contacts
I turn now to a brief consideration of broader regional influences, interactions, and contacts. An early anthropological theme concerned northeast Asian/northwest American cultural similarities and influences. The discovery and study of these was a principal motivation of the Boas-organized Jesup North Pacific Expedition. Interest in this problem has waxed and waned since the early twentieth century, but the last decade or so has seen it

increase again, spurred partly by greater contact between Russian and North American scholars (see, for example, various comments in Fitzhugh and Crowell 1988 and Fitzhugh and Chaussonnet 1994).

In recent considerations of broader regional settings, it has not been uncommon to advocate the value of an approach that recognizes three main clusters of peoples and cultures – the Northwest Coast, the Gulf of Alaska, and the Aleutians – and to suggest that we look at interactions and influences among all three as well as considering relationships with the Bering Sea region of both Alaska and Siberia (e.g., Moss 1992:13; Clark 1998:181). Most of these suggestions have, like this chapter, been more programmatic than substantive, but some recent work has analyzed regional materials in order to improve our understanding of particular local problems (e.g., Lydia Black's [1994] work on Aleut/Koniag iconography, which breaks specific new ground while echoing Boas's [1916] pioneering comparative study of myth motifs that put his Tsimshian material into a broad Northwest American and even Northeast Asian context).

To illustrate the kinds of occurrences that still need to be explained and that require culture-historical explanations, I will briefly discuss two ethnographically known traits – the ritual killing of slaves and whaling – and one archaeological and ethnographic boundary.

In an earlier section on the ethnographic Northwest Coast I briefly described the distribution of the ritual killing of slaves at the funeral of important persons, often labelled "chiefs" in the literature. In the Northwest Coast culture area itself, at least eight different kinds of occasions might lead to such killings in one society or another, but the only type of event that might invoke the killing of slaves in virtually every Northwest Coast community was the funeral of an important person. It is worth noting that, of the Gulf of Alaska coastal societies that practised true slavery (Eyak, Chugach, Koniag, Aleut), all are reported to have sometimes killed slaves at the funerals of important persons but on no other occasions. This virtually continuous distribution along the north Pacific coast from the Aleutians down to the mouth of the Columbia River suggests that the killing of slaves at the funerals of important persons is a fairly old practice throughout this wide area and that the extension of the practice to other occasions is a more recent and much more localized development. It also suggests a fairly long-standing linkage between slavery and ranking throughout this area. Obvious questions include: Where and how did these two traits originate? Did they indeed develop together? And what was the history of their spread throughout the arc of the north Pacific coast?

If the ritual killing of slaves is a continuous distribution that still requires an explanation, then whaling is a discontinuous distribution that also begs explanation. In late precontact times, whaling was important and often quite elaborate (both technologically and ideologically) in a number of North

Pacific, Chuckchi Sea, and Bering Sea societies (for a good brief treatment of Aboriginal whaling in the North Pacific see Rousselot, Fitzhugh, and Crowell 1988:163-172.) The part of this whaling distribution that interests me runs from the Aleutians along the Gulf of Alaska coast and south along the Pacific coast of North America into northern Washington State. As usually reported in the literature, the Aleut and Pacific Eskimo whaled, but the northern Northwest Coast peoples did not. Whaling is present again, however, among the Nuu-chah-nulth of the west coast of Vancouver Island, the Makah, and two other peoples on the Olympic Peninsula just south of the Nuu-chah-nulth. There were two basic types of Aboriginal whaling in the North Pacific area: poison dart whaling and harpoon and float whaling. The Aleut and Pacific Eskimo practised poison dart whaling, as did such Asian peoples as the Ainu and Itelman. The Northwest Coast peoples practised harpoon and float whaling, as did the whaling communities in the Bering Sea. While this distribution of major whaling types adds another twist to the discontinuous distribution of whaling itself, there are also important similarities in social customs and ideology between Northwest Coast whaling and Gulf of Alaska whaling. Lantis (1938) identified thirty-two elements of what she called "the Alaskan whale cult" (i.e., the social and ideological side of whaling). Many of her elements are, as she acknowledges, complexes of traits. Of her thirty-two elements, twenty-one were reported for the Nuu-chah-nulth and fourteen for the Koniag. The Nuu-chah-nulth and Koniag shared twelve of the traits. Many will feel that this degree of similarity is too great to explain by independent development and chance. As Rousselot, Fitzhugh, and Crowell (1988:171) put it: "Similarities between Siberian, Alaskan, and Northwest Coast whaling methods, material culture, and customs have been noted for many years [citing Lantis 1938]. It seems unlikely that whaling developed separately in each separate geographic region, but the timing and nature of the supposed cultural connections are not yet understood."

About the distribution of Aboriginal whaling along the north Pacific coast I say "as usually reported in the literature" because recently Steven Acheson (1998:77-78) has put together some bits of historic evidence that suggest the distribution may not have been as discontinuous as is usually believed. In the course of archaeological research in the southern Queen Charlotte Islands (Haida territory), Acheson and his associates recovered a quantity of whale bone from a number of the sites that they excavated. The usual explanation for such finds in sites in territories without ethnographically or historically reported whaling has been that the bones are from drift whales, which are known to have been eagerly exploited by both whaling and non-whaling peoples in the region. However, in late- eighteenth- and nineteenth-century sources, Acheson was able to find some fairly clear (if brief) references to whaling by both Haida and Tlingit. The data are too brief to infer much about such whaling, although it is likely from these statements that, like the Nuu-chah-nulth and Makah, the Haida and the Tlingit undertook harpoon and float whaling. Missing from the Queen Charlotte Islands sites so far are the large blades and harpoon heads and very large pieces of whale bone found in some Nuu-chah-nulth and Makah sites. What is missing from the ethnographic and ethnohistoric record is information about the ritual and social associations of whaling among these two peoples. These aspects of whaling are well represented in the Nuu-chah-nulth and Makah ethnographic record, and it is puzzling that they are absent from the very rich Tlingit and quite good Haida ethnographic record (assuming that whaling was indeed important among these groups).

More archaeological research and analysis may well help us with at least the technological side of whaling, although the prospects for archaeological help with the prehistory of slavery in the region seem fairly remote.

As Donald Clark has pointed out in a discussion of recent Kodiak Island prehistory, we find a number of traits present in prehistoric Kodiak sites (and elsewhere along the Gulf of Alaska coast) that are often identified with the Northwest Coast. One interesting boundary that does seem to set the Pacific Eskimo and peoples to the west of them off from the Northwest Coast as traditionally defined involves the stone lamp. Stone lamps have a history of usage in the Pacific Eskimo area that goes back at least 7,000 years, but it is doubtful if such lamps were ever used south and east of Yakutat (Clark 1998:181). Although many traits probably moved east and then south along the Gulf of Alaska coast, stone lamps did not. Too much should not be made of the distribution of a single trait (although this is an extremely important one in the history of Arctic adaptation), but the fit between this boundary and the historical limits of the classic Northwest Coast cultures is worthy of note.

In his treatment of external influences and relationships with the Northwest Coast, Kroeber was not so much interested in the region's immediate relationships with the Gulf of Alaska coast as with possible Asian influences and contacts. He saw Asian influences as likely much more important for the Northwest Coast than influences from what he saw as the most important source of ideas, practices, and traits for most of the rest of Native North America – Mesoamerica. Indeed, he notes the rarity of possible Mesoamerican influences in the Northwest Coast cultural repertories in contrast with their obvious existence elsewhere on the continent. To take but one example: throughout eastern North America and gradually diminishing as one goes west we find an elaborate culture trait complex around the torture of captives. This has obvious echoes with Mesoamerica. Captives were treated quite differently on the Northwest Coast, where torture was neither important nor highly elaborated. Indeed, for Kroeber one of the striking things about the Northwest Coast was its relative freedom from Mesoamerican influence. This gave the Northwest Coast a distinctive character and set it apart from the rest of Aboriginal North America (see, especially, Kroeber 1923).

I suspect that many of those working with Northwest Coast materials will be more interested in puzzling out regional patterns and relationships among peoples and traditions in the north Pacific coast region, but my reference to Kroeber's concerns with Asian and Mesoamerican influences reminds us that some will also see issues involving continental and even world culture history in play along the north Pacific coast.

Conclusion

A chapter that is intended to pose questions and to raise issues does not really lead to a set of definite conclusions, but some of the general implications of my discussion should be emphasized.

Much recent archaeological writing on the Northwest Coast has been conceptual and problem-oriented – interested in theory, if you like. It has focused on such topics as the rise of social stratification, the development of ranking, and the development of a complex maritime adaptation. It is all to the good not to be exclusively immersed in the details of very localized archaeological problems of the type that may be associated with a single site or small set of neighbouring sites. But even in the pursuit of such broader issues of wide comparative and theoretical interest, culture history and the working out of culture-historical problems remains important, even vital. The classic Northwest Coast cultures do not merely represent one good example of a "maritime adaptation." What makes the Northwest Coast the Northwest Coast is that these cultures are, among other things, particular maritime adaptations involving particular practices and cultural characteristics. In order to understand just how these maritime adaptations came about (or stratification developed, to take another example), we will need to understand the development, history, and spread of particular characteristic traits and bundles of traits. A broad regional context will allow us, indeed will challenge us, to do this.

What most interests me in conceiving of the Northwest Coast as a culture area or interaction sphere is the prospect of using the idea to focus on the dynamics of local prehistoric development and change within the Northwest Coast. Particularly since, to invoke Kroeber (1939:28) one last time, on the Northwest Coast we find the

> unusual degree to which its material, native and imported, has been worked over into its own patterns. This area is evidently one of unusual intensity of cultural activity ... This powerful repatterning has probably disguised the foreign origin of much Northwest Coast culture material. The historic source

of material of this kind should prove discernible when intensive knowledge of the area is combined with a willingness to consider remote origins. The present indications are that perhaps as much of the reworked material derives from Asiatic as from distant American centers.

Kroeber's remote influences interest me, but I confess that I regard achieving an understanding of the reworkings of both local and imported ideas an even more engrossing challenge.

Acknowledgments

I thank Donald Mitchell and Joseph Jorgensen for careful readings of an earlier version of this chapter and for their many useful comments and suggestions. R.G. Matson gave valuable editorial advice on a number of points, and Susan Matson turned my very rough drafts of the maps into the polished versions seen here.

Notes

1 The range of western red cedar in relation to Kroeber's mapping of the Northwest Coast culture area is shown in Figure 13.2.

2 Some large chinook runs are found in a few major Oregon and California rivers, but in general, in recent times at least, chinook runs everywhere are small compared to the major runs of other species.

3 This is an impression only, as the generally available published sources on both catch and escapements for the Oregon coast tend to be included with Columbia River data rather than being given separately, making quantitative comparisons impossible. It is also true that Euro-American activity such as mining and forestry had an earlier impact on California rivers than it did on rivers further north, making assessments of salmon resources in precontact times more difficult for the latter. The most important California runs were much larger than were those on the Oregon coast south of the Columbia. Baumhoff (1963) argues that the California runs were much more significant for the indigenous economies located along the major California salmon rivers than I have suggested here, although in a later overview of the environment of aboriginal California (1978:19) he minimizes "meaningful relations between environment and society" within the Northwest Coast province of California. Chartkoff (1989) is also relevant to this issue.

4 This paragraph and the one that follows are based on the discussion in Hebda and Frederick (1990).

5 The best general book-length descriptions of the culture area are still Drucker (1955b and 1965).

6 For a brief but useful discussion of many of the versions of the culture area see Suttles (1990c:5-12).

7 For a full account of Northwest Coast slavery see Donald (1997).

8 The most accessible accounts of the Dancing Societies are in Drucker (1955b:163-169); and Drucker 1965:158-167. More detailed information is in Boas (1897) and Drucker (1940).

9 Some publication anomalies need to be noted here: Kroeber 1936 was substantially written in 1928, and Kroeber (1939) was substantially written in 1931. For my area of concern, the differences between the two probably reflect as much the difference in perspective of the two manuscripts as any change of mind on Kroeber's part: the 1936 manuscript focuses on the cultures that fell within the boundaries of the state of California, while the 1939 manuscript adopts a North America-wide perspective.

10 Marpole, a cultural phase found in the Gulf of Georgia, is the best known and described archaeological culture belonging to the early stages of the Developed Northwest Coast Pattern.

11 For the Eyak, see de Laguna (1990a) and the sources cited therein. For the Tlingitization of northern Tlingit country and their origins in the Nass/Skeena area, see de Laguna (1990b:205-206).

12 For the origin of Tlingit slaves see Donald (1997:107, 146), which indicates both the capture of Chugach by Yakutat Tlingit and trade for slaves with the Chugach by the Yakutat. The Pacific Eskimo sources known to me are contradictory about whether or not they held Tlingit slaves (e.g., Birket-Smith 1953:93-94).

Epilogue
Leland Donald

As R.G. Matson writes in his introduction, the original versions of the chapters in this book were presented in a session of several sittings at the 1998 Canadian Archaeological Association Annual Meetings. Those published here represent only a sampling of these papers, for the session as a whole probably brought together the largest number of papers on Northwest Coast archaeology and closely related topics ever presented at one time.

The first paper on the schedule at the 1998 session was intended, in part, as an overview that offered a regional context for the more spatially and temporally focused papers that were to follow. That paper appears as the last chapter in the volume offered here. As is typical at meetings, most of the participants were unfamiliar with the other contributions until they heard them at the session. Nevertheless, as the papers were reworked for publication here, a number of them did influence how the authors made their respective revisions. That said, all of the chapters in the present book, except for the concluding overview of the culture area, focus on specific problems or topics and not the culture area as a whole.

I have been asked to offer the reader a kind of epilogue to this volume – one that considers how some of the specific problems and topics raised in the various chapters relate to the areal themes discussed in the final chapter. When I reread the chapters in preparation for this task, many ideas and possibilities suggested themselves to me – enough, indeed, to keep me writing until I had another chapter at least the length of the one I had already written for this book! The reader will be glad to learn that I will keep in mind the *Oxford Encyclopedic English Dictionary*'s definition of an "epilogue": "a speech or short poem addressed to the audience by an actor at the end of a play." I will not try my hand at verse, but I will be short – short, at least, for an aging academic.

My contribution to this book focuses on problems concerning the culture history of the Northwest Coast culture area and, to some extent, on the usefulness to north Pacific coast archaeological, ethnohistoric, and ethnological studies of the culture area concept itself. None of the other chapters published here (or given at the original session) attempts to deal with the culture area as a whole or as a unit, and none considers the continuing viability of the culture area concept. Yet all the authors have in their background the premise that the "Northwest Coast" is a meaningful framework within which to pursue their particular topic. And I think it clear that all assume that the identifier Northwest Coast implies more than a contiguous geographic or ecological region. The notion of the Northwest Coast implies a set of linked prehistoric and historic traditions that influenced each other and whose various Aboriginal populations shared a broadly similar set of accommodations to their natural environments and to each other. In other words, the concepts of culture area and culture history are in the background and exert influence, even as various researchers on the Northwest Coast work on problems and topics not obviously tied to either of these ideas.

Since all the other chapters in this book have a narrower focus than the entire culture area, I must now turn to the question of how some of their specific concerns play into the regional themes of my areal survey and discussion.

Boundaries

The boundaries of the Northwest Coast culture area are given considerable attention in the overview chapter. They are given little direct attention in the other papers in this book since they focus by and large on matters within the culture area. Chapter 9 does offer some useful reminders of connections both prehistoric and historic to peoples and places outside the Northwest Coast. Steve Acheson's discussion of the possibility of prehistoric metal use and prehistoric metal-working traditions within the culture area cannot be conclusive because of the modest amount of available evidence. But there is enough evidence of both prehistoric copper and iron to require us to give more attention to prehistoric metal than we usually do. Drift metal from shipwrecks, and trade and diffusion from Siberia are the most likely sources in prehistoric times. As Acheson implies, any indigenous metal-working tradition is likely the result of influences diffused from Siberia via Alaska. Such influences would be consistent with fairly obvious Siberian influences and pan-Beringian themes in a number of cultural domains.

Whaling

As discussed in the overview chapter, historically whaling has an interesting, discontinuous distribution on the north Pacific coast: whaling was important in the Gulf of Alaska and on the southwestern coast of Vancouver Island and just south of the Strait of Juan de Fuca. Between these two areas, most find little if any historical evidence for whaling as opposed to the utilization of drift whales. The peoples of the northern Northwest Coast did not whale, while some peoples to their south – the Nuu-chah-nulth and Makah – did. The archaeological evidence confirms the prehistoric importance of Nuu-chah-nulth and Makah whaling but so far offers little solid support for prehistoric whaling in the northern part of the culture area. Obviously one is tempted to see Nuu-chah-nulth and Makah whaling as somehow connected to Gulf of Alaska, Siberian, and Bering Sea whaling – especially since there are some striking similarities in various aspects of whaling, both technological and ideological, across this wide area. How did whaling "leap" over the peoples of the northern part of the culture area? Or will we in fact find that whaling was once significant in at least some places on the northern coast? If these questions can be answered it will be with archaeological data. Greg Monks's chapter (Chapter 8) on the taphonomy of Nuu-chah-nulth whale bone assemblages is important in this regard because it is only by such careful studies of what the archaeological results of known whaling activities look like that we will have comparative baselines to place archaeological finds of whale bone on the northern parts of the culture area into an appropriate interpretative context. Since whaling is another cluster of traits, both technological and ideological, that points towards Siberian connections, more is involved in sorting out the culture history of whaling in the region than an improved understanding of whaling itself.

Stratification and Big Houses

One of the most striking features of the ethnographic Northwest Coast is its tripartite system of social stratification. The constellation of features associated with stratification are among the principal traits that distinguish the Northwest Coast culture area from other parts of Native North America. The evolution of stratification has been an important topic of investigation for many archaeologists currently doing research on the culture area. Recently, household archaeology has also begun to flourish as a research focus for Northwest Coast researchers. These two themes go hand in hand in our region since a principal outcome and indicator of stratification in the area is the "big house" – the large relatively permanent plank structures that housed significant numbers of people and demonstrated the power and importance of their owners. Chapters 4, 5, and 6 (by R.G. Matson; Al Mackie and Laurie Williamson; and Gary Coupland, Roger Colten, and Rebecca Case, respectively) report on archaeological investigations of big houses. All add to our knowledge of what prehistoric and protohistoric big houses were like and, in the process, illuminate the nature of and development of stratification in the region. It is especially encouraging that each of these chapters reports on research done in areas occupied by different ethnolinguistic groups in ethnographic times – Halkomelem Salish, Ohiaht Nuu-chah-nulth, and Coast Tsimshian, respectively. As indicated in the discussion in these chapters, investigations of big houses in still other parts of the culture area are also ongoing, and we should soon have a widespread sample of excavated big houses to compare. The household studies published here and elsewhere, then, should give us a broad view of one of the most striking technological features of the culture area – the big house – and contribute insights into the character and development of Northwest Coast stratification in prehistoric times.

The nature of the relationship between types of stratification and forms of political organization is a long-standing question in anthropology. Almost all students of Northwest Coast culture have found ranking present in the traditional cultures, and some, including myself, have argued that true class stratification was present. Most students of the area do not believe that political unification above the local community level occurred in traditional Northwest Coast societies, and many have noted that, even at the community level, true political unification was often lacking. Some, usually non-specialists writing overviews, have considered that the Coast Tsimshian were organized as a chiefdom in early contact times. Many regional specialists have not agreed. In Chapter 2, Andrew Martindale argues that, for a brief period before 1840, the Gispaklo'ots leader, Ligeex, was able to act as a paramount chief, exerting control and not merely influence over a number of Coast Tsimshian villages, while both before and after this time such political unification under a single personality did not occur. This reminds us of the ability of individuals of talent and energy to greatly influence and alter their societies, and it also raises the question of what to conclude about the local occurrence of a political form that appears in such a transient fashion during a period of dramatic social and cultural change.

Social and Economic Interaction Spheres

In my discussion of cranial deformation and labrets (Chapter 13), I noted that these and some other traits are often considered as markers for subareas of the Northwest Coast, where social and economic interaction was much more intense and important than it was between communities in different interaction spheres. These interaction spheres were almost certainly important in protohistoric times. Their time depth and the question of whether and how the boundaries of these spheres changed over time are matters for archaeological investigation. In many parts of the culture area the archaeological record is still insufficiently explored to allow for an area-wide consideration of this problem. In one area at least, however, the record is beginning to be complete enough to allow a start to be made. This area is often called the Gulf of Georgia. Focusing on a single site, Colin Grier (Chapter 7) investigates how the inhabitants of a Marpole-age (2100-1200 BP) village might have interacted with those occupying other parts of the Gulf of Georgia. Such efforts to situate particular locales and their inhabitants within larger contexts of interaction should enable us to gradually build up a picture of just how and when the protohistoric interaction spheres found in the culture area developed and changed.

One kind of event that contributed to changes in the extent and character of interaction spheres was the movement of people, especially in the form of the expansion, contraction, or replacement of ethnolinguistic groups. Alan McMillan's chapter (Chapter 11) reviews changing perceptions of cultural development on the coast, focusing on the shift from interpreting change as a result of migration to an emphasis on in situ change. He then adds considerably to our understanding of the spread of the Wakashan-speaking peoples southward along the west coast of Vancouver Island. An archaeological understanding of the Wakashanization of some Salish-speaking areas at least gives us a model of how population movements and changes might have occurred elsewhere on the coast, although obviously we can't assume that such events always happened in the same way or always had similar results.

New Kinds of Data

All of the chapters in this book report on original research, and most report new data as well as reconsidering previously known information. But two of them – Chapter 10 by Kathryn Bernick and Chapter 3 by Dale Croes – use a relatively new kind of data for Northwest Coast archaeological studies: artifacts of wood and other plant materials recovered from wet sites. As Croes points out, such artifacts enable us to understand aspects of prehistoric technology and its use that are not easily inferred from stone and bone artifacts alone. The increasing attention that wet sites are receiving is also important because most studies of the technology and resource exploitation patterns of the region have focused almost exclusively on the procurement of faunal resources. The procurement and utilization of floral resources is relatively neglected, but, as I suggest in Chapter 13 when I focused on two major resources – one floral (cedar) and one faunal (salmon) – the ecological possibilities of both plant and animal resources provided the opportunities that prehistoric and ethnographic Northwest Coast peoples used to create their distinctive cultures. Without wanting to overemphasize the importance of either, we should acknowledge that both cedar and salmon are fundamental to the development of the classical Northwest Coast cultures. Increasingly, the investigation of wet sites will add to our knowledge of some now poorly understood aspects of Northwest Coast culture history.

Bernick's chapter reminds us that baskets are more than utilitarian objects for storing or carrying. They offer many opportunities in both manufacturing technique and decorative style to convey ethnic identity and many other quiet but significant symbolic messages. They also, as in this case, offer opportunities to connect and illuminate the past and the present. Bernick is able to show connections in manufacturing technique between a 1,000-year-old basket from a wet site in what is historically a Salish area and some unusual modern Salish baskets. This basket-making technique has quietly survived, reminding us that, in spite of enormous cultural and social change and the impact of European occupation of their homelands, many of the descendants of the prehistoric Northwest Coast peoples remain attached to and participate in cultural forms that are very ancient.

New Analytical Approaches
Quentin Mackie's chapter (Chapter 12) adds location-allocation modelling to the analytic tool-kit of those studying the Aboriginal Northwest Coast. Location-allocation analysis strikes me as perhaps more promising than central place approaches for regions like the Northwest Coast because it recognizes the interdependency of locations (places that have been the focus of human activity) in ways that don't require a "centre" – something that must be rather arbitrarily assumed for the Northwest Coast archaeological record. A powerful quantitative technique and some cogent and provocative reflections on various conceptual attempts to understand human behaviour and culture are brought together to suggest ways of considering aspects of the archaeological record (in this case site location) as the products of the undirected outcome of the history of human activity on a portion of the west coast of Vancouver Island. There is not space here for an attempt to tease out the full implications of Mackie's work, but, perhaps to his surprise, I will suggest that he has both introduced an important new technique of analysis to Northwest Coast culture history studies and applied some interesting concepts drawn from broad social science theorizing to the study of Northwest Coast culture history. Older approaches to culture history remain valuable and viable, but it is encouraging that newer approaches and ideas continue to be drawn into our efforts to understanding this fascinating region's people and their history.

I will end this epilogue with the observation that this book includes the work of several generations of scholars. The work here of the newer members of this scholarly community suggests that the challenges of recovering and understanding the human career on the north Pacific coast of North America continues to fascinate and to draw able new workers to the task.

References

Acheson, Steven
  1991   In the Wake of the ya'áats' xaatgáay (Iron People): A Study of Changing Settle-
         ment Strategies among the Kunghit Haida. PhD diss., Oxford University, Oxford.
  1995   In the Wake of the Iron People: A Case for Changing Settlement Strategies among
         the Kunghit Haida. *Journal of the Royal Anthropological Institute* 1:273-299.
  1998   *In the Wake of the ya'ats'xaatgay ("Iron People"): A Study of Changing Settlement Strat-
         egies among the Kunghit Haida.* BAR International Series 711, Oxford.

Acheson, Steven, and Rebecca J. Wigen
  1996   Evidence for a Prehistoric Whaling Tradition among the Haida. Paper presented at
         the Circum-Pacific Prehistory Conference, August 1989, Seattle. (Revised March
         1996.)

Adams, William H.
  1983   Ethnoarchaeology as a Merging of Historical Archaeology and Oral History. *North
         American Archaeologist* 4(4):293-305.

Adams, William Y., Dennis P. Van Gerven, and Richard S. Levy
  1978   The Retreat from Migrationism. *Annual Review of Anthropology* 7:483-532.

Adovasio, James M.
  1986   Artifacts and Ethnicity: Basketry as an Indicator of Territoriality and Population
         Movements in the Prehistoric Great Basin. In *Anthropology of the Desert West,* ed-
         ited by Carol J. Condie and Don D. Fowler, pp. 43-88. University of Utah Anthro-
         pological Papers 10. University of Utah Press, Salt Lake City.

Ames, Kenneth M.
  1981   The Evolution of Social Ranking on the Northwest Coast of North America. *Ameri-
         can Antiquity* 46:789-805.
  1994   The Northwest Coast: Complex Hunter-Gatherers, Ecology, and Social Evolution.
         Annual Review of Anthropology 23:209-229.
  1995   Chiefly Power and Household Production on the Northwest Coast. In *Foundations
         of Social Inequality,* edited by T. Douglas Price and Gary M. Feinman, pp. 155-188.
         Plenum, New York.
  1996   Life in the Big House: Household Labor and Dwelling Size on the Northwest Coast.
         In *People Who Lived in Big Houses: Archaeological Perspectives on Large Domestic Struc-
         tures,* edited by Gary Coupland and E.B. Banning, pp. 131-150. Monographs in
         World Archaeology No. 27. Prehistory Press, Madison, Wisconsin.
  1998   Chinookan Cellars. Paper presented at the 31st Annual Canadian Archaeological
         Association Conference, Victoria.

2001 Slaves, Chiefs and Labour on the Northern Northwest Coast. *World Archaeology* 33:1-17.

Ames, Kenneth M., and Herbert D.G. Maschner
1999 *Peoples of the Northwest Coast: Their Archaeology and Prehistory.* Thames and Hudson, London.

Ames, Kenneth M., D. Raetz, S. Hamilton, and C. McAfee
1992 Household Archaeology of a Southern Northwest Coast Plank House. *Journal of Field Archaeology* 19:275-290.

Anthony, David W.
1990 Migration in Archaeology: The Baby and the Bathwater. *American Anthropologist* 92:895-914.
1997 Prehistoric Migration as Social Process. In *Migrations and Invasions in Archaeological Explanation,* edited by John Chapman and Helena Hamerow, pp. 21-32. BAR International Series 664, Oxford.

Arcas Consulting Archeologists Ltd.
1988 Native Settlements on Meares Island, BC. Report on file, British Columbia Archaeology Branch, Victoria.
1991 Archaeological Investigations at Little Beach Site, Ucluelet, BC. Report on file, British Columbia Archaeology Branch, Victoria.
1992 Little Beach Site, Ucluelet, BC: 1991 Archaeological Investigations. *The Midden* 24:2-4.

Archer, David J.W., and Kathryn Bernick
1990 Perishable Artifacts from the Musqueam Northeast Site. Manuscript on file, British Columbia Archaeology Branch, Victoria.

Arctander, John W.
1909 *The Apostle of Alaska: The Story of William Duncan of Metlakhatla.* Fleming H. Revell, New York.

Arima, Eugene Y.
1983 *The West Coast People: The Nootka of Vancouver Island and Cape Flattery.* British Columbia Provincial Museum Special Publication No. 6, Victoria.
1988 Notes on Nootkan Sea Mammal Hunting. *Arctic Anthropology* 25:16-27.

Arnold, Jeanne
1993 Labor and the Rise of Complex Hunter-Gatherers. *Journal of Anthropological Archaeology* 12:75-119.

Aro, K.V., and M.P. Shepard
1967 Pacific Salmon in Canada. In *Salmon of the North Pacific Ocean.* Part 4. International North Pacific Fisheries Commission, Bulletin 23:225-327, Vancouver.

Ashley, Clifford W.
1944 *The Ashley Book of Knots.* Doubleday and Company, Garden City, New York.

Ashmore, Wendy, and Richard R. Wilk
1988 Household and Community in the Mesoamerican Past. In *Household and Community in the Mesoamerican Past,* edited by Richard R. Wilk and Wendy Ashmore, pp. 1-27. University of New Mexico Press, Albuquerque.

Assu, Harry, (with Joy Inglis)
1989 *Assu of Cape Mudge: Recollections of a Coastal Indian Chief.* UBC Press, Vancouver.

Atkinson, C.E., J.H. Rose, and T.O. Duncan
1967   Pacific Salmon in the United States. In *Salmon of the North Pacific Ocean*. Part 4. International North Pacific Fisheries Commission, Bulletin 23:43-224, Vancouver.

Bailey, Trevor C.
1994   A Review of Statistical Spatial Analysis in Geographical Information Systems. In *Spatial Analysis and GIS,* edited by S. Fotheringham and P. Rogerson, pp. 13-44. Taylor and Francis, London.

Bancroft, Hubert Howe
1884   *History of the Northwest Coast.* The Bancroft Company, New York.

Barbeau, Marius
1917   Growth and Federation in the Tsimshian Phratries. In *Proceedings of the 19th International Congress of Americanists*, pp. 402-408. US Government Printing Office, Washington.
1961   Tsimsyan Myths. National Museum of Canada, Anthropological Series 51, Bulletin 152, Ottawa.

Barnett, Homer G.
1937   Culture Element Distributions: VII Oregon Coast. *University of California Anthropological Records* 1:155-204, Berkeley.
1955   *The Coast Salish of British Columbia.* University of Oregon Press, Eugene.

Barrett, John
1994   *Fragments from Antiquity: An Archaeology of Social Life in Britain, 2900-1200 BC.* Blackwell, Oxford.

Barton, Andrew John
1994   Fishing for Ivory Worms: A Review of the Ethnographic and Historically Recorded Dentalium Source Locations. MA thesis, Department of Archaeology, Simon Fraser University, Burnaby.

Baumhoff, Martin A.
1963   Ecological Determinants of Aboriginal Populations. *University of California Publications in American Archaeology and Ethnology* 49:155-236.
1978   Environmental Background. In *Handbook of North American Indians*. Vol. 8: *California*, edited by Robert F. Heizer, pp. 16-24. Smithsonian Institution, Washington.

Bates, Ann M.
1987   Affiliation and Differentiation: Intertribal Interactions among the Makah and Ditidaht Indians. PhD diss., Department of Anthropology, Indiana University, Bloomington.

Beaglehole, J.C. (editor)
1967   *The Journals of Captain James Cook on His Voyages of Discovery.* Cambridge University Press, Cambridge.

Beals, Herbert K.
1989   *Juan Perez on the Northwest Coast: Six Documents of His Expedition in 1774.* Oregon Historical Society Press, Portland.

Bell, Thomas L., and Richard Church
1985   Location-Allocation Modeling in Archaeological Settlement Pattern Research: Some Preliminary Applications. *World Archaeology* 16:354-371.

1987   Location-Allocation Modeling in Archaeology. In *Spatial Analysis and Location-Allocation Models,* edited by A. Ghosh and G. Rushton, pp. 76-100. Van Nostrand Reinhold, New York.

Bell, Thomas L., Richard Church, and Larry Gorenflo
1988   Late Horizon Regional Efficiency in the Northeastern Basin of Mexico: A Location-Allocation Perspective. *Journal of Anthropological Archaeology* 7:163-202.

Bernick, Kathryn
1983   *A Site Catchment Analysis of the Little Qualicum River Site, DiSc1: A Wet Site on the East Coast of Vancouver Island, BC.* National Museum of Man Mercury Series, Archaeological Survey of Canada Paper 118. National Museums of Canada, Ottawa.
1987   The Potential of Basketry for Reconstructing Cultural Diversity on the Northwest Coast. In *Ethnicity and Culture,* edited by Reginald Auger, Margaret F. Glass, Scott MacEachern, and Peter H. McCartney, pp. 251-257. Proceedings of the 18th Annual Chacmool Conference, University of Calgary Archaeological Association, Calgary.
1989   Water Hazard (DgRs 30) Artifact Recovery Project Report, Permit 1988-55. Report on file, British Columbia Archaeology Branch, Victoria.
1998a   Introduction. In *Hidden Dimensions: The Cultural Significance of Wetland Archaeology,* edited by Kathryn Bernick, pp. xi-xix. UBC Press, Vancouver.
1998b   Stylistic Characteristics of Basketry from Coast Salish Area Wet Sites. In *Hidden Dimensions: The Cultural Significance of Wetland Archaeology,* edited by Kathryn Bernick, pp. 139-156. UBC Press, Vancouver.
1999   Lanaak (49XPA78): A Wet Site on Baranof Island, Southeastern Alaska. Report of June 1999 Archaeological Investigations. Permit 99-10. Submitted to Kiks.ádi Clan, Sitka Tribe of Alaska, and to Alaska Office of History and Archaeology, Anchorage.

Berreman, Gerald D.
1981   Social Inequality: A Cross Cultural Analysis. In *Social Inequality: Comparative and Developmental Approaches,* edited by G. Berreman, pp. 3-40. Academic Press, New York.

Bettinger, Robert L., and Martin A. Baumhoff
1982   The Numic Spread: Great Basin Cultures in Competition. *American Antiquity* 47:485-503.

Beynon, William
1969   *The Beynon Manuscript: The Literature, Myths and Traditions of the Tsimshian People.* University Microfilm International, Ann Arbor.

Biggild, O.B.
1953   The Mineralogy of Greenland. *Meddelelser om Groonland* 149:1-442.

Birket-Smith, Kaj
1953   *The Chugach Eskimo.* Nationalmuseets Skrifter. Etnografish Raekke 6. Copenhagen.

Birket-Smith, Kaj, and F. de Laguna
1938   *The Eyak Indians of the Copper River Delta, Alaska.* Levin and Munksgaard, Copenhagen.

Bishop, Charles
1967   *The Journal and Letters of Captain Charles Bishop on the North-West Coast of America, in the Pacific and in New South Wales 1794-1799,* edited by Michael Roe (Hakluyt Society, 2nd series, No. 81). Cambridge University Press, Cambridge.

Black, Lydia T.
1994   Deciphering Aleut/Koniag Iconography. In *Anthropology of the North Pacific Rim,* edited by William W. Fitzhugh and Valérie Chaussonnet, pp. 133-146. Smithsonian Institution, Washington.

Blake, Michael, and Douglas R. Brown
1998   Mounds for the Ancestors: Ancient Burial Practices in the Coast Salish Region. Paper presented at the 31st Annual Canadian Archaeological Association Conference, Victoria.

Blenkinsop, George
N.d.   Report to the Indian Commissioner on the Tribes of Barkley Sound, 1874. Provincial Archives of British Columbia, Black Series, Microfilm Reel B280, File 4105. Victoria.

Boas, Franz
1889   Preliminary Notes on the Indians of British Columbia. *Report of the British Association for the Advancement of Science* 58:236-242.
1891a The Lku'ngEn. In *Sixth Report on the North-Western Tribes of Canada. Report of the 60th Meeting of the British Association for the Advancement of Science for 1890,* pp. 563-592, London.
1891b The Nootka. In *Second General Report on the Indians of British Columbia. Report of the 60th Meeting of the British Association for the Advancement of Science, 1890,* pp. 582-715. London.
1897   *The Social Organization and Secret Societies of the Kwakiutl Indians.* Report of the US National Museum for 1895. Washington.
1905   The Jesup North Pacific Expedition. *Proceedings of the International Congress of Americanists,* 13th Session, 1902, pp. 91-100 (Krause Reprint 1968).
1912   Tsimshian Texts (New Series). *Publications of the American Ethnological Society* 3:65-285.
1916   Tsimshian Mythology: Based on Texts Recorded by Henry W. Tate. *31st Annual Report of the Bureau of American Ethnology for the Years 1909-1910,* pp. 29-1037. US Government Printing Office, Washington.
1921   Ethnology of the Kwakiutl (Based on Data Collected by George Hunt). *35th Annual Report of the Bureau of American Ethnology for the Years 1913-1914.* US Government Printing Office, Washington.

Borden, Charles E.
1950   Notes on the Pre-History of the Southern North-West Coast. *British Columbia Historical Quarterly* 14:24-46.
1951   Facts and Problems of Northwest Coast Prehistory. *Anthropology in British Columbia* 2:35-52. British Columbia Provincial Museum, Victoria.
1952   Results of Archaeological Investigations in Central British Columbia. *Anthropology in British Columbia* 3:31-43. British Columbia Provincial Museum, Victoria.
1962   West Coast Crossties with Alaska. In *Prehistoric Cultural Relations between the Arctic and Temperate Zones of North America,* edited by John M. Campbell, pp. 9-19. Arctic Institute of North America, Technical Paper No. 11, Calgary.
1969   Discussion (Current Archaeological Research on the Northwest Coast symposium). *Northwest Anthropological Research Notes* 3:255-263.
1970   Culture History of the Fraser Delta Region. *BC Studies* 6-7:95-112.
1979   Peopling and Early Cultures of the Pacific Northwest. *Science* 203:963-971.

Bouchard, Randy, and Dorothy Kennedy
1991   Preliminary Notes on Ditidaht Land Use. Report prepared for Millennia Research, Ditidaht Indian Band, and British Columbia Heritage Trust. Copy on file, British Columbia Archaeology Branch, Victoria.

Bourdieu, Pierre
1977 *Outline of a Theory of Practice.* Cambridge University Press, Cambridge.
1990 *The Logic of Practice.* Polity Press, Cambridge.

Boyd, Robert
1990 Demographic History, 1774-1874. In *Handbook of North American Indians.* Vol. 7: *Northwest Coast,* edited by Wayne Suttles, pp. 135-148. Smithsonian Institution, Washington.
1996 *People of the Dalles: The Indians of the Wascopam Mission.* University of Nebraska Press, Lincoln.

Brandt, K.
1948 *Whaling and Whale Oil during and after World War II.* Food Research Institute, Stanford University, Palo Alto.

Brooks, A.H.
1900 *A Reconnaissance from Pyramid Harbor to Eagle City, Alaska, Including a Description of the Copper Deposits of the Upper White and Tanana Rivers.* US Geological Survey, 21st Annual Report, Part 2, General Geology, Economic Geology, Alaska, pp. 331-392. US Government Printing Office, Washington.

Brooks, Charles W.
1876 *Japanese Wrecks Stranded and Picked up Adrift in the North Pacific Ocean.* California Academy of Science. (Reprint, Ye Galleon Press, Fairfield, 1964.)

Brown, Douglas
1996 Historic and Ancient Social Interaction in the Halkomelem Culture Region of the Central Northwest Coast. Paper presented at the 61st Annual Meeting of the Society for American Archaeology, New Orleans.

Burch, Ernest, and L. Ellana (editors)
1994 *Key Issues in Hunter-Gatherer Research.* Berg Publishers, Providence.

Burley, David V.
1979 Specialization and the Evolution of Complex Society in the Gulf of Georgia Region. *Canadian Journal of Archaeology* 3:131-143.
1980 *Marpole: Anthropological Reconstructions of a Prehistoric Northwest Coast Culture Type.* Department of Archaeology Publication No. 8. Simon Fraser University, Burnaby.
1989 *Senewélets: Culture History of the Nanaimo Coast Salish and the False Narrows Midden.* Royal British Columbia Museum Memoir No. 2. Royal British Columbia Museum, Victoria.

Burley, David V., and Christopher Knusel
1989 Burial Patterns and Archaeological Interpretation: Problems in the Recognition of Ranked Society in the Coast Salish Region. Paper presented at the Conference, Development of Hunting-Fishing-Gathering Maritime Societies along the West Coast of North America, Seattle.

Butler, Virginia
1987 Distinguishing Natural from Cultural Salmonid Deposits in the Pacific Northwest of North America. In *Natural Formation Processes and the Archaeological Record,* edited by D. Noah and M. Petraglia, pp. 131-149. BAR International Series 352, Oxford.

Byram, Scott
1998 Fishing Weirs in Oregon Coast Estuaries. In *Hidden Dimensions: The Cultural Significance of Wetland Archaeology,* edited by Kathryn Bernick, pp. 199-219. UBC Press, Vancouver.

Caamano, J.
1938   The Journal of Jacinto Caamano. *British Columbia Historical Quarterly* 2:189-222; 265-301. (Translated and edited by Harold Grenfell, H.R. Wagner, and W.A. Newcombe.)

Calvert, S.G.
1980   A Cultural Analysis of Faunal Remains from Three Archaeological Sites in Hesquiat Harbour, BC. PhD diss., Department of Anthropology and Sociology, University of British Columbia, Vancouver.

Campbell, Lyle
1997   *American Indian Languages: The Historical Linguistics of Native America*. Oxford University Press, Oxford.

Carlson, Roy L. (editor)
1983a   *Indian Art Traditions of the Northwest Coast*. Archaeology Press, Simon Fraser University, Burnaby.

Carlson, Roy L.
1983b   Prehistory of the Northwest Coast. In *Indian Art Traditions of the Northwest Coast,* edited by Roy L. Carlson, pp. 13-32. Archaeology Press, Simon Fraser University, Burnaby.
1990   Cultural Antecedents. In *Handbook of North American Indians*. Vol. 7: *Northwest Coast,* edited by Wayne Suttles, pp. 60-69. Smithsonian Institution, Washington.
1994   Trade and Exchange in Prehistoric British Columbia. In *Prehistoric Exchange Systems in North America,* edited by Timothy Baugh and Jonathan Ericson, pp. 307-361. Plenum, New York.
1996   The Later Prehistory of British Columbia. In *Early Human Occupation in British Columbia,* edited by Roy L. Carlson and Luke Dalla Bona, pp. 215-226. UBC Press, Vancouver.

Carlson, Roy L., and Philip M. Hobler
1993   The Pender Canal Excavations and the Development of Coast Salish Culture. (Special Issue, *Changing Times: British Columbia Archaeolgy in the 1980s,* edited by Knut Fladmark) *BC Studies* 99:25-52.

Carmichael, Alfred
1922   *Indian Legends of Vancouver Island*. Musson, Toronto.
N.d.   Notes Relating to Kee-hin. Provincial Archives of British Columbia. Manuscript 2305, Box 3, File 9. Victoria.

Cavanaugh, D.M.
1983   Northwest Coast Whaling: A New Perspective. MA thesis, Department of Anthropology and Sociology, University of British Columbia, Vancouver.

Chapman, John, and Helena Hamerow (editors)
1997   *Migrations and Invasions in Archaeological Explanation*. BAR International Series 664, Oxford.

Chartkoff, Joseph L.
1978   Exchange, Subsistence, and Sedentism along the Middle Klamath River. *Research in Economic Anthropology* 11:285-303.

Chatters, James C.
1981   Archaeology of the Sbabadid Site, 45KI51, King County, Washington. Office of Public Archaeology, University of Washington, Seattle.

1988 Tualdad Altu (45KI59): A 4th-Century Village on the Black River, King County, Washington. First City Equities, Seattle.
1989 The Antiquity of Economic Differentiation within Households in the Puget Sound Region, Northwest Coast. In *Households and Communities,* edited by S. MacEachern, D. Archer, and R. Garvin, pp. 168-178. Proceedings of the 20th Annual Chacmool Conference, University of Calgary Archaeological Association, Calgary.

Clamhouse, Louis, Joshua Edgar, Charles Jones, John Thomas, and E.Y. Arima
1991 From Barkley Sound Southeast. In *Between Ports Alberni and Renfrew: Notes on West Coast Peoples,* edited by E.Y. Arima, pp. 203-315. Mercury Series, Canadian Ethnology Service Paper No. 121. Canadian Museum of Civilization, Hull, Quebec.

Clark, Donald W.
1977 *Huhanudan Lake: An Ipiutak-Related Occupation of Western Interior Alaska.* National Museum of Man Mercury Series, Archaeological Survey of Canada Paper No. 71. National Museums of Canada, Ottawa.
1998 Kodiak Island: The Later Cultures. *Arctic Anthropology* 35:172-186.

Cole, Douglas, and David Darling
1990 History of the Early Period. In *Handbook of North American Indians.* Vol. 7: *Northwest Coast,* edited by Wayne Suttles, pp. 119-134. Smithsonian Institution, Washington.

Collins, June McCormick
1974 *Valley of the Spirits: The Upper Skagit Indians of Western Washington.* University of Washington Press, Seattle.

Colnett, J.
N.d. A Voyage to the NW Side of America, 1786-1788. Unpublished journal, Public Record Office, London.

Cook, James
1967 *The Journals of Captain James Cook on his Voyages of Discovery: The Voyage of the Resolution and Discovery, 1776-1780,* edited by J.C. Beaglehole. Hakluyt Society. Vol. 3. Cambridge University Press, Cambridge.

Cook, James, and James King
1784 *A Voyage to the Pacific Ocean ... Performed under the Direction of Captains Cook, Clerke and Gore, in His Majesty's Ships the* Resolution *and the* Discovery. *In the Years 1776, 1777, 1778, 1779, and 1780,* edited by G. Nicol and T. Cadell (3 vols.). J. Stockdale, London.

Cook, Sherburne F., and Robert F. Heizer
1968 Relationships among Houses, Settlement Areas, and Population in Aboriginal California. In *Settlement Archaeology,* edited by K.C. Chang, pp. 79-117. National Press Books, Palo Alto.

Coupland, Gary
1988a Prehistoric Economic and Social Change in the Tsimshian Area. In *Prehistoric Economies of the Northwest Coast,* edited by Barry Isaac, pp. 211-243. *Research in Economic Anthropology,* Supplement 3. JAI Press, Greenwich.
1988b *Prehistoric Cultural Change at Kitselas Canyon.* Mercury Series, Archaeological Survey of Canada Paper No. 38. Canadian Museum of Civilization, Hull, Quebec.
1996 This Old House: Cultural Complexity and Household Stability on the Northern Northwest Coast of North America. In *Emergent Complexity: The Evolution of Intermediate Societies,* edited by Jeanne Arnold, pp. 74-90. International Monographs in Prehistory, Ann Arbor.

1999   A Chief's House on the Northern Northwest Coast. Paper presented at the 64th Annual Meeting of the Society for American Archaeology, Chicago.

Coupland, Gary, Craig Bissell, and Sarah King
1993   Prehistoric Subsistence and Seasonality at Prince Rupert Harbour: Evidence from the McNichol Creek Site. *Canadian Journal of Archaeology* 17:59-73.

Coupland, Gary, Andrew Martindale, and Susan Marsden
2001   Does Resource Abundance Explain Local Group Rank among the Coast Tsimshian? In *Perspectives on Northern Northwest Coast Prehistory*, edited by Jerome Cybulski, pp. 223-248. Mercury Series, Archaeological Survey of Canada Paper No. 160. Canadian Museum of Civilization, Hull, Quebec.

Couture, A.
1975   Indian Copper Artifacts from Prince Rupert. *Physical Metallurgy Research Laboratories Report* MRP/PMRL-75-3 (IR). Canadian Centre for Mineral and Energy Technology, Ottawa.

Couture, A., and J.O. Edwards
1963   Origin of Copper Used by Canadian West Coast Indians in the Manufacture of Ornamental Plaques. *Contributions to Anthropology*, 1961-62, Part 2, Paper No. 6, Bulletin 194, pp. 199-220. National Museums of Canada, Ottawa.

Cressman, Luther S., D.L. Cole, W.A. Davis, T.M. Newman, and D.J. Scheans
1960   Cultural Sequences at the Dalles, Oregon. *Transactions of the American Philosophical Society*, New Series, Vol. 50, Part 10. Philadelphia.

Croes, Dale R. (editor)
1976   *The Excavation of Water-Saturated Archaeological Sites (Wet Sites) on the Northwest Coast of North America*. National Museum of Man Mercury Series, Archaeological Survey of Canada Paper No. 50. National Museums of Canada, Ottawa.

Croes, Dale R.
1977   Basketry from the Ozette Village Archaeological Site: A Technological, Functional and Comparative Study. PhD diss., Department of Anthropology, Washington State University, Pullman. University Microfilms 77-25, 762, Ann Arbor.
1980   *Cordage from the Ozette Village Archaeological Site: A Technological, Functional, and Comparative Study*. Project Reports 9, Laboratory of Archaeology and History, Washington State University, Pullman.
1988   The Significance of the 3,000 BP Hoko River Waterlogged Fishing Camp in Our Overall Understanding of Southern Northwest Coast Cultural Evolution. In *Wet Site Archaeology*, edited by Barbara Purdy, pp. 131-152. Telford Press, Caldwell, New Jersey.
1989a Prehistoric Ethnicity on the Northwest Coast of North America: An Evaluation of Style in Basketry and Lithics. *Research in Anthropological Archaeology* 8:101-130.
1989b Lachane Basketry and Cordage: A Technological, Functional and Comparative Study. *Canadian Journal of Archaeology* 13:165-205.
1992a An Evolving Revolution in Wet Site Research on the Northwest Coast of North America. In *The Wetland Revolution in Prehistory*, edited by Bryony Coles, pp. 99-111. Wetlands Archaeological Research Project (WARP) Occasional Papers No. 6, Department of History and Archaeology, University of Exeter, Exeter.
1992b Exploring Prehistoric Subsistence Change on the Northwest Coast. In *Long-Term Subsistence Change in Prehistoric North America*, edited by Dale R. Croes, R.A. Hawkins, and B.L. Isaac, pp. 337-366. *Research in Economic Anthropology*, Supplement 6. JAI Press, Greenwich.

1993 Prehistoric Hoko River Cordage: A New Line on Northwest Coast Prehistory. In *A Spirit of Enquiry: Essays for Ted Wright*, edited by John Coles, Valerie Fenwick, and Gillian Hutchinson, pp. 32-36. Wetlands Archaeology Research Project (WARP) Occasional Paper No. 7, Department of History and Archaeology, University of Exeter, Exeter.

1995 *The Hoko River Archaeological Site Complex, The Wet/Dry Site (45CA213), 3000-1700 BP.* Washington State University Press, Pullman.

1997 North-Central Cultural Dichotomy on the Northwest Coast of North America: Its Evolution as Suggested by Wet-Site Basketry and Wooden Fish-Hooks. *Antiquity* 71:594-615.

2001 North Coast Prehistory: Reflections from Northwest Coast Wet Site Research. In *Perspectives on Northern Northwest Coast Prehistory*, edited by Jerome S. Cybulski, pp. 145-171. Mercury Series Paper, Archaeological Survey of Canada Paper No. 160. Canadian Museum of Civilization, Hull, Quebec.

2002 Birth to Death: Northwest Coast Wet Site Basketry and Cordage Artifacts Reflecting a Person's Life-Cycle. In *Enduring Records: The Environmental and Cultural Heritage of Wetlands*, edited by Barbara A. Purdy, pp. 92-109. WARP Occasional Paper No. 15. Oxbow Books, Oxford.

Croes, Dale R., Jonathan O. Davis, and Henry T. Irwin
1974 *The Use of Computer Graphics in Archaeology: A Case Study from the Ozette Site, Washington.* Reports of Investigations No. 52. Laboratory of Anthropology, Washington State University, Pullman.

Croes, Dale R., and Rhonda Foster
2001 Perishable Artifacts from Northwest Coast Wet Sites: A Critical Need for Native American Expertise. Paper presented at the 66th Annual Meeting of the Society for American Archaeology, New Orleans.

Croes, Dale R., and Steven Hackenberger
1988 Hoko River Archaeological Complex: Modeling Prehistoric Northwest Coast Economic Evolution. In *Prehistoric Economies of the Pacific Northwest Coast*, edited by Barry L. Isaac, pp. 19-86. *Research in Economic Anthropology*, Supplement 3. JAI Press, Greenwich.

Cross, Guy
1995 Archaeological Remote Sensing: Shingle Point Site, Valdes Island, BC. Report on file, Laboratory of Archaeology, University of British Columbia, Vancouver.

Cutter, Donald
1969 *The California Coast.* University of Oklahoma Press, Norman.

Cybulski, Jerome S.
1975 *Skeletal Variability in British Columbia Coastal Populations: A Descriptive and Comparative Assessment of Cranial Morphology.* National Museum of Man Mercury Series, Archaeological Survey of Canada Paper No. 30. National Museums of Canada, Ottawa.

1991 Observations on Dental Labret Wear at Crescent Beach, Pender Canal, and Other Northwest Coast Prehistoric Sites. Appendix to 1989 and 1990 Crescent Beach Excavations, Final Report. The Origins of the Northwest Coast Ethnographic Pattern: The Place of the Locarno Beach Phase, edited by R.G. Matson, H. Pratt, and L. Rankin. Report on file, British Columbia Archaeology Branch, Victoria.

1996 Conflict and Complexity on the Northwest Coast: Skeletal and Mortuary Evidence. Paper presented at the 61st Annual Meeting of the Society for American Archaeology, New Orleans.

Davis, Horace
1872a *Records of Japanese Vessels Driven upon the Northwest Coast of North America and Its Outlying Islands.* American Antiquarian Society, Worcester, MA.
1872b Japanese Wrecks in American Waters. *Overland Monthly* 9:353-360. John H. Carmany, San Francisco.

Davis, Stanley Drew
1996 The Archaeology of the Yakutat Foreland: A Socioecological View. PhD diss., Department of Anthropology, Texas A & M University, College Station.

Dawson, George M.
1879 *Preliminary Report on the Physical and Geological Features of the Southern Portion of the Interior of British Columbia, 1877.* Geological Survey of Canada, Dawson Brothers, Montreal.
1880 Report on the Queen Charlotte Islands, 1878. *Geological Survey of Canada Report of Progress for 1878-79,* Vol. 4. Dawson Brothers, Montreal.

Day, Gordon M.
1973 Oral Tradition as Complement. *Ethnohistory* 19:99-108.

Dean, Johnathan R.
1994 Those Rascally Spackaloids: The Rise of Gispaxloats Hegemony at Fort Simpson, 1832-40. *BC Studies* 101:41-78.

Deans, James
1885 On the Copper Images of the Haidah Tribes. *Proceedings of the Numismatic and Antiquarian Society of Philadelphia,* pp. 14-17. Philadelphia: The Society.

Deetz, James
1967 *Invitation to Archaeology.* Natural History Press, Garden City, New York.

de Laguna, Frederica
1960 *The Story of a Tlingit Community: A Problem in the Relationship between Archaeological, Ethnological, and Historical Methods.* Bureau of American Ethnology, Bulletin 172. Smithsonian Institution, Washington.
1972 *Under Mount Saint Elias: The History and Culture of the Yakutat Tlingit.* Smithsonian Contributions to Anthropology 7, Washington.
1990a Eyak. In *Handbook of North American Indians.* Vol. 7: *Northwest Coast,* edited by Wayne Suttles, pp. 189-196. Smithsonian Institution, Washington.
1990b Tlingit. In *Handbook of North American Indians.* Vol. 7: *Northwest Coast,* edited by Wayne Suttles, pp. 203-228. Smithsonian Institution, Washington.

de Laguna, Frederica, F.A. Riddell, D.F. McGeein, K.S. Lane, and J.A. Freed
1964 *Archaeology of the Yakutat Bay Area, Alaska.* Bureau of American Ethnology, Bulletin 192. Smithsonian Institution, Washington.

Department of Indian Affairs, Dominion of Canada
1889 *Annual Report of the Department of Indian Affairs for the Years 1881-89.* Queen's Printer, Ottawa.

Dewhirst, John
1978 Nootka Sound: A 4,000-Year Perspective. In *Nu.tka.: The History and Survival of Nootkan Culture,* edited by Barbara S. Efrat and W.J. Langlois, pp. 1-29. Sound Heritage, Vol. 7, No. 2. Provincial Archives of British Columbia, Victoria.
1980 The Indigenous Archaeology of Yuquot, a Nootkan Outside Village. In *The Yuquot Project.* Vol. 1: *History and Archaeology.* Parks Canada, Ottawa.

1982 The Origins of Nootkan Whaling: A Definition of Northern and Central Nootkan Ecological Orientation for the Past Four Millennia. *Abhandlungen der Volkerkundlichen Arbeitsgemeinschaft*, Heft 33. Nortorf.

Dixon, George
1789 *A Voyage Round the World; but more Particularly to the North-West Coast of America: Performed in 1785, 1786, 1787, and 1788, in the* King George *and* Queen Charlotte. Geo. Goulding, London.

Dohm, Karen
1992 Architecture and Privacy in Pueblo Housing. *Visual Anthropology* 5:1-15.
1996 Rooftop Zuni: Extending Household Territory beyond Apartment Walls. In *People Who Lived in Big Houses: Archaeological Perspectives on Large Domestic Structures*, edited by Gary Coupland and E.B. Banning, pp. 89-106. Monographs in World Archaeology No. 27. Prehistory Press, Madison, Wisconsin.

Donald, Leland
1983 Was Nuu-chah-nulth-aht (Nootka) Society Based on Slave Labor? In *The Development of Political Organization in Native North America*, edited by Elizabeth Tooker, pp. 108-119. American Ethnological Society, Washington.
1985 On the Possibility of Social Class in Societies Based on Extractive Subsistence. In *Status, Structure and Stratification: Current Archaeological Reconstructions*, edited by M. Thompson, M.T. Garcia, and F. Kense, pp. 237-244. Proceedings of the 16th Annual Chacmool Conference, University of Calgary Archaeological Association, Calgary.
1990 Liberty, Equality, Fraternity: Was the Indian Really Egalitarian? In *The Invented Indian: Cultural Fictions and Government Policies*, edited by James Clifton, pp. 145-167. Transaction Publishers, New Brunswick.
1996 Slavery and Captivity: A Comparison of Servitude on the Northwest Coast and among the Interior Salish. In *Chin Hills to Chilouin: Papers Honoring the Versatile Career of Theodore Stern*, edited by Don E. Dumond, pp. 75-86. University of Oregon Anthropological Papers, No. 52, Eugene.
1997 *Aboriginal Slavery on the Northwest Coast of North America*. University of California Press, Berkeley.

Donald, Leland, and Donald Mitchell
1975 Some Correlates of Local Group Rank among the Southern Kwakiutl. *Ethnology* 14:325-346.
1994 Nature and Culture on the Northwest Coast of North America: The Case of Wakashan Salmon Resources. In *Key Issues in Hunter-Gatherer Research*, edited by Ernest Burch and L. Ellana, pp. 95-117. Berg Publishers, Providence.

Draper, John A.
1989 Ozette Lithic Analysis. Department of Anthropology, Washington State University, Pullman.

Drucker, Philip
1940 Kwakiutl Dancing Societies. *University of California Anthropological Records* 2:201-230.
1943 *Archaeological Survey on the Northern Northwest Coast*. Bureau of American Ethnology, Anthropological Papers No. 20. Smithsonian Institution, Washington.
1951 *The Northern and Central Nootkan Tribes*. Bureau of American Ethnology, Bulletin 144. Smithsonian Institution, Washington.
1955a Sources of Northwest Coast Culture. In *New Interpretations of Aboriginal American Culture History*, pp. 59-81. Anthropological Society of Washington, Washington.
1955b *Indians of the Northwest Coast*. Natural History Press, Garden City, New York.

1963   *Indians of the Northwest Coast* (reprint). Natural History Press, Garden City, New York.
1965   *Cultures of the North Pacific Coast.* Chandler Publishing Company, San Francisco.
1967   *To Make My Name Good: A Re-examination of the Southern Kwakiutl Potlatch.* University of California Press, Berkeley.

Duff, Wilson
1952   *The Upper Stalo Indians of the Fraser Valley, British Columbia.* Anthropology in British Columbia, Memoir 1. British Columbia Provincial Museum, Victoria.
1956   Prehistoric Stone Sculpture of the Fraser River and Gulf of Georgia. *Anthropology in British Columbia* 5:15-51.
1965   *The Indian History of British Columbia,* Vol. 1. Anthropology in British Columbia, Memoir 5. Provincial Museum of British Columbia, Victoria.
1975   *Images: Stone: BC: Thirty Centuries of Northwest Coast Indian Sculpture.* University of Washington Press, Seattle.

Dumond, Don E.
1998   The Archaeology of Migrations: Following the Fainter Footprints. *Arctic Anthropology* 35:59-76.

Dunn, John A.
1976   Tsimshian Internal Relations Reconsidered. Unpublished report. Archaeological Survey of Canada. National Museums of Canada, Ottawa.
1984   International Matri-Moieties: The North Maritime Province of the North Pacific Coast. In *The Tsimshian: Images of the Past, Views for the Present,* edited by Margaret Seguin, pp. 99-109. UBC Press, Vancouver.

Eldridge, Morley
1991   The Glenrose Cannery Wet Component: A Significance Assessment. Permit 1990-24. Report on file, British Columbia Archaeology Branch, Victoria.

Ellis, David W., and Luke Swan
1981   *Teachings of the Tides: Uses of Marine Invertebrates by the Manhousat People.* Theytus Books, Nanaimo.

Elmendorf, William W.
1960   *The Structure of Twana Culture* (with comparative notes on the structure of Yurok culture by A.L. Kroeber). Research Studies, Monographic Supplement No. 2, Washington State University, Pullman.
1990   Chemakum. In *Handbook of North American Indians.* Vol. 7: *Northwest Coast,* edited by Wayne Suttles, pp. 438-440. Smithsonian Institution, Washington.

Elsasser, Albert B.
1978   Basketry. In *Handbook of North American Indians.* Vol. 8: *California,* edited by Robert F. Heizer, pp. 626-641. Smithsonian Institution, Washington.

Embleton, Sheila M.
1985   Lexicostatistics Applied to the Germanic, Romance, and Wakashan Families. *Word* 36:37-60.

Emmons, George T.
1993   *The Basketry of the Tlingit.* (Reprinted and bound with *The Chilkat Blanket.*) Sheldon Jackson Museum, Alaska State Museums, Sitka. (Originally published in 1903, *Memoirs of the American Museum of Natural History,* Vol. 3, Part 2. New York.)

Erlandson, Jon M., Madonna Moss, and Mark Tveskov
1998 Return to Chetlessenten: The Antiquity and Architecture of an Athapaskan Village on the Southern Northwest Coast. *Journal of California and Great Basin Archaeology* 19:226-240.

Erlandson, Jon M., Mark A. Tveskov, and R. Scott Byram
1998 The Development of Maritime Adaptations on the Southern Northwest Coast of North America. *Arctic Anthropology* 35:6-22.

ESRI
1995 *ArcDoc 7.0* (Relational Database Manual for Arc/Info). Environmental Systems Research Institute, Redlands.

Ewing, Anne
1951 A Study of the Shed-Type Houses of the Musqueam. Report on file, Laboratory of Archaeology, University of British Columbia, Vancouver.

Fifield, Terence E., and David E. Putnam
1995 Thorne River Basket: Description, Context, and Opportunity. Paper presented at conference held by the UBC Museum of Anthropology in Vancouver, British Columbia, 27-30 April 1995 (Hidden Dimensions: The Cultural Significance of Wetland Archaeology).

Firth, Raymond William
1951 *Elements of Social Organization.* Watts, London.

Fisher, Robin
1977 *Contact and Conflict: Indian-European Relations in British Columbia, 1774-1890.* UBC Press, Vancouver.

Fisher, Robin, and J.M. Bumstead (editors)
1982 *An Account of a Voyage to the North West Coast of North America in 1785 and 1786, by Alexander Walker.* Douglas and McIntyre, Vancouver.

Fiskin, M.
1994 Modifications of Whale Bones. Appendix D in *Ozette Archaeological Project Research Reports.* Vol. 2: *Fauna,* edited by S.R. Samuels, pp. 359-377. Reports of Investigations 66, Department of Anthropology, Washington State University, Pullman.

Fitzhugh William W., and Aron Crowell (editors)
1988 *Crossroads of Continents: Cultures of Siberia and Alaska.* Smithsonian Institution, Washington.

Fitzhugh William W., and Valérie Chaussonnet (editors)
1994 *Anthropology of the North Pacific Rim.* Smithsonian Institution, Washington.

Fladmark, Knut R.
1973 The Richardson Ranch Site: A 19th-Century Haida House. In *Historical Archaeology in Northwestern North America,* edited by R. Getty and K. Fladmark, pp. 53-95. University of Calgary Archaeological Association, Calgary.
1975 *A Paleoecological Model for Northwest Coast Prehistory.* National Museum of Man, Mercury Series, Archaeological Survey of Canada Paper No. 43. National Museums of Canada, Ottawa.

Fladmark, Knut R., D.E. Nelson, T.A. Brown, J.S. Vogel, and J.R. Southon
1987   AMS Dating of Two Artifacts from the Northwest Coast. *Canadian Journal of Archaeology* 11:1-12.

Fleurieu, C.P.C.
1801   *A Voyage Round the World Performed during the Years 1790, 1791 and 1792, by Etienne Marchand, T.N. Longman and O. Rees* (2 vols.). Printed for T.N. Longman and O. Rees, London.

Foster, Michael K.
1996   Languages and the Culture History of North America. In *Handbook of North American Indians.* Vol. 14: *Languages,* edited by Ives Goddard, pp. 64-110. Smithsonian Institution, Washington.

Francis, D.
1990   *The Great Chase.* Penguin Books, Toronto.

Franklin, Ursula M., E. Badone, R. Gotthardt, and R. Yorga
1981   *An Examination of Prehistoric Copper Technology and Copper Sources in Western Arctic and Subarctic North America.* National Museum of Man, Mercury Series, Archaeological Survey of Canada Paper No. 101. National Museums of Canada, Ottawa.

Fried, Morton
1967   *The Evolution of Political Society: An Essay in Political Anthropology.* Random House, New York.

Friele, Pierre
1991   Holocene Relative Sea-Level Change: Vargas Island, British Columbia. MA thesis, Department of Geography, Simon Fraser University, Burnaby.

Galm, Jerry R.
1994   Exchange in the Northwestern Interior Plateau. In *Prehistoric Exchange Systems in North America,* edited by Timothy G. Baugh and J.E. Ericson, pp. 273-305. Plenum, New York.

Gamble, Clive S.
1995   Making Tracks: Hominid Networks and the Evolution of the Social Landscape. In *The Archaeology of Human Ancestry: Power, Sex and Tradition,* edited by J. Steele and S. Shennan, pp. 253-277. Routledge, London.
1998   Palaeolithic Society and the Release from Proximity: A Network Approach to Intimate Relations. *World Archaeology* 29:426-449.

Garfield, Viola
1939   Tsimshian Clan and Society. *University of Washington Publications in Anthropology* 7:167-340, Seattle.
1947   A Research Problem in Northwest Coast Indian Economics. *American Anthropologist* 47:626-630.
1951   The Tsimshian and Their Neighbors. In *The Tsimshian Indians and Their Arts,* edited by Viola Garfield and Paul Wingert, pp. 3-70. Douglas and McIntyre, Vancouver.

Gibson, James R.
1992   *Otter Skins, Boston Ships, and China Goods.* McGill-Queen's University Press, Montreal.

Gleeson, Paul (compiler)
1980a *Ozette Archaeological Project, Interim Final Report, Phase XIII.* Project Report No. 97, Washington Archaeological Research Center, Washington State University, Pullman.

Gleeson, Paul
1980b Ozette Woodworking Technology. PhD diss., Department of Anthropology, Washington State University, Pullman.
1980c Ozette Woodworking Technology. Project Report No. 3, Laboratory of Archaeology, Washington State University, Pullman.
1981 Analysis of Pandora's Box: The Ozette Experience. Paper presented to the 46th Annual Meeting of the Society of American Archaeology, San Diego.

Goddard, Ives
1996 Introduction. In *Handbook of North American Indians.* Vol. 14: *Languages,* edited by Ives Goddard, pp. 1-16. Smithsonian Institution, Washington.

Gosden, Christopher
1994 *Social Being and Time.* Blackwell, Oxford.

Gough, Barry M.
1992 *The Northwest Coast: British Navigation, Trade, and Discoveries to 1812.* UBC Press, Vancouver.

Graves, William M., and Katherine A. Spielmann
2000 Leadership, Long-Distance Exchange, and Feasting in the Protohistoric Rio Grande. In *Alternative Leadership Strategies in the Prehispanic Southwest,* edited by B.J. Mills, pp. 45-59. University of Arizona Press, Tucson.

Green, Joanne
1999 Shellfish Analysis of a Coast Salish Shed-Roof House: Shingle Point, BC. Paper presented at the 60th Annual Meeting of the Society for American Archaeology, Chicago.

Grier, Colin
1998 Household Archaeology at Dionisio Point (DgRv 3). Report on file, British Columbia Archaeology Branch, Victoria.
2001 The Social Economy of a Prehistoric Northwest Coast Plankhouse. PhD diss., Department of Anthropology, Arizona State University, Tempe.

Groot, Cornelis, and Leo Margolis (editors)
1991 *Pacific Salmon Life Histories.* UBC Press, Vancouver.

Grumet, Robert S.
1975 Changes in Coast Tsimshian Redistributive Activities in the Fort Simpson Region of British Columbia, 1788-1862. *Ethnohistory* 22:294-318.

Gunther, Erna
1960 A Re-evaluation of the Cultural Position of the Nootka. In *Men and Cultures: Selected Papers of the 5th International Congress of Anthropological and Ethnological Sciences,* edited by Anthony F.C. Wallace, pp. 270-276. University of Pennsylvania Press, Philadelphia.
1972 *Indian Life on the Northwest Coast of North America as Seen by the Early Explorers and Fur Traders during the Last Decades of the Eighteenth Century.* University of Chicago Press, Chicago.

Haeberlin, H.K., James A. Teit, and Helen H. Roberts
1928   Coiled Basketry in British Columbia and Surrounding Region. *Bureau of American Ethnology Annual Report* 41:119-484.

Haggarty, James C., and Richard I. Inglis
1983   Westcoast Sites: An Archaeological and Macro-Environmental Synthesis. In *Prehistoric Places on the Southern Northwest Coast,* edited by R. Greengo, pp. 11-33. Burke Museum, University of Washington, Seattle.
1985   Historical Resources Site Survey and Assessment, Pacific Rim National Park. Report on file with Parks Canada (Canadian Heritage) and Archaeology Branch Library, Victoria.

Hajda, Yvonne
1984   Regional Social Organization in the Greater Lower Columbia, 1792-1830. PhD diss., Department of Anthropology, University of Washington, Seattle.

Hale, Horatio
1889   Remarks on North American Ethnology: Introductory to the Report on the Indians of British Columbia. In *Fifth Report of the Committee on the North-Western Tribes of the Dominion of Canada, Report on the 59th Meeting of the British Association for the Advancement of Science,* pp. 1-5. London.
1890   Introductory to the Second General Report of Dr. Franz Boas on the Indians of the Province. In *Sixth Report on the North-Western Tribes of Canada, Report of the 60th Meeting of the British Association for the Advancement of Science,* pp. 1-10. London.

Halpin, Marjorie M., and Margaret Seguin
1990   Tsimshian Peoples: Southern Tsimshian, Coast Tsimshian, Nishga, and Gitksan. In *Handbook of North American Indians.* Vol. 7: *Northwest Coast,* edited by Wayne Suttles, pp. 267-284. Smithsonian Institution, Washington.

Harkness, David
1997   The Effects of Opportunistic Shellfish Gathering on Human Settlement during the Late Prehistoric Period at the McNichol Creek Site, Prince Rupert Harbour. Report on file, Laboratory of Archaeology, University of Toronto.

Harris, Cole
1997   *The Resettlement of British Columbia: Essays on Colonialism and Geographical Change.* UBC Press, Vancouver.

Hart, J.L.
1973   *Pacific Fishes of Canada.* Bulletin of the Fisheries Research Board of Canada No. 180, Ottawa.

Hayden, Brian (editor)
1992   *A Complex Culture of the British Columbia Plateau: Traditional Stl'atl'imx Resource Use.* UBC Press, Vancouver.

Hayden, Brian
1994   Competition, Labor, and Complex Hunter-Gatherers. In *Key Issues in Hunter-Gatherer Research,* edited by E.S. Burch Jr. and L.J. Ellanna, pp. 223-239. Berg, Oxford.
1996   Thresholds of Power in Emergent Complex Societies. In *Emergent Complexity: The Evolution of Intermediate Societies,* edited by J. Arnold, pp. 50-58. International Monographs in Prehistory, Ann Arbor.

Hayden, Brian, and James Spafford
1993 The Keatley Creek Site and Corporate Group Archaeology. *BC Studies* 99:106-139.

Hayman, John (editor)
1989 *Robert Brown and the Vancouver Island Exploring Expedition.* UBC Press, Vancouver.

Haynes, Kingsley, and A.S. Fotheringham
1984 *Gravity and Spatial Interaction Models.* Scientific Geography Series 2. Sage, London.

Healey, M.C.
1991 Life History of Chinook Salmon *(Oncorhynchus tshawytscha).* In *Pacific Salmon Life Histories,* edited by C. Groot and L. Margolis, pp. 311-393. UBC Press, Vancouver.

Hebda, Richard, and S. Gay Frederick
1990 History of Marine Resources of the Northeast Pacific since the Last Glaciation. *Transactions of the Royal Society of Canada.* Series 1(1):317-342.

Hebda, Richard J., and Rolf W. Mathewes
1984 Holocene History of Cedar and Native Indian Cultures of the North American Pacific Coast. *Science* 225:711-713.

Hillsman, E.L.
1984 The *p*-Median Structure as a Unified Linear Model for Location-Allocation Analysis. *Environment and Planning A* 16:305-318.

Hill-Tout, Charles
1907 Report on the Ethnology of the South-Eastern Tribes of Vancouver Island, British Columbia. *Journal of the Royal Anthropological Institute of Great Britain and Ireland* 36:306-374.
1978 *The Salish People: The Local Contribution of Charles Hill-Tout.* Vol. 2: *The Squamish and the Lillooet.* Talonbooks, Vancouver.

Hilton, Susanne F.
1990 Haihais, Bella Bella, and Oowekeeno. In *Handbook of North American Indians.* Vol. 7: *Northwest Coast,* edited by Wayne Suttles, pp. 312-322. Smithsonian Institution, Washington.

Himmelman, John H.
1978 Reproductive Cycle of the Green Sea Urchin, *Stronglyocentrotus droebachiensis. Canadian Journal of Zoology* 56: 1828-1836.

Hobler, Philip M.
1990 Prehistory of the Central Coast of British Columbia. In *Handbook of North American Indians.* Vol. 7: *Northwest Coast,* edited by Wayne Suttles, pp. 298-305. Smithsonian Institution, Washington.

Hoff, Ricky
1980 Fishhooks. In *Hoko River: A 2,500 Year Old Fishing Camp on the Northwest Coast of North America,* edited by Dale R. Croes and Eric Blinman. Reports of Investigations 58:160-188. Laboratory of Anthropology, Washington State University, Pullman.

Hoffmeyer, Jesper
1997 The Swarming Body. In *Semiotics around the World. Proceedings of the 5th Congress of the International Association for Semiotic Studies, Berkeley, 1994,* edited by Irmengard Rauch and Gerald F. Carr, pp. 937-940. Mouton de Gruyter, New York.

Holm, Bill
1988 Art and Culture Change at the Tlingit-Eskimo Border. In *Crossroads of Continents: Cultures of Siberia and Alaska,* edited by William Fitzhugh and Aron Crowell, pp. 281-293. Smithsonian Institute, Washington.

Holm, Margaret
1990 Prehistoric Northwest Coast Art: A Stylistic Analysis of the Archaeological Record. MA thesis, Department of Anthropology and Sociology, University of British Columbia, Vancouver.

Holmberg, J.H.
1856 Ethnographische Skizzen ber die Volker des Russischen Amerika. *Acta Societatis Scientiarum Fennicae* 4:281-421.

Holtved, E.
1944 Archaeological Investigations in Thule District. *Meddeleser om Gronland* 141:1-308.

Hoover, Alan L.
1989 Coast Salish Split-Wood Twill-Plaited Basketry. *The Midden* 21(1):6-9.

Hoskins, John
N.d. The Narrative of a Voyage on the North West Coast of America and China on Trade and Discoveries by John Hoskins Performed in the Ship *Columbia Rediwith,* 1790, 1791, 1792 and 1793. Copy of manuscript, Special Collections Library, University of British Columbia, Vancouver.

Howay, F.W. (editor)
1941 *Voyages of the* Columbia *to the Northwest Coast, 1787-1790 and 1790-1793.* Massachusetts Historical Society, Boston.

Huelsbeck, David R.
1989 Food Consumption, Resource Exploitation and Relationships within and between Households at Ozette. In *Households and Communities,* edited by Scott MacEachern, D. Archer, and R. Garvin, pp. 157-167. Proceedings of the 20th Annual Chacmool Conference, University of Calgary Archaeological Association, Calgary.
1994a Mammals and Fish in the Subsistence Economy of Ozette. In *Ozette Archaeological Project Research Reports.* Vol. 2: *Fauna,* edited by S. Samuels, pp. 17-91. Reports of Investigations No. 66, Department of Anthropology, Washington State University, Pullman.
1994b The Utilization of Whales at Ozette. Part 5. In *Ozette Archaeological Project Research Reports.* Vol. 2: *Fauna,* edited by S. Samuels, pp. 265-303. Reports of Investigations 66, Department of Anthropology, Washington State University, Pullman.

Hutchinson, Ian
1992 *Holocene Sea-Level Change in the Pacific Northwest: A Catalogue of Radiocarbon Dates and an Atlas of Regional Sea-Level Curves.* Simon Fraser University Institute for Quaternary Research, Discussion Paper No. 1. Burnaby.

Huu-ay-aht First Nations
2000 Kiix7in Agenda Paper. In *Nuu-Chah-Nulth Voices, Histories, Objects and Journeys,* edited by Alan Hoover, pp. 33-65. Royal British Columbia Museum, Victoria.

Inglis, Richard
1976   Wet Site Distribution – The Northern Case, GbTo-33 – the Lachane Site. In *The Excavation of Water-Saturated Archaeological Sites (Wet Sites) on the Northwest Coast of North America,* edited by Dale R. Croes, pp. 158-185. National Museum of Man, Mercury Series, Archaeological Survey of Canada Paper No. 50. National Museums of Canada, Ottawa.

Inglis, R.I., and J.C. Haggarty
1983   Provisions or Prestige: A Re-evaluation of the Economic Importance of Nootka Whaling. Paper presented at the 11th International Congress of Anthropological and Ethnological Sciences, Vancouver.

Ingold, Tim
1992   Culture and the Perception of the Environment. In *Bush Base: Forest Farm. Culture, Environment and Development,* edited by E. Croll and D. Parkin, pp. 39-56. Routledge, London.
1993   The Temporality of the Landscape. *World Archaeology* 25:152-174.
1996   The Optimal Forager and Economic Man. In *Nature and Society: Anthropological Perspectives,* edited by P. Descola and G. Palsson, pp. 25-44. Routledge, London.

Ingraham, J.
1971   *Voyage to the Northwest Coast of North America, 1790-1792,* edited by Mark Kaplanoff. Imprint Society, Massachusetts.

Jacobsen, William H. Jr.
1979   Wakashan Comparative Studies. In *The Languages of Native America: Historical and Comparative Assessment,* edited by Lyle Campbell and Marianne Mithun, pp. 766-791. University of Texas Press, Austin.

Jenness, Diamond
N.d.   The Saanich Indians of Vancouver Island. Unpublished manuscript, Special Collections Library, University of British Columbia, Vancouver.

Jewitt, John R.
1896   *A Narrative of the Adventures and Suffering of John R. Jewitt,* edited by Robert Brown. C. Wilson Company, London.
1967   *Narrative of the Adventures and Sufferings of John R. Jewitt: Only Survivor of the Crew of the Ship Boston, During a Captivity of Nearly Three Years among the Savages of Nootka Sound.* Ye Galleon Press, Fairfield. (Originally printed in 1815.)
1988   *A Journal Kept at Nootka Sound.* Ye Galleon Press, Fairfield.

Johnson, Allen W., and Timothy Earle
1987   *The Evolution of Human Societies: From Foraging Group to Agrarian State.* Stanford University Press, Palo Alto.
2000   *The Evolution of Human Societies: From Foraging Group to Agrarian State.* 2nd ed. Stanford University Press, Palo Alto.

Jones, Joan Megan
1976   Northwest Coast Indian Basketry: A Stylistic Analysis. PhD diss., Department of Anthropology, University of Washington, Seattle. University Microfilms, Ann Arbor.
1982   *The Art and Style of Western Indian Basketry.* Hancock House, Surrey, BC.

Jopling, C.
1978   Report on the Investigation of the Northwest Coast Coppers. Report on file, Arctic Institute of North America, Calgary.

Jordan, Richard H.
   1994   Qasqiluteng: Feasting and Ceremonialism among the Traditional Koniag of Kodiak Island. In *Anthropology of the North Pacific Rim,* edited by William W. Fitzhugh and Valérie Chaussonnet, pp. 147-174. Smithsonian Institution, Washington.

Jordan, Richard H., and Richard A. Knecht
   1988   Archaeological Research on Western Kodiak Island, Alaska: The Development of Koniag Culture. In *The Late Prehistoric Development of Alaska's Native People,* edited by Robert Shaw, Roger Harritt, and Don Dumond, pp. 225-306. Alaska Anthropological Association Monograph Series 4, Aurora.

Jorgensen, Joseph G.
   1969   *Salish Language and Culture.* Indiana University, Bloomington.
   1980   *Western Indians.* W.H. Freeman, San Francisco.

Kaufman, G.D., and P.H. Forestell
   1986   *Hawaii's Humpback Whales: A Complete Whalewatcher's Guide.* Island Heritage Publishing, Aiea.

Keddie, Grant R.
   1981   The Use and Distribution of Labrets on the North Pacific Rim. *Syesis* 14:59-80.
   1990   *The Question of Asiatic Objects on the North Pacific Coast of America: Historic or Prehistoric?* Contributions to Human History No. 3. Royal British Columbia Museum, Victoria.

Kelly, Robert L.
   1995   *The Foraging Spectrum.* Smithsonian Institution, Washington.

Kendrick, John
   1985   *The Men with Wooden Feet: The Spanish Exploration of the Pacific Northwest.* NC Press Limited, Toronto.

Kennedy, Dorothy I.D., and Randall T. Bouchard
   1990a Bella Coola. In *Handbook of North American Indians.* Vol. 7: *Northwest Coast,* edited by Wayne Suttles, pp. 323-339. Smithsonian Institution, Washington.
   1990b Northern Coast Salish. In *Handbook of North American Indians.* Vol. 7: *Northwest Coast,* edited by Wayne Suttles, pp. 441-452. Smithsonian Institution, Washington.

Kew, Michael
   1992   Salmon Availability, Technology, and Cultural Adaptation in the Fraser River Watershed. In *A Complex Culture of the British Columbia Plateau: Traditional Stl'atl'imx Resource Use,* edited by Brian Hayden, pp. 177-221. UBC Press, Vancouver.

Kidder, A.V.
   1924   *An Introduction to the Study of Southwestern Archaeology.* Rev. ed. 1960. Yale University Press, New Haven.

Kinkade, M. Dale
   1991   Prehistory of the Native Languages of the Northwest Coast. In *Proceedings of the Great Ocean Conferences,* Vol. 1, pp. 137-158. Oregon Historical Society, Portland.

Kinkade, M. Dale, and J.V. Powell
   1976   Language and the Prehistory of North America. *World Archaeology* 8:83-100.

Klein, R.G., and K. Cruz-Uribe
   1984   *The Analysis of Animal Bones from Archaeological Sites.* University of Chicago Press, Chicago.

Koppert, Vincent A.
1930 *Contributions to Clayoquot Ethnology*. Anthropological Series No. 1, Catholic University of America, Washington.

Kroeber, A.L.
1923 American Culture and the Northwest Coast. *American Anthropologist* 25:1-20.
1925 *Handbook of the Indians of California*. Bureau of American Ethnology, Bulletin 78, Washington.
1936 Culture Area Distributions: III Area and Climax. *University of California Publications in American Archaeology and Ethnology* 37:101-116.
1939 Cultural and Natural Areas of Native North America. *University of California Publications in American Archaeology and Ethnology,* 38.

Laforet, Andrea
1984 Tsimshian Basketry. In *The Tsimshian, Images of the Past: Views for the Present,* edited by Margaret Seguin, pp. 215-280. UBC Press, Vancouver.

Lagrand, James B.
1997 Whose Voices Count: Oral Sources and 20th-Century American Indian History. *American Indian Culture and Research Journal* 21:73-105.

Lang, Janet, and Nigel Meeks
1981 Report on the Examination of Two Iron Knives from the Northwest Coast of America. In *Artificial Curiosities from the Northwest Coast of America: Native American Artefacts in the British Museum Collected on the Third Voyage of Captain James Cook and Acquired through Sir Joseph Banks,* Appendix 5, pp. 103-106. Oxford University Press, Oxford.

Lantis, Margaret
1938 The Alaskan Whale Cult and Its Affinities. *American Anthropologist* 40:438-464.
1970 The Aleut Social System, 1750 to 1810, from Early Historical Sources. In *Ethnohistory in Southwestern Alaska and the Southern Yukon,* edited by Margaret Lantis, pp. 139-301. University of Kentucky Press, Lexington.

La Pérouse, Jean François de Galaup
1798 *A Voyage Round the World, Performed in the Years 1785, 1786, 1787 and 1788, Published Conformably to the Decree of the National Assembly, of the 22nd April, 1791,* edited by M.L.A. Milet-Mureau (translated from French, 3 vols.). Printed for J. Johnson, St. Paul's Church Yard, London.

Larsen, H., and F. Rainey
1948 *Ipiutak and the Arctic Whale Hunting Culture*. Anthropological Papers of the American Museum of Natural History, No. 42. New York.

Layton, Robert
1989 Introduction: Who Needs the Past. In *Who Needs the Past: Indigenous Values and Archaeology,* edited by R. Layton, pp. 1-20. Unwin Hyman, London.

Lee, Richard B., and Irven DeVore (editors)
1968 *Man the Hunter*. Aldine, Chicago.

Legros, Dominique
1985 Wealth, Poverty, and Slavery among 19th-Century Tutchone Athapaskans. *Research in Economic Anthropology* 7:37-64.

Lesser, Alexander
1961   Social Fields and the Evolution of Society. *Southwestern Journal of Anthropology* 17:40-48.

Levin, M.G., and D.A. Sergeyev
1964   The Penetration of Iron into the Arctic. In *The Archaeology and Geomorphology of Northern Asia: Selected Works,* edited by Henry N. Michael. Anthropology of the North, Vol. 5, pp. 319-326. Arctic Institute of North America, Calgary. (Translations from the Russian sources.)

Lévi-Strauss, Claude
1958   La Geste d'Asdiwal. *École Pratique des Hautes Études,* pp. 2-43. Paris.

Lincoln, Neville J., and John C. Rath
1980   *North Wakashan Comparative Root List.* Mercury Series, Canadian Ethnology Service Paper No. 68. National Museums of Canada, Ottawa.

Little, Elbert L., Jr.
1971   *Atlas of United States Trees: Conifers and Important Hardwoods.* Government Printing Office, Washington.

Lyman, R. Lee
1991   *Prehistory of the Oregon Coast: The Effects of Excavation Strategies and Assemblage Size on Archaeological Inquiry.* Academic Press, San Diego.
1994   *Vertebrate Taphonomy.* Cambridge University Press, Cambridge.

McCartney, Allen P.
1979   A Processual Consideration of Thule Whale Bone Houses. In *Thule Eskimo Culture: An Anthropological Retrospective,* edited by A.P. McCartney, pp. 301-323. National Museum of Man, Mercury Series, Archaeological Survey of Canada, Paper No. 88. National Museums of Canada, Ottawa.
1988   Late Prehistoric Metal Use in the New World Arctic. In *The Late Prehistoric Development of Alaska's Native People,* edited by Robert D. Shaw, Roger K. Harritt, and Don E. Dumond, pp. 57-79. Alaska Anthropological Association Monograph Series, Aurora.

McClellan, Catherine
1975   *My Old People Say: An Ethnographic Survey of Southern Yukon Territory.* National Museums of Canada Publications in Ethnology, No. 6, Ottawa.
1981   Inland Tlingit. In *Handbook of North American Indians.* Vol. 6: *Subarctic,* edited by June Helm, pp. 469-480. Smithsonian Institution, Washington.

MacDonald, George
1983   Prehistoric Art of the Northwest Coast of British Columbia. In *Indian Art Traditions of the Northwest Coast,* edited by Roy L. Carlson, pp. 99-120. Archaeology Press, Simon Fraser University, Burnaby.
1984   The Epic of Nekt: The Archaeology of Metaphor. In *The Tsimshian: Images of the Past; Views from the Present,* edited by Margaret Sequin, pp. 65-81. UBC Press, Vancouver.
1996   *Haida Art.* Douglas and McIntyre, Vancouver.

MacDonald, George F., and John J. Cove
1987   *Trade and Warfare: Tsimshian Narratives 2.* Canadian Museum of Civilization, Ottawa.

McDonald, George F., and Richard Inglis
1981   An Overview of the North Coast Prehistory Project. *BC Studies* 48:37-63.

McDonald, James A.
1984 Images of the Nineteenth-Century Economy of the Tsimshian. In *The Tsimshian: Images of the Past; Views of the Present*, edited by Margaret Seguin, pp. 40-54. UBC Press, Vancouver.

McIlwraith, T.F.
1948 *The Bella Coola Indians* (2 vols.). Reissued 1992. University of Toronto Press, Toronto.

McLay, Eric
1999 The Diversity of Northwest Coast Shell Midden Sites: Late Precontact Settlement-Subsistence Patterns on Valdes Island, British Columbia. MA thesis, Department of Anthropology and Sociology, University of British Columbia, Vancouver.

McMillan, Alan D.
1969 Archaeological Investigations at Nootka Sound, Vancouver Island. MA thesis, Department of Anthropology and Sociology, University of British Columbia, Vancouver.
1996 Since Kwatyat Lived on Earth: An Examination of Nuu-Chah-Nulth Culture History. PhD diss., Department of Archaeology, Simon Fraser University, Burnaby.
1998 Changing Views of Nuu-chah-nulth Culture History: Evidence of Population Replacement in Barkley Sound. *Canadian Journal of Archaeology* 22:5-18.
1999 *Since the Time of the Transformers: The Ancient Heritage of the Nuu-chah-nulth, Ditidaht, and Makah.* UBC Press, Vancouver.

McMillan, Alan D., and Denis E. St. Claire
1982 *Alberni Prehistory: Archaeological and Ethnographic Investigations on Western Vancouver Island.* Theytus Books, Penticton, BC.
1991 The Toquaht Archaeological Project: Report on the 1991 Field Season. Report on file, British Columbia Heritage Trust, British Columbia Archaeology Branch, Victoria, and the Toquaht Band, Ucluelet.
1992 The Toquaht Archaeological Project: Report on the 1992 Field Season. Report on file, British Columbia Heritage Trust, British Columbia Archaeology Branch, Victoria, and the Toquaht Band, Ucluelet.
1994 The Toquaht Archaeological Project: Report on the 1994 Field Season. Report on file, British Columbia Heritage Trust, British Columbia Archaeology Branch, Victoria, and the Toquaht Band, Ucluelet.
1996 The Toquaht Archaeological Project: Report on the 1996 Field Season. Report on file, British Columbia Heritage Trust, British Columbia Archaeology Branch, Victoria, and the Toquaht Nation, Ucluelet.

McMurdo, Anne
1972 A Typological Analysis of Barbed Bone and Antler Projectile Points from the Northwest Coast. MA thesis, Department of Archaeology, Simon Fraser University, Burnaby.

Mackie, Alexander P.
1992 Nuu-chah-nulth Culture History: Is Something Missing? Paper presented at 45th Annual Northwest Anthropology Conference, Simon Fraser University, Burnaby.

Mackie, Alexander P., and Bert Wilson
1995 Archaeological Inventory of Gwaii Haanas, 1994. Report on file, Parks Canada, Victoria, and the Council of Haida Nation.

Mackie, Quentin
1998   The Archaeology of Fjordland Archipelagos: Mobility Networks, Social Practice and the Built Environment. PhD diss., Department of Archaeology, University of Southampton, Southampton.
2001   *Settlement Archaeology in a Fjordland Archipelago: Network Analysis, Social Practice and the Built Environment of Western Vancouver Island, British Columbia, Canada since 2,000 BP.* BAR International Series 926, Oxford.

Madsen, David B., and David Rhode (editors)
1994   *Across the West: Human Population Movement and the Expansion of the Numa.* University of Utah Press, Salt Lake City.

Marsden, Susan
1990   Controlling the Flow of Furs: Northwest Coast Nations and the Maritime Fur Trade. Paper presented at the BC Studies Conference, Vancouver.

Marsden, Susan, and Robert Galois
1995   The Tsimshian, the Hudson's Bay Company, and the Geopolitics of the Northwest Coast Fur Trade, 1787-1840. *Canadian Geographer* 39:169-183.

Marshall, Yvonne M.
1993   A Political History of the Nuu-Chah-Nulth People: A Case Study of the Mowachaht and Muchalaht Tribes. PhD diss., Department of Archaeology, Simon Fraser University, Burnaby.

Martin, John
1973   On the Estimation of the Sizes of Local Groups in a Hunting-Gathering Environment. *American Anthropologists* 75:1448-1468.

Martindale, Andrew R.C.
1999a The River of Mist: Cultural Change in the Tsimshian Past. PhD diss., Department of Anthropology, University of Toronto, Toronto.
1999b The Tsimshian Household: Shifting Foundations through the Contact Period. Paper presented to the 64th Annual Meeting of the Society for American Archaeology, Chicago.
2000   Archaeological Stories of the Tsimshian: Change in the Context of Contact. In *The Entangled Past,* edited by M. Boyd, J.C. Erwin, and M. Hendrickson, pp. 90-97. Archaeological Association of the University of Calgary, Calgary.

Maschner, Herbert D.G.
1997   Settlement and Subsistence in the Later Prehistory of Tebenkof Bay, Kuiu Island, Southeast Alaska. *Arctic Anthropology* 34:74-99.

Maschner, Herbert D.G., and Julie Stein
1995   Multivariate Approaches to Site Location on the Northwest Coast of North America. *Antiquity* 69:61-73.

Mason, Otis T.
1904   *Aboriginal American Basketry: Studies in a Textile Art without Machinery.* Annual Report of the Smithsonian Institution, Washington.
1988   *American Indian Basketry.* Reprinted. Dover, New York. (Originally published in 1904.)

Matson, R.G. (editor)
1976   *The Glenrose Cannery Site.* National Museum of Man, Mercury Series, Archaeological Survey of Canada Paper No. 52. National Museums of Canada, Ottawa.

Matson, R.G.
1974 Clustering and Scaling of Gulf of Georgia Sites. *Syesis* 7:101-114.
1992 The Evolution of Northwest Coast Subsistence. In *Long-Term Subsistence Change in Prehistoric North America,* edited by D.R. Croes, R.A. Hawkins, and B.L. Isaac, pp. 367-428. *Research in Economic Anthropology* Supplement 6. JAI Press, Greenwich.
1996 Households as Economic Organization: A Comparison between Large Houses on the Northwest Coast and in the Southwest. In *People Who Lived in Big Houses: Archaeological Perspectives on Large Domestic Structures,* edited by Gary Coupland and E. Banning, pp. 107-120. Monographs in World Archaeology No. 27, Prehistory Press, Madison, Wisconsin.
1998 The Coast Salish House: Lessons from Shingle Point, Valdes Island, BC. Paper presented at the 31st Annual Canadian Archaeology Association Meetings, Victoria.

Matson, R.G., and Gary Coupland
1995 *The Prehistory of the Northwest Coast.* Academic Press, San Diego.

Matson, R.G., Joanne Green, and Eric McLay
1999 Houses and Households in the Gulf of Georgia: Archaeological Investigations of Shingle Point (DgRv 2), Valdes Island, British Columbia. Report on file, British Columbia Archaeology Branch, Victoria.

Matson, R.G., and Eric McLay
1996 Preliminary Report on the 1995 Archaeology Investigation of Shingle Point (DgRv 2), Valdes Island. Report on file, British Columbia Archaeology Branch, Victoria.

Mauger, Jeffrey E.
1978 *Shed-Roof Houses at the Ozette Archaeological Site: A Proto-Historic Architectural System.* Washington Archaeological Research Center Project Report No. 73. Washington State University, Pullman.
1980 Bent Corner Box Study. In *Ozette Archaeological Project, Interim Final Report, Phase XIII,* compiled by Paul Gleeson, Project Report No. 97, Washington Archaeological Research Center, Washington State University, Pullman.
1982 Ozette Kerfed-Cornered Boxes. *American Indian Art Magazine* 8:72-79.
1991 Shed-Roof Houses at Ozette and in a Regional Perspective. In *Ozette Archaeological Research Reports.* Vol. 1: *House Structure and Floor Midden,* edited by S.R. Samuels, pp. 29-173. Reports of Investigations 63, Department of Anthropology, Washington State University, Pullman.

Miller, Bruce, and Daniel Boxberger
1994 Creating Chiefdoms: The Puget Sound Case. *Ethnohistory* 41:267-293.

Miller, Jay
1997 *Tsimshian Culture: A Light through the Ages.* University of Nebraska Press, Lincoln.

Mitchell, Donald H.
1967 Archaeological Investigations, Summer, 1966. Report to the Archaeological Sites Advisory Board. Report on file, British Columbia Archaeology Branch, Victoria.
1968 Archaeology of the Gulf of Georgia Area, a Natural Region and Its Culture Types. PhD diss., Department of Anthropology, University of Oregon, Eugene.
1969 Site Survey in the Johnson [sic] Strait Region. *Northwest Anthropological Research Notes* 3:193-216.
1971a *Archaeology of the Gulf of Georgia Area, a Natural Region and its Culture Types. Syesis* 4, Supplement 1, Victoria.
1971b The Dionisio Point Site and Gulf Island Culture History. *Syesis* 4:145-168.

1979   Bowker Creek: A Microblade Site on Southeastern Vancouver Island. *Syesis* 12:77-100.
1981   Sebassa's Men. In *The World Is As Sharp As a Knife*, edited by D. Abbott, pp. 79-86. British Columbia Provincial Museum, Victoria.
1982   *The Gulf of Georgia Sequence*. Pictures of Record, Weston.
1983a Tribes and Chiefdoms of the Northwest Coast: The Tsimshian Case. In *The Evolution of Maritime Cultures on the Northeast and the Northwest Coasts of America*, edited by Ronald Nash, pp. 57-64. Publication No. 11, Department of Archaeology, Simon Fraser University, Burnaby.
1983b Seasonal Settlements, Village Aggregations, and Political Autonomy on the Central Northwest Coast. In *The Development of Political Organization in Native North America*, edited by Elizabeth Tooker, pp. 97-107. Proceedings of the American Ethnological Society, Washington.
1984   Predatory Warfare, Social Status, and the North Pacific Slave Trade. *Ethnology* 23(1):39-48.
1985   A Demographic Profile of Northwest Coast Slavery. In *Status, Structure and Stratification: Current Archaeological Reconstructions*, edited by M. Thompson, M.T. Garcia, and F.J. Kense, pp. 227-236. Proceedings of the 16th Annual Chacmool Conference. Archaeological Association of the University of Calgary, Calgary.
1988   Changing Patterns of Resource Use in the Prehistory of Queen Charlotte Strait, British Columbia. In *Prehistoric Economies of the Pacific Northwest Coast*, edited by Barry L. Isaac, pp. 245-290. *Research in Economic Anthropology*, Supplement 3. JAI Press, Greenwich.
1990   Prehistory of the Coasts of Southern British Columbia and Northern Washington. In *Handbook of North American Indians*. Vol. 7: *Northwest Coast*, edited by Wayne Suttles, pp. 340-358. Smithsonian Institution, Washington.
1994   Residential Mobility among Northwest Coast Cultures. Paper presented at the Symposium on Complex Hunter-Gatherers of the World, UCLA, Los Angeles.
1998a Locarno Beach Culture. In *Archaeology of Prehistoric Native America: An Encyclopedia*, edited by Guy Gibbon, pp. 468-469. Garland Publishing, New York.
1998b Queen Charlotte Strait Sequence. In *Archaeology of Prehistoric Native America: An Encyclopedia*, edited by Guy Gibbon, pp. 699-700. Garland Publishing, New York.

Mitchell, Donald H., and Leland Donald
1985   Some Economic Aspects of Tlingit, Haida and Tsimshian Slavery. *Research in Economic Anthropology* 7:19-35.
1988   Archaeology and the Study of Northwest Coast Economies. In *Prehistoric Economies of the Northwest Coast*, edited by Barry Isaac, pp. 293-351. *Research in Economic Anthropology*, Supplement 3. JAI Press, Greenwich.

Monks, G.G.
2001   Quit Blubbering: An Examination of Nuu-chah-nulth Whale Butchery. *International Journal of Osteoarchaeology* 11:136-149.

Monks, G.G., A.D. McMillan, and D.E. St. Claire
2001   Nuu-chah-nulth Whaling: Archaeological Insights into Antiquity, Species Preferences and Cultural Importance. *Arctic Anthropology* 38:60-81.

Moss, Madonna L.
1992   Relationships between Maritime Cultures of Southern Alaska: Rethinking Culture Area Boundaries. *Arctic Anthropology* 29:5-17.

Moss, Madonna L., J. Erlandson, and R. Stuckenrath
1990   Wood Stake Weirs and Salmon Fishing on the Northwest Coast: Evidence from Southeast Alaska. *Canadian Journal of Archaeology* 14:143-158.

Mozino, Jose Mariano
1970 *Noticias de Nutka: An Account of Nootka Sound in 1792.* Translated and edited by Iris Higbie Wilson. University of Washington Press, Seattle.

Munsell, David A.
1976 Excavation of the Conway Wet Site 45SK59b, Conway, Washington. In *The Excavation of Water-Saturated Archaeological Sites (Wet Sites) on the Northwest Coast of North America,* edited by Dale R. Croes, pp. 86-121. National Museum of Man, Mercury Series, Archaeological Survey of Canada Paper No. 50. National Museums of Canada, Ottawa.

Murray, Peter
1985 *The Devil and Mr. Duncan: A History of the Two Metlakatlas.* Sono Nis Press, Victoria.

Myers, Grant
N.d. The Charles and Point Shed-Roof Houses, Musqueam. Report on file, Laboratory of Archaeology, University of British Columbia, Vancouver.

Nabokov, Peter, and Robert Easton
1989 *Native American Architecture.* Oxford University Press, Oxford.

Netting, Robert McC.
1977 *Cultural Ecology.* Cummings, Menlo Park.
1986 *Cultural Ecology.* 2nd ed. Waveland Press, Prospect Heights.

Newman, Stanley
1974 Linguistic Retention and Diffusion in Bella Coola. *Language in Society* 3:201-214.

Nordquist, D.L., and G.E. Nordquist
1983 *Twana Twined Basketry.* Acoma Books, Ramona, CA.

Paul, Frances
1981 *Spruce Root Basketry of the Alaska Tlingit.* Sheldon Jackson Museum, Alaska State Museums, Sitka.

Petersen, James B. (editor)
1996 *A Most Indispensable Art: Native Fiber Industries from Eastern North America.* University of Tennessee Press, Knoxville.

Pokotylo, David L.
1998 Charles/St. Mungo Culture Type. In *Archaeology of Prehistoric Native America: An Encyclopedia,* edited by Guy Gibbon, pp. 141-143. Garland Publishing, New York.

Porter, Frank W. III (editor)
1990 *The Art of Native American Basketry: A Living Legacy.* Greenwood Press, CT.

Pratt, Heather L.
1992 The Charles Culture of the Gulf of Georgia: A Re-evaluation of the Culture and Its Three Sub-Phases. MA thesis, Department of Anthropology and Sociology, University of British Columbia, Vancouver.

Rath, John C.
1982 *A Practical Heiltsuk-English Dictionary with a Grammatical Introduction.* National Museum of Man, Mercury Series, Canadian Ethnology Service Paper No. 75. National Museums of Canada, Ottawa.

Renfrew, Colin
1986 Introduction: Peer Polity Interaction and Socio-Political Change. In *Peer Polity Interaction and Socio-Political Change,* edited by C. Renfrew and J. Cherry, pp. 1-18. Cambridge University Press, Cambridge.
1987 *Archaeology and Language: The Puzzle of Indo-European Origins.* Jonathan Cape, London.
1992 World Languages and Human Dispersals: A Minimalist View. In *Transition to Modernity: Essays on Power, Wealth and Belief,* edited by John A. Hall and I.C. Jarvie, pp. 11-68. Cambridge University Press, Cambridge.

Robertson, R.B.
1954 *Of Whales and Men.* Knopf, New York.

Rocha, Jorge M.
1996 Rationality, Culture, and Decision Making. *Research in Economic Anthropology* 17:13-41.

Rosman, Abraham, and Paula G. Rubel
1971 *Feasting with Mine Enemy: Rank and Exchange among Northwest Coast Societies.* Waveland Press, Prospect Heights.

Rouse, Irving
1986 *Migrations in Prehistory: Inferring Population Movement from Cultural Remains.* Yale University Press, New Haven.

Rousseau, E., and M. Rousseau
1978 Burials from Site EiRn 15, Canoe Creek, BC. Report on file, British Columbia Archaeology Branch, Victoria.

Rousselot, Jean-Loup, William W. Fitzhugh, and Aron Crowell
1988 Maritime Economies of the North Pacific Rim. In *Crossroads of Continents: Cultures of Siberia and Alaska,* edited by William W. Fitzhugh and Aron Crowell, pp. 151-172. Smithsonian Institution, Washington.

Rowntree, Lester
1986 Cultural/Humanistic Geography. *Progress in Human Geography* 10:581-586.

Rozen, David L.
1985 Place-Names of the Island Halkomelem Indian People. MA thesis, Department of Anthropology and Sociology, University of British Columbia, Vancouver.

Ruyle, Eugene E.
1973 Slavery, Surplus, and Stratification on the Northwest Coast: The Ethnoenergetics of an Incipient Stratification System. *Current Anthropology* 14:603-631.

St. Claire, Denis E.
1991 Barkley Sound Tribal Territories. In *Between Ports Alberni and Renfrew: Notes on Westcoast Peoples,* Eugene Y. Arima, Louis Clamhouse, Joshua Edgar, Charles Jones, and John Thomas, pp. 13-202. Mercury Series, Canadian Ethnology Service Paper 121. Canadian Museum of Civilization, Ottawa.
1998 Niismakmatsukwukw Ts'ishaa7ath: "Talking About Ts'ishaa7ath Land History." Unpublished report prepared for the Tseshaht First Nation, Port Alberni.
N.d. Ohiaht Territories. Report prepared for the Ohiaht Ethnoarchaeological Project, August 1985.

Sahlins, Marshall D.
1958   *Social Stratification in Polynesia*. University of Washington Press, Seattle.

Sahlins, Marshall D., and Elman R. Service
1960   *Evolution and Culture*. University of Michigan Press, Ann Arbor.

Salo, E.A.
1991   Life History of Chum Salmon *(Oncorhynchus keta)*. In *Pacific Salmon Life Histories,* edited by C. Groot and L. Margolis, pp. 232-309. UBC Press, Vancouver.

Samuels, Stephan R. (editor)
1991   *Ozette Archaeological Project Research Reports*. Vol. 1: *House Structure and Floor Midden*. Reports of Investigations No. 63, Department of Anthropology, Washington State University, Pullman.
1994   *Ozette Archaeological Project Research Reports*. Vol. 2: *Fauna*. Reports of Investigations No. 66, Department of Anthropology, Washington State University, Pullman.

Samuels, Stephan R.
1983   Spatial Patterns and Cultural Processes in Three Northwest Coast Longhouse Floor Middens from Ozette. PhD diss., Department of Anthropology, Washington State University, Pullman.
1999   Household Production at Ozette. Paper presented at the 64th Annual Society for American Archaeology Meetings, Chicago.

Sanger, David
1968   The Chase Burial Site EeQw-1, British Columbia. *Contributions to Anthropology VI: Archaeology,* Paper No. 2, Bulletin 224, pp. 86-152. National Museums of Canada, Ottawa.

Sapir, Edward
1911   Some Aspects of Nootka Language and Culture. *American Anthropologist* 13:15-28.
1913   A Girl's Puberty Ceremony among the Nootka Indians. *Royal Society of Canada, Proceedings and Transactions,* Series 3, Part 2:67-80.
1915   Abnormal Types of Speech in Nootka. *Geological Survey of Canada, Memoir* 62:1-21. Ottawa.
1916   Time Perspective in Aboriginal North American Culture: A Study in Method. *Geological Survey of Canada Memoir* 90, Ottawa.
1949   Time Perspective in Aboriginal American Culture: A Study in Method. In *Selected Writings of Edward Sapir in Language, Culture and Personality,* edited by David G. Mandelbaum, pp. 389-462. University of California Press, Berkeley. (Originally published in 1916.)

Savelle, J.M.
1997   The Role of Architectural Utility in the Formation of Zooarchaeological Whale Bone Assemblages. *Journal of Archaeological Science* 24:869-885.

Savelle, J.M., and T.M. Friesen
1996   An Odontocete (Cetacea) Meat Utility Index. *Journal of Archaeological Science* 23:713-721.

Schwartz, Theodore
1978   The Size and Shape of a Culture. In *Scale and Social Organization,* edited by F. Barth, pp. 215-252. Universitetsforlagets, Oslo.

Seguin, Margaret
  1984a Rich Foods and Real People: A Problem with Tsimshian Food Categories in Boas's Tsimshian Mythology. *WPLC: Papers of the 19th International Conference on Salishan and Neighbouring Languages* 4:324-330, Victoria.
  1984b Introduction. In *The Tsimshian: Images of the Past, Views for the Present,* edited by Margaret Seguin, pp. ix-xx. UBC Press, Vancouver.

Service, Elman
  1962 *Primitive Social Organization: An Evolutionary Perspective.* Random House, New York.
  1971 *Primitive Social Organization: An Evolutionary Perspective,* 2nd ed. Random House, New York.
  1975 *Origins of the State and Civilization: The Process of Cultural Evolution.* Norton and Company, New York.

Sharpe, Margaret, and Dorothy Tunbridge
  1997 Traditions of Extinct Animals, Changing Sea-Levels and Volcanoes among Australian Aboriginals: Evidence from Linguistic and Ethnographic Research. In *Archaeology and Language I: Theoretical and Methodological Orientations,* edited by R. Blench and M. Spriggs, pp. 345-361. Routledge, New York.

Shelford, Victor E.
  1963 *The Ecology of North America.* University of Illinois Press, Urbana.

Shennan, Stephen
  1988 *Quantifying Archaeology.* Edinburgh University Press, Edinburgh.
  1993 After Social Evolution: A New Archaeological Agenda? In *Archaeological Theory: Who Sets the Agenda?* edited by N. Yoffee and A. Sherratt, pp. 53-59. Cambridge University Press, Cambridge.

Shinkwin, Anne
  1979 *Dakah De'nin's Village and the Dixthada Site: A Contribution to Northern Athapaskan Prehistory.* National Museum of Man, Mercury Series, Archaeology Survey of Canada Paper No. 91. National Museums of Canada, Ottawa.

Slijper, E.J.
  1962 *Whales.* Revised edition. Hutchison, London.

Snow, Dean R.
  1995 Migration in Prehistory: The Northern Iroquoian Case. *American Antiquity* 60:59-79.

Snyder, Warren A.
  1956 Sampling at "Old Man House" on Puget Sound. *Research Studies of the State College of Washington* 24:17-37.

Spier, Leslie, and Edward Sapir
  1931 *Wishram Ethnography.* University of Washington Publications in Anthropology, Vol. 3, Seattle.

Spott, Robert, and A.L. Kroeber
  1942 Yurok Narratives. *University of California Publications in American Archaeology and Ethnology* 35:143-256.

Sproat, Gilbert Malcolm
  1868 *Scenes and Studies of Savage Life.* Smith, Elder and Co., London. (Reprinted as *The Nootka: Scenes and Studies of Savage Life,* edited by Charles Lillard, Sono Nis Press, Victoria, 1987.)

1879 Correspondence as Superintendent General of Indian Affairs with Indian Reserve Commission, New Westminster, BC. 3 March 1879.

Stein, Julie K. (editor)
1991 *Deciphering a Shell Midden*. Academic Press, San Diego.

Steponaitis, Vincas P.
1978 Location Theory and Complex Chiefdoms: A Mississippian Example. In *Mississippian Settlement Patterns*, edited by Bruce Smith, pp. 417-453. Academic Press, London.

Stevenson, Anne
1989 Netting and Associated Cordage. Appendix A. In *Water Hazard (DgRs 30) Artifact Recovery Project Report*, by Kathryn Bernick, on file, British Columbia Archaeology Branch, Victoria.
1998 Wet-site Contributions to Developmental Models of the Fraser River Fishery. In *Hidden Dimensions: The Cultural Significance of Wetland Archaeology*, edited by Kathryn Bernick, pp. 220-238. UBC Press, Vancouver.

Stewart, Hilary
1977 *Indian Fishing: Early Methods on the Northwest Coast*. University of Washington Press, Seattle.
1984 *Cedar, Tree of Life to the Northwest Coast Indians*. Douglas and McIntyre, Vancouver.
1987 *The Adventures and Sufferings of John R. Jewitt, Captive of Maquinna*. Annotated and illustrated by Hilary Stewart. Douglas and McIntyre, Vancouver.

Stewart, Kathlyn
1998 McNichol Creek Site Faunal Analysis: The 1996 Sample. Report on file, Laboratory of Archaeology, University of Toronto, Toronto.

Sumpter, Ian, Daryl Fedje, and Fred Sieber
2001 The 2000 *tsuxwkwaada* Village Mapping Inventory Project, Site 291T (DeSf-2), Tsuquana I.R.2. Manuscript prepared for Ditidaht First Nation and Pacific Rim National Park Reserve. On file, Cultural Resource Services, Parks Canada, Victoria.

Suttles, Wayne (editor)
1990a *Handbook of North American Indians*. Vol. 7: *Northwest Coast* (W.C. Sturtevant, general editor). Smithsonian Institution, Washington.

Suttles, Wayne
1951 The Economic Life of the Coast Salish of Haro and Rosario Straits. PhD diss., University of Washington, Seattle.
1952 Notes on Coast Salish Sea-Mammal Hunting. *Anthropology in British Columbia* 3:10-20.
1973 *CA** comment on Ruyle (1973). *Current Anthropology* 15:622-623.
1987a *Coast Salish Essays*. Talon Books, Vancouver/University of Washington Press, Seattle.
1987b Affinal Ties, Subsistence, and Prestige among the Coast Salish. In *Coast Salish Essays*, edited by Wayne Suttles, pp. 15-25. University of Washington Press, Seattle.
1987c The Persistence of Intervillage Ties among the Coast Salish. In *Coast Salish Essays*, edited by Wayne Suttles, pp. 209-230. University of Washington Press, Seattle.
1987d The Recent Emergence of the Coast Salish: The Function of an Anthropological Myth. In *Coast Salish Essays*, edited by Wayne Suttles, pp. 256-264. University of Washington Press, Seattle.
1990b Central Coast Salish. In *Handbook of North American Indians*. Vol. 7: *Northwest Coast*, edited by Wayne Suttles, pp. 453-475. Smithsonian Institution, Washington.

1990c Introduction. In *Handbook of North American Indians*. Vol. 7: *Northwest Coast*, edited by Wayne Suttles, pp. 1-15. Smithsonian Institution, Washington.
1991 The Shed-Roof House. In *A Time of Gathering: Native Heritage in Washington State*, edited by Robin K. Wright, pp. 212-222. University of Washington Press, Seattle.
1998 The Ethnographic Significance of the Fort Langley Journals. In *The Fort Langley Journals, 1827-30*, edited by M. Maclachlan, pp. 163-210. UBC Press, Vancouver.

Suttles, Wayne, and William W. Elmendorf
1963 Linguistic Evidence for Salish Prehistory. In *Symposium on Language and Culture: Proceedings of the 1962 Annual Spring Meeting of the American Ethnological Society*, edited by Viola E. Garfield and Wallace L. Chafe, pp. 41-52. American Ethnological Society, Seattle.

Suttles, Wayne, and Aldona Jonaitis
1990 History of Research in Ethnology. In *Handbook of North American Indians*. Vol. 7: *Northwest Coast*, edited by Wayne Suttles, pp. 73-87. Smithsonian Institution, Washington.

Swadesh, Morris
1948 Motivations in Nootka Warfare. *Southwestern Journal of Anthropology* 4:76-93.
1949 The Linguistic Approach to Salish Prehistory. In *Indians of the Urban Northwest*, edited by Marian W. Smith, pp. 161-173. Columbia University Press, New York.
1950 Salish Internal Relationships. *International Journal of American Linguistics* 16:157-167.
1953 Mosan I: A Problem of Remote Common Origin. *International Journal of American Linguistics* 19:26-44.
1954 Time Depths of American Linguistic Groupings. *American Anthropologist* 56:361-364.
1955 Chemakum Lexicon Compared with Quileute. *International Journal of American Linguistics* 21:60-72.

Swan, James G.
1870 *The Indians of Cape Flattery, at the Entrance to the Strait of Juan de Fuca, Washington Territory*. Smithsonian Contributions to Knowledge, 220. Washington.
N.d. Journal of a Trip to Queen Charlotte's Islands, BC, May 1, 1883 to September 16, 1883. Suzzallo Library, University of Washington, Seattle.

Swanton, John R.
1905 *Contributions to the Ethnology of the Haida*. Memoir of the American Museum of Natural History No. 5, Part 1, New York.

Taylor, Herbert C. Jr., and Wilson Duff
1956 A Post-Contact Southward Movement of the Kwakiutl. *Research Studies of the State College of Washington* 24:56-66.

Thieme, Hartmut
1997 Lower Palaeolithic Hunting Spears from Germany. *Nature* 385:807-810.

Thompson, Laurence C., and M. Dale Kinkade
1990 Languages. In *Handbook of North American Indians*. Vol. 7: *Northwest Coast*, edited by Wayne Suttles, pp. 30-51. Smithsonian Institution, Washington.

Thompson, Nile, and Carolyn Marr
1983 *Crow's Shells: Artistic Basketry of Puget Sound*. Dushuyay Publications, Seattle.

Tobler, W., and S. Wineburg
1971 A Cappadocian Speculation. *Nature* 231:39-41.

Tønnessen, J.N., and A.O. Jensen
1982   *A History of Modern Whaling.* University of California Press, Berkeley.

Trigger, Bruce G.
1989   *A History of Archaeological Thought.* Cambridge University Press, Cambridge.
1995   Expanding Middle-Range Theory. *Antiquity* 69:449-458.

Turner, Nancy J.
1979   *Plants in British Columbia Indian Technology.* British Columbia Provincial Museum, Victoria.

Usher, Jean
1974   *William Duncan of Metlakhatla: A Victorian Missionary in British Columbia.* National Museums of Canada, Ottawa.

Vansina, Jan
1985   *Oral Tradition as History.* University of Wisconsin Press, Madison.

Vastokas, Joan Marie
1966   Architecture of the Northwest Coast Indians of America. PhD diss., Columbia University, New York.

Vaughan, Thomas, and Bill Holm
1982   *Soft Gold: The Fur Trade and Cultural Exchange on the Northwest Coast of America.* Oregon Historical Society, Portland.

Wagner, Henry R.
1968   *The Cartography of the Northwest Coast of America to the Year 1800.* N. Israel, Amsterdam.

Wagner, Henry R., and W.A. Newcombe
1938   The Journal of Jacinto Caamano. Translated by Captain Harold Grenfell, R.N. *British Columbia Historical Quarterly* 2:195-301.

Ward, Mark
1998   There's an Ant in My Phone. *New Scientist* 157 (2118):32-35.

Wason, Paul
1994   *The Archaeology of Rank.* Cambridge University Press, Cambridge.

Waterman, T.T.
1921   *Indian Houses of Puget Sound.* Indian Notes and Monographs. Museum of the American Indian, Heye Foundation, New York.
1967   *Whaling Equipment of the Makah Indians.* University of Washington Publications in Anthropology. Vol. 1, no. 1. Seattle.

Watson, Patty Jo
1991   A Parochial Primer: The New Dissonance as Seen from the Midcontinental United States. In *Processual and Postprocessual Archaeologies: Multiple Ways of Knowing the Past,* edited by R. Preucel, pp. 265-274. Occasional Paper No. 10, Center for Archaeological Investigations, Southern Illinois University Press, Carbondale.

Webb, R.L.
1988   *On the Northwest Coast: Commercial Whaling in the Pacific Northwest, 1790-1967.* UBC Press, Vancouver.

Wellcome, Henry S.
1884   *The Story of Metlakhatla.* Saxon, New York.

Wessen, Gary C.
1988   The Use of Shellfish Resources on the Northwest Coast: The View from Ozette. In *Prehistoric Economies of the Pacific Northwest Coast,* edited by Barry Isaac, pp. 179-207. *Research in Economic Anthropology,* Supplement 3, JAI Press, Greenwich.
1990   Prehistory of the Ocean Coast of Washington. In *Handbook of North American Indians.* Vol. 7: *Northwest Coast,* edited by Wayne Suttles, pp. 412-421. Smithsonian Institution, Washington.
1994   Subsistence Patterns as Reflected by Invertebrate Remains Recovered at the Ozette Site. In *Ozette Archaeological Project Research Reports.* Vol. 2: *Fauna,* edited by S.R. Samuels, pp. 93-196. Reports of Investigations No. 66, Department of Anthropology, Washington State University, Pullman.

Whitthoft, J., and F. Eyman
1969   Metallurgy of the Tlingit, Dene and Eskimo. *Expedition* 11:12-33.

Widmer, Randolph J.
1988   *The Evolution of the Calusa: A Non-Agricultural Chiefdom on the Southwest Coast of Florida.* University of Alabama Press, Tuscaloosa.

Wigen, B., and B. Stucki
1988   Taphonomy and Stratigraphy in the Interpretation of Economic Patterns at Hoko River Rockshelter. In *Prehistoric Economies of the Pacific Northwest Coast,* edited by B. Isaac, pp. 87-146. *Research in Economic Anthropology,* Supplement 3, JAI Press, Greenwich.

Wilk, Richard R., and William L. Rathje
1982   Household Archaeology. In *Archaeology of the Household: Building a Prehistory of Domestic Life,* edited by R.R. Wilk and W.L. Rathje, pp. 617-639. *American Behavioral Scientist 25.*

Willoughby, Charles C.
1910   A New Type of Ceremonial Blanket from the Northwest Coast. *American Anthropologist* 12:1-10.

Wilson, Edward O.
1975   *Sociobiology: The New Synthesis.* Harvard University Press, Cambridge.

Wissler, F. Clark
1917   *The Relation of Nature to Man in Aboriginal America.* (Reprinted in 1938.) McMurtrie, New York.

Wobst, Martin
1974   Boundary Conditions for Palaeolithic Social Systems: A Simulation Approach. *American Antiquity* 39:147-178.
1976   Locational Relationships in Palaeolithic Society. *Journal of Human Evolution* 5:49-58.

Wolf, Eric R.
1982   *Europe and the People without History.* University of California Press, Berkeley.

Wood, Raymond
1990   Ethnohistory and Historical Method. *Archaeological Method and Theory* 2:81-109.

Woodburn, James
  1988   African Hunter-Gatherer Social Organization: Is It Best Understood as a Product of Encapsulation? In *Hunters and Gatherers*. Vol. 1: *History, Evolution, and Social Change,* edited by T. Ingold, D. Riches, and J. Woodburn, pp. 31-64. Berg, Oxford.

Yesner, David R.
  1990   Fuegians and Other Hunter-Gatherers of the Subantarctic Region: Cultural Devolution Reconsidered. In *Hunter-Gatherer Demography: Past and Present,* edited by B. Meehan and N. White, pp. 1-22. Oceania Monograph No. 39, Sydney.
  1995   Whales, Mammoths, and Other Big Beasts: Assessing Their Roles in Prehistoric Economies. In *Hunting the Largest Animals: Native Whaling in the Western Arctic and Subarctic,* edited by A.P. McCartney, pp. 149-164. Canadian Circumpolar Institute, Edmonton.

Yorga, Brian
  1978   Final Report, Archaeological Reconnaissance of the Yukon Coast. Report on file, Archaeological Survey of Canada, National Museum of Man, Ottawa.

Zenk, Henry B.
  1990a Alseans. In *Handbook of North American Indians*. Vol. 7: *Northwest Coast,* edited by Wayne Suttles, pp. 568-571. Smithsonian Institution, Washington.
  1990b Kalapuyans. In *Handbook of North American Indians*. Vol. 7: *Northwest Coast,* edited by Wayne Suttles, pp. 547-553. Smithsonian Institution, Washington.
  1990c Siuslawans and Coosans. In *Handbook of North American Indians*. Vol. 7: *Northwest Coast,* edited by Wayne Suttles, pp. 572-579. Smithsonian Institution, Washington.

Notes on Contributors

Steven Acheson is a staff archaeologist with the Government of British Columbia. He completed his master's degree at the University of Victoria and his doctorate in archaeology from the University of Oxford (1991). He also holds the position of Adjunct Professor with the Department of Anthropology at the University of Victoria, with research interests in Northwest Coast archaeology and ethnohistory. His revised dissertation on the settlement archaeology of Gwaii Haanas was published as *In the Wake of the ya'áats' xaatgáay ("Iron People")*.

Kathryn Bernick (MA, University of Victoria) is a freelance archaeologist whose experience in Northwest Coast wetland archaeology spans more than three decades. She is based in Victoria, British columbia, and Seattle, Washington. Her research has focused on ancient basketry techniques, style and cultural identity, environmental archaeology, and wet sites. Her recent books include *Basketry and Cordage from Hesquiat Harbour, British Columbia* (Royal BC Museum 1998) and the edited volume *Hidden Dimensions: The Cultural Significance of Wetland Archaeology* (1998).

Rebecca Case has a master's degree in anthropology from the University of Toronto (1999). Her research interests include Northwest Coast archaeology. She is currently articling in law at the University of Toronto.

Roger H. Colten is Collections Manager in the Anthropology Division of the Peabody Museum of Natural History at Yale University, New Haven, Connecticut. He received his PhD in archaeology from UCLA in 1993. His research interests include zooarchaeology and the complex hunter-gatherers of the Pacific coast of North America.

Gary Coupland is Professor of anthropology at the University of Toronto. He received his PhD from the University of British Columbia in 1986. His interests include Northwest Coast archaeology, the study of complex hunter-gatherers, and household archaeology. He has conducted field research in northwestern British Columbia for the past twenty years. He is co-author, with R.G. Matson, of *The Prehistory of the Northwest Coast* (1995).

Dale R. Croes received his PhD in anthropology at the Washington State University in 1977. He is currently chair of the Department of Anthropology at South Puget Sound Community College in Olympia, Washington, and Adjunct Faculty with the Department of Anthropology, Washington State University. His research focus has been on Northwest Coast wet (waterlogged) archaeological sites, and especially the analysis and comparison of prehistoric basketry and cordage artifacts from these sites. His publications include *The Hoko River Archaeological Site Complex* (1995) and a number of journal articles and book chapters.

Leland Donald is Professor of anthropology at the University of Victoria, where he has taught since 1969. His interests include the historical ethnology of the north Pacific coast of North America, the relationships between environments and cultures, and inequality and warfare in small-scale societies. He edited *Themes in Ethnology and Culture History: Essays in Honour of David F. Aberle* (1987) and is the author of *Aboriginal Slavery on the Northwest Coast of North America* (1997).

Colin Grier is a lecturer at the University of British Columbia. He received his master's degree (1996) and doctorate (2001) from Arizona State University, and his BA from McGill University (1993). His archaeological research has focused on complex hunter-gatherers and the origins of social inequality, and he has explored these topics in the context of prehistoric Arctic whaling societies, Paleolithic Europe, and, most recently, the Gulf of Georgia region of the Northwest Coast.

Alan D. McMillan (PhD, Simon Fraser University) is Chair of the Department of Anthropology and Sociology at Douglas College. He is also Adjunct Professor in the Department of Archaeology at Simon Fraser University. His interests include Northwest Coast archaeology, oral traditions, and art. His field research has focused on the Nuu-chah-nulth people of western Vancouver Island. His recent book *Since the Time of the Transformers: The Ancient Heritage of the Nuu-chah-nulth, Ditidaht, and Makah* (1999) summarizes his research in that area.

Alexander P. Mackie is a staff archaeologist with the Government of British Columbia. He completed his BA at the University of Victoria in 1981. His research interests are in Northwest Coast archaeology. He is currently coordinating, with the Champagne and Aishihik First Nation, research into the "Kwäday Dän Ts'ínchi" human remains and artifacts found melting from a glacier in northwestern British Columbia. Results from an inventory of Early Period sites in Gwaii Haanas will appear in a forthcoming UBC Press book in the Pacific Rim Archaeology Series about the prehistory of Haida Gwaii.

Quentin Mackie is Assistant Professor of anthropology at the University of Victoria, specializing in the archaeology of the Northwest Coast. His thematic interests include settlement archaeology, lithic analysis, environmental archaeology, and the first peopling of the Northwest Coast. Currently, he is investigating early Holocene human occupation and environments in Haida Gwaii, with a focus on the Richardson Island archaeological site.

Andrew R.C. Martindale is Assistant Professor in the Department of Anthropology at McMaster University. He received his master's degree from Trent (1994) and his PhD from the University of Toronto (1999). His current research investigates the nature and consequences of the contact relationship between Tsimshian and European people during the eighteenth to the twentieth centuries, and includes a comparison of data from documentary sources, archaeological sites, and indigenous oral traditions.

R.G. Matson is Professor of archaeology in the Department of Anthropology and Sociology at the University of British Columbia, where he has taught since 1972. His advanced degrees (PhC, 1969; PhD, 1971) are from the University of California, Davis. His interests include the US Southwest, as illustrated by *The Origins of Southwestern Agriculture* (1991), and the Northwest Coast, as shown by *The Prehistory of the Northwest Coast* (1995), which he wrote with Gary Coupland.

Gregory G. Monks is Associate Professor in the Department of Anthropology at the University of Manitoba, where he has taught since 1977. His BA (1967), his MA (1972) (both from the University of Victoria), and his PhD (University of British Columbia, 1977) were all earned under the direct or indirect mentorship of Donald H. Mitchell. His research interests lie in Northwest Coast archaeology, zooarchaeology, and subsistence in complex hunter-gatherer societies. His chapter in this book is the third publication on whales to stem from his collaboration with Alan D. McMillan and Denis E. St. Claire on the Nuu-chah-nulth of western Vancouver Island. He has also conducted research and published articles on Gulf of Georgia archaeology.

Laurie Williamson graduated with a BA in anthropology from the University of Victoria in 1977, with an emphasis on British Columbia archaeology, ethnography, and history. She has over thirteen years of fieldwork experience in archaeological survey, excavation, and ethnographic research along the BC coast, and abroad in Micronesia and Thailand. She has also worked at the Royal British Columbia Museum, cataloging the archaeology collection, researching museum holdings, and assisting with the compilation of the Westcoast Research File. More recently, she has been working as a research consultant, collecting and compiling archaeological and archival data, and transposing map data.

Index

(f) after a page number refers to a figure, (t) to a table

Printed and bound in Canada by Friesens

Set in Stone by Artegraphica Design Co. Ltd.

Copy editor: Joanne Richardson

Proofreader: Deborah Kerr